Principles of Social Justice

Principles of
Social Justice

DAVID MILLER

HARVARD UNIVERSITY PRESS
Cambridge, Massachusetts
London, England

Copyright © 1999 by the President and Fellows of Harvard College
All rights reserved
Printed in the United States of America
Third printing, 2003

This book has been digitally reprinted. The content remains identical
to that of previous printings.

First Harvard University Press paperback edition, 2001

Library of Congress Cataloging-in-Publication Data

Miller, David (David Leslie)
    Principles of social justice / David Miller.
        p.   cm.
    Includes bibliographical references and index.
    ISBN 0-674-70628-5 (cloth)
    ISBN 0-674-00714-X (pbk.)
    1. Social justice.   I. Title.
HM671.M55   1999
    303.3'72—dc21   99-21281

For Sue, Sarah, Jamie, and Daniel

Contents

Preface

Social justice is an idea that is central to the politics of contemporary democracies. Not everybody is for it. Some believe that the pursuit of social justice is a snare and a delusion and that we should be guided by other ideals—personal freedom, for instance. Among those who support it, it is not at all clear what the idea means. Often it seems little more than a rhetorical phrase used to add luster to some policy or proposal that the speaker wants us to support. People may be committed to social justice in the abstract, and yet disagree bitterly about what should be done about some concrete social problem such as unemployment. This increases our suspicion that the term may have emotive force, but no real meaning beyond that. It looks as though we are giving an argument in favor of a political measure when we say that it will promote social justice, but perhaps we are doing no more than emphatically expressing our support.

I do not share this skepticism about social justice. I think that a clear meaning can be given to the idea, and I do not think that the pursuit of social justice is politically misguided. On the other hand, it would be wrong to disregard or downplay the fact that people disagree about it in practice. We need to explore this disagreement, to see what its sources are, and also to see how far differing views about what justice requires can be reconciled by showing that they stem from shared beliefs at a deeper level. My aim in this book is to discover the underlying principles that people use when they judge some aspect of their society to be just or unjust, and then to show that these principles are coherent, both separately and when taken together. To do this I shall look fairly closely at empirical research on popular conceptions of justice. If we want to describe what social justice means in contemporary political debate, then sooner rather than later we must look at what the people themselves think.

In saying this I do not mean to imply that our theory of justice should be nothing more than an aggregate opinion poll. Popular beliefs about social justice may turn out to be defective in various ways; for instance, they may prove to conceal deep contradictions, or involve serious factual errors. We need to analyze the principles at stake to show that they can withstand philosophical scrutiny. My focus here will be on principles of *desert,* of *need,* and of *equality*—particularly on the idea of desert, which is not only the most widely applied but also the most problematic ingredient in popular understandings of social justice.

Because of its starting point, the theory of justice set out in this book has a different character from most theories developed in recent political philosophy. Besides being more sensitive to popular opinion, it also pays closer attention to the social contexts in which principles of justice are applied. This focus gives the theory a less abstract character. It also, I believe, increases its political relevance. I have felt acutely aware, while writing the book, of the huge gap that exists between the conceptions of social justice defended by political philosophers, particularly those we might describe as egalitarian liberals, and the kind of policy changes it is feasible to propose for the liberal societies of today. Of course social justice has always been, and must always be, a critical idea, one that challenges us to reform our institutions and practices in the name of greater fairness. But it should not be simply utopian. It is a striking fact about contemporary politics that although many democracies are now governed by parties of the left or center-left, these parties have without exception pared down their commitment to policies of social justice almost to the vanishing point, even while continuing to use the term rhetorically. There is a widespread perception that each country is tightly constrained in what it can do by global economic forces that quickly punish any deviation from orthodox free-market public policy. I examine this issue in the last chapter of the book, but here I want simply to draw attention to the way in which theorizing about social justice has become detached from questions of political feasibility.

Is it merely an accident that popular views of social justice have greater political saliency than the theories propounded in the literature of political philosophy? I believe not. Of course, one might argue that the thinking of the public at large about questions of justice is distorted by the ideological weight of existing social structures and institutions. Friedrich Engels said that justice was nothing but "the ideologised, glorified expression of the existing economic relations" and called it "social phlo-giston." Against this, I hope to show that a theory of justice rooted in popular beliefs can retain a sharp critical edge: if we take its principles seriously, they will guide us toward making substantial changes in our institutions and practices.

I am grateful to many colleagues for the helpful critical comments I received while preparing this book. I would particularly like to thank Jerry Cohen, Julian Lamont, Adam Swift, Andrew Williams, and Jo Wolff for reading the whole of the penultimate draft and making many valu-able suggestions. I am also very grateful to those who have commented on one or more individual chapters: Tony Atkinson, Brian Barry, John Charvet, Matthew Clayton, Ronald Cohen, Janet Coleman, Geoff Evans, Cécile Fabre, Denis Galligan, Bob Goodin, John Horton, Chandran Kukathas, Robert Lane, Anton Leist, Gordon Marshall, Andrew Mason, Philip Pettit, Jo Raz, Volker Schmidt, George Sher, Marc Stears, and Stefan Svallfors. Collectively they possess a breadth of expertise that far exceeds my own, and they have saved me from many rudimentary errors. My thanks go, too, to the several audiences who have had versions of chapters tried out on them, especially the Nuffield Political Theory Workshop, whose members (some named individually above) have been an unfailing source of rigorous criticism. And finally, as always, I am deeply grateful to my family, Sue, Sarah, Jamie, and Daniel, for their tolerance and support while I was writing the book. There is justice within families as well as within political societies, and they have a large sum of accumulated credit that will one day soon need to be repaid.

Principles of Social Justice

The Scope of Social Justice

When we talk and argue about social justice, what exactly are we talking and arguing about? Very crudely, I think, we are discussing how the good and bad things in life should be distributed among the members of a human society. When, more concretely, we attack some policy or some state of affairs as socially unjust, we are claiming that a person, or more usually a category of persons, enjoys fewer advantages than that person or group of persons ought to enjoy (or bears more of the burdens than they ought to bear), given how other members of the society in question are faring. But to state the question in these general terms is to conceal a host of difficulties. Three of these stand out as soon as we reflect on the precise meaning of the terms used in the sentences above.

First, what exactly are the goods and bads, the advantages and burdens, whose allocation is the concern of social justice? We tend to think immediately of income and wealth, jobs, educational opportunities, and so forth, but how far should the list be extended and what is the rationale for including or excluding particular items? Second, if social justice has to do with distribution, what precisely does this mean? Must there be a distributing *agency* that brings about the outcome whose justice or injustice we are trying to assess? And are we thinking narrowly about how government policies, say, affect the fortunes of different groups in society, or is our concern much wider than that, encompassing all kinds of social activities that determine the shares of goods that people have (for instance, exchanges and transfers within families or among friends)? Finally, what is meant here by a human society? If social justice presupposes that a boundary has been drawn inside of which its principles are applied to the circumstances of different members, how is the boundary to be fixed? Should all human beings be included, or only some?

These questions have to be answered before we can begin to examine in detail what the principles of social justice are and how they should be applied. I begin by looking briefly at how the idea of social justice first entered our political vocabulary, at the implicit assumptions that were made by those who first regularly used the idea. For this, I believe, will help us to understand the idea itself; in particular, it will throw light on what I shall call "the circumstances of social justice," meaning the circumstances in which social justice can function as an operative, policy-guiding ideal, an ideal with political relevance rather than an empty phrase. It is surely not an accident that the idea appeared in the particular social and political context that it did—the economically developed liberal societies of the late nineteenth and early twentieth centuries—but by the same token the circumstances of its appearance may suggest limits on its scope; if we try to stretch the concept too far, we may find that the assumptions needed to make it function cease to hold. And we must also ask, as I do in the last chapter, whether changes that are now taking place in the societies where social justice has been pursued for most of the twentieth century mean that the circumstances of social justice no longer obtain. Is it possible that the era of social justice is drawing to its close?

IN THE WRITINGS of most contemporary political philosophers, social justice is regarded as an aspect of distributive justice, and indeed the two concepts are often used interchangeably.[1] Distributive justice is an idea with a very long pedigree. It forms one element in the classic division of justice found in Aristotle's writings and passed down to the Christian tradition through Aquinas and others.[2] In this tradition, distributive justice meant the fair distribution of benefits among the members of various associations: in giving his account, Aristotle probably had in mind not only the distribution of public funds to office-holders and citizens in need, but also the distribution of benefits within clubs and other such private societies. Aquinas refers to the distribution of honors and wealth within a political community, but also, for example, to appointments to professorships.[3] Since these are among the issues that we expect a theory of social justice to address, it seems natural to regard the idea as simply an expanded version of distributive justice as understood by these older philosophers—distributive justice pursued more systematically and with respect to a wider range of benefits. This is a convenient way of marking the line that divides social justice from other kinds of justice that fall outside its scope—most notably retributive justice, or the justice of punishments—and it draws attention to continuities between what we see as fair in small-scale settings, such as clubs and work groups, and what we see as socially just.[4] But it has the disadvantage of obscuring what was new and distinctive about the idea of social justice itself. To grasp that we need to go back and observe how the early sponsors of the term were using it, in what context and with what background assumptions.

These early sponsors were in the main liberal social philosophers, writing at a time when the prevailing set of economic and social institutions was coming increasingly under ethical scrutiny and political challenge, and the responsibilities of the state were steadily expanding. There was no sudden leap to adopt the new term; instead, it was introduced in a fairly haphazard way in various late-nineteenth-century treatises of political economy and social ethics, in which issues such as the justification of different forms of private property or the merits of alternative forms of economic organization were being debated. British authors such as John Stuart Mill, Leslie Stephen, and Henry Sidgwick referred from time to time to social justice, although without marking it off sharply from distributive justice generally.[5] In continental Europe progressive Catholics had begun to develop notions of social justice by the end of the century, although it took another twenty-five years or so before the idea was officially endorsed in papal encyclicals.[6]

It is an interesting fact that the term "social justice" was more readily embraced by liberals and progressives than by socialists proper—partly, no doubt, as a result of the ringing denunciations by Marx and Engels, who believed that to speak of justice was to place oneself on the terrain of bourgeois ideology.[7] Nonetheless, the arrival of socialist movements as serious contenders for political power was pivotal to the development of ideas of social justice, since it was precisely the socialist challenge that forced liberals to look more critically at landownership, private ownership of industry, inherited wealth, and other such features of capitalism, and to investigate the various socialist and communist schemes of industrial organization advocated by those further to the left. What emerges, typically, is a discriminating defense of the market economy in which some existing property rights are criticized and others vindicated, and the state is charged with enacting those reformist policies that will lead to a just distribution of social resources.

Theorizing about social justice became a major concern in the early years of the twentieth century, and conveniently enough the first book actually called *Social Justice* was published in New York in 1900.[8] Its author was Westel Willoughby, a professor of political science at Johns Hopkins University who was influenced by the late idealist philosophy of the school of T. H. Green. Willoughby begins by observing that in an era of popular sovereignty we cannot avoid subjecting our existing social and economic institutions to critical appraisal, and in particular asking whether they treat individuals justly. The quest for social justice is a natural consequence of the spread of enlightenment: "the peoples of all civilized countries are subjecting social and economic conditions to the same tests of reasonableness and justice as those by which they have questioned in the past the rightfulness of political institutions."[9] In particular, Willoughby claims, it is imperative that we find ways of rebutting socialist arguments, and indeed much of the book is a critique of socialist or semi-socialist doctrines such as the land tax scheme of Henry George, the doctrine that the worker has a right to the whole product of his labor, various communist proposals, and so on.[10]

One interesting aspect of Willoughby's work that is also shared by other works from this period, such as *The Elements of Social Justice* by the British social philosopher L. T. Hobhouse, is its invocation of an organic conception of society.[11] Society is viewed as an organism in which the flourishing of each element requires the cooperation of all the others, and the aim of social justice is to specify the institutional arrangements that will allow each person to contribute fully to social well-being.[12] Principles like need, desert, and equality are examined from this perspective. To some extent this reflects the influence of idealist philosophy, which fosters a vision of society as an integrated whole, but we can also draw a more general lesson about the presuppositions needed to make social justice a workable ideal.[13] Social justice requires the notion of a society made up of interdependent parts, with an institutional structure that affects the prospects of each individual member, and that is capable of deliberate reform by an agency such as the state in the name of fairness.

To elaborate, at least three assumptions have to be made before we can begin theorizing about social justice. First we have to assume a bounded society with a determinate membership, forming a universe of distribution whose present fairness or unfairness different theories of justice try to demonstrate. This assumption is most obviously needed when the principles of justice we apply are comparative in form—that is, they concern the relative shares of advantages or disadvantages accruing to different groups of people. Is it fair that skilled workers should earn higher wages than unskilled workers? Is it fair that women should perform more domestic labor than men? In asking questions such as these we presuppose that the groups in question belong to a single universe of distribution whose overall justice we can meaningfully assess.

Other principles of justice are not comparative in this straightforward sense: for instance, we might ask whether it is just for people to be forced to live below the poverty line, say, having to sleep in cardboard shelters. But even here the question is asked against the background of a society whose members for the most part enjoy ample resources, some of which, by implication, might be diverted to aid the homeless. The bounds of this social universe are usually taken for granted and left unspecified. The early theorists of social justice simply assumed that they were talking about justice within the borders of politically organized communities, in other words, what we would today call nation-states. In later theorists the assumption is made more explicit, but it is still treated as relatively unproblematic. John Rawls, for instance, says that his principles of justice are worked out to apply to a society conceived as a closed system: "it is self-contained and has no relations to other societies. We enter it only by birth and exit only by death."[14] His assumption is that "the boundaries of these schemes are given by the notion of a self-contained national community."[15]

Connected to this first premise—that in speaking of social justice we tacitly or openly envisage a connected body of people who form the universe of distribution—is a second, namely, that the principles we advance must apply to an identifiable set of institutions whose impact on the life chances of different individuals can also be traced. The early theories of social justice were heavily influenced by nineteenth-century textbooks of political economy, one of whose important tasks was to explain the division of the social product among factors such as land, capital, and labor. Here it was taken for granted that there were discoverable social laws that determined distributive outcomes, and that also allowed one to predict the result of changing one of the institutions—say, taking land into public ownership. Once again we can refer to Rawls' work to see this assumption made explicit. According to Rawls, the subject-matter of social justice is the basic structure of society, understood as the major social institutions that "distribute fundamental rights and duties and determine the division of advantages from social cooperation. By major institutions I understand the political constitution and the principal economic and social arrangements . . . [that] taken together as one scheme . . . define men's rights and duties and influence their life-prospects, what they can expect to be and how well they can hope to do."[16] Rawls assumes that we can understand the basic structure well enough to regulate it by principles of justice.

The third premise follows naturally from the second, namely, that there is some agency capable of changing the institutional structure in more or less the way our favored theory demands. It is no use setting out principles for reforming the basic structure if in fact we have no means to implement these reforms. The main agency here is obviously the state: theories of social justice propose legislative and policy changes that a well-intentioned state is supposed to introduce. I don't mean to imply that the theories in question are exclusively addressed to legislators and other state officials. Very often the cooperation of citizens is needed to make the reforms work, so we can say that the theory is put forward as a public doctrine that ideally every member of the political community is supposed to embrace.[17] Nevertheless, given that the theory is meant to regulate the basic structure, and given that the structure is a complex of institutions with its own internal dynamics, an agency with the power and directing capacity that the state is supposed to have is essential if a theory of justice is to be more than a utopian ideal.

These three premises together define the circumstances of social justice: if we do not inhabit bounded societies, or if people's shares of goods and bads do not depend in ways we can understand on a determinate set of social institutions, or if there is no agency capable of regulating that basic structure, then we no longer live in a world in which the idea of social justice has any purchase. As noted, we must eventually ask whether our existing world has not already passed beyond these circumstances. But for present purposes I will assume that the circumstances of social justice still obtain, and examine more closely certain key questions concerning its scope. These questions are, first, how should we decide which advantages and burdens fall within the ambit of a theory of social justice? Second, what should be included within the basic institutional structure to which the theory applies, and how much space does this leave for individuals to act freely in pursuit of their own goals? Third, do we narrow the concept unduly if we think of it as applying to issues of material distribution, or should we expand it beyond what Iris Young has called "the distributive paradigm" to embrace phenomena such as power, domination, and oppression? Finally, can we still think of theories of social justice as applying within the boundaries of national political communities, or must we now enlarge the universe of distribution to embrace transnational constituencies or even the world as a whole? These are all large questions, but no theory of social justice can be elaborated without at least giving preliminary answers to them.

LET ME BEGIN, then, by trying to delimit the subject-matter of social justice, in the sense of the advantages and disadvantages whose distribution it seeks to regulate. A preliminary list of advantages must include at least the following: money and commodities, property, jobs and offices, education, medical care, child benefits and child care, honors and prizes, personal security, housing, transportation, and leisure opportunities. Alongside these must be placed a shorter list of disadvantages or burdens that are not punishments: military service, hard, dangerous, or degrading work, and care for the elderly. What makes these concerns of social justice is that they are valued goods (or disvalued goods in the case of the burdens) whose allocation depends on the workings of the major social institutions. Let us now look a little more closely at the rationale for including or excluding particular items. One thing that finds no place on the list is welfare (or happiness) interpreted as a psychic state of individuals. Social justice has to do with the means of obtaining welfare, not with welfare itself. This may seem paradoxical. Given that the goods matter because of the way in which they enhance individual lives, why not look more directly at this enhancement when assessing justice? One important reason is that between having access to a good and experiencing the well-being that may result there often stands a personal decision. In the most extreme case a person may simply choose not to avail him- or herself of the opportunity to enjoy a good—for instance, someone may turn down an offer to attend a particular college. Who gets admitted to college is a matter of social justice, but who actually enjoys the ensuing benefits is not, at least insofar as this reflects free choice rather than, for instance, economic constraints.[18]

The line I have just drawn is not easy to maintain consistently, particularly, as we shall see in Chapter 10, when the criterion of justice at stake is *need,* which at first sight appears to stand in close proximity to welfare. Here I want to explore a related point. Social justice often has to do with the relative value of the advantages received by different people. Wages received, let us suppose, should reflect the productive worth of different employees, so that if A's contribution is twice that of B's, his income should be twice as high; the first prize in a literary competition should be worth significantly more than the second prize; and so on. When we make these judgments, we appeal to values standardized across the relevant group of potential recipients, not to values for particular persons. The fact that A attaches a low value to income above a certain minimum because he lives an ascetic lifestyle—so that in some intuitive sense $20,000 paid to him is hardly worth more than $10,000 paid to B— should not affect the way we apply our criteria of just distribution. It may be that by voluntary exchange or gift people can move to an outcome that gives each of them more welfare than the just allocation, and in general there will be no objection to this. Thus if the first prize for the literary competition is a valuable book and the second prize one that is less valuable, then it would be quite all right for the winners to swap books after the event if this happens to suit their tastes. But it would be quite wrong for the judges to do so in anticipation, even if they are fully confident about what each party would prefer. Justice is about assigning benefits whose values are established by their worth to the relevant population taken as a whole, and it must be blind to personal preferences.

It follows that the idea of social justice makes sense only if we assume there is a broad consensus about the social value of a range of goods, services, and opportunities, some disagreement in private valuations notwithstanding. We can intelligibly argue about the justice or injustice of a certain distribution of income because we can recognize money as having a standard value no matter who possesses it, despite the contrasting personal valuations of ascetics and epicureans. Some of us might think that public honors are not worth having, or college education a waste of time, but because we understand that these benefits are socially valued in a way that cuts across individual opinion, we can see the injustice when rich people buy honors or college places for their children. Equally, where this consensus begins to dissolve, we encounter advantages and disadvantages whose inclusion on the list of social justice concerns becomes controversial. Let me illustrate with two such cases.

The first is meaningful work. We know that for many people one of the main benefits of employment is the opportunity it gives to develop and exercise their talents in a context in which the exercise has clear value to others (this is what "meaningful work" refers to). A question then arises whether this is an advantage that justice should take into account; whether, in particular, work that is meaningful in this sense should be paid at a lower rate than nonmeaningful work by virtue of the fact that the people who are doing it are already getting "rewarded" in a psychic sense. The problem is that the way people experience these rewards varies a great deal, depending partly, perhaps, on how they themselves understand the meaning of work. Think by way of contrast about work that is physically unpleasant, such as garbage collecting. We can agree fairly readily that such work should be paid more highly than other work to compensate for its unpleasantness. If people are nonetheless able to take a certain kind of pride in doing the work, this should be seen as a bonus that wage justice must disregard.[19] We can acknowledge this because there is widespread consensus about the disutility of work of this nature, so we can treat it as a burden with standard value. Meaningful work is a difficult case precisely because of the very wide differences of opinion about its value.

For a second case consider recognition, or status in the sense of the differential prestige that may attach to jobs, offices, and achievements of various kinds. Again we are dealing with a good that may play a big part in deciding how well a person's life is going, and so it seems a prime candidate for inclusion among the stuff of social justice. The problem is that, when we look at the good more closely, it has an objective and a subjective side, and the two may not correspond at all closely. The objective side consists in the opinions of others about, let us say, the job that someone holds, and the way that they convey these opinions through speech and behavior (showing deference, for example). The subjective side consists in the person's own estimation of his or her position, and the way this translates into self-esteem. Thus someone might be a successful accountant and get all the usual marks of esteem and other rewards provided by that job, but because he inwardly despises the work he is doing, or counts himself a failure because there are goals beyond the job that he thinks he really should have achieved, he takes no pleasure in the trappings of his position. This is an extreme case, but in general the range of possibilities is so wide that we may be reluctant to think of recognition as something whose allocation can be regulated by interpersonal principles of justice.

These, then, are borderline cases: social justice has to do with the way in which benefits and burdens are assigned to individuals on the assumption that these benefits and burdens can be assigned a value independent of the particular person who receives them. To the extent that we can attach a general value to the assignment of goods like meaningful work and recognition, there is good reason to include them within the orbit of social justice. The difficulty of doing so explains why we tend to focus on the tangible manifestations of a good such as recognition (we worry about job titles, who gets a company car and who doesn't, and so forth) rather than on the thing itself.

Something similar applies to another broad category of goods whose provision might seem to raise questions of justice, namely, public goods, in the familiar sense of goods that are made available to everyone (or at least to everyone in a certain geographical area) without restriction, such as recreational facilities provided free of charge or environmental features such as national parks that anyone can enjoy. Since a significant proportion of most state budgets is used to provide such goods, and given that priorities have to be set between different goods and the costs of provision met by retrenching on private consumption through taxation, we would expect social justice to encompass the fair allocation of public goods. Of course parks and the like are not distributed to individuals in a literal sense; nonetheless, access to parks or, to take another example, access to a public transportation system is something that different people may possess to different degrees (if I cannot make my way to a national park, then although in some sense the park is "available" to me, it would be odd to treat it as a benefit that I enjoy). So why do theories of social justice focus almost exclusively on privately held benefits like money and commodities? The answer, I believe, is that in many cases individuals' valuations of public goods are likely to diverge so radically that it is hard to discover a social value we could then say accrued to those who had access to the good in question. This is plainly not a satisfactory state of affairs, and more effort needs to go into developing a metric that would enable us to value public goods in such a way that they could be incorporated centrally into theories of social justice.[20] But meanwhile most public goods occupy a somewhat peripheral place in debates about justice.

To conclude, we should not be dogmatic about delineating the sub-ject-matter of social justice. We can identify certain resources whose distribution must be of central concern to any theory of (social) jus-tice—income and wealth, jobs and educational opportunities, health care, and so forth. Beyond this core there will be other benefits and burdens whose inclusion will be more arguable, but we must be prepared to listen to those who claim that being deprived of access to an adequate share of X, or having Y imposed upon them, makes the people concerned worse off in terms that anyone should be able to recognize. There is no canonical list of primary goods, in Rawls' sense, but instead a moveable boundary between justice-relevant and justice-irrelevant goods, the posi-tion of the boundary depending partly on the technical capacities of our social institutions, and partly on the degree of consensus that can be reached about the value of particular goods.[21]

IN SAYING THAT social justice has to do with how advantages and disadvantages are distributed to individuals in a society, we must be careful not to take "distributed" in too literal a sense. In particular, we must avoid thinking that there is some central distributing agency that assigns resource quotas to persons. Instead we are concerned with the ways in which a range of social institutions and practices together in-fluence the shares of resources available to different people, in other words, with the distributive effects of what Rawls calls "the basic struc-ture of society." But what exactly do we mean by "the basic structure," and in particular, when are the actions of individuals to be included within the structure and when are they not to be?[22]

There is no question that the state is the primary institution whose policies and practices contribute to social justice or injustice. If we look at the list of advantages on p. 7 above, we see that in each case the state, through its various branches and agencies, has a major influence on the share going to each person: it enacts property laws, sets taxes, organizes (directly or indirectly) the provision of health care, and so forth. Yet in nearly every case, the effects of state action interact with those of other agencies. Money and commodities are allocated through markets as well as through the public system of taxes and transfers; medical care is allocated by hospitals and health centers with varying degrees of auton-omy (and finally by individual doctors); and access to housing is deter-mined partly by state provision, partly by housing associations and other such independent agencies, and partly by the property and rental markets.

Without the collaboration of other institutions and agencies, the state itself would be largely impotent. If we are genuinely concerned about social justice, therefore, we must apply its principles to substate institutions that individually or together produce distributive effects that range across a society.[23] Take as one example college admissions. Here we have a number of semi-autonomous institutions each producing an allocation of benefits (offers of admission) that may itself be the aggregate result of many small decisions. Yet the overall result is important from the point of view of social justice, not only because higher education is a good in its own right, but because who receives it also determines in the long run the allocation of many other benefits. Thus assessing admissions procedures in terms of social justice is in order, as is looking at the way housing associations choose their tenants, or the way employers decide whom to promote in their firms. Although practices of these kinds affect only a few people directly, they need to be seen as part of a wider practice that has quantifiable social consequences. Thus if most employers discriminate against women when deciding on promotion, there is not merely individual injustice to the particular women denied advancement, but social injustice too. The "basic structure of society" must be taken to include practices and institutions like these whose individual repercussions are quite local but, when taken together, produce society-wide effects.

Indeed, it may be too restricting to confine social justice entirely to the assessment of practices and institutions, understood as formally organized patterns of human activity. Suppose that in the housing market there is widespread reluctance on the part of the members of the majority community to sell houses to members of an ethnic minority, simply because of racial prejudice. As a result, the minority has a restricted choice of houses and typically must bid somewhat over the normal range of market prices for housing. This would be a social injustice brought about by a pattern of spontaneous behavior on the part of individuals acting as private persons.

This example suggests more generally that institutions can produce socially just outcomes only if there is general compliance with their governing principles. This is obviously the case for those who staff the institutions, but it applies to the public at large as well. It may be an objective of public policy to make housing available on equal terms to all the groups who together form a political community, but this objective will be frustrated if large numbers of individuals behave in a discriminatory way when buying and selling their homes. Hence social justice cannot only be an ideal that guides politicians and officials and voters at the ballot box. It must also constrain everyday behavior: people need not see themselves as acting in direct pursuit of social justice, but they do need to recognize that it sets limits on what they can do. Justice does not necessarily prohibit people from acting competitively in pursuit of their interests—trying to outbid their rivals for a desirable house or competing for jobs or promotions—but it does require them to recognize rules and principles that prohibit some ways of winning these competitions (offering bribes to the relevant officials, for instance). There has to be a culture of social justice that not only permeates the major social institutions but also constrains people's behavior even when they are not formally occupying an institutional role.

This raises the question whether social justice and individual liberty are necessarily at odds with each other. Strong libertarians argue that people's legitimate freedom to use their justly acquired resources is so extensive as to leave no space for policies and practices of social justice.[24] A more widely held view is that public policy should trade off the conflicting demands of liberty and justice—for instance, when imposing nondiscrimination legislation on employers. What both views overlook is the way in which conceptions of social justice affect our understanding of liberty itself.

They do so in two ways. First, a central element in any theory of justice will be an account of the basic rights of citizens, which will include rights to various concrete liberties, such as freedom of movement and freedom of speech. The exact nature and extent of these rights will depend on how citizenship is understood within the theory in question, but in general we can say that an extensive sphere of basic liberty is built into the requirements of social justice itself. Second, one of the most contested and intractable issues to arise in debates about freedom is whether and when lack of resources constitutes a constraint on freedom. If we say that the extent of a person's freedom depends on how far he is prevented or otherwise constrained from performing actions that he might want to perform, then we have to ask, for example, whether only laws or other coercive impediments count as constraints, or whether lack of material means—say, the money to put your child through college—also counts.

In my view this question cannot be answered without appealing (openly or tacitly) to a conception of social justice. This is because I hold a version of the responsibility view of freedom, according to which an obstacle to someone's action counts as a constraint on their freedom if and only if another agent (or set of agents) is responsible for the existence of that obstacle.[25] But since "responsible" here means "morally responsible," this in turn can be established only by looking at what people owe one another as a matter of justice. Thus if we think that suitably qualified people have a right to higher education, then we owe it to our fellow citizens as a matter of justice to secure this right materially, and someone who is prevented from attending college by lack of resources can properly claim that her freedom has been restricted. By contrast, someone who can't afford to buy a racing yacht can't claim an impairment of his freedom, because there is no obligation of justice to provide yachts, and so no one can be held morally responsible for the financial obstacle this person faces.

I am not claiming here that individual liberty and social justice can never conflict. Clearly they can: to take the most mundane of examples, when people are taxed to provide social services for others, their freedom is reduced in the name of justice. It may, however, be that *overall* freedom is increased, taking into account the range of actions now open to the recipients of the services that were not open before, in which case the conflict is as much between freedom and freedom as it is between freedom and justice. My point is that we cannot confront aspirations to social justice with a predefined conception of individual liberty, because what counts as liberty, as well as how it should be distributed, will depend on how we understand justice itself.

I HAVE DEFINED the scope of social justice broadly, both in terms of the range of advantages and disadvantages whose distribution its principles seek to regulate, and in terms of the institutional structure to which it applies. Some critics will argue, nonetheless, that the account given stills falls within "the distributive paradigm" by virtue of its focus on the distribution of material resources like income, education, and health care.[26] For that reason, such critics argue, the account is too narrow, and must at the very least be broadened to include aspects of social relations that do not fall readily under the rubric of distribution. For Iris Young, for instance, social justice centrally requires "the elimination of institutionalized domination and oppression," and distributive issues should be tackled from that perspective.

This critique requires some unpicking. It has three main strands. First, theories of social justice that fall within the distributive paradigm are charged with focusing their attention on distributive outcomes rather than on the processes that gave rise to those outcomes, especially the hierarchical structures of power that may explain why the final distributions—of wealth and income, say—have the shape they do. At first sight it might seem that this charge simply misses the point, because the reason for focusing on distributive outcomes is not simply to label them just or unjust, but to indict the institutions and practices that create unjust outcomes. If the capitalist organization of industry produces distributions of income, working conditions, and so forth that fail the test of justice, then that gives us good reason to attempt to find a better alternative. Young claims, however, that decision-making processes can be unjust independent of their distributive consequences, simply by virtue of the fact that they give some people power to decide issues that they should not possess.

I accept this claim insofar as I believe that procedural justice has a value of its own that cannot be reduced to outcome justice. I consider this further in Chapter 5, where I argue that procedures are fair when they satisfy a number of independent criteria having in common the quality that they show respect for the people who are subject to them. Wherever decision-making power is concentrated in the hands of one person or a small number of people, it is less likely that the decisions taken will satisfy these criteria. Thus far I agree with Young's claim. I am not convinced, however, that all claims for the greater democratization of social life are best understood as claims for social justice. Consider the (persuasive) case for industrial democracy. Part of the argument is that when employees manage their own firms, the distribution of income and other benefits within the firms is more likely to be fair—this is an argument about social justice.[27] Part of the argument is that the experience of self-management—of being involved in decision-making, of taking responsibility for the firms' achievements—encourages the employees to develop and use personal capacities that would otherwise remain dormant. This (good) argument is not about justice; it concerns personal autonomy and personal development. Unless someone wants to maintain that social justice should encompass all the features of a good society, there is no point in stretching the concept to include these values.

A second strand in Young's argument has to do with the division of labor. She points out that whereas conventional theories of distributive justice can address discrimination on grounds of race or sex in getting access to jobs, they cannot capture the injustice involved when tasks are divided in such a way as to make certain tasks seem appropriate to some groups (for example, women) and not others, with the result that these tasks are overwhelmingly performed by members of the designated groups. (She points out that in the United States, for instance, menial service jobs are nearly always filled by members of racial minorities.) Only an expanded conception of social justice such as the one she favors can address this issue.

The problem in assessing this argument is that in the real world such patterning is almost certain to arise from conscious or unconscious discrimination on the part of those who have to fill jobs, and so it will be condemned by "distributive" theories that include, for instance, a principle of equal opportunity. But suppose this were not so, and the patterning arose simply because members of group X were convinced that they were only capable of performing tasks belonging to category C, or that it was only proper for them to perform such tasks. We would certainly think that the members of X were suffering from a form of false consciousness and were self-destructively limiting their opportunities. We would also want to raise questions about how these beliefs had come into common circulation. But the mere fact that the group in question holds such beliefs, and acts accordingly, cannot be described as an injustice.[28]

My response to the third strand in Young's argument, which concerns the cultural representation of different social groups, for instance, the way in which the mass media portray women and blacks, is much the same. Is it an injustice to blacks if, as Young claims, the media regularly represent them as "criminals, hookers, maids, scheming dealers, or jiving connivers"?[29] This state of affairs immediately raises two concerns about social justice. First, is it possible for employers and others to give genuinely equal opportunities to blacks if they are constantly being bombarded with such negative images? Second, is it possible for blacks to think of themselves as equal citizens along with others if the public media routinely portray them in this way? These questions connect Young's concern to principles, which, as I shall show, fit naturally within a conception of social justice that belongs within what she calls the distributive paradigm. By contrast, if the focus is simply on the way in which media representations might tend to encourage blacks or other groups to adopt certain roles (and so be self-fulfilling), I am less sure that this is a violation of justice. Certainly, following John Stuart Mill, we want people to choose their plan of life for themselves, and exercise faculties other than the ape-like one of imitation, but it is not an injustice if this fails to happen.[30]

Conceiving social justice in terms of how the basic structure of a society distributes advantages and disadvantages to its members need not be unduly restrictive so long as both "advantages and disadvantages" and "basic structure" are understood broadly. Relations of domination and oppression are drawn into this picture because the systematic presence of such relations is clear evidence that the basic structure is unjust. At the same time the centrality of ideas of social justice to contemporary political debate should not induce us to pack into the concept everything we might find socially desirable. As Isaiah Berlin has often reminded us, to assimilate distinct political ideals to one another is not only to court confusion, but to obscure the need for choices that involve some sacrifice of one value, which might be justice itself, in the name of others—democracy, individuality, or social harmony.

THROUGHOUT THE DISCUSSION I have spoken about "distribution among the members of a society" and "the basic structure of a society" without indicating what "a society" means in these phrases. I pointed out that theorists of social justice down to Rawls have assumed that their theories are to be applied within a self-contained political community without trying to justify this assumption. But the assumption is open to challenge from two directions. First, it is often argued that nowadays people's shares of resources and their life prospects generally depend not just on the working of domestic institutions within states, but also on transnational economic and political forces. The "basic structure" (if we continue for the moment using this term), therefore, must now be understood to include institutions (such as global capital markets) that are not subject to control by the state at national level. Second, from a normative perspective, there is no reason principles of distributive justice should be applied within national societies rather than across humanity as a whole. We should be thinking of global justice, not of social justice understood parochially.

I will return to the first challenge in the final chapter of the book, when I have finished laying out the theory of social justice I want to defend. As to the second challenge, I argued earlier that when we apply principles of justice such as those analyzed and defended in this book—primarily principles of need, desert, and equality—we presuppose a social universe within which distributions can be judged fair or unfair.[31] This universe can be small or large: we are concerned about justice within small groups like families or workplaces as well as within wider societies. But nation-states have a special standing here, because where a state is constituted in such a way that its citizens share a common national identity, the resulting political community has three features that make the application of principles of justice feasible and fruitful.

First, national identities tend to create strong bonds of solidarity among those who share them, bonds that are strong enough to override individual differences of religion, ethnicity, and so forth. The community that is formed in this way becomes a natural reference group when people ask themselves whether the share of resources they are getting is fair or not. They compare themselves primarily with fellow members rather than with outsiders when thinking about whether their income is too low or whether the educational opportunities available to their children are adequate. My claim is not that justice formally *requires* this particular scope restriction, but that the principles we use are always, as a matter of psychological fact, applied within bounded communities, and that the integrating power of national identity is sufficiently great to make the national community our primary universe of distribution. Sometimes our sense of justice may be more forcefully engaged by distribution in smaller units such as workplaces, but it is very hard to imagine this happening within units *larger* than nation-states. A Spaniard who feels that he is being underpaid may be comparing himself with other Spaniards generally, or with other workers in his factory or village, but he will not be comparing himself with Germans or Americans, say.[32]

Second, national political cultures include a range of shared understandings that form an essential background to principles of social justice. As I have shown, the idea of social justice presupposes that there is agreement both about the basis on which people can make just claims to resources and about the value of the resources that are being distributed. Thus principles of desert presuppose that we can identify valued activities (such as performing well in education, or contributing to the production of goods and services), forming the basis on which individuals come to deserve benefits of different kinds; principles of need presuppose shared understandings of what someone must have in order to lead a minimally adequate human life. On the other side of the equation, justice sometimes requires that people should receive benefits in proportion to their deserts, and sometimes that they should receive equal benefits. In each case there must be common standards of value that allow us to compute the worth of what someone is receiving. Because these shared understandings are so easily taken for granted *within* national communities, we may overlook the difficulty involved even in specifying what distributive justice would mean across such communities.

Finally, for social justice to become an operative ideal that guides people's everyday behavior, those concerned must have sufficient assurance that the restraint they show in following fair principles and procedures will be matched by similar restraint on the part of others. There is little point in pursuing social justice singlehandedly if everyone else is taking part in a free-for-all. Nation-states can help to provide such an assurance, partly because the solidarity they generate encourages mutual trust, and partly because the state is on hand to penalize defaulters. Such penalties can never be wholly effective, but if, say, I have to decide whether to fill in my tax return honestly—which I am willing to do, provided that others do likewise—then the thought that cheats stand some chance of being caught and punished is reassuring. What can motivate adherence to principles of social justice, then, is trust backed up by compulsion, and it is this combination of forces that nation-states are uniquely able to provide.

The absence of these three features at world level means that global justice cannot be understood on the model of social justice, at least not for the foreseeable future. Here and now we must continue to think of social justice as applying within national political communities, and understand global justice differently. I have argued elsewhere that our thinking about global inequalities should be guided not by comparative principles, such as principles of equality, but by the noncomparative ideas of *protecting basic rights* and *preventing exploitation*.[33] Thus to say that the scope of social justice should be limited by the boundaries of national political communities is not to say that we owe no duties of justice to people living outside those boundaries. But we should not confuse the two, in theory or in practice. The pursuit of social justice is a special project, bounded in time and space, and one that is sufficiently complex by itself to fill the pages of the present book.

2

A Sketch of a Theory of Justice

What is the point of elaborating a theory of justice? All morally competent adults have a well-developed sense of justice that enables them to cope with the practical questions they confront from day to day. How should my neighbor and I share the cost of the new fence that will run between our properties? Which child in my class ought to get the academic prize? Should I give Smith, my employee, the leave he has asked for to look after his sick mother? We know how to think about such questions, and we can answer them without any knowledge of the many abstract theories of justice that political philosophers from Plato to Rawls have advanced. So why bother to develop such a theory? Intellectual curiosity aside, how does having a theory at our disposal help us in knowing how to act justly?

We need theories, we are usually told, because of *uncertainty* and *disagreement* about what justice requires of us. Although we may know roughly in what terms to think about problems like those described above, we are often in the end unsure which principles we ought to be applying; faced with what is essentially the same problem on different occasions, we may give different answers because our intuitions are differently engaged. For the same reason, we may disagree with one another over what justice requires of us in some cases, and this is inherently unsatisfactory, because it means that at least one of us will be left bearing a grievance. Justice is a social virtue—it tells us how to order our relationships, what we must rightly do for one another—and so our hope must be that we can all agree about what justice demands of us, that everyone can feel that his or her legitimate claims have been met. A successful theory would persuade people to regulate their intuitive sense of justice by its principles and allow this hope to be realized.

In elaborating such a theory, the usual strategy is to look for some abstract principle or set of principles that, it is claimed, underlie and inform people's intuitive judgments—or most of them, at least. We hope to achieve unanimity by stripping away the concrete material and leaving only the general framework in place. Thus, it is said, justice fundamentally requires us *to treat people as equals;* or we should understand justice as *what people would agree to in advance of knowing their own stake in the decision to be reached.* This strategy may buy agreement, but it does so at a very high price. In the process of abstraction we abandon much of our intuitive sense of what justice requires of us in particular cases, but the result is that the principle or principles we end up with can't give us the practical guidance we need. How do general conceptions such as those just mentioned help us decide how to share the cost of the fence, which child should get the prize, or how to deal with Smith's request for leave? Of course the sponsors of these theories may announce that they have practical implications, but very often the concrete judgments favored by the theorist are inserted back into the theory without it being shown that these are entailed or even strongly suggested by the abstract premises. (One test of this would be to ask people ignorant of theories like that of Rawls to say which principles of social justice *they* thought would be chosen by individuals who were ignorant of their personal characteristics and social position. If my hypothesis is correct, the answer would either be "Don't know," or else the interviewees would fill in the conception of justice they would favor in any case, quite apart from the abstract setting of the question.)[1]

If we reject the usual method of abstraction for this reason, what alternatives are left to us? We may decide to adopt some form of skepticism about justice, a view implying that no general theory of justice has any claim to objectivity. One form of skepticism holds that claims about justice simply express the emotions of the person making them— if someone takes strong exception to some action or state of affairs, that person calls it an injustice. This view is likely to form part of a more general emotivist account of moral judgment, such as that advanced by twentieth-century logical positivists.[2] Another skeptical view holds that beliefs about justice are purely conventional, in the sense that they reflect the customs and practices of a particular society; when social arrangements change, people's beliefs about the justice of those arrangements will alter in tandem. Pascal expresses this with characteristic force: "Justice is what is established; thus all our established laws will necessarily be regarded as just without examination since they are established."[3]

A third form of skepticism about justice consists in maintaining that ideas of justice are imposed by powerful individuals or classes of individuals for the purpose of maintaining social relations that serve their interests. This view has a long pedigree. It is represented in Plato's *Republic* by Thrasymachus' claim that "justice is the interest of the stronger." It takes another form in Marx's assertion that every notion of justice is an idealized reflection of the prevailing set of relations of production, serving to secure acquiescence in those relations to the benefit of the economically dominant class. We find it again in Nietzsche's writings when he states that "wherever justice is practiced and maintained, we see a stronger power intent on finding means to regulate the senseless raging of rancor among its weaker subordinates."[4] Skepticism of this sort invites us to *explain* beliefs about justice, but it appears to exclude a (normative) theory of justice with any claim to general validity.[5] Finally, we may take note of recent attempts to portray justice as essentially a *fragmentary* notion, one whose meaning shifts among the many practices or language games in which it plays a part, and of which it is therefore impossible to give a valid general account.[6]

Skepticism of any of these forms tells us to abandon the search for a general theory of justice. Disagreement about justice will be universal, it is irresolvable, and all we can do is observe the game being played out in its various incarnations. A less nihilistic response is also possible, however. If substantive agreement about justice cannot be achieved, it may still be possible for people to agree about procedures to be followed in resolving their disagreements. Thus, for instance, certain methods of arbitration may command general support. If my neighbor and I cannot agree about a fair division of the costs of the new fence, we may ask a third person whom we both trust to propose a solution, and we may accept her proposal even though it does not entirely tally with what either of us thinks is substantially fair. As Stuart Hampshire has put this idea, "There is a basic concept of justice which has a constant connotation and core sense, from the earliest times until the present day; and it always refers to a regular and reasonable procedure of weighing claims and counter-claims, as in an arbitration or court of law. The procedure is designed to avoid destructive conflict."[7] This notion coexists with a multitude of constantly changing substantive conceptions of justice.

It is an important aspect of our thinking about justice that we can rely on procedural justice in this way when substantive agreement fails. But I do not think the idea can be pushed too far. Our reliance on fair procedures works against a background of substantive agreement.[8] Because we agree *in general terms* about what a fair resolution of our dispute would look like, we are able to concur on a procedure to resolve fine points of disagreement. Arbitration, for instance, usually occurs when two sides have negotiated their way to positions close to each other but still not quite convergent; the arbitrator is expected to pick an outcome somewhere in the middle. If disagreement were radical, by contrast, we would probably be unable to find a mutually acceptable procedure. If my neighbor and I are poles apart in our thinking, whom should we ask to settle the dispute? Each of us is likely to have his preferred candidate, whose methods of arbitration correspond to our different background assumptions about what is at stake between us. A similar problem would arise in choosing a mechanism to resolve disagreement; different mechanisms can be expected to bias the outcome in one way or another.[9]

If our disagreements about substantive questions of justice were as radical as the skeptics suggest, therefore, we could not hope to extricate ourselves from the skeptical quagmire by putting forward an account of procedural justice that would command general support. Agreement on procedures is possible, to repeat, because we do not disagree *too much* about what justice demands substantively. Fortunately, the evidence does not bear out the skeptics' claim that ideas of justice are fragmentary and fluctuating. If we look empirically at what people believe is fair when asked to pronounce on various practical questions, we find quite stable patterns of belief.[10] Of course there are deviant views, people sometimes contradict themselves, and so forth, but we do not find the kind of random variation that would make skepticism about justice hard to fend off.

This suggests a third way of building up a theory of justice. Rather than moving directly from intuitive beliefs to highly abstract principles, we should begin by trying to discover the practical principles that guide those beliefs, leaving it an open question for the moment whether those principles are consistent with one another when considered in the abstract. We might, for instance, discover that people compartmentalized their thinking about justice—applying one principle to this class of issues, another principle to that class—but did so in a regular manner. In this case our theory would lay out a plurality of principles of justice, each having a defined area of application, and there might or might not be a single vantage point from which this diversity could be explained.

How should we begin to construct a theory of this third sort? One way might be to consider the range of benefits and burdens whose distribution is considered a matter of justice, and see whether these can be categorized in such a way that each category carries with it its own principle of distribution. This is Michael Walzer's program in *Spheres of Justice:* Walzer argues that we should take a good such as education, consider what meaning it has for us, and elicit from the meaning a criterion of just distribution.[11] Walzer's approach has a great deal to commend it, but one difficulty it faces is that it seems unable to deal with the case where people seriously and authentically disagree about how justice requires a social good to be allocated. Sometimes disagreements about justice may stem from conflicting interests, with one side arguing for distributive criterion X because that gives it greater access to the good in question, whereas deep down this is recognized to be unfair. But not all cases are like this: some people believe it is unjust for parents to purchase superior education for their children; others think that it is not unjust so long as all children have access to decent education, and those in the second group are not all prospective buyers. We have here a conflict about justice that cannot be explained away entirely in terms of interests, nor can it be resolved simply by appealing to the meaning of education. There is no reason to think that the two sides disagree about what education is and what its value consists in.[12]

I PROPOSE A DIFFERENT KIND of pluralism about justice, one that may allow us to see some of Walzer's very illuminating examples in a new light. Rather than starting with social goods and their meanings, let us begin with what I shall call "modes of human relationship." Human beings can stand in different kinds of relationship to one another, and we can best understand which demands of justice someone can make of us by looking first at the particular nature of our relationship. In the real world such relationships are very often complex and multifaceted, but it is possible to analyze them in terms of a small number of basic modes. If our aim is to discover what social justice means to the denizens of modern liberal societies, we need to consider three such basic modes, which I shall label *solidaristic community, instrumental association,* and *citizenship.*[13]

The theory of social justice that I sketch in the following pages is not intended to be complete. In particular, it ignores the fact that people who are related in one or more of these three basic ways will usually also have an institutional relationship, defined by the law or by other rules and procedures. To take a simple case, you and I might be related as buyer and seller of a certain commodity, which would make our basic relationship an instrumental one as explained below. But we may also enter into a formal contract to exchange the commodity, in which case each of us will have certain legal rights and duties with respect to the other. These rights and duties give rise to claims of justice: I can justly demand that you buy the commodity at the price we have agreed upon. In the present discussion I shall ignore such institutionally derived claims.[14] My aim is to identify the *underlying* principles of justice that spring directly from the various modes of relationship, and that, I claim, explain the shape of the associated institutions (for instance, in the case I cited, the terms of the contract will be broadly determined by the instrumental nature of our relationship).

The first of the three modes of relationship, solidaristic community, exists when people share a common identity as members of a relatively stable group with a common ethos. It begins from face-to-face relationships between people that engender mutual understanding and mutual trust, but it can extend beyond a directly interacting group to encompass a wider circle who see themselves as bound together by common beliefs or culture as well as by kinship or acquaintance. We may conjecture that this is the primordial mode of human association, and in forms such as the village community it has acted as the main source of social bonding in all premodern societies. In modern liberal societies, by contrast, it exists only in a somewhat attenuated form. For most people solidaristic relationships occur chiefly within the family. Looser forms of solidarity emerge in clubs, religious groups, work teams, professional associations, and so forth. On a wider scale nationhood offers a form of community that is indirect and mediated by common practices and common culture. To enjoy communal relations of a direct kind on a scale beyond the family, one must enter a religious community or a secular equivalent such as a kibbutz.

Within solidaristic communities the substantive principle of justice is distribution according to need. Each member is expected to contribute to relieving the needs of others in proportion to ability, the extent of liability depending upon how close the ties of community are in each case (thus I can demand more help from my brother than from my colleague at work). Needs will be understood in terms of the general ethos of the community. Each community embodies, implicitly or explicitly, a sense of the standards that an adequate human life must meet, and it is in terms of this benchmark that the much-contested distinction between needs, which are matters of justice, and mere wants is drawn.[15] This is clearest in cases where the community embodies specific ethical commitments, as in the case of the medieval Jewish communities described by Walzer in *Spheres of Justice*.[16] Here needs were understood in relation to religious ideals: this meant, for instance, that education was seen as a need for boys but not for girls; that food was distributed to the poorest members of the communities on the eve of the religious festivals; and so forth. In other cases greater weight is given to the particular aims and aspirations of each individual member, but always against a background understanding of the community's ethos. Within families the way resources are spent reflects individual ambitions, but distinctions are still drawn between legitimate needs (music lessons for the children, say) and simple indulgences (the latest video game).

The second mode of relationship is instrumental association. Here people relate to one another in a utilitarian manner; each has aims and purposes that can best be realized by collaboration with others. Economic relations are the paradigm case of this mode. We relate to one another as buyer and seller of goods and services, or we collaborate in producing some product that is to be sold in the market. But organizations more generally can also be seen as examples of instrumental association, whether or not their purposes are narrowly economic. Thus government bureaucracies or indeed charitable organizations can be seen as instrumental in nature insofar as the people who work for them do so as a means of earning pay, achieving professional advancement, or attaining other such private goals, and regard their fellow workers simply as collaborating in pursuit of these ends. In real cases, of course, work groups are likely to take on a partly solidaristic character, as I suggested earlier. We form friendships, recognize loyalties, stand prepared to help our colleagues. But this underlines the point that the modes of association I am distinguishing must be treated as ideal types, pure forms of relationship that illuminate rather than literally describe actual cases. (In the same way, almost every solidary relationship will have its instrumental aspects too—family life illustrates this point only too readily.)

Insofar as relationships among a group of people approximate to instrumental association, the relevant principle of justice is distribution according to desert. Each person comes to the association as a free agent with a set of skills and talents that he deploys to advance its goals. Justice is done when he receives back by way of reward an equivalent to the contribution he makes. A person's deserts, in other words, are fixed by the aims and purposes of the association to which she belongs; these provide the measuring rod in terms of which relative contributions can be judged. In the case of economic enterprises this criterion is in principle easy to apply. The output of the enterprise can be measured in monetary terms, and each participant should receive by way of income that portion of net output for which she is responsible. In practice such judgments can be very difficult to make for a number of reasons.

One reason is complementarities in production. In many cases a person will be working as part of a team whose joint product may be identifiable, but if each has different skills or plays a different role in the team, it may be hard to assess individual contributions. If skills were literally unique, it would be impossible: if A and B together make a product, but there is no one else who could take A's place and no one who could take B's, then we have no way of measuring their respective deserts. Fortunately, this case stands at the end of a spectrum, and more commonly a person will bring to an association a set of skills that have a general value attached to them by the labor market. Thus if an electrician joins our association and works conscientiously through a standard work week, we can form a rough judgment of her deserts by looking at what electricians generally command in the market, for this will reflect the average contribution made by electricians to the various forms of production in which they engage.[17]

A second reason desert judgments may be difficult to make in practice is that instrumental associations tend nearly always to adopt formal structures in which people are placed in graded positions, with salaries and other benefits calculated according to the place a position occupies in the enterprise's hierarchy. From the point of view of desert, there are then two questions that we need to ask: first, is a particular position

remunerated at the right level, given the contribution a competent position-holder would be expected to make to the association?; second, is
the position being held by an appropriately qualified person? In other
words, does the job deserve the rewards, and does the person holding it
deserve the job?[18] Because a person's contribution is dependent in this
way on the position to which he or she is assigned, we can't assess desert
simply by present contribution. In the case of someone who is unfairly
denied promotion, for instance, we can't say that person now deserves
the rewards that she would have deserved had she been given the promotion for which she applied; the injustice done her consists in denying her
the job she deserved, not in denying her the salary to which she would
have been entitled.

A third kind of difficulty arises when there is disagreement about the
purposes of an association, and thus disagreement about what the basis
of desert should be when relative deserts are assessed. This is less likely
to arise in economic enterprises than in associations with less narrowly
focused aims. Professional associations, for instance, may develop standards of excellence that are not always aligned with the judgments of
people outside the association, who may take a different view of the
profession's aims. Thus university staff may be judged within the profession primarily by their success in conducting basic research, whereas
outsiders may attach greater weight to teaching or to research with practical applications. Or to take a different case, the medical profession may
have the highest regard for specialists who develop the latest surgical
techniques, whereas from the public's point of view the most deserving
doctors may be general practitioners who care in an all-round way for
their patients.[19] In these cases ambiguity about the purposes of an association translates into uncertainty about the proper basis of desert.

These are some of the complicating factors that arise when we try
to apply the principle that is appropriate to instrumental association,
namely, that each associate should justly receive a return proportional to
his or her contribution. It has become common to attack this principle in
a more radical way. How can some people deserve more than others
when their contribution depends upon a greater endowment of natural
talent, for which they can claim no credit? If people deserve rewards, it is
surely only on the basis of features of their activity for which they can be
held responsible, namely, their efforts and choices. Rather than using
contribution to measure desert, we must begin by factoring out whatever

stems from innate qualities, leaving only that fraction of contribution for which the person in question can be held responsible.

Whatever the general merits of this line of argument,[20] it seems inappropriate when we are considering distributive justice in the sphere of instrumental association.[21] Relationships in this mode are voluntary; people are under no obligation to engage in them and can withdraw from them whenever they wish, subject only to the contractual agreements that they have made. Each person is a free agent who associates with others either to promote ends he happens to share with them, or to pursue strictly private purposes (in exchange transactions, for example, each party is typically ignorant of the final purpose to which the other party will put the exchanged item). It is implicit here that each person is legitimately entitled to control and deploy his or her own skills and talents. By contrast, factoring out talents when deserts are calculated is equivalent to treating talents as a common asset whose fruits are to be shared equally among all the associates.[22] Such an understanding might be appropriate in a solidaristic community, but it contravenes the principle of instrumental association.[23]

The third mode of association relevant to my theory of justice is citizenship. In modern liberal democracies, members of a political society are related not just through their communities and their instrumental associations but also as fellow citizens. Anyone who is a full member of such a society is understood to be the bearer of a set of rights and obligations that together define the status of citizen. Citizenship is, of course, formally defined in law, but beneath the legal definition lies an understanding of citizenship as a common social and political status that may be appealed to in criticism of existing legal practice. This is not to say that the meaning of citizenship is well understood: there are different conceptions of citizenship that diverge, for instance, in the extent to which they regard active participation in the political affairs of the society as an essential attribute of the citizen.[24] At the end of this chapter I shall comment on the implications of this fact for the theory of justice.

The primary distributive principle of citizenship association is equality. The status of citizen is an equal status: each person enjoys the same set of liberties and rights, rights to personal protection, political participation, and the various services that the political community provides for its members. Someone deprived of this equal enjoyment is a "second-class citizen"—a rhetorical description that emphasizes the egalitarianism implicit in citizenship as a mode of relationship. How far this equality of status should stretch is a matter of some dispute: some would wish to confine it fairly narrowly to an equality of formal rights; others would argue that citizens cannot understand themselves as political equals unless they also enjoy a substantial measure of social equality—thus equal citizenship has ramifications for the distribution of property, income, and other social resources. On this broader understanding citizenship can be seen as a status that counteracts the inequalities that a market economy generates and legitimates, as it was by T. H. Marshall in his now-classic essay on the topic.[25]

Although equality is the primary principle of justice governing relations among citizens, sometimes citizenship may ground claims of justice based on need or desert. Citizens who lack the resources necessary to play their part as full members of the community have a just claim to have those resources provided. Thus medical aid, housing, and income support may for some people be regarded as needs from the perspective of citizenship. The difficulty here is to separate what is actually implicit in the idea of citizenship from the claims people can make on one another as members of national communities. For many people these two modes of relationship will overlap to a large extent: wherever the boundaries of the state coincide with the boundaries of the nation, people will be related to one another both as fellow citizens and as compatriots. In the latter capacity they will acknowledge obligations of justice to meet one another's needs as identified within the national culture, and these obligations will tend over time to be incorporated into the definition of citizenship itself.

A good example of this process can be found in the creation of welfare states. Originally introduced as an expression of national solidarity, rights to welfare have over time entered into the definition of citizenship, so that someone whose welfare rights are not respected can claim with justice that he or she is not being treated as an equal citizen. But it is not necessary to the idea of citizenship itself that it should embrace welfare rights in this way. As Walzer points out, the Athenians set aside funds to ensure that citizens who held public office could carry out their duties, but they took little direct interest in poverty as such, or in the need for medical care.[26] Given their particular understanding of citizenship, equality in these areas was not seen as a relevant demand.

We can now see why equality is the main principle of citizenship, while need is the leading principle of a solidaristic community. The former, unlike the latter, depends upon a formal principle of membership. Among citizens, certain needs matter from the point of view of justice because if they are not met, the equal status of some citizens is put at risk. In a community, by contrast, formal equality is not valued as such. To the extent that need is used as the basis for distributing resources to the exclusion of other criteria, communities of this kind may look markedly egalitarian overall, but here the equality is only a by-product: the effect of giving more resources to those whose needs are greater may indeed be to generate equality of a certain kind, measured by people's final scores on the index of functionings that are used to define need. What justice actually requires here, however, is that the quantity of resources each person receives should depend upon the strength of his or her claims of need.[27]

I suggested that desert, too, may play a secondary role among people related as citizens. Desert is recognized in the case of those who exceed the normal obligations of citizenship in furthering the ends of the political community. Thus honors are given to those who risk their lives in its defense, or to those who serve their fellow citizens in exceptional ways—engaging in civic works, and so forth. But in recognizing desert we do not compromise equality of status; returning generals may be given medals, but they are not given extra votes or privileged medical treatment. In this respect the current democratic understanding of citizenship diverges from older views, which saw a certain kind of desert as a *prerequisite* for holding the status of citizen (a citizen must be independent, educated, a property-owner, and so on).[28]

I HAVE BEEN TRYING to understand the plurality of principles of justice by seeing them as appropriate to different modes of human relationship. We relate to one another in our communities (at the very least in our families), in instrumental associations, and as citizens. Because these contrasting relationships call forth equally contrasting principles of justice, we face various practical dilemmas in which it is not clear which principle should guide our (public or private) decisions. I shall illustrate some of these conflicts in a moment. But first let me consider the charge that there is a circularity in the analysis offered here, that the modes of relationship have been defined in such a way that it is tautologically true that each supports a different principle of justice.

In asserting that each mode of relationship carries with it a distinct principle of justice, I was appealing to the reader's understanding of what we might call the "grammar" of justice. As a general virtue, justice may be understood, as the classic definition of Justinian has it, as "the set and constant purpose which gives to every man his due."[29] This phrase suggests that there is some mode of treatment that A should give to B, some other mode (possibly the same, possibly different) that he should give to C, and so forth. Justice means treating *each* person in the way that is appropriate to that individual personally. It also suggests that the treatment is something *due* to B, C, D, and so on—in other words, something that they can rightfully claim and something that A owes to them. These, then, are the general features that distinguish justice from other ethical principles. But to fill out the formula in a substantive way, we need to know *what* B, C, and D can rightfully claim from A, and this we cannot do without considering the general relationship in which they stand to him. Once the relationship is defined, we (as competent users of the concept of justice) know the criterion by which dues should be calculated, whether need, desert, equality, or something else.

This account would be circular, however, if the relationship could not be defined without invoking the criterion in question, for example, if we could not describe A's relationship to B without specifying that A is obliged as a matter of justice to meet B's needs. But this is not so. We were able to explain solidaristic community, for instance, as a mode of relationship without saying that the appropriate distributive principle within such a community is distribution according to need. Analytically we can separate the relationship from its associated principle of justice. In a full description of a solidaristic community, we will of course often want to mention the fact that resources are distributed according to need, for this gives the reader a richer description of the kind of community we are describing. Moreover, it will often be helpful to take the principle of justice that is acknowledged and acted upon in an association as symptomatic of the general character of that association. Suppose that a group of people who have hitherto been distributing resources among themselves solely on the basis of need begin to pay some attention to desert (suppose a kibbutz begins to award special privileges to those who hold the most responsible jobs in the kibbutz factories). This would give us good reason to think that the group was becoming less solidaristic and more instrumental in character—a conjecture that we could verify by looking at other aspects of group relations, such as the pattern of social contact.

What grounds do we have for asserting these connections between principles of justice and modes of association? We may begin by looking empirically at the judgments and behavior of people when they allocate resources in different contexts.[30] In particular, we can examine groups of people who are related in ways that approximate to each of the three ideal-typical modes and see how they assign and claim benefits among themselves—we can look at justice within families, enterprises, and so forth. Moreover, in case some latter-day Pascal should try to explain the differences we observe as merely the effect of custom and practice, we can create artificial groups and manipulate their character—encouraging the members to regard their group as having a predominantly solidaristic, predominantly instrumental, etc., nature—and then ask the subjects of our experiment to say what they think a just allocation of the group's resources would be. When we do this, we find that principles of justice are applied in a manner consistent with the pluralistic theory I have been sketching. In particular, the contrast between the use of need criteria in solidaristic groups and the use of desert criteria in instrumental groups has frequently been confirmed.[31]

This evidence should be taken more seriously than it usually is by social philosophers, for it guards us against the solipsistic fallacy that each of us already has a complete intuitive grasp of the requirements of justice.[32] Nonetheless, the evidence is not decisive from a normative point of view unless we can say something more about why a certain mode of social relationship makes the corresponding principle of justice the appropriate one to use. "Appropriate" here cannot just mean "the principle people do in fact use in these circumstances." It must be possible to show that the principle is fitting or relevant in one social context but not in another. We cannot hope to show that a mode of relationship *necessitates* the use of a certain principle of justice; but we can and must establish more than a merely empirical connection.

My argument here has two parts to it. First, a certain mode of relationship may be required to make a principle of justice *feasible* to use. I have already pointed out how the notion of need becomes problematic in the absence of a community with shared standards of an adequate human life. Wherever a community exists, we can say with some precision which needs justice requires us to meet; in the absence of such a community the concept becomes amorphous. Analogously, in the case of desert, an association with specific aims and purposes provides the criteria in terms of which different individuals' contributions can be assessed. Equality remains an empty notion until we have a more concrete conception of membership that specifies the rights and duties of citizens.

Second, a mode of association makes the use of one particular principle of justice *fitting* in a more direct sense. For instance, when people share a common identity as members of a community, they see their lives and destinies as interwoven, and their sense of themselves as free-floating individuals is correspondingly weakened; their solidarity gives rise to a more or less powerful sense of mutual obligation, and this naturally expresses itself in a conception of justice as distribution according to need. In an ideal-typical instrumental association, by contrast, the participants are strangers to one another who collaborate for a particular purpose. Each recognizes the others as autonomous agents with whom he collaborates for mutual advantage alone, and the claim that is recognized is the claim of contribution—hence the appropriateness of desert criteria when the resources of the association are being allocated.[33]

These connections are not entailments. Someone who recognizes that her relationship to B, C, and D is a purely instrumental one, but yet insists on construing justice among them in terms of need, is not guilty of a logical error. But to say this may be to say no more than that any move from the description of a situation to its ethical appraisal is less than an entailment. I may describe to you how Smith plunged into the foaming river without regard to his own safety to rescue a drowning child, but if you are not willing to recognize this as an act of courage, there is no way I can compel you to do so. In the same way, someone who has an implicit grasp of what I referred to earlier as the "grammar" of justice will understand the norms of appropriateness I am appealing to, but there is not much that can be said to someone who wants to pry justice loose from these moorings and present an entirely context-free theory, except that the enterprise is unlikely to succeed. Either the conception will be so abstract that it will give us little or no help in resolving practical disputes, or else it will be substantive but highly controversial—it will fail to persuade all those whose intuitive sense of justice tells them that *this* principle must be applied in *that* context.

HOW CAN THE CONTEXTUAL APPROACH to justice that I am proposing help us to resolve the practical conflicts that we encounter? If relationships between people were clear and distinct, the demands of justice would be easy to grasp. Unfortunately, they are neither. We are often unsure about how we stand in relation to someone who is making a demand upon us; and resource scarcities mean that we are often faced with conflicting claims, where B stands in one relation to us and claims accordingly, while C stands in some other relation and makes a different, competing claim. These uncertainties are reflected at the collective level, where institutions have to adjudicate between demands that are made upon them, and so they come to infect public policy. Let us consider some of the dilemmas that are posed by the juxtaposition of the three modes of relationship I have identified.

Take first the conflicts that are generated by the juxtaposition of solidaristic community and instrumental association. In the former case, I have claimed, justice means distribution according to need, and it is implicit here that my obligations are to co-members only. This, then, justifies me in giving favorable treatment to members of my own community, at least so long as this treatment can be reasonably understood as responding to need. But that may conflict with the desert principle required by instrumental association. For instance, when hiring new employees, are enterprises obliged to accept or reject candidates purely on the basis of merit as defined by the requirements of the job, or may they give preference to relatives of existing employees, to co-religionists, and so forth? The latter, we may suppose, need jobs and are competent to do them, albeit less competent than the best qualified candidates who are strangers. In this situation should we be guided by the desert principle appropriate to instrumental association or the need principle appropriate to communitarian relationships?

We might think that the answer to this question was settled by the nature of the good being allocated: a job by definition falls into the sphere of instrumental association. Although this is the answer I would defend, it is not self-evident, and indeed popular opinion shows the ambivalence one would expect in a case of this sort: when asked in a survey about an employee who uses his influence to get his relative a job, 44 percent of respondents could see nothing wrong in this behavior, and only 8 percent regarded it as seriously wrong—implying that it is at least permissible if not positively desirable to give precedence to solidaristic (here familial) obligations in this situation.[34] Similar dilemmas arise over the question whether it is allowable for parents to buy educational advantages for their offspring, and more generally over the issue of inherited wealth, which gives the children of rich families an undeserved position of economic privilege (it gives them immediate access to capital, for instance). If a person's position in the sphere of instrumental association should depend entirely upon his or her deserts, then these expressions of family solidarity must appear as unjust intrusions.

Let us turn now to conflicts arising between instrumental association and citizenship. There is a range of benefits whose distribution might be governed either by the desert principle appropriate to the former sphere or by the principle of equality appropriate to the latter. For instance, medical care might be provided through occupational health schemes in which employers pay insurance premiums on behalf of their employees, in which case the quality of health care people receive is likely to reflect their level of income, or alternatively through a national health service, where in principle everyone has access to the same level of care. Pensions again might be occupationally based (and therefore earnings-related), or state-provided and uniform.[35] Neither arrangement is *obviously* right. The argument from the instrumental perspective is that if someone deserves a certain reward to match his contribution, there is no reason he should not take part of that reward in the form of better health care or a higher pension. From the citizenship perspective, the counterargument is that social rights are an adjunct of citizenship, an essential complement to the core political rights, and as such should be allocated equally.

Another area of dispute is social support for people who cannot, but possibly might, find work to support themselves—the old problem, in short, of the deserving and the undeserving poor. As a citizen, everyone is entitled to a level of income that meets his basic needs as a condition of equal status. As an instrumental associate, everyone ought to get out of her association an equivalent of what she puts in, and it is unjust if A, who has searched for and now holds a job, receives no more income, or not much more, than B, who could perhaps get a similar job if he tried.

Finally, we might refer again to education as a good whose distribution can be looked at in terms of different modes of association. From an instrumental point of view, education is a practice within which children with different talents work to acquire new concrete skills that they then carry forward into the labor market; for the final distribution of occupational rewards to correspond to desert, each child must have access to educational resources according to his or her demonstrated capacity to make use of them. If we start from citizenship, by contrast, education matters as the place where children acquire the capacities that enable them to function as competent citizens, not only in the sense that they learn about their social and political environment, but also in the sense that they learn how to cooperate with others, to engage in political discourse, and generally to participate in the various spheres of social life. So here the distributive principle is equality, and the contrast between this perspective and the previous one emerges practically in debates over streaming (tracking) and selective schools, as well as over the content of the curriculum. The instrumental perspective points toward differential treatment of children according to ability and performance; whereas if we start by considering children and adolescents as future citizens, we will want them to share a common experience, to learn to associate with others from different class or ethnic backgrounds.

Education also provides an interesting case where the demands of justice that stem from specific communities may conflict with the demands that stem from citizenship. Recall that "needs" will be defined in both cases in terms of norms of an adequate human life; in the case of citizenship the relevant standard is simply a person's ability to engage satisfactorily in the range of activities that constitute citizenship. The needs of citizens may not coincide with the needs of members of particular communities. For instance, religious instruction may be considered a need in some communities—you cannot be a full member of the community unless you have learned to take part in its religious practices—whereas *qua* citizen a person may need above all to develop a capacity for tolerance of others who do not share her commitments. This points to two quite different policies in the sphere of education. From the perspective of the community in question, a just educational policy will provide religious instruction in a particular faith, whereas the needs of future citizens may best be fulfilled by exposing them to a variety of faiths, or at least by teaching them that religion is a subject about which people may legitimately hold different views. From this springs the debate about educational separatism and the national curriculum.

Although the case of education is most prominent in current debate, a similar conflict may emerge with respect to other needs. Where needs are publicly provided for, how far may groups holding particular conceptions of the good demand that provision for them respect their understanding of need? Should the state support alternative medicine, for example? Ought homoeopathy to be funded by a public health service?

People who answer these questions in the affirmative are arguing for the priority of community-defined needs, perhaps even asserting that in this area citizens' needs cannot be objectively identified.

I HAVE BEEN TRYING to illustrate how uncertainty over modes of relationship produces practical conflicts over distributive justice. Because we do not know how to understand our relationship to our associates in a given case, we dispute over what justice demands of us, which principle ought to trump the others. Can a theory of justice help us here? Is there such a thing as getting it right in these cases? Or must the theory restrict itself to hypothetical claims of the type "*If* you see your relationship to B, C, and D as taking this form, *then* you should follow principle X in your dealings with them"?

I want to argue that at least some degree of correction is possible. Sometimes people misunderstand their relationships to others; by getting them to see things more clearly, we can change their conception of what justice demands of them. A common source of misconception in everyday affairs is simple self-interest: when the demands of justice are somewhat onerous, we are inclined to minimize the extent of our relationships with others, hoping in this way to lessen the weight of their demands. If someone's friend suffers an injury that requires long-term care, for instance, the person in question will be tempted to avoid the burden by playing down the extent of the friendship. Here an outside observer may be better placed to see the true nature of the relationship, and may be able to persuade the person involved that he ought indeed to sacrifice time to look after his friend.

Where questions of social justice are concerned, self-interest will also play some part in leading people to misconceive their relations to others, but its influence is not normally great. Some evidence on this matter can be obtained by looking at class differences in conceptions of social justice: if conceptions of justice were interest-driven, we would expect to find people at the bottom of the social scale supporting broadly egalitarian views of justice and people at the top supporting inegalitarian views that legitimated their privileges. But although there is indeed a gradient of this kind, it is a shallow one—what is most striking is the degree of cross-class consensus on matters of justice.[36]

More important than self-interest is the fact that modes of association differ in their *salience* to the people involved in them. Some relationships are of such a kind that we cannot fail to be conscious of them in our day-to-day lives; others are less immediately visible, and it may take a dramatic event to remind us of their importance. If we look at solidaristic community, instrumental association, and citizenship in this light, we will find that, in normal circumstances, the salience of the relationship diminishes as we pass from the first through the second to the third. We are most directly aware of our family and other community relationships; next of our immersion in economic and other instrumental relations; and finally of citizenship, which is, for most people, a remote and poorly understood mode of association. Because of these conceptual shortcomings, we are prone to give too much weight to the demands of justice stemming from our immediate communities, and too little to the demands stemming from citizenship. Consider, for instance, the issue of nepotism when jobs are being filled. In a clear view we would see that the relationship between an enterprise and the people who work for it is impersonal and instrumental, and the principle of justice that should be applied is therefore one of desert. But this requires a fairly abstract grasp of how the separate agents who make up a market economy are related to one another, whereas a person's relationship to his family is continually reaffirmed in day-to-day activities.[37] Hence the tolerance displayed by popular opinion on the question of nepotism, which a normative theory of justice will seek to correct.

In a somewhat similar way, instrumental relationships tend to override citizenship in areas where the latter ought rightly to provide the criterion of justice. I have already suggested that citizenship, as a substantive mode of association, is poorly understood by most people in contemporary societies. Citizenship as a legal status is one thing: people know that they belong legally to this society rather than to that, and have a set of rights and duties, including voting rights, in consequence. But the underlying mode of relationship, of which the legal status is supposed to be the formal expression, is much harder to grasp. One symptom of this is that people find it hard to reach agreement about the basic *obligations* of citizenship, though if citizenship is an ethical as well as a legal relationship, presumably it must entail obligations as well as rights.[38] This uncertainty over precisely what it means to be someone's fellow citizen is reflected in uncertainty over what justice requires in this domain. Are we obliged as a matter of justice to meet the needs whose fulfillment allows people to participate fully as citizens, or should we see the relief of need as a collective act of charity, with the recipients viewed not as fellow citizens but simply as poor people for whom we are in some sense responsible? From the latter perspective there is nothing wrong in allowing welfare provision to be governed by the desert criteria appropriate to instrumental relations, so long as we keep in place a safety net to cater to the (undeserving) poor.

People do have an intuitive grasp of their relationship as citizens, but this relationship rarely presents itself in concrete form; hence it tends to be lost from sight. A theory of justice should provide people with a conception of themselves as citizens as well as family members, economic agents, and so on, and in this way seek to correct distortions in everyday thinking about fairness.[39] The aim should be to build up a pluralistic theory of justice with the three criteria I have identified held in consistent balance with one another. From this vantage point we can begin to address the disputed practical questions of social justice, some of which have been touched upon in this chapter.

3

Social Science and Political Philosophy

In the course of the previous chapter, I suggested that an adequate theory of justice must pay attention to empirical evidence about how the public at large understands justice, and in particular to the way in which differ-ent norms of justice are applied in different social contexts. There is now a great deal of evidence of this sort, collected by sociologists, social psychologists, political scientists, and economists, and my aim in this and the following chapter is to try to assess the significance of this research for political philosophy. Generally speaking, political philoso-phers have been unwilling to take such evidence seriously. On the one hand, they have argued that the research reveals not people's considered opinions about what justice is, but only their momentary response to a questionnaire or a contrived experiment. On the other hand, they have pointed to the logical gulf between the beliefs that people as a matter of fact hold and the beliefs that they rationally should hold. Political phi-losophy tells us what we ought to think about justice, not what we currently do think.

This impatience has been mirrored to a considerable degree by social scientists engaged in the empirical study of justice. Even though they are often aware of the leading philosophical theories of justice, they are likely to regard disputes between the protagonists of such theories as irresolvable. This is a legacy of the positivist view that empirical and normative questions are radically distinct, and moreover that the an-swers we give to the latter depend in the end on personal value-commit-ments that are beyond the scope of rational justification. In order to avoid getting drawn into this quagmire, empirical social scientists attempt to bracket off the question what justice really is, and see themselves as investigating "justice beliefs" or "justice behavior" without theoretical presuppositions. In his Introduction to a major survey of social psychological studies of distributive justice, Kjell Törnblom writes, "An attempt will not be made here to define the concept of justice. This would appear to be a 'hopeless and pompous task' . . . is 'beyond the capacity of any scientific analysis' and 'is not the business of psychological studies of justice phenomena' anyway. Past research has convincingly shown that the notion of justice seems to mean different things to different people and in different circumstances."[1] Here, then, subjectivism about justice is combined with an implicit view about the kinds of questions that can and cannot be answered scientifically to create a sharp division between the social scientist who studies justice empirically and the political philosopher who tries to define the concept or to promulgate normative principles of justice.

In the next chapter I shall try to summarize what we know about popular conceptions of social justice, and to assess the charge that their deficiencies are such that we need not take them seriously. Here I want to show why social scientific and philosophical studies of justice are necessarily interdependent. I first argue that empirical studies of justice must rely upon a normative theory of justice in order to distinguish those beliefs and activities that are guided by justice from those that are not. Then I turn to political philosophers and, using John Rawls as an example, argue that their theories must be tested against the beliefs of ordinary people as revealed by social scientific research.

IN ORDER TO SEE why empirical studies of justice depend upon a normative theory, we need only ask, how do empirical researchers know that the object of their research is indeed some aspect of justice? Typically, when social scientists do justice research their focus is either on allocation behavior—what subjects do when asked to distribute some valuable resource within a group, where the allocator may or may not be a recipient as well—or on practices, such as the rules and procedures that are used to distribute scarce resources such as college places or medical aid; or on people's beliefs about how various items ought to be allocated, for instance, how they respond when presented with proposed pay scales for a range of different jobs. It takes only a moment's reflection to see that in all these cases the outcomes may be influenced by a range of factors other than justice; or to put the point more cautiously, it is not obvious which among the factors that might cause the observed outcomes should be counted as justice factors.

Take allocation behavior, for instance. The staple experiment in social psychology asks a number of subjects to perform some task and then to allocate a sum of money among themselves—perhaps as a way of testing whether the group subscribes to a norm of equity or a norm of equality. As Törnblom points out, however, "subjects are not always instructed to make *just* allocations, in which case motives other than justice may account for their allocation decisions."[2] What might these other motives be? One is simple self-interest—the desire on the part of each individual in the experiment to maximize his or her own material returns. In this case the participants will favor the mode of allocation that they think is likely to give them the highest return; depending on the way the experiment is set up, it may be a more or less complicated matter to determine what this maximally rewarding allocation will be. Suppose this simple motive were to prevail. Would we then be observing "justice behavior"? According to most normative theories, we would not: justice, whatever it is, must be something distinct from individual self-interest. As the "most" in the previous sentence indicates, however, even this is not entirely clear-cut. There is a family of theories of justice that shares a general conception of justice as, to use Brian Barry's phrase, "mutual advantage."[3] This conception sees justice as consisting in the set of rules that self-interested individuals would agree to in order to promote their interests most effectively in a situation in which they need to cooperate. If we adopt this perspective, then although there will still be a contrast between just behavior and the naked pursuit of self-interest, calculations of self-interest will have a legitimate role to play in determining what justice requires.

My point is that if we wish to draw a line between self-interest and justice, we need a normative theory to do so. Observed behavior cannot be properly classified unless, openly or tacitly, we employ a theory of justice. Self-interest is not the only motive that may intrude upon experimental results. For instance, in experiments in which people are unequally productive at the task they are asked to perform, there is an observed tendency for the better performers to prefer to distribute rewards equally, whereas the poorer performers want to distribute according to desert, taking a smaller share themselves. This has been described as a "politeness ritual";[4] presumably the motive at work is that of want-ing to be seen to be nice to the other group, or indeed of wanting to be genuinely nice. Once again, most theories of justice would want to draw a line between justice proper and motives such as kindness and generos-ity, which might lead people to forgo their just claims in favor of others whom they wish to help. If we interpret the experimental results as demonstrating a case of the politeness ritual's blotting out justice, we must tacitly be invoking a normative theory with that feature.

A similar point can be made in the case of empirical studies of justice that focus on institutions and practices rather than on individual behav-ior. If we ask why practices have the shape they do, then a concern for justice is likely to be only one among a range of explanatory factors. This emerges quite clearly in Jon Elster's *Local Justice,* which examines the range of mechanisms used by different societies to allocate scarce goods (such as body parts and college places) and necessary burdens (such as military service).[5] Despite the book's title, it is clear that both the rules of allocation studied and the underlying motives of the various actors shap-ing them reach far beyond the boundaries of social justice as that idea is normally understood. For instance, Elster divides such rules into the following six broad categories: egalitarian principles; time-related princi-ples (such as forming lines); principles based on status (such as senior-ity); principles defined by other individual properties (such as, need, desert); mechanisms based on power; and mixed systems. It is at least arguable whether allocation rules in several of these categories can prop-erly be described as rules of justice. Allocating goods by forming lines or making waiting lists, for example, is a way of dealing with scarcity that is simple and relatively efficient, in the sense that there is usually no room for dispute as to who comes before whom in the line, but it is hardly something we would wish to dignify by the name of justice.[6] Wherever goods are allocated by power mechanisms, such as using influence with those who control access to the goods in question, we encounter cases that would normally be thought of as paradigms of *injustice.*

I make these points not in criticism of Elster's research, which is origi-nal and very informative, but to drive home the point that if we are interested in justice, we need to make distinctions between allocative methods, and these distinctions must be drawn from a (normative) the-ory of justice. To this there is one possible line of reply, namely, that what we ought to be interested in are the rules and mechanisms people use to allocate goods and services, whether or not these should be dignified by the name of justice according to some normative theory. I shall address this challenge shortly, but before doing so I want to say something about the third research agenda mentioned above, which involves looking directly at people's *beliefs* about justice, by asking them whether they regard some procedure or some distribution of resources as fair or just. Empirical research of this kind, it appears, can circumvent the problems identified above by relying on the subjects' own understanding of how justice differs from other considerations affecting the allocation of resources.

Even here, however, we have to impose some constraints if we want to be sure that the responses we are getting are genuine expressions of our respondents' sense of justice. We have, for instance, to ensure that self-interest is not warping the judgments being made: if the verdicts people return on different resource allocations depend on how they think they would be likely to fare under each of them, then the results will need to be moderated to eliminate the effects of this factor (alternatively, the questions could be couched in such a way that it is clear to respondents that their personal interests are not at stake). This might seem a relatively straightforward condition to fulfill.[7] But consider another complicating factor. Some experimental results appear to suggest that people may choose allocation rules on grounds such as ease of implementation, as well as on grounds of justice. For instance, research suggests that people may sometimes favor using the principle of equality, not because this is regarded as inherently fairer than other principles, but because it is simple to apply: all that is required to determine individual shares is to divide the available total by the number of people with a claim on the benefit. The difference would show up in a case where two separate allocations had to be made to the same set of people—subjects who were genuinely concerned about equality of outcome would want to look at the joint effect of the two allocations, to ensure that using the equality rule in each separate case would lead to equality overall, whereas subjects who were concerned only with applying simple and consistent rules would not care about the aggregate result of their separate decisions.[8] Or again, if simplicity of application is the motive behind use of the equality rule, we should expect it to be used more frequently when resources are readily divisible—one is sharing out identical, discrete items, for instance—than when equal division involves a complicated judgment; and this conjecture has also been empirically verified.[9]

Even when genuine moral considerations—as opposed to simplicity or convenience—guide the choice of an allocation or a procedure, it may not be obvious whether *justice*, specifically, is what lies behind the respondent's endorsement. Suppose the question involves the justification of paying higher wages to people who do difficult or arduous jobs. Someone who favors this practice might do so on grounds of desert—he or she believes that people deserve reward for having taken on work of this nature rather than a less demanding job. Alternatively, the thought might be that the economy will not work efficiently unless people are given incentives to take on difficult and taxing jobs. In this case the underlying value appears to be not justice but social utility. Although these two beliefs have a different logic—one says that unequal rewards are justified by what people *have done*, the other that they are justified by their *future effects* on behavior—they may not be clearly separated in the minds of the respondents.[10] After all, the same features of a job may trigger both beliefs, in one case by showing that a person who holds that job is genuinely deserving, in the other case by underlining the importance of the job and thereby justifying a high level of remuneration to ensure that it is filled by well-qualified people.

The questions asked in survey research rarely encourage people to make sharp distinctions along these lines. For instance, people may be asked to respond to statements such as "It would be a good thing if everyone received the same income regardless of the job they do": if someone disagrees with this, there is no way of telling whether desert considerations, or efficiency considerations, or other considerations still are uppermost in his mind. Other questions may lead people in one direction without sharply excluding the alternatives. The statement "Under a fair economic system, people with more ability would earn higher salaries" probably calls to mind the issue of unequal deserts by its invocation of fairness, but it would be quite possible for someone in agreeing with it to be thinking about the effective functioning of the economy as a whole.

As a final illustration of the ambiguities that may affect people's responses to questions about their beliefs, let me return to the issue of equality. We know that people sometimes choose equality when asked to propose a principle for allocating resources, and we also know that people generally wish to see some reduction in the scale of income and other inequalities that currently exist in our societies.[11] The question is whether these preferences should be treated as revealing beliefs about *justice.* I suggested above that in some cases equality principles might be favored simply on grounds of their ease of application. I now suggest that equality may be valued for reasons that are independent of, and possibly in conflict with, distributive justice. Suppose that in a class of children there is one boy who excels in all the activities that are important to the class: he gets the highest marks in his academic work, he is by some margin the best soccer player, he takes the leading role in the school play, and so on.[12] As a result, he wins all the prizes and receives all the commendations. There is no injustice in this: let's suppose that each reward is deserved, that all the children had similar opportunities to develop their talents, and that the activities of the class have not been slanted so that this boy can display his abilities to best advantage. Nevertheless, we may feel some regret that things have turned out this way; we might believe that it would be preferable if some children were to excel at math, others at drama, others on the sports field: this would mean that no one could feel unequivocally superior to anyone else, that self-esteem was more evenly shared, and so forth. If we do feel regret in this way, then clearly we attach a value to equality even in circumstances in which there is no injustice in inequality.

Some part of the pro-equality sentiment that attitude surveys commonly detect may be due to egalitarian values of the kind just indicated, which have nothing intrinsically to do with justice. People may simply find it more congenial to live in a world in which inequalities are not too great, even though larger inequalities could be justified on, say, grounds of desert. They might regard such a world as more fraternal, less demeaning to those who are worse off, and so forth. Once again, in order to distinguish between cases in which equality is being favored because it is required by justice and cases in which it is being favored for other reasons, we need to call in a normative theory to tell us what to count as a justice requirement. If we want to get at beliefs about justice, it may help if we phrase our questions in such a way that "justice" features prominently in them, but even so we cannot be sure that the responses people give are being guided exclusively by their sense of what justice requires, as opposed to some broader notion of "what is right" or "what I would like to see happen."

By this stage readers whose interests are primarily empirical will probably be impatient with the relatively fine distinctions I have been drawing between justice and other sources of motivation and belief. They are likely to argue that, on the one hand, empirical research should be concerned with what actually motivates people, and how they behave when asked to make allocations or to support procedures for making them; and on the other hand, that the distinctions themselves derive from a philosophical conception of justice that is bound to be controversial. There are, after all, a wide range of theories of justice to be found in the philosophical literature, so how is it possible to say with confidence that *this* counts as a justice-based belief while *that* does not, as I have been doing by implication in the preceding paragraphs?

Let me take these points in turn. The first has been nicely formulated by Adam Swift:

> Social scientists do not particularly care about what people believe about principles of justice *stricto sensu*. They are interested in the vaguer, less precise distributive judgements that ordinary people ordinarily make, and if philosophers refuse to grant these the status of principles of justice, then that is their problem.[13]

But why should we suppose that social scientists are interested in judgments about distribution independent of whether these are classified as judgments of justice? One answer might be that their ultimate interest is not in beliefs at all, but in behavior: they want to know how people will allocate resources in various circumstances, which allocations will cause resentment and protest, which institutions they will support and which they will try to alter or destroy, and so forth. Let us grant this for the sake of argument. It is still of some importance whether the distributive judgments that are made are justice-based or of a different kind, as I shall now try to show.

First, knowing the basis of the judgment can help us to predict what will happen if the circumstances alter, or if the people whose behavior we are trying to analyze receive new information. Let us return to the contrast I drew above between judgments of desert, which I took to be judgments of justice, and judgments about the incentives needed for economic efficiency. If people are supporting unequal distributions on incentive grounds, then their behavior is likely to change if fresh information is produced showing that in the particular case under consideration incentive payments are either unnecessary or ineffective—for instance, if they are part of a work group in which the more talented members would continue to pull their weight even if paid the same as everyone else. If judgments are desert-based, by contrast, this information will do nothing to disturb the belief that the more talented and productive workers have a just claim to higher rewards. Again, incentive considerations are relevant only in cases in which the payments made at time t have an effect on behavior at $t + 1$, and so they will lose their force in the case of groups that will dissolve at the end of the current period. Desert, because it looks backward to what people have already done, retains its force even if there is no behavior to motivate in the future, a point dramatically underlined in a famous pronouncement by Immanuel Kant: "Even if a civil society were to dissolve itself by common agreement of all its members (for example, if the people inhabiting an island decided to separate and disperse themselves around the world), the last murderer remaining in prison must first be executed, so that everyone will duly receive what his actions are worth."[14]

Second, knowing whether evaluations of a state of affairs or a practice are based on justice or on some other criterion is of relevance if what we want to find out is how people are likely to behave. It has often been maintained—indeed it is almost a truism—that experiencing a situation as unjust is what leads people to protest against it and to take action to alter it.[15] The perception of injustice is not a sufficient condition for action of this kind, in particular because a state of affairs that is regarded as unjust may also be perceived as impossible to change, but it comes close to being a necessary condition. Obviously any negative evaluation of existing arrangements leads to a desire to change them: if institutions are seen as inefficient, for instance, then we will try to devise and implement alternatives. But this is qualitatively different from the kind of resentment and outrage that acts of injustice or unjust practices evoke. I am not suggesting that the bare knowledge that people regard some state of affairs as unjust will tell us in any detail how they are likely to behave as a result. Social psychology has generated a fairly substantial literature on the question of reactions to injustice. But I would argue that understanding the basis of people's beliefs, and in particular deciding whether an evaluation is rooted in justice or in some other value, must be part of the explanatory story.

We come, then, to the second objection the empiricists may raise to the view I am advocating. Given that theories of justice are controversial, how can one confidently deploy a philosophical concept of justice to classify everyday beliefs? In the previous part of the argument, for instance, I contrasted people's justifying inequalities by appeal to desert (which I took to be an invocation of justice) with incentive justifications that appealed to considerations of social utility. It is well known, however, that among the contending theories of justice is the utilitarian theory, which holds that rules of justice are themselves ultimately to be justified by their contribution to social utility. Incentives are also appealed to in John Rawls' theory, which I shall discuss later, as a way of showing how economic inequalities may benefit the worst-off members of society. How, then, can it be legitimate to draw distinctions of the kind I have been drawing up to now?

This challenge would be a formidable one if the concept of justice that is used to interpret the empirical evidence were simply to be handed down *ex cathedra*, or justified by means of a purely abstract argument. But that is not how I understand the basis of a theory of justice. I maintain that empirical evidence should play a significant role in justifying a normative theory of justice, or to put it another way, that such a theory is to be tested, in part, by its correspondence with our evidence concerning everyday beliefs about justice. Seen in this way, a theory of justice brings out the deep structure of a set of everyday beliefs that, on the surface, are to some degree ambiguous, confused, and contradictory.[16] Thus on the one hand, the theory allows us to clarify the findings of empirical research by drawing distinctions between different principles of justice and between justice and other social values, while on the other hand the evidence helps to confirm the theory by revealing which principles people do in fact subscribe to. The aim is to achieve an equilibrium whereby the theory of justice appears no longer as an external imposition conjured up by the philosopher, but as a clearer and more systematic statement of the principles that people already hold. To achieve such an equilibrium we would need to show that, for instance, people implicitly recognize the contrast between justice and social utility that I referred to above, even though in making their particular judgments they might often conflate the two values.

PHILOSOPHERS AND OTHERS who are concerned with developing a normative theory of justice should pay more attention to empirical evidence than they customarily do. Their reluctance to give such evidence any significant role in the construction of theory stems centrally from a distinction between *justification* and *acceptance*. Showing that certain beliefs are widely accepted, on this view, does nothing to show that they are justified; those who hold the beliefs may do so for a number of bad reasons, whereas for a belief to be justified it has to be shown to be rational, or at least reasonable. Granting this distinction, must we dismiss everyday beliefs about justice when we try to build our theories?

It is worth noting straightaway that philosophers have in fact held a range of different views about the relationship between their own accounts of justice and the beliefs of ordinary people. If we look back to the beginning of the whole enterprise, we can see this in the contrasting approaches of Plato and Aristotle. Summarizing very crudely, Plato's method (in the *Republic*) is to consider various everyday beliefs about what justice consists in, bring out their defects (especially by showing that they contradict other beliefs that Socrates' interlocutors have been persuaded to endorse), and then propose his own somewhat unusual definition as part of a general vision of the well-ordered society. This is in keeping with the sharp distinction that he draws between knowledge and mere opinion. Aristotle, by contrast, sees his task as one of identifying and clarifying what people ordinarily mean when they invoke justice.[17] Although the analysis he gives introduces ideas that would hardly have occurred spontaneously to the average Greek—for instance, his doctrine that justice (like other virtues) always represents a mean between two extreme forms of behavior—its starting point is a set of convictions about what justice requires of someone that he assumes his readers will share.[18] Moreover, he is aware of disagreements about justice, and the interests that lie behind them, as shown by his comments on the clash between oligarchic and democratic conceptions of political justice, each of which he takes to express a partial truth.[19]

The Platonic position is a difficult one to sustain, for the following reason. In saying that knowledge of justice is possible, it assumes the objectivity of the latter: the truth of the correct theory of justice is independent of its being discovered by anyone in particular. At the same time it postulates a sharp divorce between the truth discovered by the philosopher and the opinions of the common man—although, in Platonic dialogues, truth is reached through exposing the inadequacies of common opinion, it does not *incorporate* common opinion in the way that Aristotle's practical philosophy does. But then we must ask whether the criteria by which the philosopher distinguishes truth from falsehood are the same as those used by the ordinary person. If they are the same, why is there such a radical divergence between the philosopher's conclusions and those of the ordinary person?[20] If, by contrast, the philosopher appeals to different criteria, what warrant does he have for thinking that they lead to objective truth? How can he distinguish between a mere inner conviction that the truth is to be found by the method of inquiry he favors, and a warranted belief that this is the case? The notion that philosophers can discover truth by means not available to lay persons is even more difficult to defend today than it was in Plato's time.

The plausibility of the Aristotelian approach derives from the fact that, rather than resting upon esoteric epistemological claims, it seeks to correct common opinion using only methods of argument that common opinion itself endorses. If popular beliefs about justice are in some respects self-contradictory, for instance, or if they can be shown to rest on factual errors, then the normative theory that we propose as giving the best account of these beliefs may legitimately correct them in these respects. In making the corrections, we are appealing only to the common view that our beliefs should not contradict one another, and that they should be consistent with known facts. I shall seek to show that an approach of this kind ought to pay attention to the body of empirical evidence about justice that gives a sounder basis to Aristotle's intuitive appeals to the content of "the popular mind." To achieve this it is helpful to consider the highly influential work of Rawls, since his methodological position nicely exemplifies the problematic relationship between normative theory and empirical evidence.[21]

Rawls' approach to justice has at least the following two strands to it. On the one hand, he is concerned that valid principles of justice must be publicly justifiable; the people who are going to use them must be able to justify them to one another using only commonly accepted modes of reasoning. Connected to this is the claim, particularly prominent in Rawls' later work, that the principles should express "certain fundamental ideas seen as implicit in the public political culture of a democratic society."[22] The connection between these ideas seems obvious enough: if your aim is to discover publicly justifiable principles, then you should start by looking at the principles that people do in fact accept, or at least at what is "implicit" in their thinking about justice. This strand in Rawls suggests that he should be receptive to empirical evidence about the beliefs of ordinary people in liberal democracies.[23] But on the other hand Rawls, particularly in his earlier work, also aims to present his principles of justice as those that would be chosen by rational individuals behind a "veil of ignorance." This contractarian element in his thinking seems to point in the opposite direction, for there is no obvious reason to suppose that what people currently believe about justice corresponds to what they would choose to adopt in the hypothetical circumstances postulated by Rawls.[24]

Rawls' attempt to weave these two strands together is contained in his doctrine of reflective equilibrium. To test the validity of a theory of justice we should start with what he calls our "considered judgments"— those concrete beliefs about the justice or injustice of practices or institutions that we feel confident about, and that as far as we can tell are not affected by self-interest or other such distorting factors. We then consider these in the light of various general principles of justice (such as the two principles that Rawls favors), taking into account also the philosophical arguments offered in favor of those principles.[25] Principles that sharply contradict our considered judgments may be discarded for that reason, but equally the arguments supporting one particular principle may be strong enough for us to modify or abandon specific judgments that contravene it. If after due consideration we find principles and considered judgments coming into correspondence with one another, we have achieved reflective equilibrium.

The hypothetical contract fits into this picture as an argument favoring Rawls' own two principles of justice, always supposing, of course, that his argument to show that the principles would be chosen in the original position is sound. In other words, when deciding whether the drawing power of the two principles is strong enough for us to set aside some judgment that is inconsistent with them, we are to take into account the fact that these are the principles that hypothetical contractors would choose. Rawls has further arguments, which need not detain us here, as to why this feature should strengthen the principles' claim to be valid principles of justice.

Notice that according to this account, the "considered judgments" that form the starting point for this process are the judgments of one particular person; it immediately follows that the reflective equilibrium that emerges is also an equilibrium only for the person who has engaged in the thought-process Rawls describes. Rawls raises the question whether there is a unique reflective equilibrium, or whether the individual set of judgments with which we begin influences the outcome, but quickly truncates this line of thinking: "I shall not even ask whether the principles that characterize one person's considered judgements are the same as those that characterize another's." In the same vein he continues: "So for the purposes of this book, the views of the reader and the author are the only ones that count. The opinions of others are used only to clear our own heads."[26] And despite the greater importance attached in Rawls' later work to the idea that the principles of justice must express the "shared and public political reason" of citizens, he continues to draw a line between the point of view of "citizens in a well-ordered society" and that of "you and me who are elaborating justice as fairness and examining it as a political conception of justice"; only the convictions of the latter should count when the theory of justice is tested via reflective equilibrium.[27]

The question we need to ask is whether this narrowing of focus is justifiable given Rawls' general position. According to Rawls, we must select from among our beliefs about justice those that deserve to be included as "considered judgments." These are judgments that we feel confident about, and that as far as we can tell are not affected by our emotions or by our personal interests. But can we decide whether a judgment is considered simply by scrutinizing it in solipsistic fashion, relying only on internal evidence to establish how much confidence we should place in it, or whether it has been influenced by one of the distorting factors that Rawls mentions? It is surely of the greatest relevance to see whether the judgments we make are shared by those around us, and if they are not, to try to discover what lies behind the disagreement. Suppose, for example, that on some issue better-off people tend to believe p and worse-off people tend to believe not-p; I am better off and I believe p. Suppose also that adherence to belief in p serves the sectional interests of the better off—for instance, it helps to justify economic institutions from which they benefit disproportionately. Taken together, these constitute good grounds for placing rather little confidence in the truth of p. Should I not then be similarly skeptical about my own belief in p?[28] Unless I have some exceptionally strong grounds for holding p that are independent of my interests as a better-off person, I should not admit p as a "considered judgment." Or suppose that I hold strong religious views, and I also hold a belief, q, that I maintain does not stem from my religious convictions. Suppose that investigations reveal that the only other people to subscribe to q are people who share my religious outlook. This would give me strong reason to suspect that my grounds for holding q are not what I take them to be—that religious convictions are in fact what lie behind my endorsement of q. If, then, I share Rawls' view that a theory of justice must be capable of being justified to people holding a range of different religious and philosophical outlooks, I should take q not as a "considered judgment" for the purposes of developing and testing such a theory, but rather as a component of what Rawls would call my personal "conception of the good."

This point can be put more positively. Looking at what other people believe about justice, and in particular trying to understand when people disagree and what the grounds of their disagreement are, are integral to the process of deciding which of my own beliefs deserve to be taken as "the fixed points of my considered judgment." We cannot do this simply by looking within: this might tell us how strongly we hold certain beliefs, but it cannot tell us with any certainty what the grounds of those beliefs are, what factors have led to our holding them, and so forth. Conversely, if one of my beliefs is shared with many others, if as far as I can see there is nothing suspect about the reasons others hold it, then this should give me the confidence to include it as a considered judgment in my own set.

So far my argument has hinged on Rawls' notion of a considered judgment, but I also believe that Rawls should be pushed toward giving greater weight to empirical evidence about justice by his commitment to public justifiability. This, recall, is his view that a valid theory of justice must be one that the citizens of a well-ordered society can justify to one another using only commonly accepted modes of argument. It is certainly possible to distinguish between what people now believe about justice and the principles that they would be able to justify to one another under the condition just cited. But to imagine a radical contrast between the two sets of beliefs would be very implausible, for we need to ask the question, what common modes of argument (not esoteric philosophical doctrines, and so on) could be used to pry people *en masse* away from their current beliefs in favor of the principles that are supposed to meet the public justifiability condition? It seems much more plausible to regard the set of beliefs that are publicly justifiable in a given society S as the beliefs currently held in S adjusted to take account of empirical error, faulty inferences, the distorting effect of self-interest, and so on—that is, the deficiencies that are already commonly understood to produce erroneous beliefs.

As I suggested earlier, however, Rawls appears to be pulled in a different direction by his adherence to a form of contractarian reasoning. This strand in his thought is worth pursuing a little further, because a contractarian approach to justice is the most likely alternative for someone who wishes to avoid giving much weight to current opinions about what justice consists in.[29] This approach claims that valid principles of justice are those that would be agreed on by people under certain ideal conditions, specified in such a way that they embody qualities (such as impartiality) that a theory of justice should possess. In contrast to the Platonic view, which introduces a dichotomy between the philosophical elite and the remainder of society, a contractarian approach claims that anyone can in principle be a party to the contract, provided that they are willing to enter (in thought) the conditions of the contract, while leaving open the possibility that this would require jettisoning existing beliefs about justice, formed under noncontractarian conditions.

The hypothetical contract used to underpin principles of justice can, however, be understood in different ways. One interpretation, suggested by some of Rawls' statements in *A Theory of Justice,* presents the original position as one in which rational individuals pursue their own interests under conditions of uncertainty: the principles of justice are to be understood as the principles such individuals would agree should regulate their common practices. It is generally acknowledged, however, that the outcome of such a contract would not be Rawls' two principles of justice, and Rawls has dissociated himself from such an interpretation in later writing.[30] He now draws a distinction between "the reasonable" and "the rational" and claims it is a mistake to suppose that "justice as fairness attempts to select principles of justice purely on the basis of a conception of rational choice as understood in economics or decision theory."[31] Parties in the original position are supposed to be not only guided by a rational desire to promote their interests but also constrained by norms of reasonableness to ensure that they do not propose principles that some will be unable to accept once the veil of ignorance is lifted and people are restored to full knowledge of their "conceptions of the good." Rawls thinks, for instance, that it would not be reasonable to select a principle according to which the practice of some religion was banned, because this would place an unreasonable burden on those who turned out to subscribe to it.

Once the hypothetical contract is interpreted in this way, however, it is no longer clear that it plays any independent part in the argument. Why not simply say that in developing our theory of justice, we should be governed by standards of reasonableness, in the sense that we should not propose principles to which others could reasonably take objection?[32] But on this reading the "contract" is in no real sense a contract at all, but merely stands in for the idea that in working out our theory of justice we must take up an impartial perspective, looking beyond our own interests and perspectives to take account of others'.[33] That Rawls now sees it in roughly this way is suggested by the following passage:

> As a device of representation the idea of the original position serves as a means of public reflection and self-clarification. It helps us work out what we now think, once we are able to take a clear and uncluttered view of what justice requires when society is conceived as a scheme of cooperation between free and equal citizens from one generation to the next. The original position serves as a mediating idea by which all our considered convictions, whatever their level of generality—whether they concern fair conditions for situating the parties or reasonable con- straints on reasons, or first principles and precepts, or judgements about particular institutions and actions—can be brought to bear on one another. This enables us to establish greater coherence among all our judgements; and with this deeper self-understanding we can attain wider agreement among one another.[34]

On this view invoking the original position simply represents one stage in the search for reflective equilibrium as described above. It no longer constitutes an independent strand in Rawls' argument, but merely high- lights his preferred method of proceeding, which is to move back and forth between our particular beliefs about justice and the general princi- ples that might be used to systematize them, always bearing in mind that these principles are meant to serve everybody in our society and must be publicly justifiable. (Indeed, when the original position is understood in this way, it underlines the point that reflective equilibrium cannot simply be interpreted as an equilibrium among the beliefs of one particular person, but must refer to an *interpersonal* equilibrium among the beliefs held by the different members of a society.) I argued above that this method ought to push Rawls into placing much greater emphasis on empirical evidence about how people do in fact understand justice than he has so far done.[35] What I have now tried to show is that contractarian-ism does not provide an alternative. In its original form the hypothetical contract would have provided an independent argument for Rawls' two principles of justice, had he been able to show that they would have been chosen under the conditions he describes. In its amended form, as represented in Rawls' own later work, it becomes merely another way of identifying the impartial standpoint from which reflective equilibrium is to be reached.

I CHOSE RAWLS to illustrate the issue of relating normative theories of justice to empirical research because he seems a representative figure. Among recent social philosophers some, for instance, Michael Walzer, are more obviously interested in what ordinary people think about distributive justice,[36] while others, for instance, Robert Nozick, appear happy to ride roughshod over many everyday beliefs in the name of a single principle (of rights) claimed to rest on a fundamental moral insight.[37] Rawls occupies the middle ground, and his explicitly stated methodology entails a closer relationship with empirical research than he actually adopts. Let me now recapitulate briefly the reasons for thinking that such a relationship must obtain. On the one hand, the empirical researcher, the sociologist or the social psychologist, needs a normative theory both to enable him to distinguish beliefs and pieces of behavior that express justice from those that do not, and to explain such beliefs and behavior adequately. On the other hand, in setting out a theory of justice, the normative theorist who is guided by something akin to the Rawlsian ideas of reflective equilibrium and public justifiability needs evidence about what people do in fact regard as fair and unfair in different social settings. Ideally these two enterprises would be complementary, in the sense that the theory used by the social scientist to guide research would be one that has emerged through theoretical reflection on previous research, while the normative theorist would benefit from having available empirical evidence that was more discriminating because the research that produced it embodied conceptual distinctions with a theoretical basis (such as the desert-incentives and justice-equality distinctions referred to earlier in this chapter).[38]

To say this is not to conflate social scientific research on justice with normative theory. There is still a difference of focus: one enterprise aims to understand and explain as accurately as possible the norms of justice that people adhere to at different times and in different places, the other to develop a theory that should convince people that they ought to change the way they think and behave in certain respects. Although these enterprises ought to be complementary, there may also be a certain tension between them. To the extent that empirical research reveals that people are locked into beliefs about justice that they hold for bad reasons, it may come to seem somewhat pointless to develop a normative theory of justice.[39] Even if the theory is justifiable by common methods of argument, what good is that if the evidence shows us that people are in fact very unlikely to change their beliefs when confronted by the theory? Philosophers are perhaps professionally disposed to think that people hold their beliefs for reasons, and can be persuaded to change these beliefs when presented with better reasons, whereas sociologists and social psychologists are likely to see both beliefs and behavior as powerfully influenced by relatively fixed factors such as personality traits and class location.[40] Only a very strong form of social determinism, however, would make the social philosopher's task practically redundant, and the evidence does not support this. Indeed, the evidence suggests not that people are locked into fixed beliefs about justice, but that there is a very considerable degree of indeterminacy in many of their specific beliefs (they can, for instance, quite easily be triggered into aligning themselves with one or the other side of a disputed issue by the framing effect of a particular question).[41] To that extent they are ripe targets for a normative theory that works the findings of empirical research into a consistent whole.

4

Distributive Justice:
What the People Think

Having seen why a theory of justice needs to be grounded in evidence about how ordinary people understand distributive justice, we must now sift the evidence to see whether the theory sketched in Chapter 2 stands up. There is, in fact, a great deal of relevant evidence, which can be classified along two dimensions. Researchers may be interested in how distributive justice is understood in small-group contexts, or they may be interested in justice across whole societies (say, in the justice of the income distribution in a country such as the United States). By the same token, they may be concerned with *beliefs* about justice—what people will say is just or fair—or with people's *behavior* when asked to allocate some valuable resource. If we juxtapose these two dimensions, we create four boxes into which the existing research can be placed.

In a small-group setting, it is possible either to ask people to assess a distribution—say, a distribution of rewards following the carrying out of some task by the members of the group—or to perform the distribution themselves. On a society-wide scale, we can examine beliefs by, for instance, presenting people with different arrays of income distributions and asking them how fair they think they are, and we can examine behavior by looking at how institutions do in practice allocate resources (for instance, by considering how firms set pay scales for their employees). Each approach has its strengths and its weaknesses as a way of getting at what people really think about justice. When focusing on expressed beliefs we risk picking up what might be called "Sunday-best" beliefs, that is, the views that people think they ought to hold according to some imbibed theory, as opposed to the operational beliefs that would guide them in a practical situation. If behavior is the focus, by contrast, then we are likely to find mixed motives at work, with the attempt to do justice contaminated, for instance, by self-interest. Thus an allocator in a small-group situation may distort justice to get more reward himself (or conversely, as some experiments suggest, he may bend justice in the other direction in order to be seen as generous to his co-members). Again pay scales in industry are likely in practice to represent a compromise between what may generally be regarded as fair reward differentials between workers with greater or lesser skills and responsibilities and the bargaining power wielded by different sections of the workforce.[1]

Turning to the contrast between justice within groups and justice across societies, small-group research gives the researcher the greatest freedom to set up the experiment so that unwanted influences are excluded, but it also raises the question how relevant distributive decisions in small groups are to wider questions of social justice: do people in fact use the same criteria when allocating resources among two or three individuals as they do when assessing, let us say, the justice of a capitalist economy?[2] On the other hand, looking directly at beliefs about macrojustice runs the risk of introducing too much contextual constraint into the answers that people give. For instance, if we ask people what an ideally fair distribution of income across society would be, their answers may be influenced by their perceptions of the current distribution; or if we ask them what responsibility society has to meet people's needs, they may draw for their answers on existing welfare practices.

Although for these reasons we should always be cautious in the inferences we draw from any particular piece of research about distributive justice, by combining the evidence we may still be able to produce a general picture. In particular, when we find convergence in the results of research that falls into different boxes in the micro-macro, beliefs-behavior matrix, we should feel confident that we have discovered something about how people understand justice that is quite general and is not tied to a particular form of investigation. My task here will be to try to unearth common elements of this kind. As I indicated in the last chapter, any undertaking of this kind depends upon some prior assumptions about which beliefs and which behavior can be regarded as expressing people's sense of justice. Having taken *principles of desert, principles of need,* and *principles of equality* to be the main constituents of distributive justice, I shall attempt to establish two claims: first, that people's views of justice are pluralistic, and that very often people decide what a fair distribution consists in by balancing claims of one kind against claims of another; second, that the social context in which the distribution has to be made—or more precisely how that context is perceived by those making the judgment—will determine which principle stands out as the relevant principle to follow.

The review that follows does not aim to be comprehensive. In particular, it does not aim to cover two aspects of popular thinking about justice that are very important from a practical point of view. One aspect concerns the just distribution of specific goods such as housing or medical treatment. It seems likely that both people's intuitions about how such goods should be distributed, and the practices that have evolved to effect such thinking, will vary from good to good.[3] I shall focus instead on generalized resources, such as money, that do not immediately invoke any particular beliefs about how they should be distributed. Another topic that I shall neglect here is beliefs about procedural justice—beliefs about what counts as a fair procedure for deciding on the allocation of a certain good. Again, beliefs of this kind carry a good deal of weight in practice, and I shall return to them in Chapter 5. Here the focus will be on outcomes, that is, on which final distribution of resources people in different situations will regard as just.

WHEN WE COMPARE DESERT, need, and equality as criteria of distribution, we find one point of contrast between the first two and the third. Whereas appeals to desert or to need to justify a distribution must imply that these considerations carry positive moral weight, equality may be invoked on grounds of simplicity or convenience rather than because an equal distribution of resources is regarded as substantively just. We may run into difficulty when trying to determine how to divide resources in such a way as to match the different deserts or needs of several individuals. Alternatively, if we are told that several people have made different contributions to achieving some goal, but are not told how big those contributions are—or do not have much faith in the information we have been given—we may opt for equality as the fairest distribution available. Exactly the same reasoning applies in a case in which needs may be different but we do not have reliable information about what the differences are.[4] Thus, when we find people opting for equality in preference to one of the other two principles, we need to ask whether an equal distribution is being valued positively as the fair distribution in the circumstances, or whether it is being chosen by default.

There has been much research at the micro-level on the factors influencing people's preference for distribution according to desert on the one hand or equality on the other.[5] In a typical scenario a number of people engaged in some activity have made contributions of different sizes, and respondents are asked to allocate income or other rewards, or to say what they think a fair allocation would be. Sometimes subjects are made to believe that they are participants themselves; sometimes they are simply asked to make an external judgment. Contributions may be quantified so that subjects have the option of following a proportionality rule in rewarding them. Under these circumstances the general rule is that the subjects will take account of desert in allocating rewards, but their commitment to this principle is moderated by a number of factors.

These factors appear to operate through the perceived character of the group within which the distribution is to take place. To the extent that the group is seen as made up of independent individuals whose relationships to one another are simply instrumental, the desert principle is employed. To the extent that group solidarity emerges, the preferred distribution is shifted toward equality. Some experiments contrast team activities, such as soccer, with activities involving separate individuals, such as long-distance running. Asked to allocate bonuses to successful performers, people will opt for a greater degree of equality in the team case.[6] The assumption here, presumably, is that joint activity creates a degree of camaraderie that makes greater egalitarianism appropriate. Similar results are found when subjects are given work tasks that are either competitive or cooperative in nature.[7] Moreover, it can be shown that the *experience* of working cooperatively tends to shift people who originally favor the contribution principle toward greater support for equality.[8]

Another approach is to focus more directly on the quality of interpersonal relations within the group. This can be done either by characterizing the group as a circle of friends or by providing information which suggests that members of the group share similar attitudes. Here again, respondents are drawn to equality in place of differential desert when distributing within like-minded groups (this effect is particularly marked in the case of those who have performed better than others and therefore stand to gain more from following the contribution principle).[9]

There is one qualification to this. Fairness requires that when the size of contributions depends on each person's efforts, people who make less effort should receive less reward.[10] The explanation for this is presumably that in "friendship" contexts, there is a norm that each person should exert him- or herself on behalf of the group; thus people who break the norm should be sanctioned by receiving less income. In this setting, in contrast to instrumental settings, it is not that there is something positively valuable in reward being proportional to contribution, but rather that free-riders must pay a forfeit.

Two further factors help to shift the criterion of justice from desert toward equality. One is expectations about how long the group will remain in existence. Temporary groups tend to favor the contribution principle, whereas people who expect to interact with their partners in the future are more favorably disposed toward equality.[11] The other is discussion within the group. Groups who are permitted to decide for themselves which distributive principle to adopt are more likely to favor equality.[12]

It seems fairly clear that these findings all point to the same underlying contrast, referred to above, between "groups" that are made up of separate individuals either competing with one another or having merely instrumental relations, and groups in which there is a sense of common identity and solidarity. For groups of the first kind, justice is done when what each takes out is proportional to what he or she has put in; groups of the second kind, by contrast, see equal distribution regardless of inputs as appropriate (since we have not yet considered cases in which need differences are relevant, it is not clear thus far whether equality is being valued *per se*, or whether it is being used as a proxy for distribution according to need). This general result also has an interesting converse, namely, that when asked to choose the principle of distribution they think most likely to realize specified group goals, people who are instructed to raise efficiency, productivity, and so on will suggest the contribution principle, whereas those asked to promote group harmony and good working relations will opt for equality.[13] Thus the distributive principle chosen not only *reflects* the character of group relations but also helps to constitute those relations for the future.

Thus far I have been looking at factors affecting the desert-equality choice without specifying the precise basis of desert that is being used (I have spoken about "contribution," but that is helpfully ambiguous as between the size of the product someone creates and the part of the product for which he or she is personally responsible). Some experimental studies have, however, attempted to isolate the aspect or aspects of contribution thought to deserve reward.[14] Usually distinctions are made among ability (the talents or capacities someone brings to a performance), effort expended, and the performance itself (how much is actually produced or achieved). The upshot is that ability *per se* tends to be discounted as a basis for desert (unless the ability is seen as being a result of previous efforts, as in the case of voluntary training), whereas desert is assessed through some amalgam of performance and effort. That is, people judge that the appropriate reward depends on what each person achieves, but they qualify this to some degree when presented with data about effort so that it is possible for a person who achieves less but tries harder to deserve more than another who tries less but achieves more. Effort does not obliterate achievement, however: with effort held constant, the one who achieves more deserves more; thus presumably the view is that ability can count toward desert when it is combined with effort, but not when it stands alone.[15]

Here one is tempted to ask, which counts for more, effort or achievement, when practical desert judgments are made? I am not sure that this question can be answered sensibly, since it would first be necessary to establish comparable scales for measuring the two inputs before we could analyze their impact on judgments of desert. Moreover, even if there is some natural solution to the first problem, the answer may vary from case to case. In the first of the two experimental studies referred to above, subjects had to assign deserved rewards on the basis of performance in a high jump.[16] They were told about jump performance (high or low), effort (greater or lesser), bodily capacity (shorter or taller), and training, and could assign rewards on a scale from 0 to 100. Leaving training aside, this produced a scale running from about 95 (high jump, greater effort, shorter body height) to about 28 (low jump, lesser effort, taller body height) at the other extreme. Ratings of deservingness were affected most strongly by performance and effort, with effort slightly the more prominent—with the other factors held constant, shifting from lesser to greater effort increased the rating by about 35 points on average, while shifting from low to high jump performance increased the rating by about 27 points on average. The subjects were instructed in such a way, however, as to suggest that the rewards were also to act as incentives, which perhaps explains the weight given to the factor that was directly subject to voluntary control.

In the second experiment subjects, given information about exam performance, immediate effort, usual level of effort, and ability, had to award stars to hypothetical schoolchildren.[17] In this case exam performance had the biggest effect on the fair allocation of stars, with immediate effort second. Here the instructor's emphasis was on "conveying information back to the pupil" via the star system, and in this context it appears that the due recognition of achievement became the main priority. So, given some intuitive grasp as to how effort and achievement should be quantified relative to each other, the question "which counts for most" will be answered differently according to the context of distribution and perhaps also the nature of the stuff that is being distributed.

It is interesting to compare these empirical findings with the prevailing views of political philosophers on the subject of desert. As I note in Chapter 7, it is a common view among philosophers that people can be genuinely deserving only on the basis of features such as effort that are subject to their voluntary control. I shall defend the alternative position, that although people must be responsible for their performances in order to be deserving, the performance that forms the basis of desert may also require personal characteristics such as native ability that are not voluntarily chosen. Popular opinion seems to be pulled in two ways on this issue—in some cases people will base personal desert on the level of performance that someone achieves, in other cases they will look inside the performance as a whole in an attempt to see what was directly under the control of the performer. In other cases still, we find some compromise between the two positions.

UP TO THIS POINT I have been looking at attitudes toward desert and equality in small groups. How significantly do things change when people are asked to make judgments of fairness about society-wide distributions of resources? In such cases we find the same broad pattern of beliefs, with the principle of reward according to contribution dominant but offset to some degree by egalitarianism. For instance, when people are asked to react to the proposition "The fairest way of distributing income and wealth would be to give everyone equal shares," we find up to about one-third of respondents agreeing. Much smaller numbers opt for equality, however, when forced to *choose* between the statements

"Under a fair economic system all people would earn about the same" and "Under a fair economic system people with more ability would earn higher salaries."[18] There are several reasons people may reject equal incomes: they may believe that, as a matter of justice, people deserve unequal rewards; they may think that unequal incomes are needed to provide incentives for hard work; they may think that people have different tastes and preferences and therefore ought to have the freedom to earn the amount of income needed to meet these varying desires; or they may simply believe that because of human cupidity equality would be impossible to maintain. In fact it seems likely that these lines of reasoning will be run together, making it difficult to say unequivocally that a particular person is appealing to justice as desert as opposed, say, to a claim about the necessity of having incentives. Thus we must treat the survey evidence with caution. But it is interesting that, at least at the level of verbal responses, all these arguments are represented.[19]

In a British survey, for instance, 95 percent of respondents agreed with the proposition "People who work hard deserve to earn more than those who do not," and 84 percent with the proposition "People would not want to take extra responsibility at work unless they were paid extra for it."[20] Similar questions about the need to reward responsibility and the acquisition of professional skills asked in the International Social Survey Programme typically attracted agreement rates of between 70 and 80 percent.[21] In a Swedish survey 75 percent of the sample agreed to the responsibility proposition.[22] In an American study, 78 percent of respondents agreed that "under a fair economic system, people with more ability would earn higher salaries," and 85 percent affirmed that "giving everybody about the same income regardless of the type of work they do would destroy the desire to work hard and do a better job."[23] The third and fourth considerations referred to above are represented by propositions such as "If incomes were more equal, life would be boring because people would all live in the same way" (61 percent agree, 39 percent disagree) and "Incomes cannot be made more equal because it's human nature to always want more than others" (82 percent agree, 18 percent disagree).[24] It is clear from these responses that large majorities of people cross-nationally have a favorable attitude toward economic inequalities that serve to reward and motivate people and that recognize skill and training.

Another way of approaching this question has been to present people with a series of vignettes in which a hypothetical person is described (occupation, marital status, and so on) together with his or her income. Respondents are then asked how over- or underpaid they think that person is. By aggregating the answers it is possible to construct a picture of what, in the respondents' eyes, a fair distribution of income would look like.[25] Such studies reveal that a fair distribution would be substantially inegalitarian; in an American study conducted in 1974, the set of fair incomes for individuals ranged from $7,125 at the bottom to $18,447 at the top. (This fair range of incomes is considerably narrower than the range of incomes that actually exists, a point whose significance I shall return to shortly.) The grounds for discrimination were not always based on desert: the vignette descriptions included factors such as sex, ethnicity, and number of dependents, and so it is reasonable to assume that respondents were judging what would be a fair income for a particular individual, all things considered. Two desert-related factors—occupation and educational attainments—were included, however, and both were strongly correlated with differences in fair income, with occupation having the larger impact. Indeed, occupation was by a considerable margin the most significant factor affecting judgments of fair pay.[26]

Other studies have asked people simply to judge which pay differences between occupations are fair. A survey of leaders in American political groups produced in the aggregate a scale of fair pay running from $7,954 at the bottom (for an elevator operator) to $95,230 at the top (for a chief executive); most of the groups studied favored top-to-bottom income ratios of between 9 and 12 to 1.[27] This still represented a considerable narrowing of existing differentials as perceived by the respondents, but clearly the overall pattern is substantially more inegalitarian than that presented by the vignette studies, where the top-to-bottom ratio is less than 3 to 1. This can be explained in part by the fact that the vignette studies ask for a fair income for an *individual*, with specified needs as well as deserts, whereas the occupational studies ask simply what people in various occupations deserve to earn; in part by the fact that the top job in the former case is a lawyer whereas in the latter case it is a top executive;[28] and in part by the fact that the occupational studies ask people first about actual pay and then about fair pay, thus perhaps biasing their judgments toward the status quo, whereas the vignette studies confront people with randomly assigned incomes and ask them to make judgments of under- or overpayment, thus perhaps biasing the final distribution toward the center point.[29]

Because of these difficulties, we cannot say definitively what range of earned incomes people would judge to be fair; indeed, it is very doubtful whether people themselves have a precise idea. We can say with some confidence that it would be substantially inegalitarian, but at the same time a good deal less inegalitarian than that which currently obtains in capitalist societies, even if we discount unearned incomes. Nor can we identify on the basis of the survey evidence the precise factors that lead people to say that one individual deserves to earn more than another. Here we need to turn to a different kind of evidence, such as that contained in Jennifer Hochschild's reports of intensive interviews with a small number of subjects.[30]

We may begin with education as a possible basis for desert, in view of the fact that it appears in the vignette studies and that several of Hochschild's interviewees mention it as a reason some people deserve more income than others. On closer inspection, however, it appears that education serves as a desert basis only at one remove, so to speak. Someone who acquires an education acquires skills that ought to find expression in more demanding and responsible work. Without that mediating factor, however, education does not entitle people to extra income. In a study conducted by James Kluegel and Eliot Smith, respondents were asked if, when two people are doing the same type of work, the more highly educated of the two should be paid more. The majority of respondents (73 percent) thought not.[31]

Of factors more directly related to work, we may single out occupation, effort, and results achieved. Hochschild's interviewees shift among these possibilities. Maria, a cleaner, "insists that hardworking janitors deserve more than lazy ones, but even lazy doctors deserve more than both."[32] Vincent, a factory worker, thinks that foremen should earn more than unskilled workers, but he also thinks that all workers on the same job should earn the same: "this one will do a little more than this one, and yet this one is still doing his best that he can do. You can't knock a guy for not putting out as much production as the next guy. Because everyone is not alike."[33] Pamela, a secretary, in rapid succession "invokes compensation, skill, responsibility, effort, and training as justifications for a large reward. But if these criteria clash instead of concurring, productivity supersedes effort in her eyes."[34] Such shifts appear to confirm the conclusion that people are torn between the view that we deserve reward for what we achieve and the view that we deserve reward only for what is within our control, that is, our efforts and choices.

So far we have been exploring the nature and extent of popular commitment to desert criteria in judgments of social justice. But there is also a tendency to equality even in judgments about the overall pattern of economic distribution. This tendency manifests itself in two main ways: first, in the view that the current spread of incomes is too great, and that a fair distribution would compress this range somewhat; and second, in the concern that people at the bottom end of the scale are not earning a "living wage," that is, a wage adequate to maintain a decent standard of living.

The first view is not so much a challenge to the idea of desert as an opinion about the extent to which people do in reality differ in their deserts. I noted above that both the vignette studies and to a lesser extent the studies of occupational pay produce a narrower range of "fair" incomes than the existing range. Support for this conclusion can also be found in the attitude surveys. When a sample of Americans was asked to choose not simply between equality and inequality in income, but among "complete equality," "more equality than now," "the same as at present," and "more inequality," "more equality than now" finished a close second (38 percent) to the status quo (52 percent).[35] The broader proposition "Efforts to make everyone as equal as possible should be increased" attracted the support of 57 percent of respondents, as compared with the 10 percent who thought they should be decreased.[36] In a British study, the proposition "Differences in pay between the highly paid and the lowly paid are too great" was assented to by 76 percent of respondents.[37] At the same time, however, the idea of a politically determined ceiling on incomes attracts little support in these countries.[38] This suggests that what is fueling moderate egalitarianism of the kind we are now considering is not the idea that no one could conceivably deserve, say, $250,000 a year, but rather the belief that most of those who now earn very high salaries do not in fact deserve to be paid as much as they are. Confirmation of this suggestion can be found by looking at the occupations whose pay was felt to be unfairly high or low. Groups generally thought to be unfairly overpaid included government officials, landlords, corporate executives, doctors, professional athletes, and movie stars. Groups thought to be unfairly underpaid included white-collar workers, nonunionized factory workers, teachers, and professors.[39] To-gether these beliefs point to a somewhat more compressed income distri-bution than that which currently obtains.

I have suggested that this very modest degree of egalitarianism may stem not from abandoning desert criteria but rather from applying them to a situation in which the economic system is seen to over- and under-reward various occupational groups. There is, however, another strand to this argument that appears when people are asked about various pos-sible benefits of equality. The only proposition of this kind in the Kluegel and Smith study to attract majority assent is that "more equality of incomes would lessen social conflict between people at different lev-els."[40] Here, then, we see reproduced at the macro-level the connection we discovered at the micro-level between group harmony or solidarity and equal distribution. But it is hardly surprising that this fails to become a major theme in discussions of income inequality (it surfaces only occa-sionally in Hochschild's interviews, for instance). Income is primarily earned in the economy, and the economy is predominantly a sphere of instrumental and/or competitive relationships. Thus if we are to discover support for egalitarianism at the macro-level, we must look for it in a different place.

Let me turn now to the question of low incomes. There is a common view that people at the bottom of the income scale are somehow being prevented from receiving what they deserve. For instance, the proposi-tion "Most of the people who are poor and needy could contribute some-thing valuable to society if given the chance" attracts overwhelming support (78 percent in favor, 7 percent against).[41] Alongside this we should put the finding from the vignette studies that the floor for per-ceived fair pay was considerably higher than the actual floor; that is, that occupations at the bottom of the income scale would be perceived as substantially underpaid if the facts were known.[42] Putting these two beliefs together, we can derive the conclusion that if everyone got what he deserved—if everyone had a fair chance to enter the labor market, and then was paid a fair rate for work performed—all workers would be in a position to earn an income that was adequate to meet their routine needs.[43] (One practical manifestation of this is the widespread support for government-sponsored job-creation schemes, which are far more popular than, for instance, guaranteed-income schemes.)[44] This attitude, which entails that following desert principles would eliminate a major cause of poverty, does seem to coexist alongside the attitude that the poor are to blame for their own predicament, and that is influential in perceptions of welfare provision. Thus beliefs here are somewhat ambivalent.[45] But it is important to note, in concluding our discussion of desert and equality, that applying desert criteria to current income distributions would in most people's eyes not only compress the range somewhat but also raise the floor quite sharply.

SOCIAL PSYCHOLOGISTS HAVE DONE far less research on need-based principles of justice than on the desert-based principles considered thus far.[46] As noted, when an equal distribution of resources is preferred to some alternative, it is often unclear whether equality is being valued for its own sake, or as a proxy for another principle. Thus if people choose equality over contribution as a mode of distributing money rewards, they may be exhibiting a concern that people's needs should be satisfied equally. But this could only be a tentative hypothesis: only an experiment in which equality and distribution according to need were presented as *alternatives* would give us decisive proof. Few experiments have addressed this question.

How might we separate social contexts in which need is the preferred distributive principle from those in which equality is favored?[47] In order for need to be used as the criterion, people have to be prepared to reveal enough about themselves to allow relative needs to be assessed, and others have to be confident that what has been revealed is reliable. This suggests that a fairly high degree of trust is usually required before need criteria can be used effectively. As Gerold Mikula and Thomas Schwinger have pointed out, by revealing himself to be in need, a person runs the risk of lowering his standing in the eyes of the group, and also of acquiring an open-ended obligation to reciprocate by helping other members of the group when they in turn are in need.[48] The implication is that greater solidarity will usually be required to underpin the need principle than the equality principle. If competitive or instrumental relationships encourage the use of desert criteria of distribution and highly cooperative or solidaristic relationships provoke the use of need criteria, equality may be appropriate to groups that display enough solidarity to make their members forgo claims based on differential contribution, but not so much that they are willing to go beyond mechanical equality to take account of individual circumstances.

There is limited evidence to support this last conjecture directly. In one experiment, subjects were asked to divide a monetary reward between two students who had contributed equally to a common task; one of the students was described as needing extra money to buy books for a course.[49] A few subjects advocated equal distribution, but most favored giving the needy student the money he required before distributing the surplus.[50] This, of course, shows a general willingness to take need into account when distributive decisions are made. Of particular relevance to our conjecture, moreover, is the fact that describing the students as like-minded and friendly, rather than as distant associates, increased respondents' willingness to shift from equality to need as the distributive criterion. Although they were being asked to apply a rule from outside, as it were, they were presumably choosing the rule that they thought appropriate to the situation of the people between whom they had to achieve justice.

Does it matter that the relevant difference was a difference in *need* as opposed to simply a difference in preference or utility? Here it is possible to cite some research that demonstrates quite clearly that popular belief embodies such a distinction.[51] Subjects were asked to distribute a dozen grapefruit and a dozen avocados between two individuals, Smith and Jones. In one variant they were told that Smith and Jones were interested solely in deriving a certain vitamin from the two fruits, but were able to convert grapefruit and avocado into the vitamin at different rates. Presented with a number of assignments representing different possible distributive criteria, respondents overwhelmingly selected the one that gave the respondents the highest equal amount of vitamin—as opposed, say, to an equal assignment of *fruit,* or an assignment that maximized the overall amount of vitamin extracted.[52] In a second variant, the numerical values remained the same, but subjects were told that Smith and Jones derived different amounts of utility from the fruit, as represented by the amount of money they were each prepared to pay for a grapefruit and an avocado. The pattern of responses was radically different in this scenario. The proportion favoring equal welfare fell from 82 percent to 28 percent, and the most favored option was now that which maximized overall utility. We can sum up this finding as follows: wherever needs are at stake, people will aim to equalize degrees of unmet need, which means distributing in favor of those in greater need until they are brought up to the same level as others; wherever tastes are at stake, they are much more inclined to favor individuals who can derive the most utility from the item in question at the expense of equality of welfare.[53]

In micro-contexts, as we have seen, people are willing to allocate according to need when they have the opportunity to do so; they draw distinctions between needs and tastes or preferences; and there is some evidence to back the conjecture that the group context most favorable to this distributive principle is one characterized by a high level of mutual sympathy and trust. One issue left unresolved is whether distribution according to need is regarded as a matter of justice or as a matter of generosity or humanity. In most of the research in this area, people are simply asked to express allocation preferences; they are not asked to say whether their preferences are governed by fairness or by humanitarianism. Indeed, there is a tendency on the part of the researchers to conflate these two motivations.[54] A variant of the student-book experiment described above, however, tried to isolate the role played by justice.[55] One group of subjects was asked to allocate resources between the two students in as just a way as possible, whereas a control group was asked simply to recommend an allocation with no mention of justice. Interestingly, when the students were described as distant associates, the justice group gave greater weight to need than did the control group, whereas when the students were described as close friends, the justice group gave *less* weight to need than did the control group. One possible interpretation is as follows. The first finding confirms that unequal distribution on the basis of need (giving more to the needier student) may be seen as required by justice, so that introducing the imperative to act justly brings this norm into play even when relationships are primarily instrumental in character. The second finding suggests that in contexts of friendship or solidarity, the need principle may reach beyond justice in the direction of generosity; here introducing a justice motif caused the subjects to balance the fact that the students had unequal needs against the fact that they had made equal contributions to the task at hand. In this case their generosity was reined back and they gave the needier student more than half the fee, but less than was required to satisfy his needs in full.

If this interpretation is correct, people distribute on the basis of need partly for reasons of justice and partly for reasons of generosity and humanity, and their preferences and allocation behavior are both likely to be ambiguous. This ambiguity has been reflected in the literature of political philosophy, where some have argued that the claims of need are claims of humanity or benevolence rather than of justice; others have taken the opposite view.[56] The research considered thus far does not allow us to say which view is closer to popular opinion.

One test of the distinction between justice and humanity is whether those in need are regarded as having enforceable claims to the resources that will meet their needs, and correspondingly whether potential donors are regarded as being under enforceable obligations to provide those resources. With this test in mind I turn now to macro-beliefs: must a society provide for its needy members in order to count as just? Provisional answers to this question can be found by looking at attitudes toward public welfare provision. A large proportion of the population supports such provision, at least in the case of certain needs. For instance, American respondents (whom, because of their generally individualistic outlook, one would expect to be the least favorable to welfare measures) supported by large majorities government provision of pensions, health care, and relief for those unable to support themselves.[57] Similar attitudes are displayed by British respondents.[58] Two caveats must immediately be added, however. First, support for state provision is consistent with the belief that people should be able to make private provision for pensions, health care, education, and so on.[59] Thus what we have here is not necessarily the view that certain goods and services *must* be distributed on the basis of need, but rather the view that society has a responsibility to meet needs up to a certain level, while there is nothing wrong with some people's choosing to buy superior provision.

Second, people tend to be strongly concerned that the needy not be responsible for their neediness, either in the sense that they have brought their needs upon themselves, or in the sense that they could escape them with a little effort. This concern lies behind skepticism about welfare payments, which manifests itself in the view that too much money is going to people who are needy only because of their own laziness or fecklessness.[60] Thus, as a number of authors have observed, the nineteenth-century distinction between the deserving and the undeserving poor is still alive and well. Putting the point more formally, we see desert criteria taking a certain precedence over need criteria, not in the sense that the distributive claims of desert must necessarily outweigh those of need, but in the sense that people must show themselves to be sufficiently deserving before their needs are allowed to count from the point of view of justice.

Is there agreement about what should count as a need? Old age, disability, and sickness provide uncontroversial cases, but can need be extended to other factors less tied to physiological criteria? In their study of poverty in Britain, Joanna Mack and Stewart Lansley approached this question by asking people to divide a list of items into those that were "necessary" and that adults "should not have to do without" and those that were "desirable but not necessary."[61] The results showed that the distinction was not hard and fast. At one end there was overwhelming consensus that such things as a heated house, a bath, and a bed were necessities; at the other end there was a general view that a car and a night out once a fortnight were not. In between opinion was evenly divided on the question whether a television set was a necessity or a luxury. For the most part these responses were independent of the subject's own standard of living and possession or nonpossession of the particular item in question. Thus even if we do not find a hard and fast definition of "need," there is at least a consensus about a spectrum that runs from indisputable needs through borderline needs to indisputable desires.[62]

Given that people believe (with some important qualifications) that a society's public arrangements should ensure that needs are met, and there is reasonable agreement about what counts as a need, can we say with confidence that the meeting of needs is regarded as a matter of social justice? Some doubt emerges when people are asked whether they are prepared to carry the tax burden of helping the needy. Here the generally favorable attitudes toward welfare provision noted above are counterbalanced by a reluctance to bear any significant increase in taxation. For instance, Mack and Lansley found widespread support for the general proposition that it is important to increase government spending to tackle poverty. They then went on to ask a more revealing question, namely, how big an increase in the standard rate of income tax respondents would be willing to accept if this would enable everyone to afford the items they themselves had listed as necessities. Seventy-four percent said they would accept a rise of 1p on the pound, and 20 percent said they would not. When asked about a rise of 5p on the pound, however, respondents showed a sharp reversal of opinion, with only 34 percent in favor and 53 percent against.[63]

This very marked sensitivity to the cost of welfare provision is precisely what one would expect if popular opinion were grounded in altruism rather than in social justice. People are trading off concern for the deprived against personal consumption, and are showing some reluctance to cut back significantly on their own consumption to provide for others' needs. If, by contrast, welfare were thought of as a demand of justice, then people should be willing to support tax increases up to whatever level proved to be necessary to provide it, subject only to constraints of feasibility.

One reason that it is easier to get unequivocal commitment to need criteria of justice in small-group settings than in macro-judgments about social justice may be that the character of small groups is more easily manipulable. We can arrange things so that the participants enjoy, or believe that they enjoy, a high degree of solidarity. When people make social judgments, their feelings of solidarity toward their fellow citizens are inevitably compromised by the co-presence of the prominent instrumental relationships that prevail in a market economy. Thus the claims of need will always be vulnerable to challenge by the claims of desert once we move outside a small-group context (we have already seen, in the case of welfare provision, how this challenge may make itself felt in practice). One way of avoiding the ensuing conflict of principles is to downgrade the claims of need so that they are no longer seen as claims of justice. This may explain the ambivalence we have unearthed in popular opinion. The needy have a fair claim to be helped, and I can help them. But wait, I also have a fair claim to the resources I have earned in the marketplace. So perhaps the needy can only call on my generosity.[64]

UP TO NOW I have been looking at how people switch among principles of desert, need, and equality when asked about fair distribution in different contexts, and also at how they balance the principles against one another when, say, both desert and need considerations are made relevant to a particular decision.[65] Popular conceptions of justice turn out to be pluralistic in both these senses: no single principle seems able to capture all the judgments people make or the distributive procedures they follow. How, then, should we assess Rawls' claim that the distribution of income and wealth should be governed by the difference principle—that is, the principle that social and economic inequalities are fair insofar as they act to the greatest benefit of the least advantaged members of society? This principle is equivalent to the injunction to maximize the level of primary goods (such as income) enjoyed by those who hold the smallest share of such goods.[66] Does this principle find any support in popular opinion?

Rawls argues that people will select the difference principle from behind a "veil of ignorance" that deprives them of knowledge of how they in particular will fare under alternative distributive schemes. Early evidence suggested that placing people behind such a veil increased their readiness to support redistribution from more advantaged to less advantaged people.[67] More recently, Norman Frohlich and Joe Oppenheimer have conducted a series of experiments in which subjects ignorant of their own likely place in the reward schedule are asked to choose among four alternative principles for distributing income: maximizing the minimum income, maximizing the average income, maximizing the average income subject to a floor constraint (no income to fall below X), and maximizing the average income subject to a range constraint (the gap between top and bottom incomes not to exceed Y).[68] These principles were illustrated by different schedules for distributing annual income, and the participants were then set to work on a specific task whose remuneration was fixed according to one or another schedule. Thus the judgment they were called on to make combined the narrower question "Which scheme would you prefer to work under?" with the broader question "Which scheme is fairest for society as a whole?"

Besides asking for individual rankings of the four distributive principles, the experimenters placed subjects in groups of five and asked them to reach agreement on a preferred principle (in order to simulate Rawls' notion of agreement in the original position). This produced the quite striking finding that although the difference principle (maximizing the minimum income) was the first choice of a very small minority of individuals (about 4 percent of the total sample), it was *never* selected as a group choice.[69] Instead, the overwhelmingly popular choice was to maximize the average income subject to a floor constraint. This was the individual first choice of two-thirds of the participants, and was selected by more than three-quarters of the groups. The second choice, but trailing far behind, was to maximize the average social income without either a floor or a range constraint.

The authors of these studies present their findings as confirmation of pluralism in beliefs about justice. Subjects were concerned on the one hand with ensuring that no one lived in poverty; on the other hand they wanted to ensure that the able and hard-working had a chance to reap large rewards. These two concerns were best met by imposing an income floor and then maximizing the average salary that individuals could receive above it. The difference principle was rejected because it emphasized the first concern to the entire exclusion of the second. Moreover, "groups spent *considerable* time discussing the trade-offs between setting higher constraints on the floor (and thus lowering their total income) and setting lower constraints on the floor (and thus hurting those in the lower class). Most individuals wanted to balance the security of a higher floor with the possibility of increasing the average income in the hope that they might fall into one of the higher income classes."[70]

In a further variation of the experiment, Frohlich and Oppenheimer checked to see whether people's attachment to their principles was stable in the sense that they would continue to affirm them after experiencing their effects in practice (this addresses Rawls' concern about what he calls "the strains of commitment"). In this study, subjects performed their tasks, and income was redistributed through a tax and benefit system according to the principle that had been selected. The outcome was that subjects' commitment to their principles remained undiminished; in particular, belief in the desirability of an income floor was not weakened by having to pay a "tax" to maintain it for those who earned less.

How damaging are these findings to Rawls' attempt to justify the difference principle as a principle of justice? Broadly speaking, there are two strategies that a Rawlsian might pursue given this evidence. One is to challenge the use of laboratory simulations to represent the original position. The chief argument here is that the experiments do not place people in a real situation of risk, since the amounts they stand to gain or lose by adopting the various reward schedules are relatively trivial, whereas it is integral to Rawls' argument for the difference principle that it will be used to determine people's overall life chances.[71] If one followed this argument, however, it would be difficult to explain the strong preference for having a floor constraint as opposed simply to maximizing the average income, or indeed to explain the exchanges that took place in group discussion, where participants were expressing their concern for the life chances of different groups in society. It appears that the experiments did in fact succeed in inducing the relatively conservative disposition that Rawls thinks appropriate to the making of choices of this sort, but that this expressed itself in support for an income floor rather than for the difference principle. The virtually unanimous rejection of the latter principle is arresting, and may perhaps confirm the view that such *prima facie* plausibility as it may have arises from a failure to distinguish between setting an income floor and maximizing the minimum level of income regardless of where that minimum falls. By presenting these as clear alternatives, Frohlich and his collaborators demonstrate that people's concern is to avoid the chance that they or others will experience serious deprivation, not to improve the position of the worst-off without qualification.

The other strategy open to a Rawlsian is to offer a defense of the difference principle that does not rely on the claim that it would be chosen by people ignorant of their personal characteristics and their place in society. As noted in the last chapter, Rawls has dissociated himself, in writings subsequent to *A Theory of Justice,* from an interpretation of the original position that would seek to generate principles of justice entirely from rational choice under conditions of uncertainty. Instead, he now regards the original position as a "mediating idea" that helps to bring our considered judgments into reflective equilibrium. The argument that he now offers in favor of the difference principle is "intuitive" and rests on the claim that departures from equality have to be vindicated to those who gain least from them.[72] Clearly the experiments of Frohlich and Oppenheimer become less relevant if such a strategy is adopted—though it is worth stressing their finding that the distributive scheme that maximizes average income subject to a floor constraint remains stable when people experience its results in a small-group setting, since this bears upon Rawls' claim that an adequate principle of justice must survive "the strains of commitment." More generally, the evidence surveyed throughout this chapter highlights popular attachment to desert as a major criterion for income distribution, and suggests that a distribution centered on this criterion is potentially more stable than one that aims to raise the position of the worst-off group regardless of considerations of desert and need.

ONE QUESTION THAT IS OFTEN ASKED about popular conceptions of justice is whether there is a broad consensus on what justice consists in (with, inevitably, a small amount of individual variation), or whether we find systematic differences emerging according to the subject's characteristics and background. If the latter is true, it might seem to throw in doubt the project of building a theory of justice out of the materials supplied by popular beliefs. In this concluding part of the chapter, I will investigate two claims: that popular conceptions are driven by self-interest, and that such conceptions are adaptive, in the sense that they merely reflect the existing distribution of social advantages. The first claim is most easily examined by looking for occupational and class differences in beliefs about social justice; the second by looking at cross-national differences, to see how closely beliefs in country X mirror the status quo in country X.[73]

In its starkest form, the self-interest hypothesis would assert that people select whichever conception of distributive justice best serves their material interests. How might we test this hypothesis? Two places we might look are studies of wage bargaining and class differences in attitudes toward social inequality. When groups of workers negotiate with their employers over levels of pay, we do indeed find some evidence that the criteria of justice to which they appeal are affected by the collective self-interest of the group. Thus studies of the Swedish wage-negotiation system in its corporatist heyday reveal that the Lands Organisationen (LO) representing blue-collar workers favored norms of equality, arguing that wage policy should aim to reduce the range of differentials among different groups, and appealing to a concept of "difficulty" that incorporated risk and hardship as well as skill to set wage rates for particular jobs. The white-collar union organizations (TCO and SACO/SR) argued, by contrast, that incomes should depend on criteria of desert such as an employee's productivity, his or her level of responsibility, educational qualifications, and so forth.[74] In Norway we find a similar contrast between the egalitarianism espoused by the Norwegian Federation of Trade Unions and the appeals made by the Federation of Norwegian Professional Associations to the differential importance of different jobs.[75] Studies of the rationale advanced for wage claims by unions representing skilled and unskilled workers in Britain and Ireland reveal a similar pattern.[76] Thus we might be tempted to conclude that in such cases groups of workers are simply deciding the amount of pay their bargaining power will allow them to extract from their employers, and then looking around to find a norm of justice that supports their claim.

Such a conclusion would be premature, however. There is considerably more normative consensus about wage justice than there might appear to be at first sight, and self-interest makes its impact at a different point. Let me propose three norms that I believe would command near-universal agreement. The first is that jobs with equivalent content should receive equal pay, regardless of who does them or in which economic sector (public or private, for instance) they work. The second is that every job should provide its holder with "a living wage," that is, sufficient income to allow the job-holder to meet a set of (conventionally defined) basic needs. The third is that jobs should be paid at significantly different rates on the basis of a range of desert criteria such as skill and responsibility, and also should provide compensation for factors such as physical hardship and danger. Indeed, there is sufficient agreement on this point to allow people, whatever their own jobs, to produce consensual rankings of jobs requiring different levels of skill and so forth in order of the incomes they ought to command, from unskilled workers at the bottom to doctors or company chairmen at the top.[77]

People disagree little about what justice requires at this general level. Differences begin to appear when they are asked to say *by how much* the income of the higher-ranked jobs should exceed that of the lower-ranked. Within countries we find small but significant disagreements on this issue in the direction the self-interest hypothesis would predict—the better-off favor higher differentials and the worse-off lower ones. This difference appears specifically as a difference about fair pay for jobs in the upper reaches of the range. As Jonathan Kelley and M. D. R. Evans put it, "We find substantial consensus on the legitimate pay of low-status occupations and on the legitimate hierarchy of occupational earnings. But, contrary to the consensual image, we also find socially and politically structured dissensus about the legitimate pay of high-status occupations and hence about the legitimate magnitude of inequality."[78] To give some idea of the magnitudes involved, Kelley and Evans compare an ideal-typical sixty-year-old business executive with an ideal-typical twenty-year-old unskilled worker: the executive believes that top jobs like doctor or company chairman should be paid seven times what an ordinary worker earns; the worker thinks that this differential should be only three to one.[79]

I shall return shortly to the general effect of class differences on attitudes toward social inequality. In relation to fair incomes, there is a second and possibly more significant way in which self-interest may influence judgments of justice. When deciding what counts as fair pay for those in their own occupational group, people have a marked tendency to inflate the desert-related characteristics of their jobs, and to draw comparisons with other groups who are currently better-paid on

the grounds that in relevant respects the jobs these groups are performing are similar.[80] (This presumably also accounts for the much larger
number of people who say that their income is less than they deserve
than who say that it is more.)[81] There are many examples in the literature
on wage bargaining, and in particular in discussions of "comparable-
worth" policies, whereby, in an attempt to overcome gender inequalities
in pay, different occupational groups submit evidence comparing the
work they do with that of other groups.[82] Two things seem to be going on
here. First, given that economic desert is invariably a composite of different factors such as effort, skill, and responsibility, there is scope for
weighting these factors differently. For instance, "The elements of a job
which a clerk considers particularly deserving of reward are unlikely to
be precisely those which have greatest significance for a manual worker.
And even among manual workers, different elements may 'stand out'
according to the nature of the work: steel process workers may emphasize responsibility; instrument workers, skill; foundry workers, physical
effort and conditions."[83]

Second, people tend to exaggerate how much skill, responsibility, and
so on, their own jobs require. Thus when, under comparable-worth policies, job-evaluation schemes have been applied to different jobs in the
public sector, we find each group attempting to boost its score on the
criteria being used. For example, in one scheme that gave points for
"stress and hazard," nurses complained that not enough weight was
given to the risk they ran of catching communicable diseases such as
AIDS; fire-fighters complained that their rating was no greater than "secretaries with deadlines to meet"; a librarian argued that it was "tiring to
deal with the public" and be "constantly interrupted."[84] Each group, in
other words, focused on the stressful aspects of its own work and played
down the difficulties faced by others. My point is that the impact of
self-interest here is not so much on which principles of justice someone
endorses in general, but on how these principles are applied in particular
situations. The effect is more *cognitive* than ethical: self-interest biases a
person's conception of the job he or she is doing—how much responsibility or stress it involves, for instance—more than it affects conceptions
of what a fair reward for a job with a given specification would consist in.

Let me turn now to the wider issue of what effect a person's class
membership has on his general attitude toward social inequality. A crude
self-interest hypothesis would suggest that people in the bottom half
of the income distribution would support ideals of economic equality,

whereas those in the top half would support ideals of justified inequality. Any such crude hypothesis can be dismissed at once. If we examine people's responses to statements justifying inequality such as "People who work hard deserve to earn more than those who do not" we find at most weak class differences in beliefs. Although nations differ somewhat in this respect—the United States, for instance, having an unusually high degree of cross-class consensus on legitimate inequality—the finding appears to hold good across borders. In a recent study James Kluegel and Petr Matějů constructed an inequality index using the above statement plus two others: "People are entitled to keep what they have earned—even if this means some people are wealthier than others" and "People are entitled to pass on their wealth to their children."[85] The correlation between this index and occupational status was not sufficiently high to be statistically significant; there was a stronger correlation with income, but this only reached significance in some countries, most notably in postcommunist Eastern Europe. The main point to keep in mind is that a substantial majority (up to about 75 percent) of lower-class respondents continue to endorse statements like "People with more ability should earn higher salaries."[86]

Kluegel and Matějů also suggest that class differences in attitudes toward *equality* are bigger than class differences in attitudes toward (justified) *inequality*. This might appear paradoxical until we recall my earlier suggestion that these may not be simply the contraries of each other: it is not inconsistent to believe that inequalities are justified on grounds of desert, say, while at the same time wanting the overall spread of incomes to be smaller than it now is. So, do we find that manual workers and/or people on low incomes are more likely than others to endorse ideals of equality? Adam Swift and his collaborators have constructed an equality index from the following three items:

1. "The fairest way of distributing wealth and income would be to give everyone equal shares."
2. "It is simply luck if some people are more intelligent or skilful than others, so they don't deserve to earn more money."
3. "The government should place an upper limit on the amount of money any one person can make."

They examine data for Britain, the United States, and West Germany. In Germany the effects of class on belief in equality are trivial. In Britain a significant correlation can be found when education level and class are combined, and in the United States class alone has a significant effect.[87] These last two cases bear out Kluegel and Matějů suggestion that in capitalist societies higher- and lower-class respondents are closely aligned in their beliefs about justified inequalities, but further apart in their enthusiasm for equality itself. Once again, however, it is important not to overstate working-class egalitarianism. Strong egalitarian claims such as "Under a fair economic system all people would earn about the same" are endorsed only by a small minority.[88]

What of class differences in relation to the principle of distribution according to need? If we look, for instance, at attitudes toward welfare provision, we find once again that the differences are quite weak.[89] A British study using a social welfare index that aggregated attitudes toward spending on social services, welfare benefits, poverty, and the National Health Service (NHS), as well as the redistribution of wealth, found overall a small but significant relationship between pro-welfare attitudes and low occupational status.[90] When a tripartite distinction among managers, nonmanual workers, and manual workers was drawn, however, the intermediate group had attitudes similar to those of the managers, and in some cases—for instance, in their attitude toward increased spending on social services—they were a little more opposed to welfare provision. Interestingly, beliefs about expenditure on the NHS showed no significant class differences. This corresponds broadly to the findings of a second British study, which asked respondents specifically about their willingness to be taxed to finance a range of welfare services.[91] In a few cases—for instance, pensions—the manual-nonmanual divide was significantly correlated with pro-welfare beliefs, but in the case of the overall index the relationship was very weak: 52 percent of manual workers and 48 percent of nonmanual workers were classified as generally supporting more expenditure on welfare. The relationship with income level was weaker still.

Finally, we may refer to vignette studies that provide information on how respondents balance desert- and need-related factors against each other when asked to make overall judgments of fair pay. The desert-related factors were education and occupation, the need-related factors marital status and family size. It is interesting to note that lower-class respondents particularly play down educational level (and to a lesser extent occupation) as a determinant of fair income; by contrast, they give greater weight than high-class respondents to number of dependents.

These differences are significant whether class is measured by income or by occupational prestige.[92]

To sum up, there is no good reason to write off popular beliefs about social justice as mere rationalizations of self-interest. There is a high degree of agreement in those beliefs even over questions where the interests of different sections of society appear to diverge quite sharply. Where significant divergence occurs, it is less over the principles of justice themselves than over the way they are applied in concrete situations. The direct effects of self-interest, I have suggested, are more likely to be cognitive than ethical: interests tend to bias the way in which we see the world rather than the principles we apply to it. The ethical effects are secondary. It is well known, for instance, that there are significant class differences in *explanations* of wealth and poverty—those who are better off themselves tend to prefer explanations in terms of individual responsibility, whereas those who are worse off point to structural features such as unequal opportunities.[93] These differences will affect the verdict people return on the justice of present social arrangements, but not the principles they use to reach that verdict.

AS INDICATED EARLIER, another reason is sometimes given for lending little credence to popular beliefs about social justice. It is claimed that such beliefs are to a very considerable extent adaptive, in the sense that they merely reflect the existing distribution of social advantages. People do not use independently grounded principles to assess the way their society allocates its resources; rather, their beliefs are molded so that they come to mirror that allocation: something is deemed unfair simply if it departs from the usual way in which advantages are allocated in the society in question.

This adaptation hypothesis is quite hard to test. Suppose we find that people's judgments of justice closely track their perceptions of existing social distributions. Two explanations are possible. One is that their judgments are adaptive and would change as real-world distributions changed. The other is that the distributions in question are the result of people's putting their (independently derived) principles of justice into effect. For example, a study of group leaders in the United States, Japan, and Sweden asked about occupational pay differences and found that the inequalities that the subjects regarded as fair were strongly correlated with prevailing inequalities of income. Thus, whereas the American respondents perceived the existing top-to-bottom income differential (between a top executive and an elevator operator) to be 29 to 1 and regarded a differential of 15 to 1 as fair, the Swedish respondents estimated the existing differential (in this case between a top executive and a dishwasher) to be only 3.4 to 1 and wished to reduce this marginally to 3.1 to 1. (The Japanese respondents held views somewhere in between.)[94] At first sight it might seem that subjects in each country were making their fairness judgments simply by taking their cue from the existing pattern of income distribution and compressing it somewhat. But suppose instead that Americans have a rooted sense of justice that tells them that executives deserve around 15 times more income than unskilled workers, while the more egalitarian Swedes believe a much smaller differential is fair. These beliefs will affect the way pay scales are set in companies and the kind of wage demands individuals and groups think it legitimate to make. So perhaps the causal arrow runs mainly in the other direction, from beliefs about justice to the distributive outcomes we observe in the real world.

Even if beliefs about distributive justice corresponded exactly to prevailing practice, therefore, the adaptation hypothesis would not be conclusively verified. But in fact the correspondence is a good deal less than exact. We can see this if we look at an international study of beliefs about justice carried out in 1991 that included both Western and ex-communist states. If the adaptation hypothesis were true, we would expect to find significant contrasts between these two groups of countries, reflecting the different ways in which capitalist and communist systems allocated income and other resources to their members. Broadly speaking, we would expect people in ex-communist states to have a greater belief in material equality than people in Western states, and a lesser inclination to justify inequalities by reference to the kinds of desert displayed in market economies.

Clearly there are differences between countries, but very often not of the kind one would expect if the adaptation hypothesis were true.[95] There are also some surprising similarities. For instance, Americans and Russians, whose beliefs we might have expected to stand at opposite ends of the spectrum, registered almost identical degrees of agreement with the propositions "It's fair if people have more money or wealth, but only if there are equal opportunities," "People are entitled to keep what they have earned—even if this means that some people will be wealthier than others," and "People who work hard deserve to earn more than those who do not." Or to take a different pairing, East Germans ran a little ahead of West Germans in their endorsement of these statements. By contrast, people in ex-communist countries tended to respond somewhat more favorably than people in capitalist countries to the proposition "The fairest way of distributing wealth and income would be to give everyone equal shares," though there were larger variations within the two groups than between them, and the highest agreement rating was found in Japan, not a country with a history of egalitarian practice. The apparent incongruity here—if citizens of different countries hold broadly similar views about deserved inequalities, why do pro-equality statements attract more support in some places than others?—can perhaps be explained by different expectations about the role of the state. In 1991 people in ex-communist countries still looked to the state to offset the effects of market competition by providing jobs, guaranteeing a minimum income, and holding down high salaries; the statement "The government should place an upper limit on the amount of money any one person can make" tended to attract higher levels of support in these countries than in Western countries.[96] They also expected need considerations to weigh more heavily in public policy than did their Western counterparts.[97] The adaptation hypothesis seems to apply much more to policy questions such as these than it does to the justice beliefs that lie behind them. People's basic sense of justice may be quite similar cross-nationally—particularly if we confine our attention to the inhabitants of modern industrial societies—but when we ask about the institutions and policies that might implement social justice, judgments are then affected by what already exists, or has existed in the recent past.

There are also differences in the cognitive schemes used to decide whether existing practices are fair or unfair—for instance, explanations of why people become rich or poor. Thus if we take the International Social Justice Project (ISJP) findings on capitalist and postcommunist countries (but set aside East Germany), we find that people in capitalist countries are somewhat more likely to explain the possession of wealth by reference to personal ability, and considerably more likely to explain it by reference to hard work, than members of postcommunist societies, whereas the latter regard dishonesty as the leading cause of wealth.[98] When it comes to explaining poverty, people from the latter societies give much greater weight, somewhat paradoxically, both to the lack of opportunities for the poor *and* to their "loose morals and drunkenness."[99] Without judging the validity of these explanations, we can say that the perceptions on which they rest are adaptive in the sense I am considering; they are the products of prevailing practice. The point I want to insist on, however, is that this cognitive adaptation does not seem to affect people's basic beliefs about justice. Even if Russians are considerably less likely than Americans to think that those who now possess wealth deserve it on the basis of ability and/or hard work, they are no less likely to think that this is how the possession of wealth *should* be justified.[100]

FROM THE EVIDENCE DISPLAYED THUS FAR, we can draw several conclusions about popular conceptions of social justice. First, people seem to be perfectly at home with the notion of social justice itself: they are prepared to apply criteria of distributive justice to existing social arrangements, and to say in broad terms what a just society would look like (even if they are skeptical about the chances of achieving one). The views of thinkers such as Friedrich Hayek who argue that the whole notion of "social justice" is fundamentally misguided find very little resonance in popular beliefs.[101]

Second, people's thinking about distributive justice is pluralistic in the sense that they recognize several different criteria of justice: depending on the issue they are being asked to address, they may either apply a single criterion to determine what justice requires or look for a compromise solution that invokes two or more. Their thinking is also contextual, meaning that the favored criterion or criteria will vary according to the social background against which the distributive decision is being made—especially the character of the group within which the allocation will take place. In both these respects, popular understandings of justice conform to the sketch provided in Chapter 2.

Third, desert and need criteria feature prominently in this thinking. In the case of desert, we saw that it is often difficult to disentangle beliefs about rewarding desert from beliefs about the necessity of giving people incentives and allowing for diversity; nevertheless, we cannot make sense of the evidence unless we assume that for most people the backward-looking idea of desert carries weight apart from these other considerations. We also found some uncertainty about what should be the proper basis for desert in cases in which it was possible to separate the voluntary aspects of people's behavior from their performance as a whole.

In the case of need, there was clear evidence that people see an important distinction between genuine claims of need and mere wants or preferences. There is a reasonable degree of consensus, for instance, about which items of current consumption are to be regarded as necessities. When people think about need at the social level, they see it as setting a floor or baseline below which no one should be allowed to fall, rather than as making a claim on all of society's resources. This is reflected in a strong preference for schemes that specify a minimum income, as against the Rawlsian idea that one should try to improve the position of the worst-off group to the greatest extent possible.

What of situations that bring both desert and need principles into play? We have found that in these cases subjects try to balance the two sets of criteria, endorsing distributions that reflect a composite of desert and need. This is true even where the context might appear decisively to favor desert: it is interesting that people think justice requires employers, for example, to take some account of their employees' needs when setting wages and implementing layoffs.[102] (This suggests that firms are seen not purely as instrumental associations, but as embodiments of at least a small degree of solidarity—or perhaps the view is that employers are also *citizens* with social responsibilities.) But we have also seen how desert may displace need, in cases where people feel that a person who is in need thereby reveals himself to be undeserving (for example, through having failed to look for a job).

The third principle I have been considering after need and desert is equality. Its role in popular thinking about distributive justice is not straightforward. Sometimes equality seems to be favored on grounds of simplicity, or because of lack of evidence about people's different deserts or needs. Here it carries no independent moral weight. But we have also found, in people's thinking about social distribution, a tendency to favor more equality than presently exists in liberal democracies. This is partly to be explained by considerations of desert and need: people do not regard income inequalities of the size that currently obtain as deserved, and at the bottom of the scale they think it unfair that people cannot earn enough to meet their needs. At least some subjects, however, seem to hold the view that the quality of life in contemporary societies would be improved if the differences between rich and poor could be narrowed. As suggested in the last chapter, this should perhaps be interpreted as a commitment to social equality that is independent of justice, though for the reasons given not in practical conflict with it.

According to the theory of justice sketched in Chapter 2, to find equality defended on grounds of justice, we should look primarily to the sphere of citizenship. I have not paid much attention to this sphere in my discussion, although it is not hard to find evidence to show that people believe citizenship rights should be equally distributed as a matter of justice. Hochschild's investigation, for instance, reveals a strong attachment to ideals like equality before the law and equal access to political decision-makers.[103] She also brings out the tensions that exist between these commitments to equal citizenship and people's willingness to allow desert criteria to govern the allocation of advantages in the economic domain. Thus on questions such as the funding of political parties or the progressive taxation of income, people tend to move back and forth between ideas of equality and ideas of deserved inequality. This research tends to bear out my earlier claim that citizenship and its demands are not well understood, and thus people have difficulty in deciding at what point equal citizenship should trump the principles of desert that are appealed to in order to justify the inequalities generated by a market economy.

Besides showing how popular understandings of justice correspond in their substance to my proposed theory, I have tried to show that they cannot be dismissed simply as rationalizations of self-interest or as adaptive responses to prevailing patterns of distribution. They deserve to be taken more seriously than that. But this is not, of course, sufficient to show that popular beliefs are defensible. For that we need to look more closely at the concepts and principles that underpin these beliefs.

5

Procedures and Outcomes

Societies are just, I have argued, to the extent that their major institutions conform to principles of need, desert, and equality—principles that together specify an overall allocation of advantages and disadvantages to individual members. But this picture has been fiercely criticized by those who hold that justice must be understood as a property of *procedures* rather than of *outcomes,* and who therefore reject wholesale the notion of social justice as understood in this book. To assess this criticism we must first clarify the distinction between procedures and outcomes. A procedure is a rule or mechanism whereby one agent—an individual or an institution—assigns benefits (or burdens) to a number of others. The focus here is on the actual process whereby people come to have entitlements to benefits of various kinds. Thus examples of procedures might be an employer's paying wages to his employees using a fixed salary scale, or a hospital administrator's assigning beds to patients by following some priority rule. An outcome, by contrast, refers to the state of affairs whereby at any time different individuals enjoy various resources, goods, opportunities, or entitlements. Among outcomes we might include the overall distribution of wealth in a particular country at any moment, or the types and quantities of medical treatment received by people with a specified range of illnesses, or the set of degree classes received by students graduating from the University of Oxford in 1998.

In terms of this distinction, it is evident that the three criteria of social justice we have been exploring so far—need, desert, and equality—apply to outcomes. When we ask whether people have what they deserve, or what they need, or have equal rights, we are looking at a final result or end-state in which people securely enjoy certain material or nonmaterial benefits. When we do this, of course, we are looking at a distribution at a certain moment of time, and what counts as a just distribution need not be conceived statically: people's entitlements, deserts, and needs change with time, and so the shape of the just distribution must change, too. Up to now, however, our theory of justice has been concerned with results, not with the processes or mechanisms by which they come about. But is this perspective the correct one? Others have claimed that justice is fundamentally a quality of procedures, and when we call outcomes just, all that we can properly mean is that they have been arrived at by just procedures.[1]

Connected with this question about procedures and outcomes is the issue of whether the idea of social justice has any validity at all, for in invoking that idea one is supposing that it makes sense to assess the distribution of benefits and burdens across a whole society in the name of justice. If, by contrast, justice is a property of procedures rather than outcomes, then, although any specific agent (person or organization) may commit an injustice by violating just procedures in its treatment of other agents, there are no independent grounds for considering the final distribution of benefits or burdens unjust. Any such distribution, whatever its shape, *might* be just so long as it has arisen in a procedurally correct manner. For this reason advocates of an exclusively procedural interpretation of justice have dismissed the idea of *social* justice as involving a fundamentally misleading attempt to treat "society" as though it were an organization with concrete aims and purposes.[2] Clarifying the relationship between procedural and outcome justice thus forms an essential part of any defense of that idea.

The position I shall develop maintains that there is indeed a justice of procedures that can be identified independent of the outcomes to which these procedures lead; and it is an important requirement of social justice that a society's institutions and practices should comply with this. In most cases, however, outcomes can also be judged as just or unjust independent of the procedures that gave rise to them, and so one main quality that we will look for in procedures is precisely that they should be well calculated to produce just results. As I shall show, in certain cases procedural and outcome justice may collide, and it will then be a matter of judgment as to which should yield. But there is no reason to build this up into an all-or-nothing choice between the two kinds of fairness.

SUPPOSE FOR THE MOMENT that we are committed both to using fair procedures and to producing just outcomes, and so we choose procedures intended to bring about the results we want. Why might this fail to happen? One reason is cognitive fallibility. The procedure requires the person implementing it to make judgments about the people with whom he or she is dealing, but the judgments are subject to a degree of uncertainty, and so the outcome is not the one that the procedure was designed to produce.[3] For instance, suppose our aim is to select the most able candidates for admission to a university. We administer a series of tests that are designed to reveal ability. The tests are not mechanical, but instead require the tester to make comparative evaluations of different pieces of work. Because the tester doesn't always get it right, the people admitted through this procedure are not the most able applicants. (Note that this is not the result of the procedure's being misapplied; the tester tried conscientiously to mark the exams fairly.)

Another reason procedures and outcomes may come apart is that background conditions external to the procedure may have an effect on the final outcome. Suppose that when treating her patients a doctor always prescribes medicine according to need, with the intention that each person in the same medical condition should have a similar chance of recovery. Recovery rates, however, are also affected by environmental factors of which the doctor is ignorant, such as diet or the quality of housing that the patient enjoys. The fair procedure will not then produce the intended just outcome.[4] In other cases, a procedure may pick up an extraneous feature of the individuals to whom it is applied, thus biasing the outcome in a certain direction. If a language test is used as part of the procedure for admitting students to a university, this may count against applicants from ethnic minorities for whom English, say, is only a second language. Sometimes such biases are inadvertent, and sometimes the procedure may be used deliberately to obtain an outcome that the institution knows cannot be defended publicly in its own right.[5]

A third source of divergence occurs when two or more procedures intersect with one another, so that the outcome is the combined resultant of the various procedures. Suppose, for instance, that two neighboring hospitals employ the same criteria for selecting people to have a certain operation for which there is a waiting list. The capacity of each hospital relative to the population it serves is different, however, so though the outcome in terms of speed of treatment is just when we look at each hospital separately, if we combine their two catchment areas then those served by hospital A appear to be unfairly advantaged compared with those served by hospital B. Or for a different case, consider what may happen when an unemployed person receiving cash benefits from a number of state sources decides to take a job. The classic case of a poverty trap arises because this previously unemployed person begins to receive income from an employer but simultaneously loses some or all of what he was getting from the state social security system; thus there is little financial advantage in working at what may be an unpleasant job. Both institutions have employed fair procedures, but the outcome, when the worker's overall position is compared with that of his twin brother, who stayed unemployed, seems unjust to us.

We have identified three reasons—cognitive fallibility, background conditions, and intersecting procedures—that a fair procedure may nonetheless produce an outcome that offends our sense of justice. In these circumstances, what should be done? How much weight should we give, respectively, to procedural justice and outcome justice in our thinking about social justice generally? Let's start by noticing that the answer may vary from case to case. At the extremes we have cases in which only the outcomes seem to matter, or only the procedures.

Outcomes alone seem to matter when some discrete and finite good is being allocated, the good is essential, and the criteria for allocating it are uncontroversial. Suppose we are on a sinking ship and there are enough life jackets to go around. Justice requires that each person have a life jacket, and the fair procedure to follow in allocating life jackets is simply that which ensures this most effectively. This case is perhaps unusual: once we alter it to say that there are fewer life jackets than passengers, then immediately questions of procedural justice as well as outcome justice are likely to arise. It is not easy to think of an instance of distributive justice on a wider scale that has this simple structure (perhaps the allocation of gas masks to a population threatened by gas attack might be one). As an extreme case, however, it illustrates how outcome justice may dominate procedural justice.

At the other extreme stand cases in which the outcome raises no questions of justice aside from that of the procedure employed to reach it. One instance occurs when the good we are trying to allocate is indivisible and there is no compelling reason for giving it to one claimant rather than another. Since we have no grounds for judging one outcome as fairer than another in these circumstances, all the weight must fall on the method used for the allocation. These are the cases that Rawls describes as exemplifying "pure procedural justice."[6] One example is a lottery: provided that the lottery is fairly conducted, any distribution of prizes among individuals can be regarded as fair merely by virtue of the fair procedure used to arrive at it.[7] Another example might be an auction, seen as a procedure for allocating a set of items among individuals. Provided again that the auction is fairly conducted, that the participants are properly informed about the goods being sold, and that they are justly entitled to the resources with which they bid, the final allocation— your having the china elephant, my having the basket of fruit, say—is just merely by virtue of the procedure used to reach it: no independent criteria seem to apply.

Once again the extreme cases may be relatively rare: even in the case of the auction, it may be that there is some notion of justice applying to the outcome that helps to form our understanding of a fair procedure. (When people come to the auction with equal purchasing power, the auction tends to produce a final distribution of resources that is equal in the sense that no one envies anyone else the set of items he has acquired; an equal division of this kind might in certain circumstances be regarded as a just division.)[8] At any rate, my interest here is in cases in which we have relatively strong beliefs both about the justice of a procedure and about the justice of an outcome, with neither apparently derivable from the other, giving rise to practical dilemmas in which it is not clear whether procedural justice or substantive justice ought to prevail.

LET ME BEGIN with an example of this kind that falls strictly outside my remit insofar as it deals with criminal rather than distributive justice, but is nonetheless valuable for the light it throws on procedural justice. The film *The Accused* tells the story of a woman who is brutally raped in a bar by three men. Because no one besides the victim is initially prepared to come forward to testify that the rape occurred, the prosecuting attorney engages in plea bargaining with the defense before the case comes to court, as a result of which the three rapists agree to plead guilty to a charge of assault, which nonetheless carries a prison sentence similar to that standardly imposed for rape. The trial is therefore curtailed. The rape victim, however, is incensed because she has not been able to present to a jury her own account of what occurred, and the rest of the film traces the events that eventually allow her to do so. Here, then, we have a case in which taking the course of action most likely to lead to a just outcome—bringing it about that the three rapists got what they deserved by way of punishment—violated the victim's sense of procedural justice.[9] Instead of a deal behind closed doors, the victim wanted the full procedure of a criminal trial, which would enable the facts of the case to be made public, even if there was a considerable chance that the accused men would be acquitted of the charge of rape. The just procedure is not the one that maximizes the chance of achieving a just outcome.

Let us turn now to an example of a distributive case in which procedural and outcome justice seem to come into conflict.[10] Suppose we have to choose a procedure for assigning donated kidneys to patients who need them, where the supply of kidneys is smaller than the demand for them. The position is this: all the potential recipients are between the ages of twenty and forty, and we have good grounds for thinking that any transplant is likely to be successful. The chances for success are slightly higher at the bottom end of the age range than at the top, however. We have to choose between two possible procedures for assigning the available kidneys: one is to rank the patients by date of birth and to give the n kidneys to the n youngest patients on the list; the other is simply to conduct a lottery among all the patients on the list until n names are chosen.[11]

If we were guided solely by considerations of outcome justice, we might well want to adopt the first rule. By assigning the kidneys to the n youngest patients, we maximize the chances of each transplant's being successful, and it seems an obvious extension of the distributive rule "to each according to his needs" that in cases where not all needs can be met and the goods we are assigning are indivisible, we should decide in favor of those most capable of making use of the resources we are distributing.[12] But against this the first procedure seems in some sense unfair to the older patients, who have a good claim to the kidneys but whose claim is completely overridden by the competing claim of the young. The lottery procedure, although it does not guarantee that any particular person's claim to the available kidneys will actually be honored, does nonetheless give equal recognition to all the claims. It seems procedurally more fair even though the expected justice of the outcome is less than in the case of the age-ranking procedure.

In contrast to the simple life jacket example with which we began, both these cases (the rape trial and the kidney-allocation problem) suggest that we cannot in general explain the fairness of procedures simply by saying that these are the procedures that are *most likely* to lead to just outcomes. How people are treated by allocating agencies matters *as much as* what they finally end up with by way of benefits (or burdens). Certainly many of our concerns about procedural fairness can be explained by our desire to avoid unfair outcomes. But the examples suggest that procedures may have qualities that recommend them to us over and above their tendency to produce outcomes that are substantively just. Let me draw attention to four such qualities.[13]

1. *Equality.* A fair procedure requires that everyone who has a *prima facie* claim on the good that is being allocated should be afforded equal treatment. This means in the first instance formal equality, and explains why procedural justice lays heavy emphasis on rule-following, which serves to protect individual claimants from favoritism or arbitrary behavior on the part of those operating the procedure. But equal treatment in the sense that matters to us here means more than formal consistency. The kidney-donation example given above brings this out. Allocating kidneys by age respects formal equality—a consistent rule is followed—but it does not give equal recognition to all claims. The rule must be formulated in such a way that it does not immediately exclude some morally relevant claims. To give a British example, suppose university places are allocated strictly on the basis of A-level examination scores. Someone who has taken the International Baccalaureate in place of A-levels applies for entry. If the admitting official makes no attempt to translate this qualification into an A-level equivalent, but simply applies the existing formal rule, then he is not giving equal treatment to this candidate. Moreover, equality in this sense is violated in cases where claims once advanced are dealt with on an equal basis, but where potential claimants have a greater or lesser prospect of putting their claim forward—say, because it is difficult to discover where to apply in order to be consid-

ered. These examples show that equality, far from being a simple or straightforward property of procedures, can be an exacting requirement, to be set against other qualities such as speed and efficiency.

2. *Accuracy.* A fair procedure must attempt to uncover all the information that is relevant to the allocation being carried out. This is so even in cases in which a more peremptory approach can be shown to yield good results overall. Short-circuiting devices are regarded as unfair because they ignore aspects of individual claims that ought to be considered in the course of reaching a decision. People want to be able to put their own case to the deciding body, and to know that the considerations *they* think important are given a hearing. This sense of fairness lies behind the age-old legal maxim that both sides of a case should be heard even when the verdict seems obvious.[14] People not only want the right outcome; they want those deciding that outcome to arrive at it in the right way, namely, by attending to all the relevant facts. This feature is prominent in the rape case described earlier: the victim's complaint was that the court had not made a determined effort to get at the truth.

   For another example, consider a question that Jon Elster has examined at some length: who should get custody of the children when a husband and wife divorce?[15] In many jurisdictions courts currently employ long and elaborate procedures in an attempt to determine which partner has the greater claim to look after the children. Elster argues that these procedures, which are quite fallible, often exacerbate the harm to the children that the divorce inevitably causes. There is therefore a case for employing a much simpler and quicker procedure, such as, subject to rudimentary vetting to eliminate wholly unsuitable parents, always giving custody to the wife, or arriving at a decision by drawing lots. But he concedes that this would conflict with our sense that in such a crucial matter, a conscientious attempt should be made to discover which parent's having custody would be in the best interests of the child. Again this illustrates the idea that a fair procedure must be an accurate one, even when, paradoxically, the outcomes it produces may be less good overall than those obtained by some other method.[16]

3. *Publicity.* This requirement is closely linked to the second. A fair

procedure must be an open procedure in which the rules and criteria being used are clear to those to whom they are applied. Moreover, as far as possible these criteria and rules should be explained to the claimants, so that the latter can understand the reasons behind their getting or failing to get the benefits at issue. If this is done, then all those involved can identify with the procedure being followed. They may not like the outcome, but they can put themselves in the place of the person who has to administer the rules and see that they, too, would have come to a negative decision in this particular case. Of course the publicity requirement does not get around the problem of substantive disagreement about the criteria that should be used to allocate a certain benefit. If someone thinks that preferential treatment should be given to members of ethnic minorities in the labor market, she won't be assuaged by being told that a particular firm hires its employees strictly on the basis of merit. But at least this person does not inhabit a Kafkaesque world in which rules, apparently, are followed, but no one knows what they are; she can see that justice is being done, even if not on the basis that she would ideally wish.

4. *Dignity.* This requirement falls into a different category from the first three, insofar as it is a constraint on procedures rather than a positive characteristic that procedures may exhibit.[17] Some procedures may in principle have just outcomes, but in order to obtain those outcomes, the personal dignity of the recipients has to be violated. In criminal cases there are ways of obtaining evidence that may be effective, but they are degrading to those who are subject to them; for instance, compulsory stomach-pumping might be used to discover whether someone suspected of consuming illegal drugs had in fact done so.[18] In cases involving the assignment of benefits, indignity is likely to take the form of requiring people to divulge information about themselves that is normally kept private in order to obtain the benefit. If, for instance, a social security system makes special payments to single parents that are not made to cohabiting couples, this may involve inquiring into people's personal circumstances and checking up on them in a way that is offensive to their dignity. Thus we can say that a fair procedure is one that does not require people to behave in undignified ways or to have things done to them that would normally be thought of as offensive or degrading.

Following these four standards of procedural fairness has a general tendency to improve the justice of the outcome, and it is good that this is so, for a wholesale divorce between procedural and substantive justice would make achieving social justice an even more difficult task than it already is. Nevertheless, I have been at pains to stress that procedural justice is a value standing over and above the justice of the results it achieves, and we can best understand this distinct quality of procedures as involving a respect for the people who are subject to them.[19] It is disrespectful of people not to give equal attention to their claims, not to attempt to gain an accurate picture of their circumstances, not to explain the reasons for decisions, and to use methods that violate their dignity. Short-cut methods aimed directly at outcomes, which might be defensible in dealing with herds of animals, say, are not acceptable when human beings are the subjects of a distributive procedure. This idea that procedural justice has a value that is not merely instrumental finds support in studies of popular opinion, which have found that people's reactions to distributive practices are conditioned more strongly by the procedures that are used to reach the outcomes than by the outcomes themselves; even if a person does quite badly in the final result, provided that it is arrived at by methods that match her standards of fairness, she will accept the outcome as a legitimate one.[20]

This suggestion that it is respect for persons that underlies our (noninstrumental) concern for procedural fairness can be reinforced by considering the role of procedures in supporting equal citizenship. As Charles Beitz points out, the procedures followed in public life may on the one hand strengthen people's sense of themselves as equal citizens, or on the other hand lead certain groups to feel demeaned and insulted.[21] He gives as an example a voting system that is weighted in favor of the racial majority in a political community: this will plainly tend to produce unjust legislative outcomes, but perhaps more important, it signals publicly to the racial minorities whose votes are negatively weighted that they are less worthy of concern and respect than are other citizens. Procedural fairness, in the form here of equal treatment for members of different racial groups, is necessary if group members are to be shown equal respect, and hence to enjoy an equal status as citizens.

ONE CRITERION THAT I HAVE NOT INVOKED in giving my account of procedural fairness is free agreement or voluntary consent. It is sometimes suggested that all considerations of procedural justice can in the end be reduced to free agreement: what makes procedures fair is that the people to whom they apply agree to their use; other features such as equality and accuracy count only because, in general, they are the features that people will insist on incorporating before they give their consent. This view is implicit in Nozick's account of justice; having first defined justice largely in procedural terms, he then identifies voluntary transfer as the sole legitimate procedure for reallocating resources.[22]

There are broadly two ways in which we might consider free agreement to be a criterion of procedural justice. On the one hand, it may itself constitute a procedure, as it does in Nozick's case when he contemplates exchanges between individuals in a market. If a minute ago I had five dollars and you had a joint of beef and now it is the other way around, then our voluntary agreement to exchange is itself the process that accounts for the outcome. On the other hand, we may agree to institute a procedure to settle some allocative problem. Unable to agree directly on a price for the beef, we may appoint a mediator and agree to abide by the price he sets. Or, for instance, a group of us may consent to decide certain issues by majority vote. Here free agreement is not the procedure itself, but the condition that (it is claimed) makes the procedure, whatever it is, a legitimate or fair one.

In whichever way we interpret free agreement there is reason to doubt the claim. We can freely agree to processes that violate norms of procedural and/or substantive justice, and in these cases the agreement does not cancel the injustice; at best it mitigates it a little. Why might this happen? Two obvious causes are ignorance and unequal bargaining power: we agree to take part in exchanges or to enter into practices because we don't fully understand the nature of what we are doing, or because we badly need access to some resource and the alternatives are all worse still. Indeed, *exploitation* (or at least one important form of it) consists in engaging in transactions that are unjust but are nevertheless consented to by both parties—such as purchases made at an inflated price by a person who is in dire need of the items purchased.[23]

Faced with this challenge, someone who wants to defend the primacy of free agreement might respond in one of two ways. One is simply to deny that injustice can occur in the course of voluntary transactions. The only way to support this claim is to narrow the concept of justice so that only forcible infringements of people's rights can count as injustice. It would take us too far afield to spell out the arguments for and against such a narrow understanding of justice, so I will merely signal the high price that attaches to the first response. The second response is to toughen up the conditions for free agreement so that agreements made in ignorance or in conditions of necessity will not count as genuinely voluntary. Although this may save the position in some cases, it is a dangerous move to make, for it suggests that our notion of what counts as a free agreement is finally controlled by our understanding of a just outcome. While we may be able to explain what is illegitimate about agreements made under duress simply by an appeal to the idea of freedom, once we begin adding other conditions—such as that the parties to an agreement should be equally astute, or equally determined to drive a hard bargain—it looks as though we are deriving our criteria for a fair procedure from prior beliefs about what can count as a just result.[24]

Even if this last suggestion is mistaken, it seems plain that procedural justice cannot be explained away as an epiphenomenon of voluntary agreement. William Nelson has argued, contrary to the Rawlsian notion of pure procedural justice, that the justice of lotteries and other such devices can be explained entirely in terms of the free disposition of resources to which people are antecedently entitled.[25] But people may for various reasons agree to enter biased lotteries or to decide issues by the roll of a loaded die, and their agreement does not make these procedures fair ones. When the blacksmith's team plays the squire's team at cricket, the blacksmith may indulge the squire by tossing the latter's loaded coin and allowing the squire to call; but this is not a fair way of starting the game unless there is a tacit agreement of a more substantive sort that, say, the game will go better if the squire's team bats first. A properly conducted lottery (or a toss with a true coin) is fair because each participant has an equal chance of winning: it embodies the equality criterion in its simplest form.[26] A compulsory lottery is inherently as fair as a voluntary one, although there are, of course, other reasons for not compelling people to enter lotteries against their will.

How, then, should we understand the relationship between free agreement and social justice? Rather than serving as a foundation of justice, free agreement is better understood as operating within a neutral zone marked out by justice. Suppose, for instance, that we have allocated a set of (qualitatively different) resources in the way that justice demands. If the people concerned decide to exchange items in a mutually agreeable way, this can be justified in terms both of liberty (people should be free to do what they like with whatever has been justly assigned to them) and of efficiency (people will swap items that are less useful to them for items that are more useful). These benefits will outweigh such small departures from justice as may occur as a result of the exchanges; the new outcome is not positively fair, but any unfairness it may possess is obliterated by the voluntary nature of the process by which it was reached. But this zone of indifference has its limits: very large departures from the original just allocation, particularly those that are neither intended nor desired by the participants, call for rectification, even if this means undoing some of the transactions that have been voluntarily concluded.[27]

To see how the same idea may apply in another procedural domain, consider the following. Suppose an association of people—a state, perhaps, or a smaller group within the state—has to decide some issue collectively. There are many possible decision rules that might be used. Some of these are plainly unfair, in the sense that they give an arbitrary advantage to some members of the group over others. But of those that remain, it may not be possible to say that one is intrinsically fairer than the rest.[28] Under these circumstances, universal agreement on a particular decision rule would make the use of that rule a procedurally fair way of making the decision. Again, justice creates a zone within which free agreement may serve to select a precise outcome.

Having argued that free agreement plays at most a subordinate role in our understanding of fair procedures, I now return to the wider question of the relationship between procedural justice and outcome justice. We have seen that there are distinct values associated with procedural justice, and also that the two kinds of justice can come apart in the sense that following fair procedures may in some instances lead to outcomes that are less just than those that might be obtained by other methods. Leaving aside the practical dilemmas that this raises, I wish to defend an account of social justice that focuses mainly on outcomes: one that attaches primary significance to the final allocation of resources among individuals, and only secondary significance to the mechanisms used to arrive at that allocation (or in Elster's pithier formulation, "the cart of procedural justice ought not to be put before the horse of substantive justice").[29]

The first point to note is that in most cases we cannot begin to specify what a fair procedure for allocating some good consists in without knowing in advance what distributive result we are trying to achieve. Although more than merely formal, the requirements of procedural justice are quite weak. To say, for instance, that a fair procedure must treat everyone with a claim on the good in question equally presupposes that we know what counts as a claim. If we object to university places being allocated rigidly on the basis of A-level results, this is because we have in the background the goal that the n available places should be assigned to the n most talented applicants. Examination results only come into the picture at all because we regard them as an (imperfect) means of measuring academic ability. Again, when we say that a fair procedure must be an accurate one, we presuppose some understanding of which facts count as the relevant facts about people that a fair procedure should unearth—say, facts about the medical condition of a number of patients among whom we have to allocate a scarce resource. The exceptions to this are lotteries and other such mechanisms embodying pure procedural justice. But these play a somewhat peripheral role in contemporary distributive arrangements.[30]

Next we must ask why fair procedures might fail to produce just outcomes. We have dwelt on cases in which the pursuit of outcome justice would require us to violate one of the norms of procedural fairness—for instance, we would require information about people that should properly remain private. But in other cases the failure arises simply because of the fallibility of the procedure when placed in its larger context, where other factors besides the procedure itself contribute to the outcome (recall the examples of the doctor prescribing medication for patients in different circumstances and the two hospitals with different catchment areas). Here it would be bizarre to defend the procedure if by modifying it we could get closer to the overall outcome we are trying to achieve. It is important to bear in mind that we are approaching this issue from the standpoint of social justice, asking which properties we would like our basic social institutions to display. This is not the perspective of the person who is directly responsible for allocating benefits of a certain kind—say, the administrator distributing resources, the employer paying wages, or the university teacher admitting and grading students. In our day-to-day activities in these roles we are properly guided mainly by considerations of procedural justice; were we to try to promote social justice more directly by bending the procedures, we would very likely end up creating more injustice than we avoided, because our decisions would be inconsistent with those made in institutions parallel to ours. (For instance, if an individual admissions officer tries to compensate for differences in school background when considering applicants from poor schools, then unless this is a general policy throughout his institution, he will be creating unfairness vis-à-vis candidates admitted by his colleagues, who rely entirely on academic qualifications.) Moreover, as we have already seen, from the individual recipient's point of view, being treated in a procedurally fair way may matter more than the justice of the outcome.

When we are concerned about social justice, however, our perspective is a very different one. We stand back from existing procedures and ask what the effect would be if one of these procedures were universally modified—for instance, if all universities asked their admissions officers to give some weight to the academic backgrounds of their applicants when reaching decisions. Of course we would need to be sure that the modified procedure was workable and did not violate the general requirements of procedural fairness, such as the dignity condition (would candidates from poor schools find it degrading if their entry scores were weighted to take account of this fact?) But our aim would be to identify what a just distribution of the good in question would look like, and then discover the procedure that is likely to get us closest to that outcome.[31]

Having staked out this position, I am now ready to consider the challenge that F. A. Hayek has posed to the whole idea of social justice. In Hayek's view to speak of social justice is to imply that some agency has intended to bring about the distribution of resources that obtains at any moment, whereas in any society in which the market economy plays a significant role, this "distribution" will be the unintended consequence of the activities of many separate individuals, each moved by his own aims and purposes. While social justice might have some meaning in a command economy, it is an irrelevant but nonetheless politically damaging idea in a "catallaxy" based upon the free market.[32]

It should be clear from what has been said so far that Hayek's claim about intentionality rests on a misunderstanding. When we assess the allocation of benefits and burdens across a society in terms of justice, we are looking at the way in which current institutions and practices produce distributive outcomes, and by implication we regard both the mechanisms and the outcomes as alterable; but we need not suppose either that the institutions and practices were consciously chosen or that the outcomes are intended.[33] All that we assume is that we might decide to do things differently in the future. But having set this misunderstanding aside, we still confront a substantive issue: is the pursuit of social justice possible in a Hayekian catallaxy, or market economy? Is there some aspect of the market that makes attempts to regulate the market's outcomes by appeal to standards of social justice either futile or destructive?

An economic market may be viewed as a procedure whereby individuals who are entitled to various resources, including their own capacity to work, deal with other individuals through the mechanisms of contract and exchange to reach a final allocation different from the initial one. Seen in this way, it does not differ in any essential respect from the other procedures considered in this chapter, except perhaps that whereas most allocative procedures are operated by designated officials, in a market each person is responsible for his or her own transactions. It is possible to study the distributive outcomes of a market and to consider how a change in the ground rules might alter these outcomes. Changes of this kind might be of two sorts: changes in people's basic entitlements, which they bring with them to market transactions, and changes in the rules governing these transactions themselves—for instances, changes in the law of contract.

It is sometimes suggested or implied that once we begin to tinker in this way with the basic framework that supports a market economy, the benefits that accrue to processes of free exchange will inevitably be lost. I can see no reason to believe this, however, and an example may help to bring the point home. Consider the effects of introducing legislation preventing employers from discriminating on grounds of race or sex in making their hiring decisions. Before this legislation was introduced, we had a labor market in which employers chose which jobs to advertise and which terms and conditions to attach to them, potential recruits weighed the costs and benefits and decided whether to apply or not, and employers finally decided which of the applicants best displayed the qualities they were looking for. With the legislation in place this labor market still exists, with the sole difference that employers may no longer take account of race or sex in deciding whom to employ. The assumption behind the legislation is presumably that in this way a fairer allocation of jobs and income will be produced, and this assumption can be tested empirically. This particular segment of the market has not been abolished: its ground rules have been altered in the name of social justice. Essentially the same process occurs when the respective rights of landlords and tenants are changed, when consumer protection legislation is introduced, when cartels to fix prices are made illegal, and so forth.

It is of course possible to argue that the market functions best when it operates according to classic *laissez-faire* principles, with the fewest possible restrictions placed on exchange, contract, hiring of labor, and so forth. This might be argued for on grounds of justice, or alternatively by appealing to efficiency or some other social value. Whatever one thinks of this claim, it is surely the right way to go about defending market freedom (indeed, there are places in Hayek's writings where he offers a defense of broadly this kind). To attempt to cut the debate off before it starts, by simply *asserting* an incompatibility between ideals of social justice and a viable market economy, is, by contrast, an indefensible maneuver. The proper approach is to begin by identifying and clarifying our substantive criteria of social justice, and then to review existing procedures, including the ground rules of market exchange, in the light of those criteria. There is no reason to assume that market procedures must lose out when this assessment is made. Indeed, as subsequent chapters will reveal, for some aspects of social justice there may be a strong positive case for preferring market allocations to other, more formal mechanisms for assigning benefits.

My main purpose in this chapter has been to guard against a certain naive and over-simple view of what social justice consists in, a view that is open to easy caricature by the enemies of the notion. The naive view presents the problem of social justice as follows: there is a set of individuals who make up a society, there is a stock of benefits or resources to be distributed, and there is a distributing agency responsible for making the allocation. What principle should the distributing agency use? Should it distribute the resources equally, or according to need, or in such a way that the worst-off recipient gets the greatest possible quantity of resources, or in some other way? Conceived in this way, the problem of social justice is simply a grander version of the problem faced by a parent at a children's tea party with a cake to divide among ten hungry children. Should the parent share the cake equally, should she take account of need, or merit, and so on? It is easy for the enemies of social justice to ridicule this view. As they quite rightly point out, there is no single distributing agency in society, nor is there a fixed stock of resources waiting to be distributed. Resources are all the time being created, transferred, and consumed in a multitude of different ways, through a wide range of mechanisms. This is perhaps especially apparent in societies in which the primary economic mechanism is the free market and "distribution" is the outcome of a huge number of voluntary transactions among different individuals.

In contrast to this naive view, I have insisted that the aim of a theory of social justice must be to provide criteria by which to assess a society's major institutions and practices, not directly to prescribe a distribution of resources. Although I have insisted on the priority of substantive or outcome justice in making this assessment, I have also tried to show why procedural justice matters, and why sometimes our pursuit of the ideally just outcome needs to be tempered with respect for procedural fairness.

6

Virtues, Practices, and Justice

In this chapter I subject to close critical scrutiny the theory of justice proposed by Alasdair MacIntyre in *After Virtue* and *Whose Justice? Which Rationality?* MacIntyre's account of justice contrasts sharply with mine—he would no doubt reject the idea of social justice, on grounds very different from those given by Hayek and other libertarians—but it repays study for at least two reasons. First, MacIntyre recognizes, as I do, that the philosophy of justice cannot be separated from its sociology; in other words, that conceptions of justice make sense only when placed in their appropriate social contexts. In MacIntyre's case, this context is provided specifically by those forms of human activity that he calls "practices," a term whose meaning will be explained shortly. Second, although the particular requirements of justice will differ from practice to practice, a common thread running through these various manifestations is the idea of *desert*. According to MacIntyre, "Justice is a disposition to give to each person, including oneself, what that person deserves and to treat no one in a way incompatible with their deserts."[1] Thus here we find a theory of justice that ties the virtue of justice tightly to the idea of desert, while at the same time offering an interpretation of desert that is very different from the one I shall give in the chapters that follow. In the present chapter I shall attempt among other things to expose the weaknesses of MacIntyre's interpretation.

MacIntyre's general view is that modern liberal societies cannot sustain the practices within which notions of justice find their proper home. Although we still use the vocabulary of justice in moral and political argument, this is little more than a relic from earlier forms of social life in which the truth of claims about justice and injustice could be properly assessed. By contrast, contemporary liberal moral and political philosophy presents a spectacle of continuing deep disagreement between rival theories of justice. Each theory claims to embody demonstrable truth, but there is no reason to think that the contest between them will ever be resolved. Liberalism, MacIntyre claims, has become a tradition within which inquiries into the nature of justice are ceaselessly pursued, but it is tacitly taken for granted that the search will never, in fact, come to an end.

In giving this brief sketch of MacIntyre's claims I have drawn upon both *After Virtue* and *Whose Justice? Which Rationality?*, but before beginning the substantive inquiry I need to say a little about the relationship between the two books.[2] MacIntyre's own view is that the second is a continuation of the first and was written primarily in order to fill a major lacuna in *After Virtue*, namely, the omission of any account of practical rationality that would enable us to say in what sense moral disputes could be rationally resolved within a tradition of thought, as well as to adjudicate between competing traditions.[3] This methodological shift is, however, also accompanied by a change of substance that is more germane to my inquiry here. It can be summed up by saying that whereas Aristotle is the hero of *After Virtue*, Aquinas is at least nominally the hero of *Whose Justice? Which Rationality?* In the first book, the preferred alternative to liberalism is a morality of the virtues, which explicates the virtues primarily in terms of their role in sustaining practices, and the account given of justice exemplifies that pattern. Aristotle is presented as the main protagonist of this position. In the second book, however, the Aristotelian account of justice is presented as being incorporated in, and superseded by, the Thomist account. But in the Thomist account practices no longer occupy a central place (if indeed any place at all), and justice is understood first and foremost in terms of legality—to be just is to do what the law, natural or positive, requires of you.

MacIntyre signals this shift of approach in the Postscript to the second edition of *After Virtue* and in the Preface to *Whose Justice? Which Rationality?* But he fails to explore its implications for the contrast between premodern and modern conceptions of morality and justice that provides both books with their main organizing idea. It seems that we have here two very different premodern understandings of justice, and also that the Thomist account to which MacIntyre eventually gives his blessing is in several respects closer than the Aristotelian account to the liberal view of justice that he rejects, especially in the latter's Lockean and Kantian incarnations.

Thus we face a problem in deciding which of the two texts to focus on if we want to give a critical assessment of MacIntyre on justice. I think that we should be guided not by temporal sequence but by the interest and cogency of the ideas expressed. And here *After Virtue* scores inasmuch as we are given a clear exposition and defense of the Aristotelian position, whereas in *Whose Justice? Which Rationality?* that account is repeated in its essentials, but then juxtaposed to a second view that, as I have just argued, is inconsistent with the first; moreover, MacIntyre gives only the most cursory of indications as to why he prefers the Thomist view to the Aristotelian. I shall therefore identify as MacIntyre's main doctrine the practice-based account of the virtues developed in *After Virtue* and reiterated in the case of justice in the early chapters of *Whose Justice? Which Rationality?* Most of the chapter will be devoted to the analysis and critical appraisal of that doctrine, and only toward the end will I turn to consider, briefly, whether the Thomist position might provide a more promising account of justice than the Aristotelian.

LET US NOW TURN to MacIntyre's argument that the virtues, including, of course, the virtue of justice, must first be explained in terms of those forms of human activity that he calls "practices." To show that a quality is a virtue is to show that its possession is essential to sustain one or more practices and to achieve those goods that the practices serve to foster. As the argument proceeds, this initial claim is qualified in certain respects. The concrete virtues that are displayed as someone engages in a series of practices must knit together in such a way that a life of virtue can be seen overall as a coherent good life for a particular person. Moreover, a society's range of practices must harmonize with one another so as to allow the formation of a community with an overarching conception of the good life, within which specific virtues have a well-defined place. In this way MacIntyre imposes coherence conditions—individual and communal—on his original account. Nonetheless, the original account remains central to his claim that modern society can no longer sustain a morality of virtue, for the basis of that claim is precisely that modern society lacks the practices that might give the virtues a determinate content.

What, then, does MacIntyre mean by a practice? It is, he says, "any coherent and complex form of socially established co-operative human activity through which goods internal to that form of activity are realized in the course of trying to achieve those standards of excellence which are appropriate to, and partially definitive of, that form of activity, with the result that human powers to achieve excellence, and human conceptions of the ends and goods involved, are systematically extended."[4] Among the examples he gives are games (chess and football), productive activities (farming and architecture), intellectual activities (science and history), artistic pursuits (painting and music), and politics (creating a political community). Other activities are firmly ruled out: tic-tac-toe, bricklaying, and planting turnips. To make sense of the inclusions and the exclusions, we need to pay attention to two elements in the lengthy definition cited above: the idea of internal goods and the idea of standards of excellence.

Goods internal to a practice are distinguished from those external to it by the fact that the former can necessarily be achieved *only* through participation in the practice in question. To borrow MacIntyre's example, the good that consists in playing chess well is an internal good, whereas the money one may earn through being a champion chess player is an external good: it is merely contingent that playing chess should be the means whereby somebody enriches himself, whereas the good of playing well can for obvious reasons be achieved only by the actual playing of chess. Moreover, one can achieve the good in question only by attempting to excel, that is, by endeavoring to rival or outdo those previous practitioners whose activities make up the history of the practice. Thus (presumably) the ground for excluding tic-tac-toe, bricklaying, and turnip-planting from the list of "practices" is that, although there may be specific kinds of pleasure to be had from engaging in them, there are no historically developed standards of excellence to apply, and hence no internal goods of the right kind to be enjoyed.

To understand the virtues, primary examples of which include truth-telling, courage, and justice, we must examine the ways in which these qualities are essential to achieve the goods that are internal to a range of such practices. Without, say, honesty or courage, we may succeed in obtaining some of the external goods that a society's institutions attach to practices (for instance, we may win prizes by means of deception), but we cannot attain the internal goods. To attain such goods, we must be guided in our actions by the relevant rules, and we must also sustain the appropriate relationships with our fellow practitioners, which is possible only if we possess qualities of character of the kind just identified.

To see what justice means when understood in this light, we need to focus our attention on *Whose Justice? Which Rationality?*, in which MacIntyre adopts a slightly different vocabulary to present what is nevertheless essentially the same position.[5] Instead of "practices" he speaks of "types of systematic activity," and the distinction between internal and external goods is replaced by a distinction between "the goods of excellence" and "the goods of effectiveness." The former are the intrinsic goods that consist in excelling in practices such as games, the arts and sciences, or politics, whereas the latter are the various material rewards—wealth, social status, and power—that one may contingently acquire by performing successfully in one of these fields. The fundamental requirement of justice is that one should be guided in one's participation in any practice by a quest for the goods of excellence, and this issues in two secondary requirements: first, that one allow one's actions to be governed by the rules and conventions that do indeed foster excellence (rather than attempting to win or succeed by any means or at any cost), and second, that when rewards are to be distributed, they should be allocated on the basis of desert as defined by the standards of excellence internal to the practice. Thus there are, one might say, two kinds of justice, the justice of the participant and the justice of the spectator-cum-assessor, but both are to be guided by the basic principle that the rewards of performance—both internal and external—should go to the genuinely deserving, those who manifest to the highest degree the qualities that the practice in question seeks to foster.

MacIntyre is thus claiming that an understanding of practices is essential to our understanding of the virtues in two related respects. On the one hand, we cannot know what it means in concrete terms to possess a virtue unless we are familiar with the range of practices within which that virtue is displayed. To know what justice is, we must know what the criteria of desert are in practices like games, scientific research, and so forth. On the other hand, we cannot understand why justice, say, is a virtue unless we grasp its role in sustaining such practices. If we cared only about the goods of effectiveness, we would value only such qualities as were maximally useful in achieving such goods, either for the individual or for society as a whole. This, MacIntyre asserts, is what lies behind those lists of pseudo-virtues found in modern moral philosophy—for instance, Benjamin Franklin's catalogue of the qualities useful for achieving earthly prosperity and heavenly rewards.[6]

I noted above that, in MacIntyre's view, a complete account of the virtues, and *a fortiori* the virtue of justice, would also have to examine the way in which specific practices could be brought into harmony with one another, both from the perspective of the unity of a person's life and from the point of view of the community as a whole. How would this alter the account just given? First of all, a quality that served a person well in achieving excellence of a particular kind would not count as a virtue if it simultaneously prevented him or her from achieving the goods that are internal to other practices. The example MacIntyre gives here is that of relentlessness in the sense of the ability to drive oneself single-mindedly in the pursuit of a specific goal.[7] This quality is valuable in games or in exploration, say, but it is likely to prevent one from successfully sustaining a family life, for example, and this disqualifies it from being a virtue.[8] Second, if a society's practices are to knit together in the required way then participants have to have a sense of the relative demands that each makes on them, and so a full account of justice (especially) will need to refer to the proper ordering of goods *among* practices as well as within them.[9] Finally, there are forms of behavior that are universally destructive of any form of community—MacIntyre cites the taking of innocent life, theft, perjury, and betrayal—and these will give rise to moral injunctions (and precepts of justice) that are not tied to any specific practice. Thus MacIntyre claims that such a communitarian perspective allows us to understand those aspects of justice that concern the upholding of basic moral laws.[10]

HAVING SPELLED OUT the way in which MacIntyre ties his account of the virtues to an account of practices, I now turn to a more critical examination of his position. Here we must begin by looking closely at the related notions of a practice and of an internal good. It is immediately apparent that the list of practices that MacIntyre supplies to illustrate his position is somewhat heterogeneous, and this complicates our understanding of the latter notion. There is an important distinction to be drawn between practices whose *raison d'etre* consists entirely in the internal goods achieved by participants and the contemplation of those achievements by others (I shall refer to such practices as "self-contained") and practices that exist to serve social ends beyond themselves (I shall refer to these as "purposive"). Games, from which much of MacIntyre's thinking about practices seems to be drawn, are the main exemplars of the first category. Here the contrast between internal and external goods has its clearest and most straightforward application. The good that consists in playing a fine innings at cricket is obviously incomprehensible in the absence of the game itself, and moreover the standard of excellence involved—what it is that makes the innings a fine one—can be identified only by reference to the history of the game, to the canons of judgment that have been developed by practitioners and spectators.[11] This is obviously distinct from the money or prestige that a successful player may additionally acquire.

By contrast, in the case of a productive activity such as architecture or farming, or in the case of an intellectual activity such as physics, there is an external purpose that gives the practice its point and in terms of which it may be judged—in the cases in question we might say, respectively, the creation of attractive and comfortable buildings, the production of food for the community, and the discovery of scientific truth. This introduces a certain complexity into the argument. There is still a distinction to be drawn between the good of being an excellent architect, farmer, or physicist and the various extrinsic goods that may be achieved by being successful in these fields. But the former good is not simply constituted internally to each practice. Indeed, one might say that insofar as it is so constituted, the practice is to that extent a deformed one.

Take the example of medicine, a practice not included in MacIntyre's initial list, but mentioned in the course of his discussion (and surely properly so in view of its Aristotelian associations). In contrast to the external goods such as money, the internal good provided by this practice is the good of being an excellent doctor. But this in turn may mean, simply, "an excellent healer of the sick" or "an exemplar of those standards of excellence that have evolved in the medical community." To the extent to which these two meanings diverge—say, if the medical community has come to attach special weight to the capacity to perform certain spectacular operations whose long-term efficacy is doubtful—the practice has fallen victim to professional deformation. A good practice here is one whose standards of excellence are related directly to its wider purpose.

The distinction between self-contained and purposive practices seems clear enough in itself, but it may in certain cases be disputed whether a particular practice has an external purpose or not. The visual arts, for instance, may be seen as practices whose development is governed entirely by internal canons of excellence, or alternatively they may be seen as serving social needs for the embellishment of public and private space. The view taken will determine who should be counted as a good artist. There is a somewhat similar dispute in the case of the practice of politics (compare the views of, say, Oakeshott and Lenin).

But let us continue with the cases in which the distinction can be applied without controversy. A major difference between the two kinds of practice is that, in the case of self-contained practices, critical assessment can only be carried out from within the practice itself, whereas in the case of purposive practices, the whole practice may be reviewed in the light of the end it is meant to serve. The rules of cricket may be changed to encourage the batsmen to play more ambitious strokes, or to discourage the bowlers from bowling merely defensively. Here the point of the change is to foster those excellences already recognized in the practice. By contrast, it makes perfect sense to compare entire forms of medicine (say, Western medicine and Chinese medicine) in respect of their effectiveness in curing the sick. (I do not mean to imply that the result of such a comparison will necessarily be a straightforward preference for one form over the other regardless of context.) Or one might wish to compare the results of a private system of medicine with the results of a state-funded system. If the outcome of such a comparison becomes widely known and accepted, standards of excellence may be changed: a good acupuncturist is not the same as a good surgeon. This follows immediately from the fact that, in the case of purposive practices, the relevant standards should be related directly to the ends of the practice.

MacIntyre does not make the distinction I have been making between self-contained and purposive practices. It is nevertheless clear that, for the sake of developing his account of the virtues, he regards all practices as if they belonged to the self-contained category, even in cases (such as farming) in which the practice clearly serves an external purpose.[12] This is indicated both by the examples he considers in greatest detail and by his depiction of standards of excellence as developing through internal debate within each practice, rather than in response to wider needs. It is this assumption that practices are self-sustaining that allows him to present the ethics of virtue as categorically distinct from both teleological and deontological ethical theories, as these are usually understood. To interpret virtues as qualities needed to achieve some goal such as the general welfare, or as qualities that allow their possessor to conform to certain rules, is to fall victim to the error of liberal individualism. Instead, as we have seen, a virtue properly understood is a quality that is necessary to achieve the goods internal to one or more practices. These goods may change over time as practices develop—thus the virtues themselves are not immutable—but at any moment the list must be taken as given.[13] It cannot be revised by invoking some social goal or purpose in the light of which different personal qualities would take on the character of virtues.

But suppose instead that the virtues were to be understood primarily in terms of purposive practices. It would then be impossible to defend any particular list of virtues without making reference to the social purposes which the practices that require them are meant to serve. To the extent that there is controversy about the proper form of any practice— of the kind that I tried to bring out through the example of medicine— such controversy is almost certain to spill over onto the associated virtues. Thus the virtues will no longer be self-sufficient; although it may still be impossible to *reduce* them to other kinds of moral considerations (considerations of goodness or rightness), they will nevertheless have a dependent status. It will be impossible to understand them except by reference to the needs and purposes that predominate in a particular society.

The issue we must therefore face is whether the practices with which the virtues are centrally connected are (in the terms I have been using) self-contained or purposive. Here I want to make two observations about the self-contained practices. The first is that they can exist only on the proviso that more basic social functions have been discharged. They are in that sense luxury items: they can flourish to the extent that a society's resources and human capacity are not required to meet the demands of material production, the maintenance of social order, and so forth. No doubt it is an important feature of human beings that they engage in play (understood here in a broad sense to mean rule-governed activities that have no immediate instrumental purpose). Yet it seems reasonable to suppose that originally forms of play were linked more closely than they currently are to wider social needs (for instance, that games were developed in order to encourage those skills and abilities required in hunting or battle). From this point of view, it is by no means clear whether the transition from premodern to modern society should be seen as beneficial or harmful to the self-contained practices. On the one hand, MacIntyre might argue (as it seems likely he would) that the acquisitive culture that modern market societies foster diverts people away from the pursuit of goods internal to practices toward the pursuit of money, status, and the other goods of effectiveness. On the other hand, the astonishing material productivity of these societies also creates the resources and the leisure time that allow self-contained practices—sports, the arts, and so forth—to flourish if people choose to engage in them. This ambivalence has worrying consequences for MacIntyre's general thesis, for if the virtues are to be understood in terms of self-contained practices, and if there is no reason to think that modern social conditions are less hospitable to these practices than, say, the Athens of Aristotle's time, then it is surely paradoxical that the contemporary world should have witnessed the almost complete erosion of the virtues, as that thesis maintains.

But my second observation is that it is in any case doubtful whether the virtues should primarily be understood in terms of their role in sustaining self-contained practices. Certainly it is possible to use such practices as a kind of training ground for the virtues, as Victorian public schools tried to do with their practices of sport. But are they the main arena in which the virtues are manifested? I shall look at the virtue of justice in greater detail in a moment, but consider first the case of courage. When would we think of people as displaying courage? First of all, and most obviously, on the battlefield; next when carrying out some humane act in circumstances of danger—say, manning a lifeboat in high seas; third, when facing intense pain with equanimity or deciding to carry out some arduous task such as raising a severely handicapped child. These are some central cases. We might also speak of courage as being displayed in certain sporting activities such as parachuting or hang-gliding, but interestingly enough we might here prefer some alternative term such as "daring." Why is this? The very fact that these activities are optional, in the sense that participants are not required to engage in them, either by physical necessity or by a sense of moral obligation, counts against the application of an essentially moral term like "courage." Unlike courage displayed in the service of a valued end, such as the saving of life or the defense of one's homeland, courage displayed merely for its own sake is hardly the genuine thing.[14]

Much the same may be said about the virtue of justice. We think of justice (or fairness) as being displayed primarily by legislators, administrators, judges, educators, employers, and so forth—people whose decisions bear crucially on the interests of others, and the quality of whose conduct therefore vitally affects the general character of a society. There *is* a justice-like quality that manifests itself in games and other such self-contained practices, namely, a willingness to abide by the rules and apply them impartially to oneself and others. But we would normally refer to this quality by some term such as "good-sportsmanship" rather than "fairness" (and certainly not "justice") in order to indicate the relatively trivial nature of the interests that are served in exercising it. (*Children* may talk a lot about fairness and unfairness in games, but children, of course, tend to think that much more is at stake in games than do adults.)[15]

Thus a plausible practice-based account of justice will have to concern itself centrally with purposive rather than self-contained practices. Purposive practices, to recall, are those forms of human activity that, although having internal standards of excellence, serve broad social ends and are therefore open to critical review in the light of those ends. What role does justice play in purposive practices? Here the distinction I drew in the last chapter between procedural and substantive justice—between justice as a quality of the rules or mechanisms by which one agent assigns goods or bads to another, and justice as a property of the ensuing states of affairs in which each person has a different share of these benefits and burdens—becomes crucially important. Practices typically require those who engage in them to exhibit both forms of justice, but the role of justice is very different in the two cases. Procedural justice is required at the moment of engagement, because the practice cannot be sustained unless its procedures are followed in a fair way. In order for excellence to be manifest, and the wider ends of the practice promoted, all those who participate in it must do so under the same conditions, and this requires, for instance, that those who are charged with applying the rules that govern the practice must do so impartially. Substantive justice, by contrast, is invoked at the point at which the practice is being brought under critical review. I don't mean that the main end of a practice will normally be to promote substantive justice, although this may be the case in some instances. Rather, the main aim must be pursued in a way that is consistent with substantive justice. Thus if we take a practice such as medicine, its main aim is not justice but the healing of the sick;

nevertheless, it is also important that this end be pursued in a fair way, so that, for instance, two equally sick people should as far as possible have the same chance of being cured.

It is possible, of course, for a practice to have as one of its procedural requirements that a person (or a committee) should at some point make a judgment of substantive justice. Consider, for instance, a literary competition. This will typically have all sorts of rules and qualifying conditions ("Only books published in 1990 are eligible to be considered") that require its administrators to exercise merely the most straightforward kind of procedural justice. But there will be a moment at which the jury has to make a judgment of literary merit and decide which book deserves first prize. At this point the procedures require the participants to be guided by considerations of substantive justice. Notice, however, that the basis of the judgment is whatever is specified in the rules of the competition, and the jury's job is to identify merit so defined, and to go no further. Thus the rules or conventions may require that only works published in the English language be considered, that only works of fiction are "literature" from the point of view of this competition, and so on. A different kind of substantive justice would be invoked if we were to ask whether the competition as it is now run is "fair" from the point of view of the whole world of literature it is meant to serve. Thus we can acknowledge that practices may require practitioners, on occasion, to make judgments of substantive justice, while still continuing to distinguish between procedural justice, which helps to sustain the practice in its present form, and substantive justice, a criterion in terms of which the practice may be assessed from the outside.

THE RELEVANCE OF THIS POINT to MacIntyre's argument will now become clear. MacIntyre, as we have seen, defines justice in terms of desert, but at the same time he regards justice as something constituted internally to practices.[16] How can this be? "Desert" must here be taken to refer to the specific forms of desert that a particular practice at any moment takes to correspond to its notions of excellence. That is, the practice establishes standards of achievement, and justice is done when everyone behaves in such a way that the highest achievers receive the highest rewards, and so forth. Let us call this a practice-defined notion of desert.

How adequate is such a notion? Observe first of all that what practices require of people by way of procedural justice has very often nothing directly to do with desert. In competitions, for example, the proper role of officials is likely to be that of applying the same rules and criteria to each participant so that desert may manifest itself spontaneously, so to speak, whereas an official attempting to implement desert criteria directly will very likely distort the result.[17] Thus although norms of procedural justice may be guided by the general aim of ensuring that people are treated according to their deserts, it is by no means clear that this is the best way to capture the quality of justice that practitioners must exhibit. Second, we have seen that the criterion of desert employed in any practice at any moment may be challenged by reference to wider social purposes. An example I gave earlier was that of medicine, where, because of professional deformation, the most "deserving" practitioners come to be seen as those who are most accomplished at performing organ transplants and other such spectacular operations. Here one would like to appeal to an alternative criterion of desert, deriving from the social purposes of medicine, such that a highly competent and hard-working family doctor who cares for his patients in an all-around way can be seen as more deserving (of both the internal and the external goods of medicine) than the transplant specialist.

I am suggesting here that the practice-defined notion of desert favored by MacIntyre misconceives the primary role that desert plays in relation to practices. That role is above all a critical one. We appeal to desert in order to show that a practice is not working as it should, either because its rules and procedures are badly calculated to ensure that participants get goods in proportion to their deserts, or (more radically) because the criterion of desert that underlies the present practice is misjudged.

Since this claim about the critical role of desert criteria is crucial to my argument, it may be worth citing a well-known example of an appeal to desert of precisely this kind. Stripped of its utilitarian trappings (in this case relatively superficial), John Stuart Mill's *The Subjection of Women* is an extended and eloquent plea for current practices—family life, professional employment, and public office—to be reformed in such a way that women's deserts are given due recognition. Mill's argument is partly that women share relevant qualities with men and partly that they have complementary qualities, but in general that there is no basis in desert for an enforced division of labor in the family, for the exclusion of women from political life, and so forth. If desert (and justice) were indeed ideas defined internally to practices, it is difficult to see how an argument such as Mill's could coherently be made, for it would be open to a defender of existing arrangements to make the conclusive retort that politics (say) is a practice the qualifying criteria for which simply include that of being male. It is precisely because we are able to reflect on the ends that politics should serve, and therefore on what it means genuinely to excel in this field, that arguments such as Mill's are able to take hold.

MacIntyre has an implicit reply to this claim about the critical role of desert, namely, that outside of practices notions of desert lose their determinacy, so that what we would expect to find is an interminable debate in which no one is able to establish to the satisfaction of the other parties that he has come up with the correct criterion of desert for assessing a particular practice. MacIntyre believes, for instance, that contemporary disputes about the justice of positive discrimination are irresolvable in this way. In a society from which genuine practices have almost disappeared, "we have all too many disparate and rival moral concepts, in this case rival and disparate concepts of justice, and . . . the moral resources of the culture allow us no way of settling the issue between them rationally." Thus "modern politics is civil war carried on by other means, and *Bakke* was an engagement whose antecedents were at Gettysburg and Shiloh."[18]

What are we to make of this? I have already expressed some skepticism about the claim that the modern world has been denuded of the practices that used to flourish in the ancient, and I am now equally skeptical about the idea that general notions of justice (and desert) are more contestable among ourselves than among our predecessors. Here it may be useful to begin with an observation of Aristotle's that MacIntyre cites, but whose deeper significance seems to escape him. This is his report of the dispute between democrats and oligarchs over the proper basis for holding political office. Both sides agree that those who are equally meritorious should be equally eligible to hold office, but they disagree about what the relevant test of merit consists in: "The oligarchs think that superiority on one point—in their case wealth—means superiority on all: the democrats believe that equality in one respect—for instance, that of free birth—means equality all round."[19] In reporting this dispute Aristotle was recording the views of two opposing and irreconcilable factions in Greek politics, and he was equally clear that the dispute stemmed to some degree from the conflicting interests of the two parties, who, he said, "are judging *in their own case;* and most men, as a rule, are bad judges where their own interests are involved."[20] So here we find a cardinal dispute about the conception of desert that is relevant when public office is to be allocated; and although Aristotle has his own proposal to make, he is under no illusion that he is likely in practice to persuade the conflicting parties to agree. If we were to apply the same standards of political realism to fourth-century Athens as MacIntyre applies to contemporary America, we might conclude that Athenian politics was civil war carried on by other means, and that Aristotle's *Politics* was an engagement whose antecedents were Cleisthenes' revolution of 508 B.C. and the oligarchs' coup of 411 B.C.[21]

In general, in any complex society that contains a variety of practices, each having its own internal standards of excellence, we should expect to find some agreement about criteria of desert and some disagreement, with the disagreement attributable in part to the conflicting interests of different groups in the society who stand to gain or lose from having their favored criterion generally adopted, as blacks and whites do from having different criteria of merit used in university admissions today, and oligarchs and democrats did from having different criteria of merit used for political office in fourth-century Athens. To this commonplace observation I want, however, to add a qualification. Contrary to MacIntyre's belief, the modern age has not witnessed the decline of the notion of desert, but if anything its apotheosis. The reasons for this lie in the comparatively open and fluid social structure of contemporary market societies, by virtue of which it is easier than it was in Aristotle's time to draw a line between people's personal qualities and accomplishments and their ascribed social position. We no longer have any inclination to think that people can deserve goods by virtue of their rank or station, whereas Greek thinkers had to work within an ethical vocabulary that tended to conflate the claims of personal merit and social standing: it was, for instance, an open and disputed question whether key terms of appraisal such as *agathos* should apply to those who were well-born and wealthy or to those who displayed moral virtues.[22] In contemporary discourse we use the term "merit" to refer broadly to a person's admirable qualities, while tending to reserve "desert" more specifically for cases in which someone is responsible for the results he or she brings about. There is no Greek equivalent for "desert" in this specific sense. The Greek term *axia*, which corresponds to "merit," has broad connotations:

to Aristotle there is nothing unintelligible about judging merit by wealth or noble birth, even though his own recommendation is that it should be gauged by moral virtue.[23] (It is therefore potentially misleading when translators use "desert" and "merit" interchangeably when rendering Aristotle into English.)

MacIntyre might concede that the notion of desert retains a strong hold on popular moral consciousness.[24] In his discussion of the competing liberal theories of justice advanced by Rawls and Nozick, he points out that these theories are separated from the more popular views of justice to which they would otherwise correspond precisely by their overt repudiation of that notion. But he presents this as a case of the liberal philosophers' being clear-sighted about what justice has to mean under modern conditions (essentially a set of rules whereby everyone may successfully pursue the goods of effectiveness), whereas the common man is simply inconsistent in wanting to hold together with modern ideas of rights and utility a notion of desert that belongs within a traditional conception of justice. This diagnosis, however, depends on establishing that desert criteria cannot be applied successfully to the institutions and practices of contemporary societies. Such a view is hard to sustain. Think, for instance, of higher education and public employment as two kinds of goods to which access is continually being reshaped by criteria of desert. Or think of job-evaluation schemes as involving a systematic attempt to bring the rewards and perquisites of job-holding in line with the comparative merits of the job-holders.

This last example, however, challenges one of MacIntyre's principal reasons for seeing modern society as the graveyard of desert. He believes that in a market economy there can be no genuine apportionment of reward to desert: "There is no relationship of desert or merit connecting work and its products on the one hand and endeavour and skill on the other. Of course in a market economy endeavour and skill will receive their rewards insofar as they have been embodied in successful attempts to give what they want to those who have money in their pockets. But even so the reward is not for success in whatever form of activity of doing or making is in question, but for having done or made that for which there is economic demand."[25] What is being claimed here is that work, or more generally economic activity, in contemporary societies does not take place within practices in the MacIntyrean sense: there are no internal goods to achieve or standards of excellence with which to comply.

Granting this—and at best it is a partial truth, for many work communities do embody just such standards of excellence and offer their members the internal goods of recognition and esteem—why is it inconceivable that people should deserve rewards simply for their success in providing others with what they want, as shown by their willingness to pay?[26] A valuable activity is being undertaken voluntarily; economic demand gives a measure, albeit an imperfect one, of that value. Even if we believe that in existing markets the rewards people receive are often disproportionate to the contributions they make, we may still go on to claim that by reshaping the property rights and other institutions surrounding the market, we can achieve a closer fit. Here the notion of desert is employed in its critical capacity, as a criterion against which existing arrangements, and the distribution of goods that flows from them, can be judged.

In presenting this case, I do not mean to imply that economic desert of the kind just identified is the only kind of desert available to the denizens of modern societies. On the contrary, I have been at pains to stress that MacIntyre's decline-and-fall-of-the-practices thesis is at best a gross exaggeration, and it follows that there are many contemporary forms of human activity within which different criteria of justice apply. The deserts of doctors, teachers, and public administrators are not assessed in the same way as the deserts of businessmen or manual workers. But I do want to claim that the arrival of societies in which the market economy has a central role also ushers in desert as a key criterion for assessing the distribution of goods. For the first time, perhaps, almost everyone can aspire to a state of affairs in which her merits are recognized and duly rewarded. In earlier societies, including the Greek city-states, the majority of men and women were excluded from the practices—politics, the arts and sciences, the professions, and so forth—within which notions of desert or merit had a place. Desert was publicly recognized and rewarded only among those who inhabited a social plateau, access to which depended almost entirely on birth, sex, and other ascriptive qualities.

WITH THIS IN MIND, we can turn finally to look at MacIntyre's endorsement of a Thomist view of justice in the later parts of *Whose Justice? Which Rationality?* Although in passing from Aristotle to Aquinas we are moving forward in time, we should not assume too readily that the social and political context provided by Paris in the thirteenth century A.D. is closer to our own than that of Athens in the fourth century B.C. In some respects the former seems more distant: the scope of the market economy was more narrowly circumscribed, there was greater fixity in social ranking (though of course slavery had disappeared), and there was a lesser degree of popular participation in the government of the polity. So it may turn out that Aquinas' understanding of the virtues and of justice rests on assumptions that make it less relevant to our contemporary predicament than that of Aristotle.

Two points emerge clearly from even the most cursory reading of Aquinas' account of justice. The first is that justice, along with the other virtues, is not defined primarily in terms of its role in sustaining practices (in MacIntyre's sense of "practice"). The second is that desert features only peripherally in that account. Justice is defined, in accordance with a long-standing tradition, as "a habit whereby a man renders to each one his due by a constant and perpetual will."[27] This is then subdivided into general justice, which Aquinas identifies with legal justice, adherence to the precepts of natural and positive law; and particular justice, which again has two subdivisions, commutative and distributive. Commutative justice is not our concern here, though it is worth underlining that much of Aquinas' discussion is taken up with matters of legal procedure—with the principles of compensation, with the conduct of trials, and so forth. One could sum this up by saying that for Aquinas justice has centrally to do with the law: its primary requirement is that we should abide by the law in our dealings with our fellow citizens, and its main secondary requirement is that when the law is broken, just procedures should be used to compensate the victim and punish the offender. In most cases the law in question will be the positive law of a particular polity, though if positive law should conflict with the rational precepts of natural law, then justice requires us to obey the latter.

This brief sketch already indicates the distance that separates Aquinas' account from any practice-based understanding of justice. But now let us look at what he has to say about distributive justice, where we might expect to find that distance lessened. Distributive justice concerns the division of the common resources of a community among its members, and the principle is that each person's share should be proportional to his or her "due." How is the latter established? Aquinas tells us to look toward the common good of the community to see what a person's "due" is in a particular case. If people are destitute and the community's resources can help them, then need becomes the criterion.[28] If the question is who should be promoted to a professorship, then the relevant quality is the extent of a person's knowledge.[29] In other cases social standing is the criterion: "The rich ought to be honoured by reason of their occupying a higher position in the community" (though not merely for being rich).[30] We would say that desert was being recognized in the second case but not the third, but interestingly Aquinas draws no such sharp line. For instance, in considering the issue whether the doctrine of the mean applies in the same way to commutative as to distributive justice, he poses the following objection:

> In order to observe the mean in distributive justice we have to consider the various deserts of persons. Now a person's deserts are considered also in commutative justice, for instance, in punishments; thus a man who strikes a prince is punished more than one who strikes a private individual.[31]

To which Aquinas replies as follows:

> In actions and passions a person's station affects the quantity of a thing: for it is a greater injury to strike a prince than a private person. Hence in distributive justice a person's station is considered in itself, whereas in commutative justice it is considered in so far as it causes a diversity of things.[32]

It is surely remarkable (from our point of view) that Aquinas would reply to an argument couched in terms of desert—and this is one of the few places in his discussion of justice where the term is explicitly used—by talking about the different ways in which a person's *station* is relevant to the two kinds of justice. This suggests very strongly that we have here once again a world view in which the claims of personal merit and of social standing have not been disentangled, so that to Aquinas it would not seem incongruous to speak of someone as "deserving" something merely by virtue of his rank within the community. This is hardly surprising given the hierarchical nature of the society to which Aquinas belonged, but it confirms our earlier speculation that his social experience is, if anything, more remote from our own than that of the Greek philosophers of democratic Athens, and his account of justice to that degree less relevant to us.

MacIntyre might want to see this remoteness as a virtue rather than as a vice. He points out that Aquinas' conception of justice, particularly his views on usury, would condemn "the standard commercial and financial practices of capitalism."[33] But my claim is not merely that a Thomist theory of justice would be critical of present-day market societies, but that it would be critical in a way that renders it unavailable to us, for the Thomist view presupposes an ordered community within which people occupy well-defined positions whose respective contributions to the common good can be meaningfully compared. We do not have such a community, nor can we aspire to have one. Many of MacIntyre's critics have pointed out that his general account of the decline of morality tells us virtually nothing about how we might hope to revive it under modern conditions. In the case of justice, we can be more specific: to the extent that MacIntyre now wishes to defend a Thomist account of justice in place of an Aristotelian account, he is committing himself to the revival of a form of life that is categorically, and not merely contingently, excluded by the social structures of the modern world.[34]

TO SUM UP, while it may be possible to develop a theory of justice as a practice-sustaining virtue, one cannot at the same time define it in terms of desert. Nor is there much warrant for attributing such a theory to the two main protagonists of MacIntyre's books, both of whom endorse the notion of distributive justice as a set of criteria to govern the allocation of a society's common resources. Thus both conceptually and historically MacIntyre's thesis is suspect; and we have seen already that it cannot help us in our search for a conception of justice to guide the development of modern societies.

7

The Concept of Desert

MacIntyre is not alone among contemporary writers in pointing to the large and significant gap between the role played by desert in popular conceptions of justice and the role assigned to it in recent political philosophy.[1] As we have seen in Chapter 4, popular thinking appears to attach a good deal of weight to desert when assessing the justice of a distribution of resources. Political philosophers, by contrast, have mostly been suspicious of the idea of desert, many thinking it either inherently confused or at least indeterminate in its application. This suspicion cannot be interpreted simply as a wish to promote some rival principle of justice such as need or equality. There *have* been attacks on desert by strong egalitarians, but the idea has also been attacked by thinkers located firmly in the liberal mainstream, by rightist liberals such as Hayek as well as by leftist liberals such as Rawls.[2]

This gap is bound to worry anyone who holds a view about the relationship between theories of justice and popular conceptions similar to the one defended in Chapter 3. For the political philosophers I am referring to here have not been engaged in clarifying or refining pretheoretical notions of desert; they have wanted to throw them out altogether, or at least to transform them into something radically different. Even if the *words* "desert" and "deserve" are not blacklisted, the concepts that these words centrally express in ordinary discourse are declared redundant. This may, as Samuel Scheffler speculates, also affect the practical prospects of liberal political philosophy.[3] For if notions of desert are as deeply embedded in popular understandings of justice as I believe, then it may be difficult to win support for policies whose justification depends on the assumption that desert is an incoherent or irrelevant idea.

I shall attempt here to defend the idea of desert against these charges of incoherence and irrelevance. By way of preliminary mapping, it may be helpful to distinguish three positions one may adopt on desert in general, and a further three on the relationship between desert and distributive justice.

On desert in general we can distinguish:

1. *The Positive View.* It is possible to identify a single, coherent notion of desert that, while it may not make sense of everything that people commonly say using the language of desert, will at least make sense of most of it.
2. *The Negative View.* There is no coherent conception of desert to be extracted in this way. Claims about desert must be translated into another form if they are to be meaningful. Sidgwick provides a classic illustration of this view: "The only tenable Determinist interpretation of desert is, in my opinion, the Utilitarian: according to which, when a man is said to deserve reward for any services to society, the meaning is that it is expedient to reward him, in order that he and others may be induced to render similar services by the expectation of similar rewards."[4] This is not, of course, the only version of the Negative View.
3. *The Pluralist View.* The notion of desert is used to make a variety of claims, of which some at least have moral force and cannot be reduced or translated in the way that the Negative View demands. But there is no single thread running through all these claims, no core idea that constitutes *the* concept of desert.[5]

On the relationship between desert and justice, we have once again:

1. *The Positive View.* Justice is to be understood exclusively or at least centrally in terms of desert. A just distribution of resources, in other words, simply is one in which each party gets what he or she deserves.
2. *The Negative View.* Desert is irrelevant to justice. When deciding what justice requires we should make no reference to desert. This might be (a) because the notion of desert makes no sense at all; (b) because although the notion makes sense, we are not morally required to give people what they deserve;[6] or (c) because although

the notion makes sense and has moral force, the demands it imposes are not obligations of justice.[7]

3. *The Pluralist View.* Desert is relevant to justice. In deciding what
   justice requires we should consider what different people deserve.
   But this is not the only, nor even necessarily the main, relevant
   consideration. It may conflict with other criteria, such as need, in
   which case we may have to balance the various criteria against one
   another in deciding what justice requires.

These are the broad possibilities, and refinements may be added to
each of them. The relationship between the two triads should be fairly
evident: if one holds the Negative View about desert itself, one must also
hold the Negative View about desert and justice; but Positive and Pluralist Views about desert can and do consort with any of the three positions
about desert and justice. It will be clear from Chapter 2 that I hold the
Pluralist View about the relationship between desert and justice. My
main task here will be to defend the Positive View about desert itself,
though with some concessions to the Pluralist View, and a subsidiary
task will be to defend the Pluralist View about desert and justice against
the Negative View; in other words, to show that the concept of desert I
wish to elaborate does have relevance to justice.

LET ME BEGIN BY TRYING to pin down the notion of desert itself.[8]
Consider the wide range of cases in which we make judgments to the
effect that a person deserves some benefit by virtue of some performance
or attribute. I propose to distinguish *primary* desert judgments, which
fall within the core of the concept, *secondary* desert judgments, which
still invoke the concept but are parasitic on primary judgments, and
sham desert judgments, which use the language of desert but are really
appeals to some other ethical idea.

When primary desert judgments are made, some agent A is said to
deserve some benefit B on the basis of an activity or performance P. A is
most often an individual but may also be a collective such as a football
team. B is something generally considered beneficial to its recipient: a
prize, a reward, income, a promotion, an honor, praise, recognition, and
so on. P may be a single act or a course of activity extending over time.
The important thing is that P should be in the relevant sense A's performance; that is, A should be responsible for P. This rules out a number of

possibilities. One is the case in which A is coerced or manipulated into performing P—for example, under hypnosis I accomplish some danger- ous task that I would normally be too scared to perform.[9] Another is the case in which A performs P inadvertently: he intends to perform Q but because of circumstances beyond his control he ends up performing P. Yet another is the case in which A's performing P is some kind of fluke; although he intends to perform P, the fact that he succeeds is very largely a matter of luck. For example, suppose that I am a very poor archer but manage to persuade the local archery club to let me take part in its annual tournament. By sheer good luck I send three arrows into the gold, something I could not repeat in a million attempts. I could not on this basis deserve the trophy that is presented to me.[10]

To deserve B on the basis of P, I must intend to perform P, and the performance of P must be sufficiently within my control. But although *intention* is in this way relevant to desert, *motive* may very often not be. It is a characteristic mistake of philosophers writing on this topic to sup- pose that deserving agents must have moral motives for their perform- ances—that to deserve on the basis of P, one must have performed P out of a sense of duty, or in order to confer benefits on others.[11] Clearly there is a *kind* of desert of which this is true, namely, moral desert; people who display virtuous qualities when they act deserve praise and moral com- mendation, and possibly though not necessarily certain kinds of honor. But generally speaking desert depends on the performance itself and not on the motive that lies behind it. The athlete whose performance in the marathon is such that she deserves to win may be motivated to run by ambition, greed, or simply the wish to prove something to herself. The junior lawyer who deserves a pay raise for hard work and long hours may equally be driven by a desire for income or status. Admittedly, having the wrong motive does sometimes appear to reduce a person's deserts, even when the desert in question is not moral desert. But this may be because it reveals something about the quality of the performance itself. Thus if someone carries out a hazardous rescue, but then discloses that he did it only in the hope of being rewarded by his grateful victim, we may revise downward our estimate of what he deserves because we think that some- one who did it for *that* reason isn't likely to have found the rescue as scaring as we had supposed. In other cases revealing a bad moral charac- ter may generate negative desert, which has to be set against the posi- tive desert of the performance itself. (Many Westerns have central characters who perform good and courageous deeds for what appear to be cynical reasons, leaving the heroine in a dilemma at the end, not knowing what to think of her champion; if desert required a moral motive, there would be no such dilemma.)

What of the performance itself? P must be something that is positively appraised or valued by the surrounding community, but once again this need not amount to a *moral* evaluation. The grounds of the evaluation will differ greatly from case to case. The author who deserves to win the Booker Prize does so because he has written a book that is excellent by literary standards. The employee who deserves the biggest slice of the firm's profits is the one who has done most to raise its productive output. The girl who deserves the highest examination grades is the one who has achieved the best mastery of the various subjects. No doubt in the background there often stands some idea of social utility: we appraise literary excellence, productivity, and academic achievement positively because we think that the exercise of these qualities enriches our lives in one way or another, but it does not seem to me essential to the idea of desert itself that this should be so. Although athletic competitions may create social benefits (as entertaining spectacles, for instance), the performances that form the basis of athletes' deserts, such as running down a track very fast, have no social utility in themselves. And to take a case where the performance is in fact socially harmful, there seems nothing incoherent or bizarre in saying that the man who masterminded the bank robbery deserves a larger share of the loot than the guy who merely drove the getaway car.

The concept of desert does not itself settle the basis on which people come to deserve advantages of various kinds. It imposes certain requirements—principally, as we have seen, that the performance which composes the basis should be in the right way the *agent's* performance, and that this performance should be positively appraised—but the concrete content comes from elsewhere.[12] This raises the question of whether desert is merely a conventional idea: is it merely being used to signal the benefits and advantages that are customarily attached to performances of various kinds? For the moment I simply want to distinguish claims about desert itself from more substantive claims about the kinds of performance that *ought* to constitute bases of desert.

Finally, we must explore the connection between the performance and the benefit that is said to be deserved. It is implicit in the idea of desert that it is good or desirable for A, who has performed P, to have B; the world is in a better state when he has B than when he does not have it. Furthermore, in most cases some or all of us have reason to ensure that A gets B. The exceptions are cases in which there is nothing we can do to produce this outcome or in which attempting to do so would violate some other requirement of justice. Thus we might say of a scientist who has worked hard at a problem for many years, "He really deserves to make a breakthrough," but in this case there is nothing we can do to bring about the result. Or we might say of an athlete, "She deserves to win the gold," but it would be wrong for that reason to try to tip the race in her favor, since we are bound by norms of fairness and impartiality to treat all competitors equally. But these cases are unusual and perhaps marginal. Usually desert gives us a reason to assign B to A, either by direct action or by changing our practices or institutions so that A is likely to end up with B.

This reason is a basic one. The performance has taken place, and A's being put in a position to enjoy B is the fitting or appropriate response on our part to that fact. Many people find this relationship a mysterious one, and therefore seek to translate desert judgments into another form in which they do not have the implication that A's doing P at one moment simply *is* a reason for his being given B at some later moment. For instance, it may be said that giving B to A serves as an incentive for A and others like him to perform P in the future; or it may be said that A's performing P shows the strength of his ambition to achieve B, so that by giving him B we are satisfying a strongly felt desire. But although it is often the case that requiting desert also achieves aims such as these, the suggested translations do not capture what we mean by desert. Desert belongs together with "reactive attitudes" such as gratitude and resentment within what Peter Strawson has called the "participant" perspective on human life, in which we regard others as freely choosing agents like ourselves, and respond to their actions accordingly.[13] If we switch, as we sometimes must, to the "objective" perspective, regarding others as creatures to be trained, managed, and cared for, either in their interest or in ours, we should drop all talk of desert rather than try to invent a surrogate meaning for it.

Thus far I have been trying to elucidate the meaning of what I earlier called "primary" desert judgments, and it will not have escaped the reader's attention that some parts at least of our thinking about desert do not seem to fit into the framework I have proposed. In particular, we sometimes say that people deserve things on the basis of personal qualities rather than performances: we say the ablest candidate deserves the scholarship, that the applicant who has the greatest capacity to perform the job deserves to be offered it, that (in advance of the race) the fastest runner deserves to win it. Here past performance may yield evidence that the person in question does have the qualities that we attribute to her, but the basis for desert seems to be the quality itself rather than the performance. It is sometimes suggested that we should mark this contrast by talking of *merit* rather than desert in these cases: "Merit is often understood in the same sense as desert, but it is useful to distinguish the two, using merit to refer to the personal qualities a man may possess, and desert to refer to the deeds he has done."[14]

Although this distinction is a useful one, I propose that merit judgments of this kind are best understood as secondary desert judgments deriving their moral force from others that are primary. Roughly speaking, when we say that a person deserves some benefit on the basis of a quality, we are anticipating a future performance in which that quality is displayed. When we identify A as the fastest runner and say that he deserves to win, we mean that we expect him to turn in a performance when the race takes place such that he will deserve to win.[15] Of course for unforeseen reasons the race may not take place, and even when it does there are a number of factors that may interfere with A's performance that would not lead us to revise our original judgment, so we are not offering a prediction, but something like a *ceteris paribus* judgment. The same applies to the scholarship case, in which the person who deserves it is the person who, other things being equal, will subsequently perform at the highest level, and, as I shall try to show in the following chapter, to the case of deserving a job.

If a judgment of merit cannot be linked in this way to an anticipated performance, then we do not have desert in its proper meaning. Thus when we say, to take a well-worn case, that Miss Australia deserves to win the Miss World contest because we think she's the best-looking contestant, we are simply assessing her according to the criteria used in this contest; we are saying that she fits the criteria best. The judgment involved is really no different from the judgment we might make about the finest dahlia in the annual flower show. It is what I call a "sham desert" judgment. Sham desert judgments are those in which "A deserves

B" means no more than "It is right or fitting for A to be given B" without the grounds for the judgment being performance-based desert as identified above. These include cases in which the "deserving" A is not a human agent ("Horses deserve to spend their last years in comfort"), cases in which we think A is entitled to some benefit under the rules ("They changed the closing date without telling anyone, so Smith deserves to have his job application considered"), cases in which we think A needs or can make good use of B ("All patients deserve access to the best available medical care"), and cases in which we just think that enjoying B is appropriate to the occasion ("After that piece of good news we all deserve a drink"). In all these cases we could replace "deserves" with "should have" and absolutely nothing would be lost, whereas in the case of genuine desert judgments "deserves" supplies the *ground* for "should have." We appeal to desert to explain why somebody should be given or allowed to enjoy a benefit, and it is implicit here that there might be reasons of other kinds to which we are *not* appealing.

HAVING SAID SOMETHING about the core idea of desert itself, I will now explore whether we should regard it as an *institutional* concept or as pre-institutional, as what Joel Feinberg calls a "natural" concept.[16] Do desert claims derive their force from institutional conventions, or do they have force prior to and independent of institutions? By an institution I mean any regular pattern of human activity in which people are given tasks to perform, encouraged to behave in one way or another, assigned rights and obligations, and so on. This definition is to be interpreted broadly to encompass practices like competitive sports and the public system of honors, as well as those things we might more readily think of as institutions, such as firms, bureaucracies, and schools.[17] It is clear that our ideas of desert are institution-dependent, in two ways at least. First, many of the benefits that people are said to deserve could not exist in the absence of the appropriate institutions. No one can deserve an athletics medal unless there is an institution like the Olympic Games in which medals are presented to successful athletes. No one can deserve a promotion unless there is a hierarchy of office in which people move from one level to the next. No one can deserve a Victoria Cross unless we have a system of military honors, and so on.

Second, in a number of cases the performance that constitutes the basis of the desert qualifies as such only because the relevant institution exists. The same course of action performed in other circumstances would not make the performer deserving. I can mark out a 400-meter track and run around it in 45 seconds, but in the absence of an institution of competitive sport there is nothing (except perhaps a kind of bewildered admiration) that I deserve for doing so. I can master Latin grammar and stand ready to display my mastery on paper, but if there is no Latin examination there is no grade nor scholarship nor anything else tangible that I can possibly deserve. It is the existence of the institution that makes the performance or the capacity a possible basis of desert.

It may then seem that desert cannot serve as a *basic* ground for distribution, or more particularly for just distribution. Rather, our basic principles serve to justify a framework of institutions, and then when the institutions are in place criteria of desert are established and justice is done when people get what they deserve by these criteria. To say "He deserved to get it but in fact he didn't" is to say that the institution is not functioning the way it is supposed to function. This is Rawls' view.[18] We have principles of justice that specify what shape our basic social institutions should take, people come legitimately to expect under these institutions that benefits will be attached to the performance of certain activities, and we express this by saying that those who perform the activities in question deserve the corresponding benefits. Desert here derives its ethical weight from the principles that shape the institutions; it has no pre-institutional force.[19]

The view I am describing need not involve a straightforward confusion of desert and entitlement. We become entitled to something by qualifying for it under an existing set of rules, and this is not the same as deserving it, as has often been pointed out.[20] Our terms and conditions of employment may prescribe that a man doing a certain job is to be paid 25 percent more than a woman doing the same job, but this does not show that male employees *deserve* more than their female counterparts. The institutional view of desert gets around this by saying that what one deserves is what one would be entitled to under *just* institutions, not *existing* institutions: Rawls analyzes desert in terms of *legitimate* expectations, not *de facto* expectations.[21] Thus one can in this way distinguish being entitled to something under existing rules and deserving it according to the fair rules that a just set of institutions would embody, while still treating desert as a secondary and derivative ethical idea.

Should desert be analyzed in this way as an institutional concept? I shall argue that at base desert is pre-institutional, even though particular desert judgments may contain institutionally dependent elements—they couldn't be made in that form unless the institutions in question were already in place. Let me begin by challenging the equation of desert and legitimate entitlement. For simplicity's sake, consider cases in which the institutions we are examining are unequivocally just, so that whatever people are entitled to, they are *justly* entitled to. It is revealing that we would normally use the language of desert only in cases where the entitlements are *performance-based.* For instance, suppose that the president of the company has to be selected from among the Board of Directors, and we decide to do so annually by rotation on an alphabetical basis. If Brown is president this year, then Cairns is entitled to be president next year, but to say that Cairns *deserves* to be president would be very peculiar, to say the least. Having a name beginning with "Ca" is not something that can make one deserving. Or again, if the president is chosen by lot, the fact that Smith's name comes out of the hat does not entail that Smith deserves the position, even though by the rules we are following (assumed to be just) he is plainly entitled to it.

Rawls misses this point because he is considering the case in which what justice requires is that economic rewards be attached in a certain way to jobs and offices (as mandated by the difference principle), and he then imagines individuals training for and working in these positions, and legitimately expecting the rewards that have been attached to them. In this case, clearly, legitimate expectations are generated by performances, and moreover performances of the kind that popular thinking considers to be deserving. Thus desert and entitlement run together here, and it is plausible to argue that "deserves" simply means "legitimately expects." But the plausibility is simply an artifact of the particular theory of justice that Rawls favors. If "deserves" really does mean "is entitled to under fair institutions," then this should hold when other principles of fairness are invoked, and I cannot see any reason to exclude rotation or selection by lot as putatively fair procedures.

Thus far I have argued that if deserts are to be construed as legitimate entitlements, then only a subset of legitimate entitlements are going to count, namely, those that derive from individual performances in the sense that I explained earlier. I now want to argue that desert places substantive constraints on what can count as a just set of institutions. If this is so, then clearly we cannot treat desert as merely an institutional concept.

It is helpful once again to use Rawls' theory of justice as a concrete example in making this argument. Rawls' difference principle states that social and economic inequalities are to be arranged to the greatest benefit of the least advantaged. This implies that the wages and salaries paid for performing jobs should be fixed according to whatever scheme maximizes the economic position of the least advantaged—Rawls assumes that this will be a competitive labor market plus a tax-and-transfer system to help the unemployed and the low-paid. There is nothing here to rule out the possibility that in certain jobs men and women might be paid differential wages: to take a simple example, if the labor market is such that an employer finds that to attract competent biscuit-packers he has to pay male workers one wage and female workers a somewhat lower wage, then this may well be what following the difference principle requires him to do.[22] In contrast, by appealing to desert we can argue that if two people produce equivalent performances, then they deserve the same rewards, even if one is willing to work for less than the other. Here equal pay for equal work emerges as a substantive requirement of the desert principle, so if an institution does not meet that requirement, people cannot deserve the rewards they are legitimately entitled to under it.

This equivalence requirement is not the only substantive implication of the desert principle. Although appeals to the concept of desert cannot necessarily determine which kinds of performance are to be taken as the basis of desert claims, once the performance has been identified, desert requires that superior performance attract superior recognition in whatever form the institutions mandate. Desert does not require that people be paid for productive work, but if people *are* paid for work of this kind, then those whose productivity is higher deserve, *ceteris paribus,* higher pay (something, once again, that Rawls' principles do not necessarily require).

If we use "desert" in anything like its normal sense, it cannot be understood simply as entitlement under institutions that are just by some standard not incorporating desert itself (such as the Rawlsian difference principle). So either we include desert criteria as basic elements in our account of justice, in which case desert cannot be a purely institutional concept, or else it has to be translated into something very much less determinate than the normal idea.

Finally, it is worth looking again at the original claim that both the bases of desert and the kinds of benefit that people deserve are institution-dependent. This claim looks most plausible in instances where rewards or prizes are awarded for very specific activities. If we take some athletic event such as caber-tossing that is practiced in only a few places, it would be implausible to argue that potential caber-tossers in other places deserved to have competitions established and prizes awarded. Here the institution comes first, and this generates a rather narrow basis for desert. But this is a peculiar case, or at least one that stands at one end of a long spectrum. The reason is that this particular manifestation of bodily strength is not something that we would expect every society to value. At the other end of the spectrum we find acts of courage or self-sacrifice that it is hard to believe could *not* be socially valued. If there are performances that are socially valued, then those who undertake them do have deserts, albeit rather vague ones, prior to the establishment of institutions. They deserve recognition or reward *in some form* even though the form may legitimately vary a good deal from place to place. If a society simply refuses to show its appreciation of voluntary activities that are valuable by its own standards, then its institutions are less than just. If within a kibbutz, for example, some take on positions of greater responsibility than others, they deserve to have their contribution recognized; because of the general ethos of the kibbutz, this cannot take the form of additional income, but might, for instance, come in the form of greater influence when collective decisions are made. If their deserts are not recognized at all, they can legitimately feel that they are being treated unjustly.[23]

My claim, then, is that desert is predominantly a pre-institutional notion. When we invoke it, we are very often assessing the way our institutions work in the light of prior ideas about what constitutes a fitting response to individual performances. Desert is a *critical* notion: when we say "He deserves this" or "She doesn't deserve that," we may well be challenging the way our institutions allocate benefits, either on a particular occasion or in general.

This criticism may take various forms. One kind of criticism is that the institutional allocation is tracking not performance at all, but some irrelevant characteristic like sex or geographical location: "Men and women deserve equal pay for equal work"; "A bright child from the inner city deserves as good an education as his counterpart in the suburbs." A second variety of criticism challenges the kind of performance that currently serves as the institution's desert basis: "Academics deserve to be promoted on the basis of their teaching as much as on the basis of their research"; "Tennis players whose only claim to fame is a thunderous serve don't deserve to win Wimbledon." Here there is no doubt that the benefits in question are currently being distributed on the basis of performance, but the complaint is that the wrong kind of performance is being rewarded, or that an equally deserving performance is being overlooked. Finally, the criticism may have to do with a disproportion between the value of the performance and the benefits it currently attracts: "Top athletes deserve to win medals, but they don't deserve the huge financial bonuses they now receive"; "Anyone can see that nurses who work long hours with demanding patients deserve higher pay than they're now getting." Here tacit comparisons are being made with people who are deserving in other ways. The underlying assumption is that there should be some consistency in the way a society responds to deserts of different kinds.

This, then, is the sense in which desert is pre-institutional or "natural." Concrete desert judgments most frequently refer to institutional facts—to prizes or honors, for instance—which presuppose that the corresponding institutions are already in place. But the force of the judgments is to assess those institutions critically by appeal to pre-institutional standards of equivalence and of what should count as a valuable performance. No doubt our desert judgments are in some respects causally shaped by the institutions we already have.[24] But the logic of a desert claim isn't "This is what A has coming to him as the institution now operates," but "This is what A would have coming to him if the institution operated so as to give proper recognition to his performance."

I NOW TURN BRIEFLY to the relationship between desert and *luck*. To what extent can we say that people are deserving when we know that their performances have been affected by different kinds of luck? By luck here I mean random events outside the agent's control. Luck affects performance in two ways. On the one hand, the performance itself—what the agent actually achieves—may depend to a greater or lesser extent on his luck. I gave the example earlier of a poor archer who shoots three lucky arrows and wins the competition. I shall label luck of this kind "integral luck." On the other hand, luck may determine whether someone has the opportunity to perform in the first place. The car carrying the athlete to the track meet may break down so that she has no chance to run. One soldier may be given an opportunity to show courage in battle, while another never gets within range of the enemy. Luck of this kind can be called "circumstantial luck."

Integral luck does appear to nullify desert. In other words, when we assess someone's performance in order to judge what he or she deserves, we try to factor out the effects of both good and bad luck. The athlete whose performance is affected by bad luck, such as being tripped by another competitor, may still deserve to win the race. Conversely, the entrepreneur who decides to manufacture a product that unexpectedly turns out to be a runaway success doesn't deserve all his gains—though here it will be much harder to separate genuine luck from an inspired hunch.[25]

It is a somewhat different story with circumstantial luck. It may be luck that a young scientist gets a job in a particular laboratory, but if he then does a pathbreaking piece of research, he may well deserve a Nobel Prize. The performance is entirely his, but it was to some extent a matter of luck that he was in a position to execute it. Equally it may be a matter of luck that I am walking by at the moment when a child falls into the river, but if I plunge in and rescue her then I deserve gratitude and reward in proportion to the difficulty and danger of my action. How can this be? Consider the position of a second person who claims to be equally deserving on the grounds that she, too, would have done the research or carried out the rescue if she had only been given the chance. Why would we reject her claims as unjustified?

Two reasons seem to count here. The first is epistemic: we can never really know what she might have done if luck had been on her side. Even if we know on other grounds that she is a good scientist, we can't tell whether she would have had the particular insight needed to crack the problem that the Nobel winner has cracked. Even if she can demonstrate that she has rescued other children in similar circumstances, we can't be sure that when the moment actually came she would have braced herself and jumped into the swirling river.

Even in cases where we can be relatively certain that Jones would have done what Smith actually did if his circumstantial luck had been better, however, we are still reluctant to say that Jones deserves what Smith does, because our notion of desert tracks actual performance rather than hypothetical performance.[26] As noted, when integral luck plays a part, we adjust our estimate of the performance to eliminate its effects, so that the person who finishes third in the race may deserve to have won it if his coming third is due to bad luck. But the athlete who never makes it to the race track, and so does not put in a performance at all, cannot deserve to win. We feel sympathy for her, of course, and we may think that she is the victim of unfairness if her failure to appear stems from causes that the race authorities ought to have eliminated, but the unfairness does not consist in her failing to receive the medal she deserves.

Do differences in circumstantial luck have *any* effect on how much one person deserves compared with others? Whether they do depends on at least two factors. First, the benefit that is deserved may to a greater or lesser extent be competitive as between possible claimants. There can only be one Nobel Prize for chemistry in any given year, whereas there is no limit to the amount of gratitude that can be shown toward acts of kindness or courage. In the first case people who are lucky deservedly gain at the expense of the unlucky, and this may lead us to qualify our judgments somewhat. To the extent that we are convinced that several other scientists might easily have made the discovery that led to the award of the Nobel Prize had they been in a position to do so, we will see the actual winner as less deserving. He's still pretty deserving, of course—not many could have solved that problem—but he's not much more deserving than several others who in the nature of the case are excluded from receiving Nobel prizes. In contrast, the rescuer who gets a case of champagne from the grateful parents of the salvaged child isn't standing in the way of some other rescuer's being rewarded on some other occasion.

Second, to the extent that the impact of luck is itself under human control, a decision to allow greater scope to luck will reduce desert. Suppose, for example, that we decided to allocate jobs by lottery. Those who ended up in these jobs would still be more or less deserving than others—one would work hard and skillfully, another would shirk, and so forth—but the random allocation would cast a shadow over these judgments. Many could legitimately claim that it was only their bad luck in the draw that prevented them from exercising their talents for science or music productively. How can Smith deserve more than me for the work he is doing when I would have done as well or better if given the chance? Desert is strengthened when opportunities to become deserving themselves depend on the initiative and choice of individuals, and are not artificially distributed by some other human agency.

Integral luck nullifies desert, I have argued—we have to factor it out when judging what people deserve on the basis of their performances—and circumstantial luck may lead us to qualify our judgments about the deserts of those who are its beneficiaries. But if we want to keep the notion of desert and use it to make practical judgments, we cannot compensate completely for luck of the second kind. It is luck that I was born in the time and place that I was, with the range of opportunities that my society provides. I become deserving by taking these opportunities and producing intentional performances of an appropriately valuable kind. Judgments about my deserts are not affected by the fact that other people in different physical and social circumstances may have very different sets of opportunities. Circumstantial luck always lies in the background of human performances, and only when it intrudes in a fairly clear and direct way on what different people achieve relative to one another do we allow it to modify our judgments of desert.

THE PERFORMANCES ON WHICH EVERYDAY judgments of desert are based may depend not only on people's circumstantial luck, but also on their natural talents—the capacities and abilities with which they are genetically endowed. These, too, can be regarded as a form of luck. No one has any control over his natural endowments, though he can, of course, decide which of these endowments to develop and exercise. Ought we therefore to discount natural talents when estimating desert, factoring out of people's performances whatever depends on natural talent? Many philosophers have thought so.[27]

If followed through consistently, this suggestion, I shall argue, would sabotage the whole notion of desert rather than, as its proponents believe, refine its moral quality. First, according to the concept of desert being defended here, people can deserve benefits only on the basis of intentional performances, so though the performance may depend on natural talent—as in the case of the athletic examples I have been using—it also requires choice and effort. The desert is based on the *performance,* not the talent that may be its necessary condition. Where there is not even an anticipated performance, as there is in the case of secondary desert judgments, there can be no desert. It follows that people cannot deserve anything merely for *having,* as opposed to exercising, talents. Whenever people are judged meritorious on the basis of native endowments alone—as in the beauty contest case—we have only sham desert judgments.

Second, even those who want to say that having a talent is merely luck would, I think, concede that luck of this sort has a less negative impact on desert than other kinds either of integral or of circumstantial luck.[28] Consider two mountaineers setting out to scale Everest; one succeeds, the other fails. What does each deserve? The second had bad luck in the form of adverse weather and a rope that unexpectedly broke; she was also physically weaker than the first. It would be very odd to treat these as equivalent kinds of luck. We would want to factor out the weather and the broken rope as far as we were able, because these were external to the second climber's performance, the skill and determination she showed. Perhaps on this basis she deserved to reach the top, to have her achievement commemorated in some way. But her physical strength was integral to her performance; indeed, it was partly what made it *her* performance as opposed to anyone else's. Thus to discount it, and to say that what she deserved was what she would have achieved had she been stronger, would be decidedly strange.

Conceding these points, the critic of talent-dependent desert may still argue that one person can only deserve more than another, in the morally relevant sense of desert, on the basis of those aspects of his performance that are under his voluntary control. Let us begin to think through the implications of this principle. Consider a performance that depends on natural talent, such as climbing Everest or playing a Beethoven concerto at concert level. In cases like this the performer must (a) have chosen and worked to turn a natural ability like manual dexterity into a developed talent like musical skill; and (b) have decided to deploy the talent so as to produce the performance—to spend his evening playing a concerto rather than watching television. These choices and exertions are presumably what the critic would want to count as *genuine* desert bases. But now observe that these voluntary acts take place against the background of unchosen factors: on the one hand the performer's native talents, on the other his tastes and preferences (insofar as these are not themselves subject to choice). The person who decides that she wants to become a mountaineer does so on the basis of what she knows about her physical capacities, and also on the basis of her liking for being out in the open air. Of course tastes and preferences can to some extent be cultivated, but they are usually cultivated on the basis of other existing tastes and capacities.[29]

My point is that a greater or lesser element of contingency enters into even those elements of performance that the purist about desert would want to allow in as possible bases. If we say that the concert pianist deserves applause, not for his performance as such, since this depends in part on his natural talents, but for what is left over when the effect of natural talent is removed—the choice and effort involved in raising himself to this level—then we immediately have to recognize that his making those choices and efforts itself depends on contingencies that are not under his control. He did not choose to be born dexterous and with a good musical ear. Other people have not been confronted with the same range of options as this person.

If, in the light of this argument, our critic decides to retreat still further in his search for a desert basis that is not affected by contingencies outside the agent's control, he is likely to end up saying, with Kant, that the only possible basis is good will—deciding for moral reasons to try to act in this way rather than that. If Kant is right, moral reasons are completely independent of preferences, and since all that matters is the will to act and not the outcome, the agent's natural talents as well as his external circumstances become irrelevant to his desert.[30] I happen to think that Kant is wrong, but the main point to note here is that desert shrinks to within a tiny fraction of its normal range.[31] We can no longer talk about athletes deserving medals, workers deserving wages, soldiers deserving military honors, parents deserving their children's gratitude, and so on. All we are left to talk about is people deserving moral praise or blame for deciding to act rightly or wrongly.

We therefore stand at a parting of the ways. Do we want to continue using a concept of desert that is able to guide us in making our distributive decisions, as individuals or as a political community, or should we remove it from the armory of social justice and use it only to make individual moral appraisals?[32] We may, of course, decide that the concept is so fraught with difficulties that we should dispense with it altogether, as Rawls and utilitarians like Sidgwick effectively recommend.[33] But if we decide that we want to keep the concept in a form that captures most of the desert judgments people actually make, then we cannot hope to find a basis for desert that is untouched by contingency. What we need instead is the idea of an agent and a performance, where the performance is intended and controlled by the agent, but makes use of qualities and characteristics that are integral to him or her—natural tastes and abilities among them.[34] We want to factor out luck proper—features of the environment like the fraying rope that makes the agent's performance turn out differently from what she might reasonably have expected—but if we try to eliminate contingency of every kind we find that our judgments are directed at a radically thinned-down idea of the human agent. Instead of assessing the deserts of flesh-and-blood actors who make a visible impact on the world, we find ourselves at best judging the qualities of Kantian noumenal wills.

LET US TAKE STOCK of the argument thus far. My aim has been to defend what I called the Positive View of desert by showing that it was possible to identify a single coherent notion of desert not reducible to some other ethical idea (such as legitimate entitlement). I said at the outset, however, that there would have to be some concessions to the Pluralist View, and I should state explicitly what these amount to. The core idea of desert is that of an agent's voluntarily undertaking a valuable activity, and as a result deserving benefits whose enjoyment forms a fitting sequel to what he has done. All primary desert judgments take this ethical form, and I have sought to explain how secondary judgments, in which a quality rather than a performance forms the basis of desert, can be linked to these. The pluralism emerges in two places. First, we have seen that the range of possible desert bases and the different kinds of benefits that people can deserve depend to some extent on existing institutions and may be expected to vary from place to place. There are no resources internal to the idea of desert itself that can be used to explain this. Thus if we ask why athletes in this place deserve these awards and why musicians in that place deserve those forms of recognition, no explanation in terms of desert can be given. The concrete content of desert judgments is inevitably heterogeneous and variable.

Second, if we press to get at what it means for a benefit to be a *fitting* response to a performance, once again we encounter pluralism. Some have thought that all deserved benefits are deserved as rewards: this appears to lie behind Sidgwick's suggestion that justice as the requital of desert should be understood as "Gratitude universalised."[35] But this cannot apply to cases such as athletes deserving medals or scientists' deserving Nobel prizes, where the performance in question need not involve the agent in conferring a benefit on anyone else (if Nobel prizes were rewards, they would be given for the most *useful* discoveries, not for the most original or groundbreaking pieces of research). In these cases the attitude captured by the desert claim seems closer to admiration or appreciation than to gratitude. All I want to claim here is that there is a range of attitudes of this kind that, when one of them is elicited by someone's performance, makes it morally fitting for him to enjoy certain benefits.[36] It is not possible to dig deeper here in an attempt to find some *further* value that is served when people receive the benefits they deserve. The value simply resides in the fit between the performance and the allocation of benefits.[37]

Finally, if we say that a just society must *inter alia* be one in which each person gets what he or she deserves, how strong a constraint does this place on our institutions? Let me begin by introducing two limitations on the desert principle that arise directly from my discussion in previous chapters. First, we saw in Chapter 2 that it is only to the extent that people are associated instrumentally that desert emerges as the relevant criterion of just distribution among them. In other modes of relationship need or equality may be the appropriate criterion. So in some cases social justice requires us to set desert aside in favor of one of these other criteria of distribution. Sometimes this will be relatively unproblematic because the benefit we are considering is such that no one has any claims of desert upon it. But on other occasions we have to choose between assigning a good such as housing on the basis of desert or assigning it on the basis of need, say, and here the fair policy may be to take need as the basis of distribution.

Second, as we saw in Chapter 5, if we focus not on institutional design but on the allocative decisions of particular individuals, the relevant criteria to apply will very often be criteria of procedural justice. Civil servants, employers, school administrators, and so forth should apply existing rules fairly without attempting to make direct estimates of desert. The effect will sometimes be that deserving people have their claims turned down because to recognize them would be to violate procedural norms of equality, and so forth.

Even at the individual level this limitation does not always hold. For sometimes what officials and others are called on to do is precisely to allocate some benefit according to desert. Thus civil servants drawing up honors lists, selectors awarding a scholarship, or judges conferring a literary or scientific prize are required to make substantive desert judgments about possible beneficiaries. They are given guidance about the kind of desert they are to look for ("acts of public service," for example), but there is no formal set of rules that can be applied to give the right answer. Often what is involved in these cases is the weighing of different elements in someone's overall performance, and in the background stand possibly controversial judgments about what constitutes service to the public or literary merit.

As I argued in the last chapter, however, desert is more often invoked at a different point: when existing institutions and practices and the rules they embody are being assessed from a wider perspective. Here we are asking not what particular individuals should receive, but whether whole categories of people are getting what they deserve under the present institutional set-up. The question I want to ask is how much guidance the principle of desert itself can give us at this critical juncture.

Let me answer it by dividing claims about desert into four categories according to how determinate the claim is in each case—the most determinate kind of claim being one that specifies precisely the benefit B that is due to A by virtue of P. I shall then ask what degree of confidence we can have in claims in each of these categories. The least determinate kind of claim asserts that it is unjust if benefits are allocated by criteria that are irrelevant from the point of view of desert; for instance, if hiring decisions are affected by the race, sex, or religious affiliation of job applicants. Here the claim is simply that this is an allocation that should be made on grounds of desert; thus if the allocation is in fact being made on other grounds, an injustice is being committed. To make this claim we do not have to assume very much about the grounds of desert itself (for example, in virtue of which capacities or performances people deserve to be hired for jobs). All we need to know is that race, sex, or religious affiliation *cannot* be such grounds.

Somewhat more substantial are claims that when two people are equally deserving, it is unjust if one receives more benefit than the other. Claims of this kind are often made in support of uniform treatment—for example, if workers in one part of the company are being paid more than workers in another part for doing jobs that are essentially similar in nature. On a wider scale "comparable worth" legislation is guided by the same ideal.[38] These claims require identification of the relevant desert basis, and judgments to the effect that two individuals or two groups have performed equally by that standard, but nothing stronger than this.

Next in order of determinacy are comparative claims to the effect that there is a disproportion between what group A is receiving by virtue of P and what group A' is receiving by virtue of P'. Examples here would be the claim that nurses are grossly underpaid in comparison with doctors, or the claim that it is unfair if civil servants who are simply doing their jobs receive the same honors as private citizens who have performed supererogatory acts of public service. These claims require us first to make comparative judgments about the deserts of different groups of individuals, and then to make judgments about what, comparatively, would be suitable requital. Depending on whether these judgments are ordinal or cardinal, we have more or less determinate cases falling within the third category. At one end of the spectrum we have judgments like "Managers exercise more responsibility than manual workers so they should be paid more highly"; at the other end a quite specific claim like "A doctor's work is three times as valuable as a nurse's, therefore doctors deserve salaries that are three times as great."

Finally, we reach noncomparative judgments of desert: judgments to the effect that people who have performed P deserve some identifiable benefit B without reference to what others have done or are getting: "Everyone who does a full day's work deserves an income that allows him to live in comfort"; "Anyone who performs a courageous act like that deserves a medal."[39] If precise judgments of this kind could be made across the board, we could arrive at a complete specification of what social justice requires from the point of view of desert. Given n individuals and n performances (or more strictly *sets* of performances, since as we have seen, people become deserving by virtue of a variety of different activities), we could specify a distribution of benefits that would give each of the n precisely what they deserved taken one at a time.

Can claims in these four categories be justified? To deny claims in the first category is tantamount to abandoning the concept of desert itself, for it is to say that we have no way of distinguishing features that might form a desert basis from those that cannot. So long as we are willing to use the concept at all, therefore, some claims in this category must be justified. And indeed appeals to desert in debates about social justice very often take this form: desert is invoked to protest against people's receiving benefits that are in no way related to their own performances, but depend upon some irrelevant feature like social background or sex.

Some claims in the second category are surely justifiable in the same way. If two people have done essentially the same thing, but are distinguished only by background circumstances that are irrelevant to desert—they work in different towns, or their jobs carry different titles—

then desert uncontroversially demands that they receive equal treatment. Matters become more complicated when what they have done is physically different but is judged to be of equal value by some standard. Here our confidence in the judgment will depend on whether we can agree on a standard of value, and on whether there is some reliable way of combining different features of a performance—of a job, say—to give an overall rating. This leads us directly to the difficulties we face with desert claims in category three.

Here we are not merely judging that two or more performances count equally from the point of view of desert, but making comparative judgments about how much desert different groups of people have acquired. In general we have far more confidence in ordinal rankings than in cardinal ones; we can confidently state that one person or group is more deserving than another but would often be hard pressed to put a figure on the difference in value between their performances. In a number of cases ordinal rankings are all we need. If we have to allocate prizes, we have to judge who has written the best book, perhaps also who should get second prize, but we aren't required to say that the winner has performed 10 percent better than the runner-up; the same is true if we have to allocate a limited number of college places among a pool of applicants. In other cases what we are doing is essentially grading performances, placing them in a number of bands. When implementing a system of military honors, for instance, we have to be able to say that this action displayed the highest form of courage and deserves the Medal of Honor; that action was courageous but less so and deserves the Silver Star. Where cardinal judgments do have to be made, we are most confident when performances can be judged along a single dimension: we are reasonably happy about attaching numbers to performances in academic tests ("Smith deserves a 65 for that essay, but Jones doesn't deserve more than 58 for his"), but far less happy about estimating the worth of different and unrelated jobs, say, where several possible standards of value may conflict (How much is the work of a college professor worth? It may contribute to knowledge, but how much does it contribute to the GDP?)[40]

Our concept of desert thus constrains the set of just social distributions without fully determining how different groups should be treated in comparison with one another. If one society pays its doctors five times as much as its manual workers, while another society pays them only three times as much, we cannot say simply by appealing to desert that one of them is more just than the other.[41] The judgments that we can justifiably make are not sufficiently determinate (they are, however, determinate enough for us to say that a society that pays its doctors *less* than its manual workers is virtually certain to be unjust).[42]

We must be even more cautious about claims in the fourth category. I am doubtful that we can make judgments about deserved benefits that are both specific and genuinely noncomparative. That is, I am not convinced that we can justifiably claim that A deserves some precise B by virtue of P except against a background of other people's receiving rewards for performances like or unlike P. The best examples of noncomparative judgments of justice can be found in debates about punishment.[43] When we say that no one deserves to be hanged for stealing a sheep, we are saying not merely that this penalty is disproportionate to others, but that there is an absolute lack of fit between the wrong committed and the proposed penalty. Whenever deserved benefits are at issue, we can make nonspecific judgments ("That act of courage deserves to be honored"; "He deserves some reward for going to all that trouble on your behalf"), but we cannot in the same way say what is deserved without tacitly invoking comparisons with the way others have been or are being treated.

There are two reasons this may be so, applying in different cases. One is that many benefits have a conventional character: a Medal of Honor now means what it does by virtue of the kind of actions for which it has been awarded in the past, so we cannot judge whether A deserves a Medal of Honor except by comparing his action with the actions of his predecessors. In the same way examination grades are obviously conventional in nature: there is no notion of natural fitness that tells us that a paper of this sort should be given an A. The second reason is that desert claims are often claims on a finite pool of resources; thus we cannot decide what share of the pool A deserves without first knowing how A's performance compares with that of the other members of the relevant group. Income distribution provides an obvious example. What A deserves is typically a *share* of her company's income, or in a wider compass a share of national income; the actual sum will depend upon how much is available for distribution and what others can claim by virtue of *their* deserts.[44]

If we can indeed make genuinely noncomparative judgments of good desert, these are more likely to occur in the sphere of personal relations than in the sphere of social justice. Good deeds may deserve gratitude, where the amount of gratitude it is appropriate to feel and express is not dependent on what has been shown to others on similar occasions. Feinberg has drawn attention to the justice of judgments, where the unfairness of the judgment that A's book is second-rate and derivative does not depend on the judgments passed on the works of others.[45] But if we are thinking about desert of property, positions, prizes, honors, income, and so forth, then our judgments are at best judgments about what A deserves in comparison with others.

To sum up, I have argued that we have a coherent concept of desert that is sufficiently independent of our existing institutions for it to serve as a critical weapon in the armory of social justice. A just society is, in considerable part, a society whose institutions are arranged so that people get the benefits they deserve, and many legitimate complaints about existing societies appeal to this principle. But considerations of desert do not fully determine these institutional arrangements. They do not, for instance, tell us whether we should award prizes for athletic prowess or literary merit at all; nor do they tell us precisely how wide the dispersion of incomes should be. I have tried to steer a course between the view that desert is merely a formal principle that comes into play once we have decided which institutions to establish and the view that it tells us how everything in a society should be distributed. Because it is not wholly determinate, desert leaves room for other principles of justice to operate, as well as contrasting values such as efficiency and social equality.[46] A society can give people what they deserve but also set resources aside to cater to needs, and be guided in economic matters in part by considerations of efficiency. This is a welcome result.

8

Deserving Jobs

"The greatest comfort, Camden, is that you have deserved it."
"When a man gets a good berth, mother, half the deserving must come after."[1]

According to a widely held view, when there are a number of applicants for an available job, justice demands that the job be offered to the best-qualified applicant. We express this by saying that the best-qualified applicant deserves the job or, in a slightly different formulation, that the principle involved is one of hiring by merit. This is the principle that condemns discrimination on grounds of sex, race, or religion when hiring employees, as well, of course, as good old-fashioned nepotism. Equally, the principle is often thought to pose problems for positive discrimination or affirmative action programs: a common view is that such programs may have good social effects overall, but they do so at the expense of injustice toward the best-qualified candidates, who are passed over in favor of less-qualified candidates from the groups targeted by the program.

In saying that the principle I am considering is widely held, I do not mean that there is consensus over either its weight or its scope.[2] It conflicts most obviously with the freedoms of contract and association: people's right to employ and work with whomever they choose. For libertarians these rights trump the principle that jobs must be given to the best-qualified candidates. Even libertarians, however, may concede that the principle is appropriate to public-sector employment (to the extent that there is any). Nonlibertarians will argue that the weight of the

156

principle derives from the strong association between the job that someone holds and his or her life chances generally, so that fairness in assigning jobs is a prerequisite for fairness in overall social distribution: this
justifies constraining employers' freedom of action, at least in the case of
discrimination on grounds of sex, race, and religion. But these disputes
about weight and scope will not be my concern here. Rather, I will
examine the basic conceptual issue involved in the claim that the best-
qualified applicant deserves to be given the job. What sort of desert claim
could this be? What kind of injustice, if any, is committed if the job is
offered to someone else? The answers to these questions are less straightforward than one might think. My aim, however, is to find a defensible
interpretation of the claim, and in that respect to vindicate common
opinion—although I shall also argue that the policy implications of the
desert claim are not quite what common opinion takes them to be.

I shall limit my investigation to the case in which an institution (I use
this term to cover private firms, public organizations, educational estab-
lishments, and so on) decides to appoint someone to a particular position, well-specified in terms of the work it involves, and with a predetermined salary that reflects the character of the work. This case stands at
one end of a spectrum, although it is not at all uncommon. At the other
extreme we have, say, the case in which a firm decides that it needs an
extra staff member in the marketing department, issues a very broad
advertisement, looks at the field of applicants, and, on the basis of what
it sees, juggles with the structure of the department to fit in one of the
favored candidates. Under these circumstances, it is unclear whether one
can say that any candidate in particular deserved the job. There are still
issues of procedural justice: it would obviously be unfair if all black
candidates were discarded regardless of their qualifications. But if A has a
strong claim to a secretarial position while B looks well qualified as a
sales rep, I cannot see any possibility of making meaningful comparative
desert judgments about these two candidates. To avoid such complications, I restrict myself to the simple case.

I shall also take for granted in the discussion that follows the general
understanding of desert claims set out in the last chapter. I shall assume
that people come to deserve benefits of various kinds by voluntary performances, in the course of which they make use of their native talents.
There is nothing more to say here to the critic who holds that because
people are not responsible for their native endowments, they cannot

deserve benefits for performances that depend upon those endowments. The present task is to take this general understanding of desert and to see whether and how it can be extended to the case of deserving jobs. It is possible, however, that the argument I shall make might with suitable adaptation be made to serve someone who held that people could deserve things, in the primary sense, only on the basis of characteristics and activities that were subject to their voluntary control (so that efforts and choices, for instance, could count as bases of desert, but native abilities could not). Someone who held this view would need to rewrite what I say below about economic desert to factor out the effects of native talent, but might otherwise come to agree with my analysis of what we mean when we say that the best-qualified candidate deserves the job.

THERE ARE THREE POPULAR and apparently plausible interpretations of the principle of deserving jobs, but each of them faces serious difficulties. The first of the three was offered classically by Sidgwick, and it amounts to reinterpreting the principle of hiring by merit so that it no longer qualifies as a genuine principle of desert but is regarded instead as a principle of *fitness*.[3] We begin by defining the person who merits the job as the person who as far as we can judge will fulfill the requirements of the job most successfully. It follows that he or she will contribute most to the productivity of the institution (whether measured in economic terms or in some other way) and thereby—in normal cases—to the welfare of society. Thus the principle is justified as a derivative of the principle of utility. Hiring by merit is the rule that employers should follow if they want the institutions they represent to contribute maximally to overall happiness. Such a justification looks not to the past but to the future. It treats past performance simply as evidence about candidates' likely future performance. So on this reading if we continue to say that the best-qualified candidate "deserves the job," we cannot be using "desert" in its standard sense to indicate treatment that is due to a person by virtue of his or her performances, past or present. Rather, desert has to be taken more loosely, as specifying treatment that is appropriate by some criterion, in this case by virtue of the hiring rule, adherence to which will best promote social welfare.

The problem with this reading is that it fails to capture our sense that an injustice has occurred if the best-qualified candidate is not given the job—in particular, that he or she can legitimately complain of unfair treatment.[4] The fitness construal shows that it is irrational for the employer, and unfortunate for society, not to offer the job to the best-qualified applicant, but it fails to bring out the injustice done to the person who is passed over.[5] In response, an advocate of the fitness reading might argue that, by advertising a job, an institution creates a legitimate expectation among potential candidates that the best qualified among them will be chosen—it being a well-entrenched feature of contemporary practice that this is how appointments are made.[6] Thus the best-qualified candidate deserves the job, not in the "raw," preconventional sense, but in the looser sense in which anyone who is entitled to a benefit under a standing rule can be said to deserve that benefit.[7]

But this is still too weak, because an employer might make it quite clear through public announcement that he felt under no constraint to hire by merit—indeed, he might announce that he would favor candidates from a particular religious or educational background—and in these circumstances the best-qualified candidate could have no legitimate expectation of being chosen. Yet we would want to say that such a policy was unjust and that when the employer made his arbitrary or prejudiced appointments, he was treating the various applicants unfairly. This shows that there is a principle of justice at stake that cannot be captured in terms of entitlement under established rules, nor more generally as a derivative of global principles such as social utility.

IT SEEMS THAT we must take the desert principle more literally if we want to capture the unfairness involved in discriminatory employment practices. An obvious move is to treat jobs as rewards for past performance. Over some period of time, applicants have worked hard, developed skills, and so on, whether in education or in previous employment. In allocating a job, we compare the deserts that have been accumulated in this way and award it to whomever seems on the evidence available to be the most deserving applicant.[8] The reward for past efforts comes in the form of the income, status, and satisfaction, among other things, that the new job provides.

Unfortunately, this way of construing the desert principle runs into insuperable difficulties as soon as we examine it at all closely. The only case in which it looks remotely plausible is one in which the job in question represents a promotion for applicants who have all been and will otherwise be in secure employment. There might then be a *prima facie* case for saying that the differential between the benefits offered by the new job and the benefits that the applicants are receiving in their current jobs represents a fair reward for the superior past performance of the top candidate. But suppose we took a case at the other extreme, one in which all the candidates have hitherto been unemployed, and in which the unsuccessful candidates will predictably remain unemployed. How is it plausible here to present the large income differential that will shortly open up as requital for past performance?

To this it might be replied that the most deserving candidate must have done something to become most deserving. But even if we accept this for the time being, it is easy to see where the reward interpretation falls down. Jobs are properly rewarded in the course of performing them. The job-holder contributes some amount to the performance of her enterprise or the output of her organization and deserves benefits—primarily income—in proportion to that contribution. (As noted, this formulation will need to be adjusted by anyone who wishes to exclude elements of performance that depend on native ability.) When selecting the best-qualified candidate to hold a job, the employer is not in the business of rectifying a shortfall in the rewards that person received in previous employment. First, there may have been no shortfall: income in the previous job may precisely have matched contribution. Second, even if the best-qualified candidate has performed his previous job at a level above that reflected in his income up to now, he may be less deserving in that respect than some other candidate who is quite incapable of filling the job advertised, but whose past employment history reveals consistent exploitation. Third, a new job is in any case a particularly crude instrument for rewarding past achievement, since it represents an income stream of indeterminate size, depending on what the successful candidate chooses to make of it, how long she stays in it, and so on.

For all these reasons, the reward interpretation of the desert principle we are considering seems wholly unpromising. This is not to say that jobs are never given as rewards. Clearly they are, as in "Buggins' turn," whereby promotion is routinely handed out to the longest-serving member of the department. But rather than instantiating the principle that jobs should go to the best qualified, it is instead a corruption of that principle. Jobs are not deserved *qua* rewards. Past performance is not the *basis* of desert, but rather a source of evidence about who is now deserving. Moreover, it is not the only possible source of evidence. We might in appropriate cases want to gather information more directly, for instance, by asking the candidates to take various tests. It seems that the desert basis here must be the relative ability of the candidates to perform the job, as revealed by the best means at our disposal for detecting ability. But the nature of the desert still remains obscure. In what sense does the candidate with the greatest relevant ability *deserve* the job being offered?

IF JOBS ARE NOT DESERVED AS REWARDS, might they instead be deserved as *prizes?* The person who deserves a prize is the person who exhibits to the highest degree the quality or ability that the prize was established to recognize. In some cases (for example, literary prizes) the ability will have been manifested in extended past performance; in other cases (for example, sporting competitions) the basis of desert is ability displayed at the particular moment the competition is held. The person who deserves the gold medal in the 100m is the competitor who on the day of the race is the fastest runner; past performance enters in evidentially but not criterially. The sporting example seems to correspond best to the case of jobs, where the most deserving candidate is the one who, at the time the decision is made, exhibits the greatest relevant ability. Past performance matters only as an indicator. We shouldn't appoint has-beens on the grounds that they once displayed the greatest ability, if we *know* they are has-beens. Thus the suggestion here is that in awarding jobs we are recognizing capacity in roughly the same way as when awarding certain prizes. The complaint of the best-qualified candidate who is passed over is that his ability has been slighted. Both materially and symbolically, he has falsely been declared less capable than one of his rivals.

There are, though, some significant differences between jobs and prizes. One is that, in the case of prizes, the ability comes first and the system of recognition is set up afterwards. That is, we decide (for whatever reason) to celebrate some ability—literary skill or fleetness of foot—and then establish an institution to confer prizes with appropriate rules for seeking out the ability. With jobs, by contrast, the "prize" comes first—a firm finds that it needs another fitter or accountant—and this determines the relevant ability on which desert is based. One consequence is that the best-qualified candidate is not necessarily the most talented person in the field; rather, he or she is the one who has most of the (perhaps quite peculiar) ability that the job requires. Another is that some candidates may be over-qualified; by this I mean that although the candidates in question have an ample supply of the particular skills that the job requires, they also have other skills that will not be exercised, as a result of which they will predictably become bored and finally do the job less well. Thus a job competition is not (or rather should not be) a talent contest; the aim is not to uncover talent *per se,* but to find the individual who on the basis of available evidence can be predicted to perform best in the particular role that the institution requires.

This points to a deeper and more significant contrast between jobs and prizes as deserved benefits. When we say that someone deserves a prize, we standardly base our judgment on some past or present performance in which the capacity in question has been revealed, and these judgments are not invalidated by future performance. Thus we might say of an author that he deserves to win a literary prize on the basis of the novels he has written, or of an athlete that he deservedly won the gold medal for the race he ran. These judgments would not be undermined by future performance.[9] The athlete might lose form and run badly in his next six races; the author might take to the bottle and never produce another decent book. But they would still deserve the prizes in question for what they had already achieved. As noted in the last chapter, there are also cases in which we judge that people deserve prizes on the basis of a capacity that will be revealed in a performance that has yet to occur, as when we say before the race takes place that Lewis deserves to win it. Such judgments do, I believe, play a more peripheral role in our thinking about desert of prizes; perhaps what we are doing when we make them is imagining ourselves having witnessed the race in which Lewis has displayed his capacity. In any event, let us say that prizes may be deserved on the basis of either an observed or an anticipated performance.

In the case of jobs, by contrast, the desert claim appears to rest upon a performance that necessarily has yet to occur. The best-qualified candidate, the one who deserves the job, is the one who *will* perform it best, other things being equal.[10] This can be brought out if we consider a job that begins, say, in three months' time, and for which there are two candidates—one of whose performance level is on a plainly rising curve, while the other's performance curve is equally clearly declining. What should count is not performance level now or in the past, but predicted performance level at the time the job commences. Indeed, this point can be taken further. The most deserving candidate may be the one with the greatest potential, meaning the candidate who will perform best over the period during which it is reasonable to expect the job to be held (say, over a five-year period). Obviously there are practical difficulties caused by uncertainty in making judgments of this kind, but they do not seem to be ruled out on principle.

Thus there appear to be substantial disanalogies between prizes and jobs from the point of view of desert. Again, it is worth noting that jobs *may* be treated as prizes, for instance, when a professorship is awarded purely as a mark of distinction and without reference to the capacities of the individual involved to carry out the special duties of a professor. This seems defensible, however, only insofar as what is actually being conferred is really a title rather than a job, that is, where there is no expectation that the individual so honored will change his or her existing style of work. When real jobs, not honorary jobs or sinecures, are allocated as prizes, we witness not the principle of hiring by merit but a somewhat different practice.

JOBS ARE NOT DESERVED AS REWARDS for performance in the past; they are not deserved as prizes for talent displayed at the time of appointment. But in ruling out these two interpretations of the desert principle, we appear to be driven directly back to Sidgwick's principle of fitness, which I rejected earlier. For the basis of "desert" when someone deserves a job turns out to be (predictable) future performance. The principle appears to be forward-looking, and this suggests that what is really at stake in hiring by merit is not desert or justice but productive efficiency, and thereby eventually social welfare.

Despite these appearances, we can find a reading that preserves the principle as a substantive principle of justice. Consider what happens when someone holds a job. She makes a contribution to the output of her institution and is rewarded for that contribution with income and other job-related benefits. Let us say that her rewards are fair when they are proportionate to the value she creates for her institution. It doesn't matter for present purposes how value is estimated, whether through the use of market prices or in some other way.[11] All that matters is that we have some measure of value that enables us to estimate the contribution made by different individuals to overall output, so that we can say that jobs are fairly remunerated when for each person the aggregate of income and other benefits is proportional to value contributed.

Next consider a social system that is fair throughout, in the sense that each designated job has the appropriate remuneration attached to it, and each job-holder performs at the appropriate level. We now have to choose an applicant for a vacant job whose salary has been set to reflect the contribution its holder is expected to make to our institution. If we appoint the best-qualified applicant, we bring about a situation in which rewards are as closely as possible aligned with deserts. The best-qualified applicant, let us recall, is the one who, as far as we can determine, will most successfully carry out the tasks associated with the job being offered. In the ideal case, the best-qualified candidate fits the job like a glove, so to speak, and here our anticipation is that the income he will receive will correspond precisely to his contribution. In the second-best case, no candidate has all the qualifications we are looking for, so if the job continues to be paid at the predetermined rate there will be some excess reward, but by choosing the best qualified of the contenders we minimize the excess and thereby the injustice. This gives us a defense of the hiring-by-merit rule that appeals to distributive justice rather than an aggregative principle like efficiency: appointing the best-qualified candidate will maximize justice in the future by bringing about the closest possible correspondence between contributions and rewards.

Consider some complications. We have thus far contemplated the application of the desert principle against a background in which all jobs are fairly remunerated. This background may be (and in the real world is likely to be) distorted in either or both of two ways. First, salaries may to a greater or lesser extent be out of line with the contributions that jobs require. Second, as a result of past hiring decisions, people may have been placed in the wrong jobs, so that some job-holders are at present overperforming and others underperforming in a manner that throws the benefits they are receiving out of kilter with their relative contributions. If we start from a state of affairs that is unjust in either or both of these ways, is hiring the best-qualified applicant the policy that minimizes future injustice?

The following case may suggest otherwise. We are making an appointment to a university professorship. There are two candidates. The more competent of the two already holds a senior position at another university; the other, slightly less competent, has so far failed to win promotion and remains in a junior position. Assume that the academic performance of both candidates is constant over time and is not affected by the position that either of them holds. Let's assign some crude numbers: Brown (the senior position-holder) deserves a salary of $50,000, will receive $50,000 as a professor, and is currently receiving $45,000. Green (the junior position-holder) deserves a salary of $45,000, will receive $50,000 as a professor, and is currently receiving $30,000.

Suppose we measure the injustice of a state of affairs simply by summing up the financial inequities that it involves.[12] At present Brown is underpaid to the extent of $5,000 and Green to the extent of $15,000, so injustice totals $20,000. Hiring by merit requires us to give the chair to Brown, eliminating her underpayment, but still leaving Green earning $15,000 less than he deserves. By contrast, awarding the chair to Green would mean overpaying him by $5,000 while leaving Brown still $5,000 beneath her proper salary, a total injustice of only $10,000. To minimize injustice we should give Green the chair.

Before we leap to that conclusion, however, let us consider the matter a little more carefully. The first thing to notice is that by giving Green the chair we are knowingly bringing about an injustice. Given our stipulations that the salary for the job is fixed in advance, and that the academic performance of both candidates is constant, we are permanently lodging Green in a position in which he is overpaid.[13] If we appoint Brown, by contrast, we directly bring it about that a person is fairly remunerated—precisely so, as I have set the example up—while admittedly passing up an opportunity to rectify injustice elsewhere. This contrast between perpetrating and failing to rectify injustice is reflected in the complaint that Brown would no doubt make if Green were appointed: she would say, "I agree that it's unfair that poor old Green is stuck in his junior job, but I don't see why *that* injustice should be put right at *my* expense." Brown is appealing here to an idea of procedural justice and arguing that each person's claim to fair treatment should trump a concern for the overall justice of the outcome.

Next, let us remind ourselves that the hiring-by-merit rule is supposed to guide the deliberations of many independent selection bodies, who cannot anticipate in detail what the others will do. In this context, consistent following of the rule will tend always to maximize the justice of the overall outcome.[14] Any attempt by one body to rectify injustice more directly is liable to miscarry because of the later decisions of other selection committees in the same field. Thus Green in our example may in fact be about to be promoted to the more senior position that he deserves (at a salary of $45,000). By jumping in and offering him the professorship, we mess things up for everyone else. So we have two possible defenses of the hiring-by-merit rule, even against a background in which people are not currently holding the jobs or receiving the rewards they deserve. One is deontological in character and amounts to the claim that we should follow the principle (hiring by merit) that, if universally adopted, would bring about a maximally just outcome, even though in the world as it is we cannot be certain that this will follow. The other is more consequentialist in flavor, and consists in the claim that hiring the best-qualified candidate is the rule that, in the long run, will maximize the chances of a just distribution of rewards, together with the observation that we are not justified in breaking the rule in an individual case such as the one outlined above, because of uncertainty about what other appointments are going to be made.[15]

A similar strategy can be used to deal with the case in which jobs are variously underpaid and overpaid in terms of their social contribution. What we need here is an overall reassessment of relative incomes, and it is irrational for an individual appointing body to try to correct the maldistribution by, for instance, appointing a less-qualified candidate to hold a job that it knows is underpaid. It is not possible to move toward a situation of overall justice through a series of such individual decisions. At best, what happens is that one arbitrary injustice is corrected at the expense of creating another.

To sum up, hiring by merit is the policy that in general brings about the closest correspondence between individuals' contributions and their rewards. This result is reasonably robust even against the background of substantial initial injustice. Thus the policy can be defended by appeal to justice quite apart from utilitarian considerations. Nepotism or discrimination is unfair because it predictably creates a state of affairs in which there is a discrepancy between deserts and income rewards. Moreover, the best-qualified candidate who is passed over can legitimately complain that she is the victim of an injustice through being prevented from earning rewards commensurate with her potential contribution.[16]

The connection with justice has been made, but we still have to specify precisely the sense in which the best-qualified candidate *deserves* the job. Plainly that candidate does not yet deserve the income the job brings; to deserve the income one must actually carry out the tasks associated with the job, and that has yet to happen.[17] So in what sense is there a desert claim that is not met if the job is assigned to someone else? Compare the case of the athlete who is prevented by some petty decision of an official from taking part in a race that he has a fair chance of winning. We cannot say that this athlete deserves to win the prize. The person of whom that is true is the person who actually displays the greatest speed, which in the simplest case means the athlete who arrives at the tape first (as we have seen, matters are more complicated when one of the contenders suffers a stroke of bad luck like tripping in the course of the race). Nonetheless, the excluded athlete does appear to deserve something, namely, the opportunity to compete. He deserves the chance to become deserving, one might say. Moreover, his claim rests not merely on the general rights of human beings, but on particular facts about himself, namely, his demonstrated athletic ability. He complains not about there being a selection process for entry to the race, but about the way in which he has been excluded. That is why his claim that he deserves to run is a genuine claim of desert. It is a claim that can be made not by anyone but only by those whose proven ability is such that they have a genuine chance of winning.

A similar story can be told about the best-qualified candidate for a job. The position for which she has applied is a benefit, in the sense that it represents an opportunity to earn the rewards of contribution.[18] Her claim upon it rests on facts about herself which show that she is the candidate who, if given the job, is most likely to perform it in such a way that she will deserve the remuneration that is attached to it.[19] Since we are trying to establish a claim of desert, the future performance cannot itself be the basis of this judgment: the claim is not simply "she deserves it because she will perform in such and such a way."[20] The claim, rather, is that she has, now, qualities that we can say with some degree of confidence will allow her to perform at the level required by the job and so earn the corresponding rewards. It is these qualities that form the basis of desert. Thus it seems that we do indeed have a genuine desert claim here, albeit one that makes sense only in relation to a further desert claim, namely, the claim of job-holders to the rewards that their contributions bring.[21] In the same way, we can make sense of the excluded athlete's claim that he deserves to compete only by referring to the more fundamental claim of the fastest athlete that he deserves to win the medal. The desert claim we are investigating rides piggyback on the primary desert claim of the performer to his or her reward.[22]

THE CONTRAST BETWEEN the principle of desert I am defending and a more purely forward-looking principle of fitness can be brought out by considering some predictions about future performance that are *not* relevant to a candidate's deserts. First of all, it is only performance in the job itself that is relevant. It may be that the result of hiring one particular applicant would be to allow him to take on charitable or political work outside the job, and we may know that he would do this work extremely well—so well, in fact, that simple consequential calculations would dictate that we should give this applicant the job. But this does nothing to show that he deserves the job. Alternatively, it may be that one applicant is the bearer of a well-known local name, and we can foresee that having this person visibly employed is going to raise the profile of our company and increase our business. But again, this predictable result of employing the person is not something we should consider when assessing her deserts.

For a second contrast, suppose that some of the applicants are women, and we can discover, through consulting the appropriate statistics, what the probability is that each of these will take time out of employment to have children. Suppose, too, that this interruption will result in a lower level of performance overall (I am not saying that this is true for most jobs—it is not likely to be—but only contemplating a possibility). If we were to make our hiring decision simply in terms of likely performance, we would need to discount each woman applicant's predicted level of achievement by this probability factor. But if we were following the desert principle, we would enter no such discount. The fact that I may at some future time decide to do something that lowers my performance level cannot affect the extent to which I am now deserving of jobs or other benefits.

Note that the argument here does not rely on excluding all probabilistic information about individuals, but only information that relates to the whole group or class to which someone belongs. A particular woman is not made less deserving because she happens to fall into a category of which it is true, *ex hypothesi,* that members have such-and-such a probability of reduced performance in the future. In this respect the case differs from, say, that of the injury-prone sportsman who, for reasons specific to him, has a 10 percent chance of not being able to complete the game or the series. That fact does affect his deserts; it is quite in order to say, "Jones is strong as an ox; Smith is the more talented player, but we can't risk the chance that he will break down; so Jones deserves the last place on the team." From a purely forward-looking point of view, the probabilities in the two cases may be similar, but whereas in the second case we have information about a particular individual that bears on his deserts, in the first case we cannot say of any particular woman we are considering for a position that she is liable to perform at a lower level because of a decision to have children.[23] To make that assumption is to fail to treat her respectfully as an individual, and potentially to commit an injustice.[24]

Finally, consider a case in which performance levels will depend on the behavior of other people. Suppose we have a prospective black employee whose job performance will predictably be lowered by the obstructive behavior of his prejudiced supervisor. This fact does not make him any less deserving. The predictable performance is not connected in the right kind of way to present facts about the applicant.

This example does, however, open up the wider question of what have been called "reaction qualifications" for jobs, that is, personal attributes that contribute to job performance via the responses of other people, as opposed to straightforwardly technical qualifications.[25] It is obviously relevant in hiring a salesman to consider whether his manner is likely to please customers, as well as his accuracy with figures. A line must be drawn between having black skin in an environment of racial prejudice and having a grating manner in an environment where customers expect to be treated with courtesy, but it is not easy to say precisely where. We want to say that the customers' reactions are legitimate whereas the prejudiced supervisor's reactions are not, but again it is difficult to specify the criterion of legitimacy.[26] Fortunately, we do not need to resolve this issue for present purposes. However legitimacy is defined, only job qualifications based on legitimate reactions (on the part of customers, colleagues, and so on) are relevant when we are assessing applicants' deserts. Once again there is a clear contrast with a straightforward appeal to consequences in deciding whom to employ.

These examples show not only how the desert principle I have been outlining differs from utilitarian and other such straightforwardly consequentialist principles, but also (I hope) the superiority of the desert principle. We would think it unfair to candidates if employers made hiring decisions by appealing to *general* consequences rather than by trying to isolate those aspects of future performance that depend upon each applicant's own skills and efforts. Thus our final statement of the principle of deserving jobs should read as follows: candidate A deserves the job being offered when, on the basis of specific information about A's present personal characteristics (relevant skills, motivation, and so on), he is the person likely to perform best in that job, once we discount illegitimate third-party reactions such as those stemming from racial or sexual prejudice.

I NOW WANT TO CONSIDER the objection that jobs cannot be deserved because it is up to those offering them to decide which jobs to make available, and they should therefore have a free hand in deciding which applicant has the qualities they are seeking. This position has been defended by Michael Walzer, who contrasts prizes with offices in this respect:

> A prize . . . can be deserved because it already belongs to the person who has given the best performance; it remains only to identify that person. Prize committees are like juries in that they look backward and aim at an objective decision. An office, by contrast, cannot be deserved because it belongs to the people who are served by it, and they or their agents are free (within limits I will specify later) to make any choice they please. Search committees are unlike juries in that their members look forward as well as back: they make predictions about the candidate's future performances, and they also express preferences about how the office should be filled.[27]

Walzer gives the example of appointing a hospital director. He thinks the selection committee is entitled to choose the candidate who shares its view about the general direction in which the hospital should move, rather than the candidate with the greatest managerial talent.

The contrast Walzer draws between prizes and offices amalgamates two distinctions: the distinction between backward-looking and forward-looking reasoning, and the quite separate distinction between applying objective criteria of selection and simply following your preferences. These two distinctions are logically unrelated (you could give the prize for best novel of the year by choosing the book that made you laugh the most, for instance: this would be backward-looking but based on subjective preference). We have seen already that jobs differ from prizes inasmuch as past performance is very often a sufficient basis for deserving prizes, whereas in the case of jobs past performance matters only as a source of evidence about a person's present qualities. But it does not follow that judgments about who deserves a job are forward-looking in character. They identify a fit between a person's present potential and the job in question. Earlier we saw why a hiring committee concerned with doing justice with respect to the candidates will be involved in prediction only in a highly circumscribed way.[28]

Perhaps, then, Walzer's other distinction, between objective criteria and the preferences of the hiring committee, holds the key to the assertion that jobs cannot be deserved. But let us examine it more closely. Walzer wants to rule out idiosyncratic preferences that are not relevant to the job at hand, for example, preferences for hair or skin color; he admits that to act on these would be unjust. Thus we are left only with different possible views about what the aims and goals of the job are: should the hospital director be a highly competent administrator, or a leader who changes the general spirit of the hospital? This issue has to be settled before we know what the job is for which the candidates have applied (and, of course, in practice it is quite possible for there to be dissension within the appointing committee on this question). But once that issue is settled, then the question which of the applicants deserves the job is in principle an objective one. It is a matter of seeing which candidate has the qualities to carry out the job in the way that comes closest to our specification. Judgment is of course involved here—judgments about how candidates would in fact perform, judgments about how their scores along different dimensions add up—but in this respect the case is no different from that of a jury's awarding, say, a literary prize, where again a fairly sophisticated judgment involving several dimensions of excellence has to be made.

Walzer's fear is that applying the principle of desert to offices would entail something like a universal examination system as the method of entry. But although examination scores offer a very simple, quantitative way of comparing candidates, I cannot see what forces selection committees to move in this direction if, as Walzer rightly claims, these scores are a very poor way of selecting candidates for most jobs. The British Civil Service, in earlier years notorious for the reliance it placed on written examinations as a means of regulating entry to its higher grades, now uses a broader set of criteria, taking into account relevant experience and personal skills insofar as these can be assessed through extended interviews and so forth. So long as those involved in hiring are committed to the goals of their institutions, which may be defined in economic terms or in some other way, they will want to get the best people to fill jobs, and so they have every incentive to seek out the deserving by the best available means. If there is a danger, it is that they will consider the consequences of different appointments too directly, not that they will employ excessively narrow tests of desert.

FINALLY, LET US LOOK briefly at how the principle of desert I have been defending bears on the issue of positive discrimination in the job market. I use "positive discrimination" to cover all policies that give preferential treatment to women, ethnic minorities, or other groups considered to be disadvantaged, whether these take the form of reserving places for members of these groups, awarding them extra points when hiring decisions are made, or something else.[29] In each case positive discrimination policies appear to contradict the principle of hiring by merit, and this is often given as a strong or even conclusive reason against adopting them. As I shall show, appearances may be deceptive: there is at least one form of positive discrimination that is consistent with desert. We need to distinguish both the kind of policy involved and the reasons used to support it.

Some justifications of positive discrimination are forward-looking and appeal to the benefits of having people belonging to many different categories in each occupation. A popular argument of this type appeals to the need for role models.[30] The claim here is that by placing a certain number of women, blacks, Catholics, and so on in positions where until now very few members of these groups have been found—especially high-status professional or executive positions—we encourage other women, blacks, and Catholics to aspire to and train for these positions, so breaking down the inhibiting effects of existing cultural norms. Let's assume that the empirical claim is correct, as it may well be: what value is being invoked when positive discrimination is justified by appeal to the need for role models? The value is positive freedom, or autonomy, rather than justice.[31] The argument is that it benefits members of disadvantaged groups to be presented with a wide range of occupational choices through being able to observe members of their own group already holding positions within each field. But though this argument may be valid, it fails to show that the future role model has a claim of justice to the position he is to occupy merely by virtue of being a role model. The fact that a woman who holds a professional position will serve as a role model for other women is irrelevant to the question whether she deserves that position.

In reply here it might be argued that a woman doctor, say, is doubly deserving, because besides the routine benefits that she is creating as a doctor, she is creating indirect benefits for women by serving as an exemplar; thus this would justify taking on a woman as a doctor in preference to a slightly more competent man. But there are two difficulties with this reply. The first is that the indirect benefits are a pure surplus, in the sense that they don't require the woman in question to do anything over and above what she would do in any case as part of her job. In that respect the case is rather like one in which someone does a job, more or less competently, but is simply very beautiful, so that at the same time he spreads joy and longing around him; this has no bearing on his occupational desert. Admittedly, it would be different if the woman had chosen to be a doctor at least in part in order to provide a role model for others, because this does seem to ground a genuine claim of desert. But is the desert relevant to the hiring decision?

When jobs are rewarded with income and other benefits, the desert that is at stake is desert acquired through the successful performance of the various tasks that make up the job itself. As I argued earlier, if A is more competent than B with respect to the position we are filling, we shouldn't hire B even if we know that B, in his spare time, will carry out some worthy function like running the local Scout group. We are requiting not desert across a whole life but only one particular slice of desert.[32] In the case where someone serves as a role model to others, it happens to be true that she can so serve only by virtue of the fact that she holds and carries out the job in question, but this does not make being a role model part of the job, any more than having a Famous Name and thereby raising the profile of our company increases the job-related desert of the person who bears the name.

Let me repeat that I am not dismissing the role-models argument as such, but simply pointing out that it cannot be couched in the language of desert and may therefore conflict with the principle of hiring by merit. A second way of attempting to square positive discrimination with that principle is to claim that a person's sex, ethnicity, and so on may in appropriate circumstances actually count as a constituent of merit. As Ronald Dworkin puts the argument:

> There is no combination of abilities and skills and traits that constitutes "merit" in the abstract; if quick hands count as "merit" in the case of a prospective surgeon, this is because quick hands will enable him to serve the public better and for no other reason. If a black skin will, as a matter of regrettable fact, enable another doctor to do a different medical job better, then that black skin is by the same token "merit" as well.[33]

The tacit assumption here is presumably that black doctors may be better able than white doctors to serve black communities, by virtue of inspiring greater confidence in their patients. In a similar way it is sometimes claimed that women students learn better from women teachers and professors; thus being a woman might here be a source of merit alongside the other academic and personal qualities that make someone a good teacher.

The problem with these claims is that they turn on the beliefs and attitudes of the job-holder's clients, and we must therefore ask whether the beliefs and attitudes in questions are legitimate ones. If we do not do this, then it is easy to turn the argument around in such a way that being white and male becomes a form of "merit" whenever the job in question involves dealing with customers or clients who are positively disposed toward these qualities, or prejudiced against their opposites.[34] What does Dworkin mean when he says that it is a "regrettable fact" that black doctors can perform more effectively than their white counterparts? If he means that it is regrettable that many blacks are racially prejudiced against whites, then we might agree, but at the same time we would be reluctant to regard this as a source of merit in black doctors, any more than we would in the reverse case. Perhaps he means that black patients, although not prejudiced, may be diffident about approaching or talking frankly to a white doctor, whom they see as holding a higher social status. In this case we might see having black skin as a possible source of merit, though presumably better still would be the white doctor who manages to break through the barrier of mistrust and thereby helps to create a less divided society. The general point is that merit cannot be stretched to include every feature that may in a particular case help someone perform his or her job effectively without letting in forms of discrimination that we would immediately recognize as unfair.

Having looked at two forms of positive discrimination that cannot be justified by appeal to a principle of desert, let me now turn to a form that can. Suppose it can be shown by empirical research that there are social groups whose members are generally disadvantaged by the treatment they receive in education and the job market. Suppose, for instance, that black children generally receive less attention and encouragement in schools than white children of comparable ability. It would follow that performance to date, in the form, say, of examination grades received, would under-represent the potential of members of these groups.[35] And it would also follow that if we use evidence of this kind when making hiring decisions, we should include a weighting to allow for such under-performance. This does not amount to a departure from the desert principle. Recall that the basis of desert in hiring cases is not past performance but capacity to carry out the job being offered as *indicated* by past performance and such other measures as we are able to employ. In building in a weighting factor to take account of racial or ethnic differences, we are correcting the evidence of past performance in line with known general facts.[36] A black candidate with an educational grade of 65 percent may deserve a job in preference to a white candidate with a grade of 70 percent if the first candidate's grade predicts a better job performance than the second's.

Note that this more sophisticated use of the desert principle does not amount to compensation for past injustice. It is frequently argued that positive discrimination in employment is justified in order to compensate for the past exploitation of the disadvantaged groups. There are difficulties with this proposal, some of which are suggested by my earlier discussion of jobs *qua* rewards for past performance. The present suggestion has nothing to do with compensation. If blacks or women are owed more favorable consideration than white men, this is not to rectify past injustices, but because their past performance under-represents their present deserts.[37] On the basis of what we know generally about the group or groups in question, our best estimate of a particular member's capacity to do the job we are filling requires us to apply a weighting factor to past performance. Thus, if the examination grades achieved by black students generally underestimate their capacity (as compared with white students) by 5 percent, then in the absence of specific information about the applicants, we should inflate the examination scores of all blacks by 5 percent in arriving at our judgment of desert. Here hiring by merit requires positive discrimination in the sense that we should adjust our standard tests of merit in a way that favors candidates from the relevant groups (it does not, however, license quotas for the group or other more rigid forms of positive discrimination).

This argument can be extended in one further respect. Suppose that the groups whose members have underperformed prior to the point of selection were to continue to underperform afterwards. Assume that women of equivalent ability not only get lower grades at school than men, but continue to get lower grades when admitted to a university under a positive discrimination policy.[38] Would this defeat the desert argument for positive discrimination? It depends on what causes the underperformance. Suppose that girls perform less well than boys in mixed schools because teachers tend to lavish more attention on the boys; suppose that this pattern is repeated at the university level. An admissions committee might then be justified in admitting women with lower grades, even though the committee expected them to perform less well than their male counterparts. The justification would be that their expected deserts were not reduced by the unfair or negligent behavior of university lecturers. They would be as clever as the men, work as hard, and so on, but get results that were not as good. This would parallel the case discussed earlier of a black applicant for a job who we know is going to perform less well because of the prejudice he will encounter in the workplace. Deserts are not diminished when some extraneous environmental factor comes between what a person is attempting to achieve and the actual result that ensues.

Here we have a case in which the desert principle is more favorable to positive discrimination policies than consequentialist reasoning would be. From a consequentialist point of view, if we know that somebody is likely to perform badly in our institution—for whatever reason—it is silly to select that person. Although my main task in this chapter has been clarifying rather than defending the principle of deserving jobs, I am convinced that the principle carries considerable weight in political argument, both as a separate principle and as part of the broader idea of meritocracy to be considered in the next chapter. Thus it is of considerable importance that it can justify at least one form of positive discrimination. Contrary to first appearances, hiring by merit sometimes means giving special consideration to applicants from historically disadvantaged groups.

9

Two Cheers for Meritocracy

The aim of the present chapter is to set out a qualified defense of meritocracy. By this I mean the ideal of a society in which each person's chance to acquire positions of advantage and the rewards that go with them will depend entirely on his or her talent and effort. In such a society inequalities among different people's life chances will remain, but social institutions will be designed to ensure that favored positions are assigned on the basis of individual merit and not allocated randomly, or by ascriptive characteristics such as race or gender, or by the machinations of the already powerful.

This ideal appears to have commanded cross-party support in recent political debate. To use British examples, when Conservative leaders such as John Major have proclaimed their commitment to a "classless society," they have meant by this not the old socialist ideal of a society without significant social inequalities, but what I have just described as a meritocracy. Meanwhile, the residual egalitarianism of the Labour Party has been confined to attacks on the "undeserving rich," that is, those whose wealth has not been achieved in a suitably meritocratic way. And of course the idea of meritocracy, if not the term itself, has been a cornerstone of liberal and social-democratic thought for the last two centuries. It has usually been understood as a progressive ideal, in the sense that it serves to criticize social arrangements based on inherited position or privileges: *la carriere ouverte aux talents* versus the *ancien régime*. In later incarnations—for instance, in Anthony Crosland's *The Future of Socialism*—it forms the basis for an attack on private education, inherited wealth, and so forth.[1] No doubt meritocracy has also played a role in legitimating the institutions of modern liberal societies, but at the very least it is a double-edged sword. While the principle of merit it embodies serves to endorse liberal institutions when these are contrasted with feudal or oligarchic regimes, it calls them to account for failing to live up to their own pretensions—for example, when women are denied equal treatment, when the boss's son gets a fast track to the top of the firm, or when Ivy League or Oxbridge colleges bend the rules to let in the off-spring of wealthy alumni.

The merit principle seems to have a firm grounding in popular think-ing about justice: it corresponds to the widespread belief that people deserve to enjoy unequal incomes depending on their abilities and how hard they work.[2] But since it collides in practice with the equally deep-rooted belief that people are entitled to do the best they can for their children and their other relatives, it cannot be regarded as an overriding operative ideal. As noted in Chapter 2, there is evidence that people take a tolerant view of at least the milder forms of nepotism, such as using one's influence to help get a relative a job. In cases like this, the merit principle is trumped by the needs of members of one's family or commu-nity. Thus in proclaiming meritocracy, and in insisting that those who are responsible for allocating positions of advantage should pay attention only to the ability and motivation of those who seek them, we are not simply pushing at an open door. Indeed, we are asking people to set aside principles of action that come naturally to them—favoring their families, their friends, their co-religionists, those who have done them favors in the past, and so forth—and that have cemented societies together throughout human history. Meritocracy is in one sense a profoundly unnatural way of allocating social advantages.

It is not my intention here to try to determine how meritocratic exist-ing liberal societies already are. As readers will soon discover if they attempt it, this is a difficult issue to address empirically, in part because we don't have a clear understanding of what meritocracy means, so we don't have a proper measuring rod against which to gauge social realities, saying how far they do or do not conform to meritocratic criteria.[3] Inso-far as I succeed in clarifying the merit principle, this chapter may be a useful prolegomenon to such an empirical investigation, but clearly it cannot replace it. My general assumption is that we still fall far short of the meritocratic ideal.[4] What I *do* want to show is that there is no deep-seated reason having to do with the nature of contemporary societies that prevents us from approaching it. I shall argue, in particular, that there is no profound antagonism between meritocracy and the market economy; there is no reason in principle why an advanced industrial society in which the market plays a central role shouldn't be meritocratic. The obstacles to meritocracy lie closer to the surface—in tradition, in sexual and racial prejudice, in the natural desire to favor one's friends and relations that I alluded to above, and so forth. These obstacles are undoubtedly serious, but they are obstacles that we can combat through education, legislation, and institutional change. If the critics of meritocracy were right, and the very idea of trying to allocate social advantage on the basis of merit betrays a profound misunderstanding of contemporary societies, the ideal would be nothing more than an interesting utopia.

The meritocratic ideal has been attacked in recent years from very different quarters. The neoliberal critique, represented most notably by Hayek, sees meritocracy as the Trojan Horse of socialism (or one of them). If we say that a person's share of social advantages should depend upon his or her merits, Hayek argues, we extend a principle that may at best be appropriate within an organization to cover a whole society, and in doing so we necessarily undercut the free market.[5] In a market, a person's rewards are a result of his providing services that others happen to want and are prepared to pay for, whether this comes about by effort, ability, or brute luck: the distribution of advantages will bear little relation to any recognizable pattern of merit.

Philosophers of the left, by contrast, routinely criticize meritocracy on the ground that it replaces a concern for equality of outcome with a concern for equality of opportunity: it is interested only in ensuring that positions of advantage are fairly allocated, instead of seeking to reduce or eliminate economic and other social inequalities. Moreover, in doing so it justifies these inequalities on specious grounds, for how can people be said to deserve the talents and skills that form the basis of merit? As Rawls famously puts it, "it seems to be one of the fixed points of our considered judgments that no one deserves his place in the distribution of native endowments, any more than one deserves one's initial starting place in society."[6]

A third line of attack comes from feminists and champions of ethnic minorities who see meritocracy as standing in the way of affirmative action programs that reserve educational places or jobs for members of these groups, or at least weight the selection process in their favor. The claim here is that "merit" is not a neutral and objective criterion for settling which of several candidates should be given a sought-after position, but instead a socially constructed notion that works in favor of those already entrenched in positions of power, that is, white males. Essentially we determine what kind of person we would like to fill a position, and that then settles what counts as "merit"; thus if the selectors were instead to decide that they wanted a woman, then being female would be, for the purposes of the particular position in question, a source of merit.

IN ORDER TO RESPOND to these criticisms, we must begin by distinguishing in a more analytical way between different objections to meritocracy. The first line of objection puts in question the very idea that people can deserve positions of advantage on the basis of their efforts and talents. This might stem from a wholesale rejection of the idea of desert, or from the thesis that people cannot deserve benefits on the basis of features such as talent for which they are not responsible. I have discussed this objection in the previous two chapters and shall not repeat myself here.

A second line of objection concedes that effort and talent can form legitimate bases of desert, but points out that the opportunities people have to compete for positions of advantage are strongly influenced by their social origins. A wealth of evidence indicates that in contemporary societies family background plays a large part in determining which skills people acquire through education, how well motivated they are, and so forth, so that even if access to positions of advantage was formally meritocratic, people from favored backgrounds would still enjoy undeserved advantages.[7] Short of abolishing the family, there seems little prospect of eliminating this effect.[8] This objection appears to me unanswerable in its own terms. It shows that meritocracy conflicts with other values that we are not likely to want to abandon, so that any feasible social arrangement must represent a compromise between these ideals. But it does not destroy meritocracy as an ideal, any more than democracy or liberty are destroyed when we realize that these values, too, can never be fully realized, either because we cannot prevent some people from having more political influence than others, or because some constraint is necessary for social life.

A more positive response is to see meritocracy as having two parts. One has to do with the formation of individuals' capacities and abilities in the early years of life, through the family and the education system. The other part takes these abilities and capacities as given, and looks at the opportunities that are available to people from young adulthood onward, in higher education, in the job market, and in social life generally. As far as the first part is concerned, the education system can, through head start programs and so forth, offset to some extent the antimeritocratic effects of the family, but it can never do so entirely. Let us concede this. My concern here will be with the second part of the meritocratic ideal.

Here we reach the criticism that I shall mainly be addressing, namely, that there are no objective standards of merit to which we can appeal in order to judge whether the benefits people are receiving are in proportion to merit. Since merit is a meaningless, or at best a subjectively defined, notion, the principle that people's life chances should depend exclusively on their merits is equally meaningless or subjective. This is common ground between left- and right-wing critics of meritocracy, although as we shall see the reasons they give for thinking it are somewhat different.

Let us return to the critics of meritocracy and begin with the Hayekian argument. What is interesting about this argument is that it assumes that the market is the key allocative mechanism in modern societies. Because what people receive in market transactions is determined solely by forces of supply and demand, Hayek claims, these receipts cannot correspond to personal merit. In this respect Hayek's argument appears diametrically opposed to the critique mounted by Claus Offe (and picked up by some recent critics such as I. M. Young), which holds that it is precisely the fact that a person's activity is no longer in any real way measured by the market that makes the merit principle merely ideological. Offe's claim, in other words, is that a person's contribution is now arbitrarily assessed by the organization that employs him, whereas at an earlier stage of capitalist society, when producers were directly exposed to the market, what Offe calls "the achievement principle" made at least some sense. As he puts it, "While the early liberal form of capitalism ensured a continual direct evaluation of the individual work of the commodity producers by means of market prices, the growth of large-scale organizational forms of work means an at least temporary exclusion of the working individual from the evaluative mechanisms of the market."[9] Hayek's argument rests on the contrary assumption that producers' receipts depend directly on their success or failure in market competition, rather than being determined by authoritative decision. Clearly these two critiques of meritocracy cannot both hold good at once: if rewards are market-determined, as Hayek assumes, then Offe's argument no longer applies; conversely, if rewards are determined by organizational factors, then Hayek's argument is invalid. Thus we may draw some initial comfort from the fact that the two leading attacks on meritocracy that we are considering rest upon conflicting pictures of the allocative mechanisms at work in contemporary market economies.[10]

Hayek's argument breaks down into two parts. First, he draws a distinction between value and merit and argues that a person's merits cannot be estimated by the value of his or her conduct. Second, he argues that in market contexts the idea that activity has a definable value is mistaken. Let me take these in turn.

The merit-value distinction is arrived at by identifying a person's merit with the moral character of her conduct. A person is deserving or meritorious, in other words, to the extent that she behaves in morally praiseworthy ways—which means acting from good motives and bearing costs and overcoming difficulties to reach her goals. Hayek then points out that in order to assess merit starting from what we know about a person's achievements, we would on the one hand have to discount the effects of natural abilities—"a good mind or a fine voice, a beautiful face or a skillful hand"—for which the person in question can claim no credit; and on the other hand discount the effects of luck, of being in the right place at the right time, of lighting by chance on some product for which there turns out to be enormous demand, and so on. But, he says, in market settings we cannot possibly know enough to make these judgments; we cannot say, for example, whether a successful investment was the result of prudent foresight or merely a huge gamble. He concludes that "the possibility of a true judgement of merit thus depends on the presence of precisely those conditions whose general absence is the main argument for liberty."[11]

Let us grant straightaway that productivity in a market context cannot be used to measure merit in Hayek's sense. The question is whether the kind of merit he invokes belongs among the principles relevant to meritocracy. In Hayek's discussion three possible bases of merit are run together: moral motive, effort, and pain. It is true that each of these may in certain circumstances ground a judgment that someone deserves a reward. Sometimes we praise people for acting according to good moral motives—for instance, for holding fast to their convictions when they stand to lose financially by doing so. At other times we congratulate people for making an effort—struggling to the top of Ben Nevis, for example—and we may give a prize to the hardest-working child in the class. Finally, people may deserve praise and reward, not for experiencing pain as such, but for the determination they show in soldiering on with some course of action despite the pain it brings them. But it is false to infer that because people sometimes deserve reward for acting morally, making an effort, and bearing pain, these are the only possible bases of desert. In other contexts these aspects of people's activities may be quite irrelevant.

Consider prizes, for example. As I pointed out in the previous two chapters, these are very often deserved on the basis of a person's achievements without reference to his motives or efforts. For instance, we might judge that Hayek deserved the Nobel Prize that he received for his writings on economics, and all that we would need to show in order to vindicate this judgment is that Hayek did indeed write the books in question—they weren't plagiarized—and that they are of a quality to merit the prize. Whether Hayek endured pain and suffering in the course of composing *The Road to Serfdom,* or whether the words flowed easily from his pen; whether he wrote out of a moral concern to save mankind from the follies of economic planning, or to earn sufficient royalties to keep the Hayek family in *Sachertorte* and *Einspänner;* in this context these questions are irrelevant.

The same is true if we ask on what basis people deserve the rewards of economic activity (income and so forth). Hayek is quite correct to point to the somewhat bizarre consequences that would follow if we remunerated people on the basis of their motives, their efforts, or their pains. We would need to know whether the baker who sells me my bread is a Calvinist or an agnostic. We would have to pay clumsy people more than quick and skillful people for making the same object, since the effort involved is greater. We would have to remunerate people who disliked their jobs more generously than people doing the same work who enjoyed doing it. We would have to reward effort even in cases in which the effort in question was expended on some futile project like growing fruit that nobody wants to eat and so forth. But this only shows that we are looking in the wrong direction if we want to find the basis of economic desert. People deserve the rewards of economic activity for their achievement, for the contribution they make to the welfare of others by providing goods and services that others want. Effort matters here only because it counts, along with talent and choice, as a factor in determining what a person achieves. Effort that does not emanate in a productive contribution may possibly deserve reward of some other kind, but it cannot form the basis of economic desert.

We have disposed of the claim that, because people's merit depends upon the moral praiseworthiness of their activities, we cannot use economic contribution as a measure of merit. But we still face the second Hayekian challenge to meritocracy. Hayek argues that the amount someone receives for the goods and services he produces for the market does not correspond in any real sense to their "value to society." Indeed, this notion of value is strictly meaningless in the context of a market society. Thus even if we wanted to measure merit by social contribution, it would be quite inadmissible to apply this notion in a social system that has no single overall aim or purpose, but is instead made up of many individuals with widely divergent aims and purposes.

We need to be clear about the problem here. We are considering an individual who produces goods or services for sale in a market, and we are not for present purposes considering the problems posed by market distortions such as monopoly or collusion. In other words, we are talking about a Smithian butcher or baker selling his wares in competition with other butchers and bakers and asking the question whether there is any sense in which the price such a person can command can be seen as a measure of the value he contributes to society as a whole. Hayek gives several reasons we might answer in the negative.[12] One is that we have qualitative standards of value that are not reflected in market prices. He asks whether "a man who supplies matches to millions and thereby earns $200,000 a year is worth more 'to society' than a man who supplies great wisdom or exquisite pleasure to a few thousand and thereby earns $20,000 a year."[13] Well, supposing that these sums are fairly earned in competitive markets, why not make such a judgment? In making it we would be relying on two premises that seem fairly uncontroversial: that a contribution that benefits a greater number of people is more valuable than one that benefits a lesser number, and that the benefit that someone derives from a good or a service is measured by the amount she is willing to pay for it.

The second premise could be challenged. Someone might make a qualitative value judgment to the effect that writing books of philosophy or performing Beethoven sonatas counts for more than making matches, but it is hard to see why this would have any claim to objectivity. What the market does in cases like this is aggregate a large number of individual judgments as to the relative value of matches and books of philosophy, and this does, it seems to me, have some claim to be called an estimate of overall "value to society." We might still want to argue that people would be better off if they consumed more books of philosophy and fewer matches. Even if this were true, it is not clear why we should let this affect our judgments of the relative value contributed *now* by the matchmaker and the philosopher, unless we have some Marcuse-like theory that the matchmaker is somehow preventing us from cultivating an interest in philosophy.

It is of course true that some forms of social contribution are not reflected in the market price that people can command for their labors. The benefits produced may be public goods that, because they are non-excludable, cannot be sold on the market at all. And even when what is being produced is a private commodity or service, the way it is produced may create (positive or negative) spillover effects that are not confined to the immediate purchasers. (A shopkeeper, for instance, may embellish his shop in a way that adds to the general attractiveness of the area in which it is situated.) I shall return later to the question of how one might begin to estimate the value of such contributions. For the time being, let me make it clear that I am not defending the philistine view that the only meritorious kind of social contribution is the kind to which a market price can be attached. What I do want to argue against Hayek is that if we want to establish the relative value of *economic* contributions, then the market price of the resulting good or service gives us a nonarbitrary way of totaling up the value of a contribution to the many different people who may benefit from it.

Another of Hayek's objections is that the price someone pays for a good or a service may not fully capture its value to that person. In one sense this is perfectly true. In market economies we often have what economists would call a consumer surplus: the person who buys a box of matches for fifty cents might have been willing to pay up to two dollars, say, to have the matches. The price of a commodity is set by what the marginal consumer is willing to pay for it, and what the marginal producer is willing to make it for. But in a large and competitive market, it seems appropriate to assess someone's contribution by placing him or her in the position of the marginal producer.[14] When a Smithian baker decides to bake a batch of bread, he does so against a background in which many others are already engaged in baking bread. The value of his contribution is the value of the extra bread that he is adding to the overall stock, a value that will be adequately reflected in the market price of a loaf. The fact that, because bread is regarded as an essential, many consumers would be willing if necessary to pay a much higher price for it does not increase the value of the baker's present activity.[15]

A third objection leveled by Hayek against the thesis that market prices may provide a measure of social value is that different goods and services are very often sold to distinct groups of people, which in Hayek's view undercuts the notion of their having a definable "value to society." Again the premise seems true, but it fails to support the conclusion. If the butcher supplies services for which group A will pay in total $1,000 and the baker supplies services for which group B will pay in total $500, why in the absence of special evidence should we not conclude that the butcher has contributed twice as much as the baker? Unless we have reason to think that each dollar put up by those in group A buys them more utility or welfare than each dollar put up by those in group B, why resist the obvious conclusion that, over fairly large aggregates of people at least, the money they are willing to put up to acquire goods and services provides a reasonable estimate of the value of those goods and services, and thus a reasonable estimate of the contribution of the providers?

This riposte may not seem convincing when there are substantial inequalities in consumers' incomes. Two issues arise here. The first is that the pattern of consumer demand is likely to depend upon the current distribution of income, and thus there appears to be a circularity involved in trying to defend as deserved and just a contribution-based scale of rewards when the value of each person's contribution depends in turn on the pre-existing income distribution. Whether this circularity is vicious, however, depends on whether justice-enhancing changes in this distribution lead toward an equilibrium. Suppose we start with an income distribution and pattern of consumption that are unjust in the sense that some individuals are over-rewarded and others under-rewarded when their contributions are measured in market terms. (Suppose some have succeeded in exploiting their position as monopolists.) By altering the set of property rights, or in some other way, we change the distribution to reflect relative contributions. As we do so, spending patterns are likely to change, and so further adjustments are called for (or perhaps the market itself will cause contributions to be revalued in the light of the new schedule of consumer demands). The important questions are whether this process tends toward an equilibrium, and whether the equilibrium that is reached depends upon the initial starting point. If there is an equilibrium, and it is not path-dependent, then the circularity we are considering is not a vicious one.[16]

The second difficulty arises from the reasonable assumption that the marginal utility of money diminishes as the quantity of money someone possesses increases. It appears then that those who supply goods (or services) normally consumed by the better-off will create less value than is suggested by the market prices of such goods, while those who supply goods normally consumed by the worse-off will create relatively more value for each dollar's worth of goods. For instance, the wealthy consumers of expensive perfumes are likely to derive less benefit per dollar from their purchases than the masses will from their purchases of basic commodities like boots and shirts. If producers generally know this, then the incomes of people who choose to make expensive perfumes may be inflated relative to the value they create, and basic commodity producers' incomes will be deflated. Hence, people's market-derived income may represent more or less than they deserve depending on whether the consumers of their products usually fall toward the top or the bottom of the income scale.[17]

My intention is not to deny the force of this argument entirely, but to point out two qualifications. First, everything depends on the actual degree of income inequality in the society we are considering: the greater the inequality, the more likely it is that market receipts will not accurately reflect the value of different productive activities. Or to put the point positively, the more egalitarian a market economy is, the more likely it is to allocate advantages according to merit.[18] Second, the less consumption is stratified by income, the less relevant the argument becomes. Contemporary market societies have two features whose likely effect is to reduce stratification of this kind: a generally rising standard of living and growing cultural pluralism, which together mean that consumption becomes more homogeneous across income groups and less homogeneous across subcultures. In these circumstances it becomes less plausible to claim that some producers of goods and services deserve less than others because the market price these goods or services command deviates systematically from their real consumption value.

A final Hayekian argument for dissociating the merit principle from the market economy cannot be disputed. This is simply the observation that luck plays a significant part in determining people's receipts in market settings. For instance, two people may open night clubs in the same city, the clubs may be quite similar in what they have to offer, but because people begin to congregate at the first club and not the second more or less by chance, the first club takes off and its owner gets rich, whereas the second goes under. We can't avoid or write off examples like this. I would just add, though, that a Hayekian cannot push this point too far without grave danger to his ideological health. For it is a key element in the Hayekian defense of markets that they utilize the specific local knowledge of entrepreneurs to find new ways of making and selling goods and services. We can therefore never tell, from the outside, whether the decision to situate the night club here rather than there was a simple matter of luck or a shrewd piece of entrepreneurial insight. It cannot *all* be luck, however, or else the efficiency arguments in favor of letting entrepreneurs retain most of the money they make for reinvestment would go by the board. Hayek's claim is not only that entrepreneurial rewards are needed to motivate would-be entrepreneurs, but that it is desirable for capital to stay in the hands of those who have shown that they know how to invest it. If, however, success were entirely a matter of luck, this second argument would fail, and capital for future investment might as well be randomly allocated.

I shall return to luck later, but for now let us simply concede to Hayek that because of the role played by luck in a market economy, a society that incorporates such an economy can never be a perfect meritocracy. Luck serves as a limit to the principle of merit much as does the effect of family background. But this is not a reason for throwing the principle out altogether, as Hayek recommends. There is no inherent flaw in the claim that someone may deserve the benefits she receives in a well-functioning market as a reward for the contribution she is making. In each individual case luck is likely to have played some part in the outcome, but there is merit as well as luck, and no reason to think that luck is always the dominant influence. In particular, we should avoid the error of supposing that because we rarely have exact knowledge of why someone received the benefits he did, we must attribute that outcome to luck—in other words, we should avoid using luck as a residual category to account for that part of personal success that cannot be explained by other measurable factors, as Christopher Jencks once did.[19]

HAVING NOW CRITICALLY ASSESSED the Hayekian claim that the merit principle is inherently incompatible with a market economy, I turn to the opposite line of attack found in authors such as Offe and Young. As mentioned, this radical attack on meritocracy rests on a picture of contemporary capitalist economies very different from that proposed by Hayek. In this view of things, individuals' positions and remunerations are for the most part determined not by market forces but by organizational rules and practices; furthermore, the market is not seen as exercising a determining influence on the way those rules and practices operate. There are two main claims in this argument. The first is that it is impossible to make objective judgments about the relative competence of individuals to hold jobs, and so various normative criteria are used instead to select people for positions. The second is that jobs cannot be ranked in terms of their importance or contribution to the organization as a whole. Thus the idea of rewarding job-holders according to contribution is essentially a screen for a division of rewards that reflects the balance of power among different groups within the organization.

Offe makes a number of points in defense of the first claim. Some of these depend upon a view about the technological development of industrial societies according to which labor becomes increasingly divided but also deskilled, while at the same time the opportunity to exercise what he calls "initiatory influence" on work diminishes. The picture is of an assembly-line form of production in which each person has a very limited task, requiring only the exercise of a few task-specific skills, and in which there is no room for better-than-average work. Either a person does his job and the assembly line proceeds at its predetermined pace, or he disrupts production and the line stops. Offe argues that because in these circumstances managers have no way of judging their subordinates' skill, all they can go by is their loyalty and reliability as manifested by the fact that they don't disrupt or sabotage the production process.[20]

This argument rests on assumptions about how the organization of work will develop in industrial societies that no longer seem very plausible. Most sociologists of work would probably agree that we are moving into a "post-Fordist" epoch in which the assembly-line model of production has largely been superseded.[21] Nevertheless, there are still many jobs in the service as well as the industrial sector to which one of Offe's points applies, namely, that all they require is minimal competence, which most people have, so that finer judgments of merit are out of place. I would concede that in the case of these jobs the merit principle applies only in attenuated form: it prohibits some ways of selecting people for employment, such as skin color or family connections, while not providing sufficient grounds for narrowing the field of applicants down to the number of positions available.[22] In such a situation all one could do is use some random device like first-come first-served and then be prepared to replace those who are not competent to hold the job.

One further observation is worth making here, namely, that it is not clear why "reliability," say, should not be taken as a legitimate qualification for routine clerical and service jobs. In the literature I am responding to, there seems to be an assumption that unless "merit" can be assessed by some mechanical means such as educational grades or typing tests, we are in the realm of subjective norms. But in the case, for instance, of a secretary, reliability in the form of good time-keeping and the conscientious completion of tasks is a large part of what competence in the job consists in; or to take another example, for a bartender honesty is of crucial importance. You can call these qualities normative if you like, but the norms in question are intimately involved in carrying out the job successfully; there is a pretty clear line dividing such behavioral attributes from other things that we might want to call norms, for instance, ideas about employees' hairstyles or other such aspects of their personal appearance, that can quite properly be dismissed as merely subjective. (I shall qualify this remark in one respect shortly.)

To show that the views I am opposing here are not merely those of straw persons, let me quote from Young:

> Even though the merit principle requires impartial technical definition of qualifications, the criteria actually used to determine qualifications tend to embody or include particular values, norms, and cultural attributes—such as whether those being evaluated behave according to cer-

tain social norms, whether they promote specifically defined organizational goals, and whether they demonstrate generally valued social competences and characteristics. Factory workers are often evaluated for their punctuality, obedience, loyalty, and positive attitude; professional workers may be evaluated for their articulateness, authoritativeness, and ability to work effectively in groups.[23]

Sensing, perhaps, that few readers will find these observations disturbing, Young continues, "Let me emphasize that using criteria such as these is not necessarily inappropriate; the point is that they are normative and cultural rather than neutrally scientific." My point is that you can call them what you like; the distinction that counts is the distinction between qualities that are relevant to the successful carrying out of a job, and qualities that are irrelevant but attached to it purely by social convention or the norms imposed by powerful superiors, such as that secretaries should be young, female, and physically attractive. It is a caricature of the merit principle to insist that it must be applied using scientific criteria, if that means confining oneself to IQ and aptitude tests and the like. The problem is that the relevant qualities that are *not* subject to scientific testing may be difficult to detect in advance, in the absence of reliable reports about previous employment. This means that more weight has to be placed on apprenticeships, trial periods, and the like, where performance can be observed directly, in the case of the jobs that fall relatively low in the organizational hierarchy.

Further up the hierarchy, both the nature of the problem and the solution change somewhat. For managerial and professional jobs, it is harder than in the case of lower-ranked jobs to identify specific skills that are needed to carry out the jobs successfully. Often a range of different qualities—technical knowledge, initiative, ability to communicate with others, and so on—will combine to make a successful professional, but these qualities are difficult to quantify independent of one another. By contrast, since there is more room for what Offe calls initiatory influence, it will often be easier to measure overall success. Performance targets can be set for individuals, and often these will be at least partly quantifiable: department heads can be assessed by the volume of business or sales that their departments generate, for instance. Here the authors I am discussing are handicapped by their assumption that individuals are no longer in any real sense exposed to market mechanisms. The current tendency, if I read the evidence right, is precisely to generate such exposure by assigning costs and profits to subunits within organizations, even perhaps to individual people. We may want to argue about the extent to which this remarketization can be real as opposed to a convenient fiction, but to the extent that it can, merit can be judged by results, and there is no need to disentangle the precise set of attributes that makes for a successful performance.

There is, however, one further issue that needs to be addressed here. In many positions the success of a person's performance will depend on the reactions of those around him or her, whether these are colleagues or clients or customers, and the problem is to decide whether these reactions are relevant to the deserts of the person in question.[24] At one extreme we can say that a friendly manner and an ability to empathize with others are legitimate assets in any circumstances in which team work is called for; in other words, it is simply a mistake to restrict merit to *technical* ability in any context in which cooperation with others is essential to getting the job done. At the other extreme, we have cases of, for example, bricklayers who won't work with women or customers who refuse to be served by blacks, and these reactions have to be seen as irrelevant since they are in direct contradiction to the principle of meritocracy itself.[25]

The difficult cases are the intermediate ones, and these tend to take the following form: a social norm is attached to the performance of the job such that although in one sense the job could perfectly well be carried out without conforming to the norm, this would run against people's expectations, which are not themselves of a discriminatory or antimeritocratic kind. Meanwhile, it is easier for some people to conform to the norm than others so that *de facto* some are "better" at the job than others when the norm is taken into account. Examples that fit this broad pattern come readily to mind. For people holding certain positions, there may be conventionally expected standards of dress, for instance, and this may pose problems for those who from personal conviction or ethnic membership wish to dress differently. Or it may be the practice in an office to retire to the pub at the end of the working day, and the camaraderie thus developed eases working relationships, but it is often hard for parents (in practice often women) with family responsibilities to take part.

These cases pose problems for the principle of merit, and I don't think it will be possible to draw a hard-and-fast line between behavior that is relevant to a particular position and behavior that isn't. What can perhaps be said is that meritocracy itself, together with cultural pluralism, will tend to erode the norms surrounding jobs by exposing individuals to a greater variety of people holding them. This will then lead to a narrower definition of merit than currently exists, one that focuses more closely on the requirements of the job itself. I am suggesting, in other words, that some of the difficulties we face in deciding what should count as merit stem from the existing significantly unmeritocratic order in which jobs tend to be reserved by informal means for particular categories of people, as a result of which norms specific to those groups get attached to the jobs. One of the side effects of moves toward equalizing opportunities for women may precisely be this narrowing down of our understanding of job-related merit. Thus here we may have a benign circle whereby moves in the direction of meritocracy make conceptions of merit more specific, thereby making it easier to move further in the same direction.

MY ARGUMENT SO FAR has sought to show that the principle of merit can be applied to men and women producing goods and services in a market setting. Let me reiterate my conviction that existing market economies still fall a good way short of meritocracy. Nor do I believe, as some have argued, that without political intervention the market itself will tend to eliminate antimeritocratic practices such as racial and sexual discrimination.[26] My positive argument can be summarized as follows: in market economies, the rewards people receive depend partly on the market itself and partly on the distributive practices of the enterprise to which they belong, with the independent producer at one end of the spectrum and the employee of a large corporation at the other. Provided that markets remain competitive, and provided that enterprise managers make a conscientious effort to assess the respective contributions of the people they employ, there is no reason these rewards should not correspond to desert in the form of productive achievement. Practical obstacles mean that the correspondence will never be exact, but the idea that *in principle* market-based activity cannot be measured by criteria of justice can be shown to be an error.

But much productive activity even in contemporary liberal societies is not market-based. People work to produce goods and services that are public (such as national defense), or that are not supplied through market transactions (such as most education). In these cases the idea that we can measure a person's contribution by using price as an indicator of the aggregate demand for his or her services cannot hold. Does this mean that we are finally in an area in which notions of merit are genuinely subjective, in the sense that it has to be left to public officials to decide how much a soldier or a teacher is "worth" in comparison with an auto mechanic or a bank clerk, for whose services the market sets a price?

This problem about public goods must be distinguished from a second problem, which has to do with activities outside of or over and above work itself that create social benefits. These are activities such as running the local Scout group in one's spare time, or offering help and advice to students in a way that goes beyond the expected role of a teacher. The contrast I am drawing here cannot be made precise, but it is the contrast between work in the public (nonmarket) sector of the economy, and socially beneficial activities that are counted not as work but as examples of good neighborliness or good citizenship. Both may be regarded as meritorious, but the problem in the first case is that we want equivalent expenditures of talent and effort in public and private sectors of the economy to be equally rewarded, whereas in the second case we are at a loss to know how to commensurate desert of this kind with economic desert. I shall leave the second problem aside for the time being, and return to it at the end of the chapter.

At first glance the solution to the first problem might seem relatively simple. A decision is reached on general policy grounds about which public goods should be provided and in what quantities; the labor market is then used to recruit people with sufficient skills to supply the goods at the level required. The price paid for labor adequately commensurates the deserts of people in the public sector with those in the private sector. At the individual level this may be sufficient. No one can accuse John of injustice if he chooses to work as a teacher for $25,000 rather than as an accountant for $30,000: if a salary of $25,000 has been (correctly) estimated as the salary needed to recruit a sufficient number of good junior teachers, and John works effectively as a junior teacher, then he deserves his pay.

But if we look at the matter more broadly, this account does not go far enough. If we dig down to discover what explains the accountant's salary, we find the market and the valuation that people generally in this society place upon an accountant's services. Beneath the teacher's salary, by contrast, lies a political decision; if the state had decided to recruit fewer teachers, or less qualified teachers, the price of teachers' labor would have dropped. Thus if we are to show that John's salary, and the salaries of people like him, are deserved from a wider social perspective, we have to ask what justifies the decision to provide goods such as education at a particular level.

This is the thorny question, familiar to economists, of how to determine the optimal supply of public goods in any society. Here I can provide only a very crude sketch of the issue.[27] To simplify matters, let's focus on public goods in the strict sense—goods such as roads, parks, and clean air that are in principle available to all members of society and that are therefore standardly funded through tax revenues. Given that the greater the revenue used to produce public goods the less remains available for private consumption, the problem is one of striking a proper balance between demands for public goods and demands for privately consumed goods and services. This problem is complicated by the fact that we would expect different people to place different values on each good—if I refuse to drive a car then roads have no direct value at all for me—while taxation cannot generally be tailored to reflect these different valuations: whether progressive or flat-rate, it has to be broadly uniform.[28] How, then, should we decide which goods to produce and in what quantity?

In accordance with my general approach, the obvious starting point is to value public goods entirely in terms of the preferences of potential consumers. Let's suppose that through surveys or in other ways we can discover how much each citizen would be prepared to pay to have a particular good supplied at different levels. Here we encounter the practical difficulty that individuals may have an incentive to overstate or understate the figure if they know that their answers are going to determine policy. But setting this to one side, assume that we can obtain genuine information about the value, expressed in monetary terms, each person derives from increasing amounts of the good. We still face the problem of how to combine these individual valuations to obtain a social valuation.

By analogy with the market case, we might think that the solution was simple aggregation: we should supply each good up to the point at which aggregate willingness to pay turns negative.[29] But whereas in market settings no one is forced to pay for a good that she doesn't want at the going price, in public-goods cases some people may be obliged to pay in taxes for goods to which they attribute little or no value (such as the nondriver forced to pay for road-building). Thus there is an issue of equity here that needs to be resolved before we can say what social value is created by someone who contributes to the production of a public good. Besides the aggregate gain in utility, some consideration must be given to the distribution of that utility among persons.[30] Assuming that the pretax distribution of income is fair, we might think that ideally everyone should gain the same amount from the bundle of public goods that is provided out of state revenues. A minimal condition is that the bundle should represent a Pareto-improvement, in the sense that public expenditure makes each citizen better off by comparison with a hypothetical situation in which no public goods of any kind are provided.

This general approach may, however, be challenged on the grounds that the value of public goods cannot be estimated solely in terms of want-satisfaction. Economists sometimes apply the term "merit goods" to goods whose value cannot be explained entirely in terms of their capacity to satisfy individual preferences.[31] But the examples that are given suggest that two quite different cases are being run together. First there is the case in which a particular good is taken to have its own intrinsic value, independent of existing human preferences. Features of the natural environment are sometimes regarded in this way, as having value independent of the satisfaction human beings derive from experiencing them (it's good that there are tigers living freely in the wild even if nobody gets pleasure from watching them). Somewhat similarly, it may be claimed that some human satisfactions are simply more valuable than others no matter what individuals prefer (watching opera is intrinsically superior to listening to rock music). Second, however, there is the quite different case in which goods are valued because of their effect on the social distribution of resources: we may value cheap public transportation, say, because we believe that it will provide worse-off people with greater opportunities for mobility. Public goods, suitably funded, may be seen as the best way to redistribute resources so as to guarantee that a range of basic needs are met.

From our perspective there is an important difference between the two cases. It does not seem justifiable for the social value of public goods to be affected directly by judgments of intrinsic value. Rather, such judgments should be seen as considerations that can be advanced politically, which if successfully done would then alter the content of people's preferences. Thus if you believe that wild tigers have intrinsic value, then you may try to persuade others that this is so; to the extent that you succeed, people will want to have tiger habitats preserved, and this becomes a genuine public good.[32] If by contrast people are not persuaded, then the judgment cannot ground any claims of justice: I cannot demand a reward for my activities in securing tiger habitats on the ground that this is a public good, any more than in market contexts I can claim rewards for making things that I judge are valuable for people to have but that they are not willing to buy.

When a "merit good" rests on a claim about distribution, however, our analysis must be quite different. For what explains the enhanced value of a public good, in these cases, is a demand of justice. Assume that physical mobility is a basic need that a society has an obligation to each of its members to meet; and assume also that the most effective way to meet this need is through a subsidized system of public transportation, which is redistributive because it is mainly used by worse-off people. Then justice requires this good to be provided, and its value cannot be arrived at merely by referring to preferences across society. Rather, it has to be assessed in terms of the urgency of the needs that it meets relative to other demands on resources.

Our original problem was how to assess the productive contribution of someone whose work consists in supplying nonmarket goods or services. What does a bus driver who drives a publicly subsidized bus justly deserve to be paid? What is now clear is that this question about desert and justice depends upon answering a prior question about justice, namely, whether the bus service in question is one that justice requires us to provide (at the current level). Although this complicates matters, it does not introduce any vicious circularity into the argument. The second question, which concerns needs, can be answered independent of the first. I want to conclude by conceding, however, that whenever someone's work involves the production of a public good, there is likely to be some indeterminacy in estimating the size of his or her contribution.

Recall the general issue being addressed here. Since meritocracy implies that people should be rewarded in proportion to their productive contribution, regardless of whether that contribution is made in a market or a nonmarket setting, we need to have some way of measuring the value created by the production of public goods. It turns out that we must first give an account of "justice in the production of public goods." We have to know what justifies taxing private consumption in order to provide public benefits like parks and sports facilities, and we also have to know when needs-based justice requires or at least allows us to supply goods such as subsidized public transportation. Unfortunately, the account is likely to be to some degree contestable. As we saw, there are different possible criteria for deciding when the supply of public goods is optimal; equally, claims that certain goods are "merit goods" because of their redistributive effects may run into controversy about what should count as "needs." Our account of justice in the production of public goods is therefore not likely to be complete. We may be able to say that some forms of provision are unquestionably just and others unquestionably unjust, but within these bounds there may be an area of uncertainty, and this will translate into uncertainty about what the people involved in supplying the goods really deserve.

In practice this means that the idea of meritocracy won't help us much in comparing societies that follow different policies in constituting their public sectors. Suppose for simplicity's sake that lawyers always work in the private sector, whereas doctors always work for public health services. Meritocracy can guide us in looking at how people are chosen to be lawyers or doctors, and at comparative pay for more senior and more junior members of both professions. But if in one society lawyers in general are paid considerably more than doctors, whereas in a second society the reverse is the case, we may not be able to make comparative judgments of (meritocratic) justice. It may be the case, in other words, that public good provision in the two societies is governed by criteria that are quite different, but in neither case demonstrably unjust. Both may be meritocracies, but meritocracies that value different services differently and reward their providers accordingly.

I HAVE BEEN DEFENDING the general claim that there is nothing about the conditions of economic life in modern societies that makes it radically impossible for people's life chances to depend on their merits. So why only two cheers for meritocracy? Since a meritocracy is a society in which people get what they deserve, why not say that meritocracy simply is the good, or at least the just, society, and that we should get as close to it as we feasibly can?

The reasons for refusing the third cheer were in part foreshadowed in the book that introduced the word "meritocracy" into the English language, Michael Young's *The Rise of the Meritocracy*, published in 1958.[33] In the course of his satire Young pointed out that when the meritocratic principle had been fully implemented, people would be socially segregated on the basis of merit, and moreover, those who found themselves in the lower ranks would no longer be able to console themselves with the thought that if they had been given a fair break they might have made something more of themselves. They deserved to be at the bottom of the heap, and equally the elite would have none of the diffidence that comes from realizing that it is good fortune as much as merit that accounts for one's position of advantage. The rank and file suffer from low self-esteem; the elite are overweening and self-satisfied.

In support of Young's critique, let us observe first that a meritocracy of the kind we have been considering inevitably picks out only one of a number of possible kinds of merit as its basis of distribution. In Young's satire, merit was defined as IQ plus effort in deference to the educational theories of his time. Nothing in the argument so far compels us to adopt such a narrow view of what merit consists in, but the point remains that in a market economy, merit will be defined in terms of someone's capacity to perform activities that yield marketable goods and services. We have seen that this definition can be extended within certain limits to cover public-sector employees. Nevertheless, there will be many activities that are generally seen as meritorious that cannot be captured in this way. Consider a dedicated teacher who takes a close interest in the lives of his or her pupils, who tries to help them when they run into personal problems, who takes time to give them career advice, and so forth. Merit of this sort cannot be measured in market terms, nor in the quasi-market terms—value-added and so forth—that schools are now being encouraged to use.

The danger inherent in meritocracy is that one dimension of merit will be given too great an emphasis, both in terms of the esteem that attaches to it, and in terms of the material rewards that it commands. Someone who has the skill to make arts and crafts, say, that people want to buy gets recognized and rewarded; someone whose skills are less tangible but from a wider social point of view just as valuable—such as the devoted teacher I referred to a moment ago—is liable to have her merits ignored. This criticism becomes more serious the greater the range of social benefits that are allocated on the basis of economic contribution. Up to now I have been talking in terms of jobs and the incomes, wages, and salaries that these command, but as we now know only too well, other benefits besides purchasing power can become income-related—the size of one's pension, one's access to medical care, and the quality of education available to one's children. If all these benefits are allocated, indirectly, on the basis of merit, then we have a system in which far too much turns on whether we happen to be constituted in such a way that we can provide the goods that the market or the state will pay us to provide. The defense of meritocracy I have been offering is severely weakened in these circumstances.

The remedy for this is twofold. First of all, and in line with the general theory of justice sketched in Chapter 2, the meritocratic allocation of jobs and rewards needs to be offset by a robust form of equal citizenship—robust in the sense that people have a strong understanding of their equality as citizens regardless of their different economic deserts, and robust in the sense that equal citizenship is the controlling principle for benefits such as health care and education. Merit of any sort should only be allowed to govern the distribution of a certain range of goods and services, and in particular not those goods and services that people regard as necessities, such as health care. Second, social relations as a whole should be constituted in such a way as to recognize and reward a plurality of different kinds of merit, so that rather than there being just a single pyramid of merit, as there is in the Young model and as there would be in a society in which economic desert counted for everything, there are several pyramids: economic contribution should count as one form of merit, education and scholarship another, artistic achievement a third, public service yet another, and so forth. If each of these carries its own mode of recompense, there may be sufficient incommensurability among the different kinds of merit that no single scale of deservingness can be constructed: we cannot rank people according to merit *tout court*. To the extent that pluralism in this sense can be achieved, the merit principle is compatible with egalitarianism of the kind advocated by Michael Walzer, according to whom equality is arrived at not by dividing all advantages up equally, but by enabling different people to excel in different social spheres.[34]

These last remarks have been somewhat sketchy. The general point is that meritocracy is acceptable when it is offset by principles and institutions of equality. There must be equal citizenship, which gives people both a social status and a range of tangible benefits that are independent of merit of any kind. And merit of one kind should be made to counterbalance merit of another, giving us a society in which Alf is recognized to be an excellent car mechanic, Bill an excellent father and neighbor, Clare an excellent scholar, and so on and so forth, but none of them is more deserving in an across-the-board sense than another, and each regards the others as fundamentally his or her equals.

There is one further respect in which merit and equality are compatible rather than competing principles. They both stand opposed to a distribution of advantages on the basis of luck. In my earlier discussion of Hayek, I conceded that in a market economy distributive outcomes would inevitably depend to some extent on chance as opposed to merit, even when we understand the latter notion in the sense I have been explaining rather than in Hayek's own rather peculiar sense. Although we cannot eliminate luck, we can try to ensure that its effects are not cumulative. In existing market economies, economic success can be consolidated through the ownership of capital, giving the person who enjoys it a built-in advantage in later rounds of the game. If we return to my earlier example of the two would-be nightclub proprietors, for several reasons the one who strikes it lucky in Oxford, say, is then better placed than his rival to open a second nightclub in Reading, and so on. Wherever success depends on luck, both the principle of merit and the principle of equality would point toward an alternative regime that would reduce the effects of luck by not allowing gains to be carried forward from one venture to the next, whether through progressive taxation or more radically through a system of property rights that excludes private ownership of enterprises.[35] From an egalitarian perspective, it is obviously desirable for chance gains to be shared as widely as possible; the point I am making is that meritocracy implies this too, because if the effects of luck are allowed to cumulate, people's rewards will depend less on their deserts than on their good or bad fortune in the early stages of the economic game.[36]

To conclude, it seems that a good deal of intellectual hostility to ideas of merit and meritocracy stems from a perception that they are anti-egalitarian, that is, we must choose between a commitment to equality and a commitment to ideas of desert and merit. In one obvious sense this is true, namely, that if we could envisage a society of simple equality in which everyone was entitled to the same bundle of goods and services, then ideas of desert and merit would become redundant, at least so far as economic and social distribution was concerned. But quite apart from the question whether this is the kind of equality that egalitarians should favor in principle, this vision is a utopian one. In technologically advanced societies there will continue to be quite substantial inequalities of reward attaching to different social positions. Against this background, the principle of merit demands first of all that these advantaged positions be fairly assigned. If we want to argue, as most of us will, that race, gender, and inherited class should play no part in determining access to these positions, then we need to appeal precisely to this principle. I doubt if even the most radical egalitarian would regard removing these crude forms of discrimination as ethically irrelevant. But beyond that, meritocracy in its full and proper sense does not have anti-egalitarian implications. If we say that a society is not fully meritocratic until all kinds of merit are recognized and rewarded in appropriate ways, then this can be used to support a Walzer-inspired conception of social equality. Indeed, Hayek may after all have been right to fear meritocracy as the harbinger of socialism.

10

"To Each According to His Needs"

In this chapter I turn from principles of merit and desert to the principle of distribution according to need as a principle of social justice. As I will argue, the principle of need remains cogent despite widespread skepticism, which chiefly takes two forms. One has to do with the concept of need itself. It is often said that "needs" are merely an arbitrarily chosen subset of wants or desires. Political spokesmen, on their own behalf or on behalf of the groups they represent, dress up their demands in the language of "need." Paternalistic bureaucrats justify overriding the preferences of those they are meant to serve by claiming that they are addressing their real needs.[1] The moral force of "needs" is here being applied rhetorically in order to advance goals that have no greater claim on our attention than any other aims or purposes that individual people might have. More generally, the charge is that "need" is a morally loaded term that masquerades as one having objective and empirical criteria of application. To cite John Gray:

> The objectivity of basic needs is . . . delusive. Needs can be given no plausible cross-cultural content, but instead are seen to vary across different moral traditions. Even where moral traditions overlap so as to allow agreement to be reached on a list of basic needs, there are no means of arriving at an agreed schedule of urgency among conflicting basic needs.[2]

Gray's remarks also introduce the second ground for skepticism. Even if needs can be identified in a reasonably uncontroversial way, what does it mean to distribute according to need? How can different needs be weighed against one another in circumstances in which there are not enough resources to satisfy all claims of this kind? If we commit ourselves to meeting needs, won't we be faced with demands that escalate without limit, particularly in the case of needs such as those for medical care?[3] How, in keeping with the principle, can we make choices about who is to have priority in such instances?

Let me say at once that our concern will be with distribution according to need as a principle of justice. This is worth emphasizing because we might also use "to each according to his needs" as a guiding rule when we are promoting other goals. If we are moved by a humanitarian concern to minimize human suffering, and we have to decide how to allocate a limited stock of resources among claimants—in a case of famine relief, for instance—we might use intensity of need as our guiding criterion. As I shall show, justice and humanity do not always run in parallel in such cases, and so we may face dilemmas in which we have to choose between treating individuals justly and following policies that, on humanitarian grounds, have the best results overall. But for the moment the point to bear in mind is that we are trying to see how "to each according to his needs" might be construed so as to serve as a principle of social justice.

This might seem to beg an important question. After all, it is a matter of some controversy in political philosophy whether the need principle is a principle of justice. This issue will be considered later, but for the moment we may simply take note of the fact that someone's being in need is widely regarded as grounding a claim of justice. Our first question must be whether this view is coherent: can we understand "to each according to his needs" in a way that at least potentially qualifies it to serve as a principle of justice? Having found a suitable interpretation both of the idea of need itself and of what it means to distribute *according* to need, we can then ask whether it stands up as an independent principle. Can an appeal to need ground a claim of justice *directly*? Or is it the case, as some have thought, that needs at best function indirectly here, as indicators of other factors that do directly ground claims of justice?

Regarding the need principle as (potentially) a principle of justice immediately introduces some constraints on its interpretation. One such constraint is that we want it to function in circumstances of relative scarcity, that is, in circumstances where there are fewer resources than there are individual demands waiting to be satisfied. This is not a trivial constraint. Marx, who gave the principle popular currency in *Critique of the Gotha Programme* (though he was not the first to use it) made it clear that the principle would be used in circumstances in which "the springs of co-operative wealth flow more abundantly."[4] Some have read this passage as implying a world beyond scarcity and therefore beyond justice. Clearly, if such a world could exist, familiar problems of separating needs from desires or wants and establishing priorities among needs would be bypassed. But at the same time we may be inclined to agree with Hume that in a world of abundance "the cautious, jealous virtue of justice would never once have been dreamed of."[5] My interest is in the use of the principle to establish claims of justice in circumstances where needs have to compete with other demands, and where there is no guarantee that all needs can be met. Thus the principle must be given an interpretation that allows it to deal with conflicts among different people's claims of need.[6]

A second constraint is that we want the principle to function as a social principle, meaning a principle that a society, or some smaller group within it, could use to guide its institutions. This implies that people must be able to agree about what constitutes needs and what does not, which in turn implies that there should be interpersonal criteria for deciding what counts as a need. In saying this I don't mean to suggest that disputes about needs will be easy to resolve: except in the case of very basic bodily needs, they are unlikely to be. The point is that "to each according to his needs" as a principle of social justice must embody a conception of need that is not merely idiosyncratic or confined to those who hold a particular view of the good life. Rather, it must be capable of being validated on terms that all relevant parties can agree on. There may be no such conception, but unless we can establish that there is, we shall have to join the ranks of the skeptics about need as a principle of justice.

In the analysis that follows, I shall focus on two questions. First, how should we understand "needs" if we want our conception to meet the two conditions I have just identified? What, in other words, should count as needs from the perspective of social justice? Second, what does it mean to distribute resources according to need, particularly in situations in which there are fewer resources available than are required to meet all the demands that count as needs by the criteria we have established? Does the principle suggest how conflicts should be resolved? Assuming that satisfactory answers can be found to these questions, we can then return to the broader issue of the place the needs principle should occupy in our thinking about social justice.

THE NEEDS THAT CONCERN US in this inquiry are those that in an earlier discussion I called "intrinsic" needs, and that others have called "categorical" or "fundamental" needs.[7] In particular, a distinction has to be drawn between claims of need that are merely instrumental, and those whose force depends on their being noninstrumental. If I say, "I need a car," it is open to anyone hearing me to ask, "What do you need a car for?" To this I might reply, "I need one to get to horse races on the weekends," thereby revealing that the need I was invoking was indeed merely instrumental to my goal of watching horse races. My interlocutor might then ask, "But do you need to go to the races?" and *this* question reveals the noninstrumental sense of "need." The sense of it is, "Is going to race meetings really of vital importance to you? How come?" and it is asked in a skeptical vein, because attendance at the races won't count as an intrinsic need unless some very remarkable circumstances obtain. Of course I may be able to reply to my questioner in a way that shows this need, too, to be instrumental: "There's a man who owes me a lot of money. My only chance of finding him is to go the rounds of the race tracks." But again the reply will come, "And do you really need the money?" We cannot say in advance where the chain of questions will end. The point is that the possibility of asking, in reply to "I need X in order to get Y," "But do you really need Y?" shows that our moral vocabulary contains a notion of need whose sense cannot be captured through an instrumental interpretation.[8] Moreover, it is need in this latter sense that carries independent moral force. In the case of instrumental needs, such force as they have derives from the end that is sought. If I say that I need three dollars to buy a hamburger, then the force of this claim depends entirely on how desirable it is for me to have a hamburger. The reference to need adds nothing of any weight. But if I say that a child needs to have a stable relationship with at least one adult, this does carry independent weight.

To say that in our practical discourse we recognize a categorical or intrinsic sense of need is not to justify that usage. I have not yet tried to lay down or defend the grounds for counting something as a need. What, then, do we mean when we describe someone's having X as a need in the intrinsic sense? We mean that it is necessary for that person to have X if he or she is not to be harmed. This is the analysis of need I wish to examine here.

The analysis has two parts to it. The first says that what is needed is necessary. The fact that A's having X prevents A from being harmed in some respect does not show that A needs X, for it may be possible to prevent that harm from occurring in other ways. Need refers to what is minimally necessary. A may be hungry, and cake may satisfy his hunger, but he does not need cake if bread would satisfy his hunger equally well. There may be circumstances, as Marie-Antoinette appears once to have believed, in which cake is available but not bread, in which case it would be true to say that the hungry need cake. Here cake can be called, follow-ing Garrett Thomson, a circumstantial need.[9] It is not instrumental: there is nothing that cake is needed *for*. Rather, it is that, because of the special circumstances, the generic intrinsic need for food takes the form of a specific need for cake. So when we say that what is needed is what is necessary to avoid harm, we should keep in mind that sometimes the necessity derives from general facts of the human condition (the human need for food), and sometimes from the constraints imposed by a par-ticular state of affairs (people's needs, here and now, for cake). Needs of the second sort are just a particular expression of needs of the first sort. This rather mundane point should not be confused with the much more serious question about the relativity of needs that I shall be addressing shortly.

The second part of the analysis raises more difficult issues. If we say that X is a need in that having X is necessary in order to avoid being harmed, then we have to settle what constitutes harm. This may be controversial, and reminds us of our initial anxiety that "need" may after all turn out to be a subjective term. It may be helpful here to think of judgments about harm as having three possible sources. First, there are biological or quasi-biological facts about human beings of a quite general kind that might enable us to say that the absence of certain conditions— adequate levels of vitamin C, for example—would cause a malfunction-ing of the organism. Second, there are aims and purposes specific to each individual that give rise to basic interests for that individual, and that would in turn allow us to identify as needs those conditions or resources that promoted the basic interests of each person. Thus if my ambition in life is to be a mountain climber, then boots, ropes, and oxygen equip-ment might figure among my needs. Third, there are shared social norms about what constitutes a minimally decent life for human beings, and by appealing to these norms we could define as needs those things that prevented people from slipping below this minimum. We can say that housing is a need, because our norm of a decent life excludes sleeping rough on the pavement.[10]

Which approach to harm, and thereby to need, should we take? The first route has the obvious attraction that it promises to define harm in wholly empirical terms, and to give judgments about need an unimpeachable objectivity. These are great virtues, and we should follow the route as far as it leads, but it will not lead us very far. It can enable us to identify nutritional and medical needs, but even here we may run into difficulty sooner than we think. We can show how and why diseases such as tuberculosis interfere with the natural functioning of the human organism (and therefore why there is a medical need for treatment), but how should we assess the normal span of a human life (and thus decide which life-prolonging treatments are to be counted as needs)?[11]

What we must avoid here is stretching the biological model beyond its limits and presenting as instances of "health" what may in fact be contestable ideals of human life. This is the weakness of accounts of human needs such as Abraham Maslow's that attempt to move seamlessly from biological conditions up to needs for love, creativity, and so forth, on the grounds that scientific studies of human nature can demonstrate the existence of all these "needs."[12] To avoid this we must supplement the biological approach with one of the other two approaches sketched above.

But which is to be preferred? It might seem that we should begin with individuals and their plans of life, and say that harm and need are to be judged in terms of what is necessary to carry out those plans of life.[13] There is, after all, nothing odd or unfamiliar about saying that different people have different needs. So why try to impose a uniform understanding of need on people whose purposes in life and conceptions of value may be very different?

On reflection, however, this way of understanding need has serious weaknesses. If we judge each person's needs on the basis of his or her plan of life, we may make needs dependent on the choices that people make about how to lead their lives. The problem is not that we are allowing people to define their own needs. Within the individual model, there is still room for a distinction between what people need and what they believe themselves to need: someone may be mistaken about the conditions necessary for her to fulfill her central aims and ambitions. The problem is that since needs depend on life plans, and since life plans may depend on choices, the needs principle will commit us to giving resources to people because of choices they have made, whereas with different choices their demands would have been fewer. Someone whose plan of life centers around creating monumental sculptures in bronze will have costly needs, whereas if that person had chosen to paint water-colors instead his needs would be far cheaper to fulfill. This is a serious objection if we want to treat the needs principle as a principle of justice, giving rise to obligations on others to meet the needs of the person in question. We may well believe, in line with much recent liberal thought,[14] that people should be held responsible for the choices they make about their aims of life, so that no demands of justice can stem directly from such choices.[15]

Even if people's plans of life are unchosen, we may still be reluctant to identify their needs with reference to those plans. Suppose someone has been reared in a social milieu that attaches great importance to a costly activity such as polo playing, and that this becomes his central passion. It may be wrong to say that he has chosen this way of life. Nevertheless, we may understandably be reluctant to define his needs by reference to such a contingency. Perhaps he should be encouraged to find his fulfillment in something else and to regard polo playing as a minor hobby. If he was first socialized in one way, why can't he now be socialized in another? If we take on a commitment to distributing (some) resources according to need, aren't we entitled to ask people to alter their plans of life so that their (individually defined) needs become less costly to fulfill?

The force of these questions, together with my earlier argument about need and personal choice, compels us to abandon a conception of need that defines it in terms of individual life plans.[16] The problem is not merely that needs so defined will be very extensive, or that disputes about need will be hard to settle (because they will turn on whether having X is essential to avoiding a blighted life); it is also that needs so defined seem not to ground claims of *justice* made against other people, once we recognize the contingent and alterable nature of life plans. To put it another way, what seems to be missing here is the idea that my aims and ambitions have first to be *validated* to other members of the relevant community before they will count the needs that arise from those aims and ambitions as imposing obligations on them to provide resources.

This suggests that we should take up the third route, identifying needs over and above the biological minimum by reference to shared social norms. Here the claim is that within each community there will be a shared conception of the range of activities that together make up a normal human life. Following a suggestion of Amartya Sen's, we might think of these as a set of functionings that each person is expected to be able to perform.[17] Thus we may believe that each person should be able to read and write, to move around physically, to hold a job, to marry and raise a family, and so forth. Anyone who is prevented by lack of resources from functioning in one or more of these ways will to that extent be judged to be in need.[18] This does not imply that each person must want to engage in the whole range of functionings: someone may prefer not to marry or to raise a family. Need is judged in terms of capacity to function in a variety of ways, not in terms of an individual's choice about whether to exercise a particular capacity.

In introducing this way of understanding "need," I said that needs could be identified as those conditions that allowed people to lead a minimally decent life in their society. This reference to "decency" needs explaining. It is intended to pick up Adam Smith's well-known remark that "necessaries" should be understood to comprise "not only the commodities which are indispensably necessary for the support of life, but whatever the custom of the country renders it indecent for creditable people, even of the lowest order, to be without."[19] Smith gave as contemporary examples linen shirts and leather shoes. Without these, he said, no one could appear in public without disgrace. This links clearly to the functionings approach to harm, because if one cannot enter public space without shame, a whole range of activities from work to recreation to political participation will be inaccessible, or accessible only on pain of great discomfort. So when we judge people's needs by reference to their capacity to function in socially recognized ways, we must consider not only impediments that are strictly physical but also social impediments such as those highlighted by Smith. A laborer in Smith's day didn't need a linen shirt in the same way that he needed food and shelter, but he needed it nonetheless.

It may seem that this way of understanding need is insufficiently sensitive to individual differences. Let me indicate some ways in which it is not. First, it should be obvious that each person's concrete needs will differ from everyone else's even though we are judging them all in terms of the same functionings. The specific educational resources that I require to achieve basic literacy won't be the same as the resources you require. Second, the functionings we use to define needs are only a small subset of the functionings that people will actually be able to perform in any society but the poorest. We define needs by reference to a minimal standard of life, and people will have choices to make over and above this minimum about how to lead their lives. Third, people are not forced to use what they are judged to need if they really find no value in a certain functioning; to use one of Sen's examples, the fact that having an adequately nourished body is one of the functionings that defines needs does not prevent someone from fasting voluntarily on religious or other grounds.[20]

This last example does, however, introduce a possible objection to the analysis of need I am proposing. Suppose that someone's plan of life or conception of the good is such that he attaches no value to a particular functioning, but does value an activity not on the social list that is no more costly to undertake. Suppose that a religious ascetic is content with a nomadic existence (and so has no self-ascribed need for housing), but claims that the resources that would have provided him with shelter at a minimal level should instead be used to supply him with devotional tracts. Why should he not claim these as things that he needs?

The answer is that someone's preferences, no matter how strong, cannot ground claims of need. The ascetic's willingness to forgo shelter in favor of religious tracts testifies to the importance he places on having the tracts, but it does not show that he will be harmed by not having them, at least according to the understanding of harm that prevails in his community. The strength of his desire cannot impose obligations of justice on others, given that they do not regard the unavailability of tracts as harmful.[21] This becomes very clear if we think not of categorical needs, as we have been up to now, but of the functional needs that arise in a purposive community. My college makes available a fairly generous annual allowance to be used for the purchase of computer equipment. Because my computer needs are rudimentary, I use only a small part of the allowance. I might try to argue that the balance should be paid to me in cash to help me pursue my passion for yachting. This argument would rightly receive short shrift. The allowance is given because academics need computers; it is given to meet that need, which is related to the purpose of the community. The slenderness of my particular need is good news for the college's budget, but it doesn't give me any compensating claims.

In saying that needs above the biological minimum have to be defined in terms of social norms about what constitutes a minimally decent life, I am conceding that definitions of need will vary from place to place as these norms vary. In the example of the religious ascetic I took it for granted that spiritual "needs" did not count as such, but plainly many societies have seen religious observance as an essential functioning and interpreted needs accordingly.[22] This sets limits to the objectivity of needs, but again it is important not to exaggerate the significance of this point. It does not entail that a society's operative definition of need is unchallengeable. For instance, a society may attach central importance to a particular activity, but then deny that one section of its members— women, say—has needs that relate to that activity. Here one could mount an argument that women are harmed by their inability to engage in the activity in question, and thereby argue for a reassessment of their needs. (In contemporary liberal societies we can argue in this way that women need jobs, as well as the education and training that give access to jobs.) Nor does it entail that needs have to be understood in relation to current levels of provision; a society's economy may be incapable of producing sufficient resources to meet all those needs that derive from its understanding of a minimally decent life, but that does not give grounds for revising the set of needs downward.[23]

All political concepts are shaped by background assumptions about what gives value to human lives, and to that extent they are not objective in the way that scientific concepts are. "Need" is no exception. But it is not clear why this should create a problem. Within a political community it will be possible to give interpersonally valid reasons for treating some demands, and not others, as needs, and this may give us a sufficient degree of objectivity. Critics allege that if we regard needs as culturally determined, we can no longer appeal to "need" in critical fashion, to condemn local practices or to underline the obligations that citizens of rich countries have toward poor countries.[24] But this does not follow. If A's needs are not met, A is harmed: he cannot live a minimally decent life in the society to which he belongs. That "harm" and "need" have to be understood, once we move beyond the biological minimum, by reference to the norms of that society does not weaken the force of that claim. The criticism I am considering overlooks our capacity to recognize and acknowledge harm even when we do not ourselves subscribe to the norms in question. I may lack any religious commitments, but I can understand what it means to be a religious outcast in a society in which religion plays a central role in everyday life. I can see why someone in this position is harmed, and why a society that permits deprivation of this kind is unjust. To the extent that I acknowledge an obligation to meet the needs of those outside my own community, these needs will count for me.[25]

For the purposes of the present discussion, let's note that for "to each according to his needs" to be a workable principle of justice, we require agreement about need only within the community that wishes to implement the principle. The interpretation I have given—not neglecting the biological core of "need," but emphasizing the social understanding of a minimally decent life that fills in the periphery—meets this requirement.

MOST DISCUSSION OF THE PRINCIPLE that this chapter is addressing has focused on the meaning and objectivity of "need." But there are just as many difficult issues involved in deciding what it means to *distribute according to* need. This would not be a problem in cases where the resources we have available are adequate to meet all the needs of the relevant set of claimants. In those cases the principle simply tells us to give each person whatever quantity of resources is sufficient to meet his or her need. But, as indicated, if we want to use the principle as a principle of justice, we also have to be able to apply it in situations of scarcity, when the resources we have cannot meet everyone's needs in full. This might be because there are just not enough resources available in our community; or it might be because there are conflicting demands on these resources. Besides meeting needs, we are called upon to recognize desert, or to invest in productive capital, or to protect the environment. It is not obvious that claims of need must always take precedence over these other demands; it will depend upon their urgency. So let us consider the case where we have, so to speak, a limited budget available for meeting needs and where there are more claims on the budget than we are able to fulfill.

One problem that arises here is that of weighing needs of different kinds against one another. A minimal requirement of justice would seem to be that if two people are equally needy they should be treated in the same way, but even this requires us to construct an index of need. Suppose A needs medical aid while B needs housing: how should we judge who has the greater needs? In accordance with the analysis presented earlier in the chapter, we would have to compare the functionings that A and B cannot perform because of their unfulfilled needs, but these functionings may be valued differently. Is it worse to have to live with the rest of your family in a one-room apartment than to suffer from chronic bronchitis, say? Perhaps, as Sen suggests in his discussion of functionings, the most we can hope for are partial orderings: even if we cannot say whether A or B is in greater need, we may be able to say that C, who lives in a two-bedroom apartment and suffers only from hayfever, is less needy than either.[26]

Let's leave that problem aside and consider cases in which we are dealing with needs that are all of one type and that are commensurable, so that we can place people on a scale in terms of their respective degrees of neediness. We might think of the allocation of medical resources among people who will suffer different degrees of bodily impairment if they do not receive the resources. This is admittedly a gross simplification, but unless we can attach a clear meaning to the principle in simple cases it will be virtually useless in more complicated ones. So let us suppose that for each person in need, we can find a number that represents the extent of his or her need—the greater the number, the greater the need. What does "to each according to his needs" mean if we cannot reach an outcome in which everyone's score is reduced to zero (which is another way of saying that we are assuming scarcity)?

Our first thought might be that we should distribute resources *in proportion to* need. If A scores −50 on the scale of need while B scores only −10, then A should receive five time as many resources as B.[27] We total up everyone's claims and then divide resources according to the fraction of the total that each person's claim represents. This would make the need principle a mirror image of the principle of desert, as applied, say, in cases where the income of a firm has to be shared among its employees in proportion to productive contribution. Here we would calculate each person's contribution as a fraction of the total, and then assign her that fraction of the firm's net profit.

But this interpretation of the need principle is challengeable. It faces two main objections. First, it distributes resources according to the degree of need that each person is in to start with, but it does not consider what effect the resources have on that need—it does not consider where people end up as a result of having their proportional share. Even though A receives five times as many resources as B, it may be that (for reasons peculiar to A or for general reasons having to do with the qualitative character of A's need) A moves only a small way up the scale as a result of having the resources, whereas B moves right to zero. We could adjust the principle to meet this objection. We could say that resources should be distributed in such a way that everyone enjoys the same proportionate increase in the capacity to function. If A's position improves from -50 to -25, then B's should improve from -10 to -5. This requires a more complex calculation than the unadjusted version of the principle, but it seems better to capture the idea that in cases of scarcity, we should distribute resources in proportion to need. Someone who favored that idea would, I think, mean that everyone's needs should be satisfied to the same (proportional) extent.

Even with the adjustment, however, we face a second objection. Does the principle so interpreted give sufficient weight to A's greater need? Suppose the two scores are measuring something like a nutritional deficiency. Instead of splitting resources between A and B, shouldn't we give priority to A until his level of deficiency has also been reduced to -10 (and if we still have food to distribute, then divide it between them in whatever way keeps their scores rising equally)? How can it be fair to A to do anything for B while A remains in a worse position still? These questions suggest that the correct interpretation of the need principle is one of strict priority for the most needy. We distribute according to need by going to the most needy first, helping them until their needs are no more urgent than the next group's, then addressing the remaining needs of both groups, and so on until our resources are exhausted.

The strict priority view faces a challenge posed by the practice of triage.[28] This is the practice, originating with military doctors, of dividing battle casualties into three categories: those who are so severely wounded that their chances of recovery are slight even with extensive medical treatment; those who are badly injured but who with limited medical resources can be saved and returned to active service; and those who will recover in due course without treatment. Under triage the second group is given priority even though their needs are not as great as the first group's (measured by distance from normal functioning). If time or resources run out, the most severely injured are left to die. Similar policies have been advocated and practiced outside of military contexts, for instance, in deciding who should receive scarce medical treatment such as hemodialysis or in coping with the effects of natural disasters such as earthquakes.[29]

It might seem that triage reflects a concern for efficiency rather than for justice, and indeed this appears to have been what lay behind the original practice; triage was justified as the most effective way of getting as many soldiers quickly back into active service as possible. In its more general setting, triage is defended as the way to achieve the greatest possible saving of life. But we still need to ask whether triage is always unjust, as the strict priority view would suggest.

Here we must begin by defining the problem more precisely. There is some ambiguity—perhaps a deliberate ambiguity—in common definitions of triage about whether category 1 casualties or victims are those who will eventually die no matter what is done, or whether they are those who may live, but only if considerable resources are expended on them.[30] On the first interpretation they would not seem to have any claim of justice on medical resources; "to each according to his needs" does not require me to give resources to people who cannot make use of those resources, even though their general condition is one of need.[31] The problem arises on the second interpretation. Suppose that with extensive intervention A's life could be saved and he could be restored to partial functioning. He could, let us say, be raised from -100 to -50 on the medical scale. For the same expenditure of time and resources, five individuals in category 2 could be restored to full functioning. B, C, D, E, and F can each be raised from -50 to 0 on the same scale. The strict priority view tells us to treat A. But is this the best interpretation of "to each according to his needs"?

The counterargument might be put in this way. The principle is supposed to serve as a principle of justice. As such it has to consider the potential claims of everyone who falls within its ambit. In the present case, these claims are claims of need. It is an injustice if, avoidably, some are in need and others are not (if everyone is unavoidably in need to the same extent, this may be regrettable but there is no injustice: no one thinks it unjust if the only available loaf of bread is shared equally among ten hungry people, even though this still leaves each of them somewhat hungry). The strict priority view pays lop-sided attention to those in the worst-off category (to A in our example); it considers the injustice in A's being left needier than everyone else, but it fails to consider the injustice in the fact that B-F are left needier than everyone else bar A. It doesn't weigh the injustices against one another as they should be weighed, and so it is unfair to the people in category 2 whose claims are set aside in favor of A's.

But what more positive principle of justice does this counterargument suggest? We are facing a situation in which because of resource constraints we cannot achieve a perfectly just outcome. Someone is going to have needs that are met less fully than those of others. Since perfect justice is unattainable, we should adopt the policy that minimizes the injustice in the final outcome. To measure injustice, we look at each person's position on the scale of unmet needs. Whenever two people have different scores on that scale—a difference we are assuming is removable—there is to that extent an injustice. In order to compute the overall degree of injustice, we need to invoke a measure of inequality: given several arrays of scores on the scale of need, we have to be able to say which is the most equal. Unfortunately, there are several such measures to choose from, each with some degree of plausibility, and this is not the place to try to adjudicate among them.[32] For the sake of argument, let us assume that the degree of inequality in a distribution is best measured by summing up the differences between each pair of individuals.[33] That is, we take the difference between A's score and B's, add to it the difference between B's and C's, add to that the difference between A's and C's, and so on. Whichever distribution yields the lowest sum total of differences is judged to be the most equal and therefore, in this context, the fairest.

In the case we are looking at, we first need to define the relevant community within which our principle of justice will be applied. Suppose that this community is the platoon that comprises A, B-F, and four other individuals, G-K, who have escaped injury in the preceding battle. As before, we have to choose between treating A and treating B-F. If we treat A, we eliminate the inequality between him and B-F by raising him to -50, and we reduce by half the inequality between him and G-K. If we treat B-F, we eliminate the inequality between them and G-K by raising them to 0, but at the same time we increase by a factor of 2 the inequality between them and A. If the resulting total is smaller in the second case, the triage policy is justified. We set the injustice involved in leaving A severely injured when we could help him somewhat against the injustice involved in leaving B-F less severely hurt when we could restore them to full functioning, and we choose the lesser injustice.

Note that this principle is not the same as the principle of minimizing neediness. The latter principle tells us to adopt whichever policy meets most needs in the aggregate; it is a humanitarian principle. In the case we are discussing this principle would straightforwardly favor treating B-F, since this would reduce aggregate need by $5 \times 50 = 250$, whereas treating A would reduce aggregate need by only 50. The principle of justice I am elaborating tells us to look at *differences* in unmet need; it tells us to look at where each person ends up *relative to others* on the scale of need. The calculation is a more complicated one than that involved in minimizing neediness. We start with individuals whose needs are as follows:

A	B	C	D	E	F	G	I	J	K
−100	−50	−50	−50	−50	−50	0	0	0	0

If we treat A we reach the following outcome:

A	B	C	D	E	F	G	I	J	K
−50	−50	−50	−50	−50	−50	0	0	0	0

(overall inequality in need-fulfillment 1,500)

If we treat B-F the outcome is as follows:

A	B	C	D	E	F	G	I	J	K
−100	0	0	0	0	0	0	0	0	0

(overall inequality in need-fulfillment 1,000)

Thus in this case "to each according to his needs" favors the second option, the policy of triage, in line with the humanitarian principle of minimizing neediness and in opposition to the principle of strict priority to the worst-off. But this won't always be the case. If we change the example so that B falls into the severely wounded category (that is, his score is initially −100), and we have to choose between raising A and B to −50 and fully repairing C, D, E, and F, a similar calculation shows that our principle now favors treating A and B, this time in opposition to the humanitarian principle. So whereas humanitarian considerations will usually favor triage (because the resources we devote to category 2 victims produce a much greater effect in terms of reducing need than resources devoted to the other victims), and whereas strict priority always disallows it, the need principle is more discriminating; it gives suitable weight to those who because of extensive needs are furthest from the norm (in this case full bodily functioning), but it is also sensitive to changes in the position of those who are closer to the norm.

But now we must consider two apparently serious objections to the principle as I have stated it. The first is that the policy that justice recommends is sensitive to changes in the number of people who are not themselves in need: if instead of G-K our platoon contains only one uninjured soldier, G, then, as a quick calculation will show, the need principle now recommends treating A instead of B-F. But how, it may be asked, can the justice of treating one seriously injured person instead of five who are less seriously wounded be affected by the presence or absence of others who are fully fit? In reply, let me say first that such results depend partly on the particular measure of need-inequality that I have chosen to use, which may not always capture exactly our intuitive sense of the relative degree of inequality in different distributions.[34] But second, it does not seem irrelevant in comparing the justice of two outcomes to look at the relative position of everyone falling within the universe of distribution. We should assess not merely the claims of A vis-à-vis B, C, and D, but the claims of each of them against G, H, I, and so on. The more people who fall into this last category, the more often will B be able to say, truly, "If you compare me with X, it's unfair that he is fit while I am left without medical attention." This is a morally relevant claim for B to make, and so it does not seem absurd that the overall strength of B's claim as compared with A's should depend on the number and relative standing of other members of the group being considered.

This, however, leads us into the second objection. If injustice is reduced to zero when people end up at the same relative point on the scale of need, then this appears to recommend lowering the position of some if this turns out to be the best way to achieve an equal position. Given that we cannot raise everyone's position to 0, should we not contemplate treating A and then lowering the position of G-K to −50? This would seem to ensure perfect justice. In the case as described this would mean inflicting injuries on G-K, and it might seem that this is ruled out by some independent principle prohibiting the deliberate infliction of harm. But alter the case and this line of defense vanishes. If I have to allocate food supplies during a famine, and for some reason I cannot distribute all the available food so as to achieve equal fulfillment of need, does justice not require me to withhold or destroy that part of the supply that cannot be so distributed?

There may be circumstances in which this is indeed what justice requires. Suppose it is necessary to impose a waiting time for a minor operation: it may seem fairer that everyone should have to wait for the same length of time than that some should wait for this time and some for less (to the extent that we favor the second option, it appears as though humanitarian or utilitarian considerations are displacing justice). But we are not likely to say the same when a policy of strict equality in meeting needs begins to impose real costs on those who otherwise might have escaped them. It seems *unfair* to leave some people in need just because we cannot provide the same relief for everyone.

This suggests that "to each according to his needs" actually comprises two separate injunctions. First, there is the injunction to help those who are in need. This is violated by the person who destroys resources or refuses to use them to help anyone—the doctor who turns his back on an injured patient, for example. Second, there is the injunction that the treatment given to each person should depend on his or her particular need, which as we have seen is best understood as an injunction to equalize scores on the scale of need. This is violated by the person who uses resources to meet needs but fails to consider properly the strength of different claims—the doctor who expends all the available resource on a single patient, for example. Happily, these two injunctions will often point in the same direction. But sometimes they will not: where resources are indivisible, for instance, we may have to choose between assigning them in a way that is distributively unfair—because people with equally strong claims cannot be treated in the same way—and withholding them altogether.

This shows that the contrast between *comparative* and *noncomparative* justice that we noticed in our discussion of desert also applies to the principle of need. Someone who withholds resources that might be used to meet needs inflicts a noncomparative injustice on those who might have been given relief. Someone who makes sure that every available resource is used to meet a need but doesn't weigh equally the claims of those who might be helped inflicts a comparative injustice on those who get less than their fair share.[35] There is no algorithm for deciding which form of justice should take priority in cases of conflict. Someone who wishes to apply the principle of need in such cases has simply to weigh one kind of injustice against the other and choose the course of action that seems least unjust.

One way to soften the conflict between the two kinds of justice in difficult cases is to invoke procedural justice. Suppose there is a single kidney available and several people in need of one, but no way of discriminating among them—their need is the same. Whomever we choose, there will be a comparative injustice. But to discard the kidney for that reason would be seriously unjust in a noncomparative sense. So we might apply a fair procedure: we might conduct a lottery among the patients, or we might try to resolve the dilemma by obtaining consent—it may be that the patients themselves could agree on a criterion other than medical need to break the deadlock. This does not obliterate the comparative injustice of the outcome, but it offsets it to some degree.

We have found that distribution according to need is a complex matter. The original sponsors of the principle envisaged a happy state of affairs when all needs could be met. I have been exploring what the principle must mean in circumstances of scarcity. As we saw, when goods are fully divisible and transferable, it tells us to get people as close as possible to one another's position on the scale of need: if my needs are half-satisfied, so should yours be. Usually this will mean giving priority to those whose needs are greatest, but, as our discussion of triage showed, not always. Difficult problems arise when resources are not fully divisible or transferable. Here we may have to choose between meeting needs equally (comparative justice) and not wasting or withholding need-satisfying resources (noncomparative justice). Our decision will depend on the absolute magnitude of the cost involved in withholding the resource. Wherever the cost is high, we should look for a fair procedure for assigning the resource. In this way, though we cannot treat everyone's needs equally as the principle ideally requires, we can at least show everyone a form of equal respect.[36]

HAVING NOW ANALYZED the two components of the principle we are considering—what "need" means and what it means to distribute *according to* need—I want to ask whether it is indeed a principle of justice. More precisely, I shall consider some reasons that have been offered for thinking it is not. I approach the question in this indirect way because I do not know what could be said to someone who claims that need has nothing to do with justice, or to put the point more precisely, that if justice involves rendering to each person his or her due, need is plainly irrelevant to deciding what this "due" consists in. The critics I shall be considering do not claim this; they admit that "need" is commonly invoked in debates about social justice, and in that sense is *prima facie* a relevant criterion. But they argue that its status in those debates is derivative rather than basic. We can appeal to "need" not directly to ground a claim of justice, but only in order to indicate, for instance, that people have not been given what they deserve, or that the rules of some agreed practice have been breached.

The critics' position can be put as follows.[37] The relief of need is a powerful moral imperative, but it is an imperative of benevolence or humanity rather than of justice. Justice, by contrast, has fundamentally to do with the requital of desert; in a secondary sense it has to do with keeping agreements, applying rules consistently and evenhandedly, and so forth. So when it is claimed that some institution or policy is justified because it distributes resources to people according to their needs, there are two possible ways of understanding the claim: either it is a straightforward appeal to a humanitarian principle that tells us to relieve neediness, or it is a roundabout appeal to justice, in either its desert-based or its procedural form. Bare needs, needs detached from desert or existing agreements or some such special circumstance, give rise only to humanitarian obligations.

Let me start by asking how "to each according to his needs" might be regarded as a humanitarian principle. Humanitarianism is not a precise idea, but as an opening definition we might say that the principle of humanity tells us to relieve the suffering and distress of those we are able to help. It seems to follow that we should allocate our resources according to need, because someone who is in need will suffer as a result, and the greater the need, the greater that person's suffering is likely to be. Hence as humanitarians we should be concerned not only with the fact of need but also with the extent of need, and "to each according to his needs" as a distributive rule follows naturally.

But now consider two major difficulties with this argument. If we interpret obligations of humanity as obligations to relieve suffering, then it seems that what should count is actual felt suffering, the misery of the person who is starving or in pain. But the extent to which people suffer does not always correlate with the extent of their need. Someone who is badly deprived may not suffer to any great extent (because of a stoical temperament, or because her only experience has been one of deprivation).[38] Thus if we acknowledge an obligation to meet needs that is independent of the subjective state of the person who has the need, this cannot be an obligation of humanity or benevolence in the usual sense. But it is plausibly seen as an obligation of justice, for as I have argued throughout this book, justice has to do with the fair allocation of resources to individuals, and not with the subjective sense of satisfaction or relief that any particular individual may get from having those resources.

One might of course attempt to redefine humanitarianism so that its aim became the prevention of *harm* rather than suffering. This seems to me to run counter to the core moral intuition that the principle of humanity expresses—that whenever we are confronted with human distress, our common humanity tells us that we should try to relieve it—but a redefinition of this kind might link humanitarianism more closely to the meeting of needs. But now we come to the second objection. If our humanitarian obligation is to relieve suffering or deprivation, we should relieve as much suffering or deprivation as possible with the resources at our disposal. This does not, however, always mean providing most to those whose suffering or deprivation is greatest, as our discussion of triage showed. The humanitarian principle is most naturally construed as aggregative in form—it tells us to minimize the sum total of suffering or deprivation. Sometimes the way to do this will be to help those who are not badly off in comparison with others, but who can benefit most from the resources we have available.

Tom Campbell has replied to this objection in the following terms:

> Humanity does not require us simply to relieve the sum total of suffering, but to relieve the suffering of individual human beings and the obligation is greatest where the suffering is greatest, in that the person who is suffering most has first claim on the available resources. That is, beneficence as embodied in the principles of negative utilitarianism embodies the distributive principle that those in greatest need ought to receive most assistance or, more specifically, that aid should be in proportion to need.[39]

This formulation is not entirely clear (the reference to negative utilitarianism muddies the water), but it can be read as putting forward what we may call a weighted priority principle.[40] A principle of this kind tells us to weight improvements in people's positions according to how badly off they are to begin with, so that, to revert to the terminology used earlier, raising one person from −80 to −50 counts for more than raising another person from −40 to −10. The actual improvement, whether measured in terms of relief of suffering or meeting of need, is the same in both cases, but we attach greater moral weight to improving the position of someone who is initially worse off. Depending on the size of the weighting factor, our obligation might be to raise one person from −80 to −50 in preference to two from −40 to −10.

Weighted priority principles are formally coherent in the sense that applying them will give us clear and consistent solutions to practical dilemmas such as those I have been considering. But can they be given a coherent justification? Giving priority to those who are worse off is a good rule of thumb because of the diminishing marginal utility of resources: in general, we meet more needs by concentrating our efforts on those who are in greatest need to begin with. But does our humanitarian concern justify giving extra weight to the worse-off over and above this effect of diminishing marginal utility? If humanitarian principles stem from our sympathetic response to the deprivation or suffering of others, doesn't it follow that we should give equal weight to every unit of need met or suffering relieved?

Thomas Nagel, who defends a weighted principle in *Equality and Partiality*, claims that the weighting follows when, instead of comparing people's positions in the aggregate, we try to put ourselves into each person's shoes in turn.[41] I find it mysterious how this different description of the impartial standpoint can make any difference to the outcome; even if we consider people's lives one at a time, we still have to perform an aggregation of some kind to arrive at a practical recommendation. What in fact drives Nagel's intuitions in the direction of a weighted priority principle, I believe, is a sense of fairness: a sense that it is unfair if the worst-off are left to suffer because we can do more good by concentrating our resources on the less needy. If that is so, the weighted principle cannot be treated as fundamental. Rather, it represents a compromise between our concern for comparative justice—our concern with reducing or if possible eliminating inequalities in the extent to which different people's needs are met—and our concern for overall efficiency when resources are deployed to fulfill needs. Whatever the principle's merits, it cannot be represented as simply the best expression of humanitarian concern for the needy. It must be motivated in addition by independent beliefs about justice.

It seems to me doubtful, however, whether a weighted priority principle can fully capture our ethical responses to those in need. A principle of this kind must always favor improving one person's position even if this results in increased inequality between her and others. If A, B, C, and D are each at -10, and the only possibility open to us is to raise A to -5 or leave things as they stand, the principle tells us to raise A. But as my earlier discussion suggested, situations of this kind reveal a conflict between comparative and noncomparative justice, and sometimes comparative justice should win out.[42] In a fuel shortage it may be fairer (and better overall) to ration fuel equally than to give extra fuel to a few. If we believe (as I do) that there are cases of this kind, then we should simply acknowledge the internal complexity of "to each according to his needs," rather than try to reduce it to a single weighted priority principle.

To those who want to treat claims of need as humanitarian, my answer therefore is (a) that I cannot see why humanitarian principles should attach greater intrinsic moral weight to the claims of those in greater need; (b) that principles which do this—weighted priority principles— are best seen as expressing a compromise between different moral imperatives; and (c) that the compromise so expressed is not fully satisfactory, for it fails to capture the overriding force, in some situations, of comparative justice.

I turn next to the argument that claims of need, when they are relevant to justice, are parasitic on other claims, such as claims of entitlement or desert. It would be absurd to deny that need claims are sometimes parasitic in this way. To use John Lucas's example, in a Mutual Insurance Society "we may make it an explicit principle of our community that need shall be a ground of apportionment, and then of course justice will require that each man shall receive what he needs, in the same way as under a legal system justice requires that each man shall have his legal due."[43] Need counts here because members of the society have agreed that it should count. Lucas believes that "the same principle governs the National Health Service and various other aspects of the Welfare State."[44]

But we must look more closely at the reason need is chosen as the ground of distribution in such societies. There seem to be two possible answers. One is that distribution according to need is seen as the *fair* way to apportion whatever benefit the society is set up to provide: we choose need rather than some other criterion because we regard it as the fair criterion. But if this is so, then "to each according to his needs" is seen as a principle of justice prior to its incorporation in the insurance scheme: the scheme simply formalizes what the members see as independently fair. The second possibility is that the need principle is chosen for reasons having nothing directly to do with justice, for instance, out of rational self-interest. If we belong to a group whose members all face the possibility of being injured at work, but nobody knows where the blow will fall, it may be in our interests to contribute to a need-based scheme. But this depends on very specific circumstances, in particular on our believing the chances that any one member of the scheme will find him- or herself in need to be roughly equal. Remove this perceived equality of risk, and the rationale for a need-based scheme disappears.

If we take an institution such as a national health service and ask what lies behind its taking the form that it does, the answer will have to draw on both the suggestions in the last paragraph. To some extent people endorse and support the National Health Service (in the British case, for instance) because they are uncertain what their future health needs will turn out to be; but, given that the Health Service also covers people whose needs can be anticipated in advance—the congenitally disabled, for instance—they also support it because they believe that it rests upon a principle that is fair. Without the second source of support, we would expect to find people preferring separate health insurance schemes for those with different levels of risk.[45] Thus to sum up, although need undoubtedly becomes a formal criterion of justice in mutual insurance schemes and the like, we cannot (in general) understand the shape those schemes take unless we recognize distribution according to need as having independent force for the participants.

What of the suggestion that when need claims are claims of justice, they are always parasitic on claims of desert? Campbell lists a number of possible circumstances in which this dependency might obtain: someone may experience need as a result of his or her own meritorious behavior, or as a result of blameworthy behavior on the part of another (say, in cases of exploitation); someone's being in need may indicate that the general distribution of social benefits does not properly reflect desert; or a condition of need may be an obstacle to equality of opportunity, and therefore to people's getting what they deserve in the future (a child who needs education but doesn't get it won't have the job opportunities that he or she deserves). In all such cases, he argues, we point to needs in order to indicate that people have not received, or will not receive, the benefits they deserve, and it is the latter claim that gives our argument the force of justice.

Once again we should recognize the partial truth in this argument: sometimes we are required to meet needs in order to requite desert, and indeed in societies in which desert principles play a central role in thinking about justice, the most effective way of advancing claims of need may often be to link them to claims of desert.[46] If we want to defend social benefits for the unemployed, for instance, then rather than putting forward claims based solely on need, we should in many cases underline the social contribution that unemployed people have made and may make again in the future.

The question remains whether all claims of need that we see as justice-related can be interpreted in this way. Suppose an elderly woman develops arthritis and needs a hip replacement. Resources permitting, we may think she has a just claim to one. There is no connection between her condition and any service she has rendered or any injury she has suffered at the hands of another: the arthritis is simply the result of the body's aging. The woman has not, in general, received less than her fair share of benefits; and since she has passed the age of retirement, no question of future opportunities arises.[47] It therefore seems that the claim is simply one of need and not one of desert. Of course, we might be tempted to point out in support of the claim that the person in question has contributed through taxes to the funding of the health service. But this would establish no special claim of desert; it would merely serve as a reminder that the scheme operates according to the principle "from each according to his ability, to each according to his need." If desert counted in cases like this, then we ought to establish an order of priority among arthritis sufferers according to their various degrees of merit. But in fact this would be widely regarded as repugnant. What should count is the severity of the arthritis and the likelihood of the hip replacement's being successful.[48]

If such examples are convincing, the need principle stands independent of principles of desert. But what of cases in which people have brought their needs on themselves, for instance, the heavy smoker who develops lung cancer from that cause? Don't we feel that these cases are undeserving, and that it is only humanity, rather than justice, that prompts us to meet needs in such circumstances?[49]

Cases of this sort do not show that need claims depend on desert claims; they do nothing to undermine the argument about the arthritis sufferer. What they do show is that our obligation of justice to meet needs may be subject to a responsibility condition. At one level this is obvious enough. If we provide someone with the resources that he needs, and he then promptly wastes them, we do not, in general, have a further obligation to replace what has been squandered. We expect someone to exercise common diligence in using the medicine supplied, in eking out limited supplies of food, and so forth. This can be extended to behavior that prevents needs from arising in the first place: we think differently about a farmer whose crops are devastated by drought despite his best efforts than about a farmer who loses his crops because he fails to take elementary precautions against the weather. We may not recognize that the second farmer has a just claim against us. We might express this difference by saying of the second farmer, "He doesn't deserve to be helped." This doesn't, however, show that the first farmer's claim is one of desert; it is a claim of need that, unlike the second farmer's, has not been voided by irresponsible behavior.[50]

These examples suggest that "to each according to his needs" as a principle of justice may be subject to the rider that prospective claimants should not be judged responsible for their condition of unmet need. If they are judged responsible, two possibilities present themselves. One is that their claims are no longer claims of justice, but claims of humanity or benevolence. We should help the homeless person who has lost his home through reckless behavior, but solely on humanitarian grounds: he cannot demand to be helped as a matter of justice. The other is that the claims of need are still claims of justice, but that they carry with them an obligation to pay back to the community the costs of irresponsible behavior. It is often now suggested that people who incur health risks through heavy drinking or smoking, or who engage in dangerous sports, should pay (through higher insurance premiums or in some other way) the additional costs of meeting those risks.[51] In this way the responsibility condition can be met, while those who turn out to have medical needs as a result of their behavior can claim treatment as a matter of justice.[52]

Adding the responsibility condition adds a further dimension of complexity to our principle, because it will be controversial which activities people can properly be held responsible for.[53] How far is it reasonable to expect people to know about the consequences of their dietary choices, say? How large a range of activities should be categorized as involving special risks? Where do we draw the line between, say, everyday use of a car and sports racing? These questions take us back to the communitarian setting that the need principle presupposes. We saw earlier in this chapter that the definition of need itself depends on such a setting, which yields the norm of a minimally decent life. Now we must add that such a community embodies an understanding about what is to be regarded as a matter of collective fate, and what is to be regarded as a matter of individual responsibility. This is not an empirical matter (though empirical evidence is relevant when we argue about where precisely to draw the line). Which claims count as needs in the first place; which needs give rise to demands of justice; and how to establish priorities among different qualifying claims: these questions raise complex ethical issues that belie the apparent simplicity of "to each according to his needs."

11

Equality and Justice

Thus far I have said relatively little about equality as a principle of justice. In the first chapter I argued that equality was the relevant principle of distribution when people were associated together as fellow citizens; in the fifth chapter we saw that some idea of treating people with equal respect seemed to lie behind our criteria of procedural justice. My review of empirical studies of justice also revealed some pull in the direction of equality—not a very strong pull, perhaps, but most people when asked to comment on prevailing social inequalities appear to believe that greater equality in distribution would be fairer. In this chapter I want to turn the spotlight more directly on the idea of equality, in an attempt to bring its relationship to justice into sharper focus.

Opinions about the relationship between equality and justice have tended to polarize in the following way. On one side are those who think that the two concepts must be kept radically separate. Justice has nothing to do with equality except in the purely formal sense that if, for instance, a rule is applied to everyone, it follows that it is applied equally to everyone: two people who commit the same crime deserve the same punishment, and so on.[1] Those who believe this generally also believe that whereas justice is intrinsically valuable, equality has no value in itself; they are likely to describe themselves as antiegalitarians.

On the other side stand those who think that the two values are one and the same, or at least think this about distributive justice. This is indicated by the popularity of the phrase "egalitarian justice" in the recent writings of Dworkin, Sen, Cohen, and others who have taken part in the debate about whether, if people are to be treated as equals, they should be made as equal as possible in resources, or welfare, or opportunity for welfare, or capacities, or something else again.[2] This debate has been conducted on the assumption that the principle we are looking for is simultaneously a principle of equality and of justice. A quotation from Dworkin makes this explicit: "We use 'equality' in its normative sense . . . precisely to indicate the respect or respects in which the speaker thinks people should be the same, or treated the same way, *as a matter of justice.*"[3] Here, then, there is no question about whether or why equality is valuable: it is simply subsumed under justice. Once we have identified the appropriate currency, an equal distribution of that currency will constitute a just distribution and will have value for precisely that reason.

We should pause, however, before embracing this second view. If it is true, how are we to make sense of the fact that "justice" and "equality" strike such different chords in political debate? Neither idea figures very much in political manifestos, but for quite different reasons. To declare oneself in favor of justice would be too banal even for the manifesto writers of today. One might say that one intended to achieve justice for the elderly or for deprived children, but here one would merely be signaling that a general predisposition in favor of justice, too commonplace to be worth mentioning, was to be activated in favor of these groups. By contrast, an unqualified declaration in favor of equality would be politically hazardous to say the least—almost as hazardous as saying that under a fair tax system people like me would pay a little more in taxes. Any statement about equality has to be hedged about to make it clear which specific kind of inequality is being attacked; for instance, "We intend to reduce inequalities of pay between men and women."

Apart, perhaps, from a few "half-baked neo-Nietzscheans," everyone is in favor of justice.[4] Equality, by contrast, seems only to be embraced unreservedly by political fanatics and philosophers.[5] This should be enough to make us hesitate before amalgamating the two ideals, or subsuming one under the other. Yet there does still seem to be some connection between them, a stronger connection than those in the first camp acknowledge when they say that justice entails only a formal kind of equality, such as the kind of equality implicit in the consistent application of rules. What connection could this be?

I shall suggest a third view: there are two different kinds of valuable equality, one connected with justice and the other standing independent of it. Equality of the first kind is distributive in nature. It specifies that benefits of a certain kind—rights, for instance—should be distributed equally, because justice requires this. The second kind of equality is not in this sense distributive. It does not specify directly any distribution of rights or resources. Instead, it identifies a social ideal, the ideal of a society in which people regard and treat one another as equals—in other words, a society that does not place people in hierarchically ranked categories such as classes. We can call this second kind of equality *equality of status,* or simply *social equality.*[6]

These two kinds of equality really are quite different, even though in certain cases they might be invoked to support the same broad policy. Suppose, for instance, that we wanted to argue in favor of reducing the income inequalities that exist in contemporary liberal societies. If we took our stand on distributive equality, we would try to show that those currently receiving higher incomes had no just claim to them, that justice required a more equal, or in the most extreme version a perfectly equal, distribution of incomes. Put differently, we would try to show that those with incomes below the mean had a fair claim to (some part of the) income going to those above it. If, by contrast, we invoked social equality, we would argue that income differences on the current scale unavoidably translated themselves into social divisions. We would argue, for instance, that those whose incomes fell below one-half of the mean income (say) were very likely to feel alienated and excluded from social life, would experience an immense social gulf between themselves and those living a comfortable middle-class lifestyle, and so on. But even though the burdens of inequality may be seen as weighing most heavily on those who have the least, the argument in this second case is not centrally about unfairness in distribution; the claim is that *our society should not be like that.* In objecting to inequality, we are objecting to social relations that we find unseemly—they involve incomprehension and mistrust between rich and poor, for instance, or arrogance on one side and obeisance on the other.

One way of bringing out the distinction here is to say that equality of the first kind is individualistic, whereas equality of the second kind is holistic.[7] In the first case we can explain what is wrong with inequality by pointing to particular individuals who can justly claim more than they are getting, whereas in the second case the badness of inequality resides in the character of the whole society.[8] Of course this inequality must also be bad for the members, in the sense that their social experience is colored by the inequality in a way that we (and perhaps they) find objectionable; but this cannot be spelled out in terms of particular individual claims that are not being met. To try to do so would be to distort the value we may find in social equality. Thus to the question "Is the value of equality best understood individualistically or holistically?" my answer is "both." We should not be pushed into thinking that there is just one valuable kind of equality, and that we must therefore choose between an individualistic and a holistic account of that value.

WHEN DOES JUSTICE REQUIRE equality in distribution? As already indicated, I do not share the view held by several recent political philosophers that justice is always egalitarian. If we say that in general justice requires us to render to each his or her due, in the classic formula, then as I argued in Chapter 2 what is due to a person will depend on what is being distributed and on the context in which the distribution is taking place. This may require an unequal distribution, particularly when the relevant criterion of distribution is some form of desert.[9] Here I reject the view that (valid) claims of desert always turn out finally to be claims for compensation. It is sometimes said, for instance, that when people are rewarded for their efforts, what is happening is that the costs involved in making an effort are offset by the extra income they later receive, so that the overall result is one of equality.[10] This seems to me very implausible as a general account of what is going on when efforts are rewarded, even if it holds good in a few special cases. Whether effort is costly depends on the particular kind of effort involved and on the mental attitude of the worker. So unless we want to say that people who enjoy their work or who see their work as a duty that they are enjoined to fulfill should be paid less than those who find it burdensome or intrinsically unrewarding, we must give up the idea that rewarding effort is a means of achieving equality. This holds *a fortiori* for desert of other kinds.

In which cases, then, does justice require an equal distribution of advantages? It does so, first, in cases where there is some benefit to be allocated and there is no one who can advance any particular claim to all or part of it. These are what we might call manna-from-heaven cases, cases in which a group of people find themselves in possession of a divisible good for whose existence none of them is in any way responsible and on which none has any special claim of need, say. Here an equal distribution is the only distribution that recognizes the equal moral standing of each member of the group, and it is the distribution that justice requires. This might be overridden by mutual consent—for instance, everyone might agree to pile the manna into a heap and draw straws for the whole heap—but the baseline is that everyone can justly claim a 1/nth share unless he or she voluntarily gives it up.[11]

I regard this as a limiting case.[12] Manna from heaven is exceptional both in the sense that it arrives without anyone's doing anything, and in the sense that it is a consumption good that everyone stands equally in need of. (The Biblical account of the original event is confusing on this latter point, implying both that each man was limited to gathering an equal quantity of manna, and that this somehow adjusted itself to his needs; "they gathered every man according to his eating," according to the Authorized Version.)[13] It is sometimes argued that the earth's natural resources are to be regarded as analogous to manna, and that each person can justly claim an equal share of them. But the analogy fails in several respects. Natural resources are production goods as often as they are consumption goods—think of coal and oil as well as deer and apples— and so their value depends upon the knowledge and capacities of the particular people who use them. They are not simply waiting to be picked up and used, as the manna was, but have to be appropriated by labor: the deer must be hunted, the coal mined. And there may be good reasons for not distributing these resources to individuals as private holdings—they may, for instance, play an essential part in ecological processes that are of general benefit, such as the water cycle. These considerations do not settle the issue of resource distribution, but they do show that the case for an equal distribution cannot be made by analogy with the manna case. Equality is the proper principle for distributing manna only insofar as the beneficiaries of its arrival have no distinguishing features that would bring other principles into play. This cannot be said about natural resources in general. Thus a theory of distributive equality that bases itself on the idea that every human being is entitled to an equal share of the world's nonhuman resources is resting on very shaky foundations.[14]

Distributive justice may also require equality when a distribution has to be made in conditions of uncertainty about people's respective claims. Suppose, for instance, that I assemble a team of people to carry out some task, at the end of which there is a product to distribute among them. When the task is finished I have no reliable way of knowing how much each of them has contributed. I suspect that some made more of a contribution than others, but I cannot quantify this in any way (for instance, no one left half way through the job). Under these conditions I should distribute the product equally in order to minimize the expected injustice of the distribution.

A simple example may illustrate this claim. Suppose there are five members in the team and the total product is twenty-five units. Having to decide under ignorance, I regard any array of contributions as equally probable, from, at one extreme, the case where each member has contributed five units to, at the other extreme, the case where one member has effectively contributed all twenty-five and the other four have merely gone through the motions. Let injustice be measured by adding up the shortfalls between members' contributions and the amounts they later receive as rewards so that, for instance, if actual contributions were A10, B5, C5, D3, and E2 and rewards received were A6, B4, C8, D2, E5, the unfairness of the allocation is calculated as $(10 - 6) + (5 - 4) + (3 - 2) = 6$.[15] Then an equal distribution of rewards will minimize the expected injustice.[16]

Alternatively, one might argue that under conditions of uncertainty one should act so as to minimize the maximum possible injustice done to any one individual. Once again an equal distribution achieves this. Suppose, in the worst case, that one member of the team has effectively produced all twenty-five units of product by himself. An equal distribution rewards him with five, and the injustice done to him is measured at twenty. Under any other distribution it is possible that he will receive less than five, and injustice to him will be greater than twenty. By choosing an equal distribution, we know that the worst deprivation we can inflict on anyone is twenty units of benefit; if we choose any other distribution, this figure must be higher.

The same argument will also apply when the relevant criterion of distribution is need, but we have no sure way of knowing what different people's relative needs are. Sharing resources equally will minimize the expected deviation from a perfectly just distribution. I suspect that something like this chain of reasoning may be at work in practical cases in which people who would have to make a fairly complicated calculation to divide resources fairly choose equality as the simplest solution.[17] There is, of course, a procedural aspect to this—if you divide equally no one can accuse you of bias or favoritism—but beyond that may lie the thought that if you can't be bothered to make the exact calculation, or are worried that if you make the attempt you may get it wrong, then at least by dividing equally you minimize the unfairness.

This argument about uncertainty could be taken further. Suppose, for instance, that you are quite skeptical about measuring desert, in practice if not in principle. Suppose you believe that people deserve rewards if and only if they are personally responsible for bringing about certain outcomes, but you think that in real cases it is nearly always impossible to disentangle what someone is responsible for from the effects of factors for which they are *not* responsible, such as their natural endowments; then you might support the equal distribution of income on the grounds that this will predictably get you closest to the ideally fair distribution, which would be a distribution according to desert. As will be clear from earlier chapters, I do not share this skepticism about desert, but I do believe that some egalitarians may base their egalitarianism on considerations of this kind. Notice that this would also give you a reason for resisting proposals to introduce Pareto-superior inequalities: if asked the familiar question "Why choose 5, 5, 5, 5, 5 when 12, 9, 7, 7, 6 (say) is an available alternative?" the egalitarian I am considering can reply, "Because it's fairer. Having no good reason to think that the person who gets 12 under the second distribution deserves more than the person who gets 6, I would be increasing expected injustice if I moved from the first to the second distribution."

The two justice-based arguments for equality I have considered thus far are essentially negative in character. The first says that equal distribution is required by justice when there are no relevant differences between persons (the manna-from-heaven case); the second says that equal distribution gets you closest to justice when you lack the evidence or computational skill to reach the perfectly just solution (the team-work case). The third argument is more positive. It says that there are certain social groups whose members are entitled to equal treatment by virtue of membership. The claim to equality flows from the very fact of membership. To recognize someone as a member and yet to deny her an equal share of advantages with other members is to treat her unjustly.

The groups in question may be quite varied in character. At the lowest level you might think of a voluntary association such as a squash club. Someone who joins this club should have an equal opportunity to book courts, to serve on the committee that runs the club, and so forth. At the other extreme stands membership in a political community. People who are full members are citizens, and as citizens they can justly claim equal treatment over a wide area—equal legal protection, equal voting rights, equal rights to the benefits of the welfare state, and so forth.

Two counterarguments might be brought against my claim that equality stems from membership in cases like this. The first says that membership may carry with it certain entitlements, but these are not to be understood in terms of equality. Rather, they are entitlements to absolute amounts of whatever X is in question. This interpretation is not plausible, however, as I shall try to show by exploring the case of rights of citizenship.

Consider the range of essential services provided directly or indirectly by modern states, including health, education, communications, transportation, and so forth. In many cases receipt of these services will be considered an adjunct of citizenship. It is, however, a matter of choice precisely which services will be provided and at what level. This will depend on the society's level of economic development and on cultural values that attach greater or lesser importance to particular services. Take transportation as an example. States must inevitably assume responsibility for the basic systems that allow people to move freely from place to place—for roads and rail networks, for public transportation, and so on.[18] But equally it would be quite implausible to attempt to define a right to some absolute level of free movement. It is by no means clear what terms could be used to define such a right, and in any case there can legitimately be substantial variations among states in their transportation policies: one sparsely populated country might try to achieve mobility by ensuring that everyone has access to a private car, while another, small and densely populated, might decide to create a mass transit system and discourage the use of cars.

What matters from the perspective of citizenship is not that each person should enjoy some specifiable amount of "mobility" but that whatever transportation system is adopted should as far as possible treat people equally. This condition of equality would be violated if, for instance, country dwellers enjoyed far worse access to transportation than city dwellers, or if a transportation policy that strongly favored car users left a significant minority who could not afford to buy cars with a residual, low-quality system of public transportation. Perfectly equal treatment for each individual is no doubt impossible to achieve. But any group who could show that their opportunities for free movement were significantly smaller than those of other citizens could appeal to their general rights as citizens to argue for a policy change.

Somewhat different considerations apply in the case of another aspect of citizenship, political rights. Why do we insist on equal rights to vote ("one person, one vote, one value")? The value of a vote, materially and symbolically, depends on the overall distribution of voting rights in the political community. If a scheme of plural voting such as that advocated by J. S. Mill were adopted, whereby people get different numbers of votes in proportion to their ability to decide political issues, as evidenced, for example, by their level of education, then to have one vote is not only to be politically ineffective, but also to be declared a low-grade citizen.[19] That is why plural voting has become politically unthinkable in the present century. Once the status of citizenship is extended to all competent adults, it becomes essential that every member of the political community is treated equally, and this is given material expression in equality of voting rights.

But this brings us to the second objection. Is the equality that is demanded in the groups we have been looking at anything more than a conventional artifact? To return to the squash club example, the objection runs that if club membership is constituted in such a way that each member has equal rights, then of course all members must be treated equally when the courts are allocated and so forth. But this is just contingent. In another club there may be a hierarchy of membership grades, and then justice would require unequal treatment. Moreover, justice itself cannot determine which sort of club we should have.

This second objection is not wholly off the mark, but it cannot be sustained in the form stated above. It is not merely a matter of contingency that we form our groups and associations on the basis of equality. Such groups have a special kind of value for us that would be lost if we chose a stratified form of membership. Associating as equals provides us with a kind of recognition that is essential to the modern self.[20] It is not a universal truth about human beings that they need recognition in this form, which is why I say that the objection is not wholly off the mark. But for people like us, recognition must take this form, and so we insist that our most important memberships—above all membership of the nation-state—be based on equality. Justice then demands equal treatment for everyone who is a member with respect to the advantages that membership provides. As noted, this amounts to a positive argument for equality. When we say that all people should enjoy equal political rights, this is not because there are no differences among them that might justify an unequal assignment, or because we lack confidence in our ability to discriminate in practice, but because we find it positively valuable that equality should be affirmed in this area.[21]

THESE ARE THE ARGUMENTS, negative and positive, that show why justice sometimes requires an equal distribution of rights and resources. But now I want to explore a little further the idea of social equality, which earlier I characterized as free-standing and independent of justice. One may think that a just society would also be egalitarian in this second sense. But this could only be an empirical claim, needing evidence and not merely argument to back it up.

It is possible to elucidate the ideal of social equality in various ways, but difficult to give it a sharp definition. To recall, social equality is a matter of how people regard one another and how they conduct their social relations. It does not require that people be equal in power, prestige, or wealth, nor, absurdly, that they score the same on natural dimensions such as strength or intelligence. What matters is how such differences are regarded, and in particular whether they serve to construct a social hierarchy in which A can unequivocally be ranked as B's superior. Wherever there is social equality, people feel that each member of the community enjoys an equal standing with all the rest that overrides members' unequal ratings along particular dimensions. This is expressed in the way people interact: they use common modes of address (an egalitarian society is what Michael Walzer has called "a society of misters"), they shake hands rather than bow, they choose their friends according to common tastes and interests rather than according to social rank, and so forth.[22]

The ideal of social equality is more deeply embedded in the moral consciousness of contemporary societies than political rhetoric would suggest. When people recoil from equality, as earlier I suggested they frequently do, it is across-the-board distributive equality they are rejecting. Conversely, although people often act in such a way as to reinforce class distinctions, they do not regard such distinctions as legitimate. One small piece of evidence to support this can be obtained by looking at the fortunes of the term "condescension." In a ranked society, to condescend—defined by Samuel Johnson as "to depart from the privileges of superiority by a voluntary submission; to sink willingly to equal terms with inferiours"—is a virtue; it is amiably to forgo deference that one can rightfully claim.[23] By Jane Austen's time, condescension is viewed more ambiguously. Readers (or viewers) of *Pride and Prejudice* will remember the appalling Mr. Collins, who is forever praising the condescension of his patron, Lady Catherine de Burgh. Collins is both a comic and a pathetic figure, and Austen's characterization is plainly a satirical one, but she is describing a moral world in which it was still possible to regard condescension as a virtue. Today it is not possible: to describe someone as condescending is to condemn him or her. Condescension is a vice because there are no legitimate "privileges of superiority" from which to depart, and so someone who behaves in a condescending way is claiming a superior status to which he is not entitled. The progressive acceptance of social equality as an ideal, I am suggesting, could be roughly measured by tracing the moral passage of the concept of condescension from virtue to vice.

But why call social equality a kind of equality? Why not say "a society of easy-going camaraderie" or something of the sort? Clearly, social equality is not a distributive kind of equality (though I shall suggest in a moment that it does have certain distributive implications): it does not prescribe the equal assignment of any specific type of advantage to persons. It does nonetheless identify a form of life in which people in a very important sense treat one another as equals. In their social intercourse, they act on the assumption that each person has an equal standing that transcends particular inequalities (of achievement, for instance). John may be a better doctor than Peter, in which case it is right for me to prefer seeing him when I am sick, but in every other respect I regard them as equals and treat them accordingly. I don't show John any deference that I withhold from Peter except in the particular area in which he has superior expertise.

Why is social equality valuable? It is tempting to try to answer this question by reaching for some ideal such as human dignity or respect for persons in terms of which an egalitarian society scores better than a hierarchical one. I am doubtful, however, whether this strategy can be made to work, because it seems that the two social forms we are considering each carry their own moral vocabulary. Some terms—such as the one just discussed, condescension—switch from being terms of praise to being terms of condemnation. Other terms shift their meaning but not their value sign: this is the case with both dignity and respect, which take on one sense within the value system of a ranked society and another sense within the value system of an egalitarian society. In a ranked society one gains respect by carrying out the duties attached to one's station, and dignity is a matter of behaving in a way appropriate to that station. (There is a very illuminating treatment of the contrast between aristocratic and democratic notions of dignity in Kazuo Ishiguro's novel *The Remains of the Day.*) We therefore lack neutral terms with which to compare the two forms of life. What can be said is that the first alternative, the hierarchical order, is not a real possibility for us. We could not recreate the set of beliefs and attitudes necessary to undergird such an order without first absorbing a massive dose of false consciousness. Thus if people are to have dignity and respect in this society now, it must be the kind of dignity and respect that social equality provides. In a similar way, we can argue that if we want our society to have some degree of solidarity, the only feasible basis is for people to be linked together horizontally as equals. These are contingent arguments for social equality, not rock-bottom ones, which I do not think can be found.

Social equality is not a distributive ideal in itself, but it does have distributive implications. First of all, it requires that our most important associations be formed on the basis of equality. This is particularly the case with the political community of which we are members, whose preeminence stems from the fact that it is the final authority responsible for regulating all other distributive practices. Unless we enjoy an equal status as citizens, we cannot have equal status in social life more generally—this is an empirical claim for which I cannot provide evidence, but it may seem so obvious as not to need any. This then entails the claims about distributive equality that I outlined earlier in the chapter: citizens must have equal voting rights, equal welfare rights, and so forth. If they are not being treated equally in these ways, they are not being treated as equal citizens; and if people are not associated politically as equals, they will certainly not enjoy social equality.

Second, a commitment to social equality may help shape other practices of distributive justice that are not themselves internally egalitarian, so to speak. It does so in the following way. In many instances our concern for justice will impose constraints on practices without fully determining their form. Let me give two examples, both of which in-

volve desert-based justice. On the one hand, justice may sometimes require us to reward people differently for different performances without
specifying by how much or in what way the rewards must differ. As we
saw in Chapter 4, it is a widely held view that people who take on
responsible jobs should be rewarded more highly than those who don't
carry responsibilities. But how large should the pay differential be—
should it be three to one or ten to one?—and must it be a differential in
pay, or could responsibility be adequately recognized by, for instance,
differences in the quality of someone's work environment? Justice does
not provide us with definite answers to these questions: it requires consistency and proportionality in the treatment of those holding responsible jobs, but it does not determine what precise treatment they are
owed.[24]

Equally, there are cases in which it is a matter of contingency, from the
point of view of justice, whether a certain practice exists at all, but given
that the practice does exist, questions of justice or fairness arise in the
course of its operation. It is not a requirement of justice that the University of Oxford offer a prize for rendering an English poem in Latin
hexameters, but given that the prize exists, it would clearly be unfair if
the promised sum were not paid out in full, if women were excluded
from entering, and so on.

What has this to do with social equality? If we want our society to be
egalitarian, then we will try to shape our distributive practices so that the
emergence of hierarchy is discouraged; in particular, we will try to avoid
the emergence of large-scale, cumulative inequalities of advantage that
make it difficult for people to live together on terms of equality, even if
politically they are all defined as equals. This, I take it, is the current
situation in liberal democracies: formally, everyone enjoys equal rights of
citizenship, and this is important, but materially there are large, cumulative inequalities in educational attainment, in organizational power, and
in income, and this is important too, because it means that these societies are still effectively class-divided.[25]

I have argued elsewhere that the most hopeful response to this state of
affairs can be found in the idea of complex equality—the idea, very
briefly, that if we can maintain many autonomous distributive spheres,
and if for the most part different people score highly in different spheres,
then we can achieve social equality without introducing an across-the-
board simple distributive equality which we know to be both unjust and

impossible to implement.[26] But as part of this strategy we can turn to our advantage those aspects of our practices about which, as we have just seen, justice remains silent. For instance, in a market economy it will almost certainly be inevitable, and be regarded as fair, that there should be income differentials within firms. But there seem to be no reasons, either of economic necessity or of fairness, for these differentials to be anywhere near as large as they now are in most capitalist systems. So here there is an opportunity to shape conceptions of wage fairness in the interests of social equality. Public opinion is already inclined to move in this direction; insofar as they are able to make firm judgments, people regard existing income differentials as too large.[27] What I am suggesting is that it would not be difficult to persuade people that it was fair for the managing director of a large company to be paid not more than, say, three or four times the wage of an unskilled worker, with proportionate differentials in between.

Furthermore, wherever there is a choice as to which practices to create or maintain, we can allow that choice to be guided by considerations of social equality. Suppose we decide to have a system of public honors. At one extreme, honors can be handed out to rich businessmen who make large donations to political parties—a practice that exemplifies particularly clearly the opposite of complex equality, or what Michael Walzer calls "dominance."[28] At the other extreme, we might set up the honors system so as to pick out ordinary people with no other claim to eminence than, for instance, giving up a good deal of their free time for volunteer work. Neither practice is inherently more just than the other; each corresponds to a different understanding of the purpose that an honors system is meant to serve.[29] But social equality gives us a clear reason for favoring the second.

To sum up, neither the cause of justice nor the cause of equality has been helped by political philosophers who have run the two ideas together under the heading of "egalitarian justice." Instead, we need to think about two kinds of equality: equality in distribution, which in some cases (but not others) is a requirement of justice, and the quite distinct idea of equality of status, or social equality. This, too, has implications for distribution, but they are much less direct and depend upon sociological claims about the way in which differences in income or education, say, are converted into inequalities of social class. Here, I have claimed, equality can shape the practice of justice where justice itself remains silent. It is not part of my case that the two kinds of equality must necessarily conflict; on the contrary, equal citizenship and the concrete rights that attach to it provide an essential starting point from which moves toward a wider social equality can be made. But they are different nonetheless, and draw upon different political traditions: distributive equality from the tradition of liberalism, social equality from social democracy and socialism.[30] Anyone who seeks to defend equality is open to easy caricature by critics of that notion, and so it is important to be clear from the start about precisely which form of equality is being advocated.

12

Prospects for Social Justice

My aim in writing this book has been to explore the idea of social justice used by citizens in contemporary liberal democracies when they assess the basic structure of their societies. I suggested that this idea was complex, and that the principle of justice people use depends on how they understand their relationship to the people with whom or to whom they are doing justice. Thus different principles are used in different social contexts. This explanation was confirmed by looking at empirical studies of people's beliefs about social justice. A theory of justice has to do more than simply report popular beliefs, however; it must also show that the principles in question are philosophically coherent and can be welded together to form a cohesive whole. My claim is that a theory of justice combining principles of need, desert, and equality can meet these conditions.

Yet this is not quite the same as showing that social justice remains a viable political ideal. The concept may be perfectly sound in the abstract, but at the same time social and political forces may be at work in contemporary democracies that deprive it of practical relevance. In Chapter 1 I introduced the idea of the "circumstances of social justice" to denote the conditions under which the concept had practical application—meaning that it could be used to shape legislation, public policy, and the behavior of citizens generally—and I raised the question whether the liberal democracies that gave birth to the concept might be moving beyond those circumstances. In this concluding chapter I return to that question. Are we witnessing changes in contemporary societies, within and across national boundaries, that spell the end of the era of social justice?

In particular, I am interested in the effects of two tendencies that are usually identified by the labels "globalization" and "multiculturalism." By globalization I mean the process whereby national political boundaries are eroded in such a way that people's life chances everywhere increasingly depend on the workings of a global market over which states have little if any control. By multiculturalism I mean the process whereby a variety of groups within existing states—religious groups, ethnic groups, groups defined by gender or sexual orientation, and so on—increasingly assert their separate cultural identities and demand that those identities be given political recognition. We will need to look more closely at these tendencies later in the chapter. But the issue I am addressing can now be posed in the following fairly simple way. As we saw in Chapter 1, the concept of social justice apparently presupposes a relatively homogeneous political community whose directing agency, the state, has the capacity to shape its major social institutions—and thus the final distribution of social resources—in the way the principles embedded in the concept prescribe. But this presupposition, it's argued, no longer holds: political communities are increasingly divided along cultural lines, and states are increasingly powerless to alter the resource distributions that the global market creates. Thus we appear to be moving rapidly beyond the circumstances of social justice. Whereas Hayek and other earlier critics of the idea believed that the pursuit of social justice was feasible but mistaken—the state could intervene in the market to alter the distribution of resources in accordance with ideals of distributive justice, but the effects of doing so would be economically disastrous—the view I am confronting is that the pursuit of social justice is simply impossible, so we might as well drop the idea from our political vocabulary and stop constructing elaborate theories with no practical relevance.

I shall expand upon these claims about the consequences of globalization and multiculturalism shortly, but before doing so I want to summarize the theory of social justice that our analysis up to now has suggested. For clearly the impact of these twin forces, supposing them to be real, will depend on the conception of social justice that we hold: it seems likely that some conceptions will be more vulnerable to the ravages of globalization and multiculturalism than others. Assuming for the moment, then, that our theory is to apply within the borders of a well-defined political community, what must the basic institutional structure be like for the society in question to be a just one? According to my analysis, it must comply first with principles of need, second with principles of desert, and third with principles of equality.

The institutional structure must ensure that an adequate share of social resources is set aside for distribution to individuals on the basis of need. Individuals' needs will in practice be fulfilled by a wide variety of institutions, including families, mutual aid associations, and public institutions such as health and social security services. For social justice to obtain, what is necessary is that each person's needs be met (fully or proportionately) according to a common standard of need that is recognized and applied across the whole society: as we saw in Chapter 10, the best way to understand this is in terms of the set of functionings that together make up a minimally decent life for people in the society in question. Depending on the particular need at stake, this may involve imposing a general constraint on the distribution of resources, or it may involve allocating essential items directly on the basis of need. To illustrate, food is clearly a vital need, but ensuring that everyone's need for food is met is normally (in the circumstances of economically advanced liberal democracies) a matter of constraining the income distribution so that all people are in a position to purchase sufficient food to satisfy their needs. Thus measures such as minimum-wage legislation, unemployment benefits, and pension provision may be adequate to guarantee that needs for food can be met. On the other hand, in cases where needs are perennially liable to outstrip available resources—medical needs being the outstanding example—justice requires that the allocating agencies be set up in such a way that need and need alone becomes the criterion for distributing the resources in question. As our discussion in Chapter 10 revealed, there remain vexing questions about what exactly it means to distribute according to need in situations of scarcity. But clearly in such cases the allocative mechanisms have to be detached from institutions such as the economic market whose distributive logic is very different. In other cases still, a mixed solution may work best: housing is a need that most people can meet out of earned income, but for a minority there has to be either a scheme of public housing or a system of subsidies that reduces the cost of housing for low-income families and individuals.

The institutional structure required by the need principle is likely, therefore, to be a complex one. Given that we are looking at the problems allegedly posed by globalization and multiculturalism, the key points to bear in mind are that we presuppose both a common society-wide definition of need and institutions that are capable either of correcting the market-derived income distribution or of supplying needed goods on a nonmarket basis.

Justice requires that many social resources be allocated to individuals on the basis of desert. In some cases this follows directly from the nature of the thing being allocated (prizes and honors cannot be prizes and honors unless they standardly go to those who have displayed desert of the appropriate kind), but in other cases goods such as money with no built-in distributive criterion of their own are regarded as appropriate means of recognizing and rewarding differences in desert. The institutions and practices within which desert is requited are varied and widespread, but the main issue for social justice is economic desert: how people are rewarded for the work they perform, taking work in its broadest sense to encompass productive activities such as innovation and management as well as labor.

What kind of institutional structure is necessary to ensure that people get what they deserve for their work? Let's assume that a large proportion of the economy will be market-based: I argued in Chapter 9 that there is no inherent reason a market economy should not meet (meritocratic) criteria of social justice.[1] This is not to say that existing market economies are socially just, nor that an unregulated market system left to its own devices would generate just outcomes. Indeed, in both cases the reverse is true. A just market economy will require a strong regulatory and corrective framework, and will look substantially different from the capitalist economies that we now inhabit. More precisely, it will have to meet at least the following five conditions.

First, the market must operate against a background of equal opportunities. People entering the market must as far as possible have had an equal chance to develop their skills and talents, must be encouraged to choose from a wide range of jobs and careers, and so forth. Although what justice immediately requires is that people be rewarded according to their economic performance, this requirement carries its full weight only if differences in performance stem from the talents, effort, and choices of the individuals in question, and not from differences in background conditions (such as the quality of the education they received before entering the market). Second, for similar reasons, antidiscrimination legislation must ensure that people do not lose out, whether as employees or as purchasers of goods and services, because of the prejudiced attitudes of others. Third, the market must be kept competitive, so that people are rewarded simply for their part in supplying the goods and services that others want, as opposed to enjoying monopoly rents, whether these derive from economic cartels or from licensing practices that limit access to certain professions. Fourth, the institutions surrounding the market should act so as to dampen rather than to amplify the effects of luck: given that these effects cannot be eliminated entirely, what matters is that as far as possible good and bad luck should not be allowed to accumulate in the course of particular lives. Fifth, the incomes and associated benefits received by people working in the non-market sector of the economy should be broadly comparable to those going to people doing similar work in the market sector.

These are clearly demanding conditions, and some readers may wonder whether a market can operate effectively if, say, luck is not allowed full rein. But my concern is specifically with the question whether changes in the circumstances of the advanced liberal democracies have made even modest advances in the direction of social justice impossible, and the logical first step in answering it is to describe in outline an ideally just society. One further issue needs addressing here: what range of economic inequalities does justice as desert require or permit? As my earlier discussion indicates, I do not think this question can be answered precisely. Our intuitions about desert are not sufficiently strong that we can attach absolute magnitudes to the deserts of doctors or plumbers. At the same time, we saw in Chapter 4 that the general public consistently takes the view that existing income differences are too great and that high-earning groups typically do not deserve the levels of reward they are now getting. It is plausible, I believe, to link this reaction to the conditions laid down in the last paragraph. Without crediting the public with a sophisticated grasp of economic theory, it is not far-fetched to suggest that people instinctively feel that rich landlords, executives, and doctors owe their receipts not to the market as such but to something closer to a position of monopoly, whereas sports and movie stars are enjoying a kind of amplified luck (you win a tournament or an Oscar, your name goes up in lights, and then you go on to earn considerably more than people around you with similar levels of talent). Or to put the point positively: differences in people's economic performance due to personal talents and effort are not so great as to justify very large inequalities of reward on the scale that we now see. A just distribution of income would be substantially unequal, but the range of inequality would be considerably smaller than the range that now exists in almost all capitalist economies.

This brings us to the third element of social justice: equality. As I argued in the last chapter, justice positively requires equality only as an adjunct of membership of certain social groups, and as far as social justice is concerned, the key form of membership is citizenship. In their capacity as citizens, people must be treated as equals, and this requires that they enjoy equal legal, political, and social rights. Beyond this public policy must give equal consideration to the interests and preferences of those affected by it, for instance, when the state provides benefits available to all, such as cultural and environmental goods. How can this requirement of equality be institutionalized? To some extent it can be realized through a formal constitution that specifies the set of rights that each citizen must enjoy. It is important, however, not to overstate the capacity of constitutional mechanisms here. Even in the case of social rights, it may be hard to specify the content of the right in such a way that a judicial body can determine whether a particular policy fulfills the right or not (consider what would be involved in specifying an equal right to medical care, for example).[2] To some extent, too, democratic mechanisms will ensure that people's demands receive equal attention when legislation is passed and policy is made. But much depends here on the quality of the decision-making—on the extent to which the participants are themselves committed to the ideal of equal citizenship when reaching decisions. If they are not so committed, then minority groups may find that their claims go unheard and their interests unacknowledged. The underlying ethos of the political community thus matters as much as its institutional structure. We can sum this up by saying that to achieve social justice we must have a political community in which citizens are treated as equals in an across-the-board way, in which public policy is geared toward meeting the intrinsic needs of every member, and in which the economy is framed and constrained in such a way that the income and other work-related benefits people receive correspond to their respective deserts. This is the model whose prospects I will assess against the background of globalization and multiculturalism.

"GLOBALIZATION" IS AN IMPRECISE TERM used to describe a range of economic, political, and cultural processes that, it is claimed, are making national boundaries increasingly irrelevant in today's world. I shall focus here on the economic changes that are allegedly reducing the capacity of nation-states to determine economic parameters within their borders. The claim is that increased mobility both of capital and of labor—especially highly skilled labor—together with rapid flows of information across borders, forces all states to converge on the same basic set of institutions on pain of losing both capital and labor to rival states in which economic conditions are viewed as more attractive. Thus a state that tries to regulate the market in an attempt to make firms bear the social costs of their production, or that introduces a charter of workers' rights whose effect is to raise the cost of employing labor, or that taxes individuals or corporate bodies at a higher-than-average rate, will find that investors begin to place their capital elsewhere, that multinational companies relocate their production to more favorable economic regimes, and that people with skills in high demand will choose to live and work in countries where they can maximize the return on those skills. Thus unless a state is prepared to isolate itself from the global market—a cure whose effects are likely to be worse than the disease—it finds itself in an economic strait-jacket that severely restricts the policies it might want to implement in the name of social justice. Socially just institutions presuppose a flourishing economy to support them, but, the argument goes, to have a flourishing economy in the contemporary world a country must play by the rules of the global market.

The most extreme version of the globalization thesis holds that individuals have already to a large extent broken free from the confines of the nation-state, and are now in a position to organize their economic activities on the basis of free contracts with other individuals across the globe.[3] As a result, any state that wishes to survive must reconstitute itself as a provider of services to these free-floating individuals, and indeed the state as a unitary entity may disappear, to be replaced by a range of institutions offering services to their clients on a contractual basis—people would buy personal protection from one agency, medical care from another, and so forth. In these circumstances, clearly, the state could no longer function as an instrument of social justice: in particular, it could not implement programs whose predictable effect is to transfer resources from one group of individuals to another (say, from high-earners to low-earners, or from the healthy to the chronically sick), since if it attempted to do so, those of its clients who would lose out would simply buy their services from another state (or would shop around among a number of different service providers).

"Multiculturalism" is a term no less vague than globalization, but again I shall use it here specifically to describe the fragmentation of national cultures and the rise of distinct cultural groups—whether within or across national borders—whose members' personal identities are linked to their participation in the group.[4] As this occurs, people begin to act politically as members of cultural groups, making demands on behalf of their group both for material resources and for symbolic recognition.

Multiculturalism is said to have three main consequences for social justice. First, we can no longer take for granted the idea that social justice is something to be achieved within a well-defined political community. We cannot assume that people will see themselves as having special ties to their fellow citizens that will lead them to support institutions and policies whose purpose is to create distributively just outcomes across that community. Instead, they will be concerned with seeing justice done to and within their cultural group, which in some cases will mean contemplating a universe of distribution that is considerably narrower than the nation-state and in other cases considerably broader (if the people concerned are the bearers of a transnational religious or ethnic identity, for instance).

Second, agreement about social justice will be very difficult to achieve, even if we confine our attention to groups within the borders of established states. Wherever societies are divided along linguistic, ethnic, or religious lines, the claim goes, it is unreasonable to expect any consensus on issues of distributive justice. Not only will the various groups disagree in practice, but their underlying world-views will diverge radically in such a way that there will be no basis on which a consensus might be built. Thus the hope of philosophers such as the later Rawls, that groups holding different religious, moral, and philosophical doctrines might nevertheless be able to reach an overlapping consensus on principles of justice, is held to be forlorn. It is simply not reasonable to expect people to renounce or set aside their deeply held convictions so that agreement on principles of justice can be achieved.

Third, multiculturalism is said to have the effect of displacing traditional concerns with material distribution, whether these have to do with the division of the social product among classes, or with how far the state (rather than the market) should be involved in supplying goods and services. Authors such as Iris Young and Nancy Fraser argue that as societies become multicultural, issues of material distribution decline in political significance, to be replaced by issues of cultural recognition.[5] People become less concerned about inequalities in wealth and income and more concerned about the way in which certain cultural identities are acknowledged and promoted by the state and others sidelined. These are still issues of justice in the broad sense, but they are not issues of distributive justice as political philosophers from Mill to Rawls understood them. Thus the problem is not merely one of trying to reach a consensus about social justice; the problem is that social justice itself, in its traditional sense, becomes an issue of declining importance to groups whose main preoccupation is the struggle for cultural recognition.

The argument, then, is that multiculturalism has caused people to care less, and disagree more, about social justice as traditionally understood, while globalization has given states tightly constrained policy options, so that steps in the direction of social justice would be blocked even if there existed the political will to take them. Seen in this light, the prospects for social justice appear very dim. I want to reject quite decisively one response to this argument. It holds that we should respond to the challenges of globalization and multiculturalism by inventing new and more complex forms of justice: if nations are no longer the primary site of justice, then let's have ethnic justice and regional justice and transnational justice all thrown together in one glorious casserole! This solution to the problem simply cannot withstand serious scrutiny. No matter what else it requires, justice minimally demands consistency in the treatment of individuals and groups. Whatever the exact criterion of just treatment that is employed—whether need, desert, equality, or something else—it is an elementary requirement that any two people who resemble each other along the dimension that justice tracks must be treated in the same way. This cannot be achieved unless there is a single, coherent institutional structure that provides the resources in question. If my neighbor and I suffer from the same illness, then we should have access to equally good health care: the fact that we may belong to different ethnic groups, or have different transnational affiliations, is simply irrelevant at this point. Moreover, it will be experienced as irrelevant: if I get hospital treatment that my neighbor is denied, telling him a fancy story about the fragmentation of political identities is hardly going to satisfy him. Postmodern justice is no justice at all.

Thus we must respond more directly to the challenges posed by globalization and multiculturalism. One way to do this would be to argue that the significance of both processes has been vastly overstated in general: the evidence that economies are being exposed to global forces in an unprecedented manner, and that societies are now multicultural in a way that they have not been hitherto, is hardly decisive. The issues here are extremely complex, however, and it would take at least a book to do justice to them. Instead, I want to look only at those aspects of globalization and multiculturalism that might have a direct bearing on the pursuit of social justice. What precisely are the reasons an increasingly globalized economic system, and increasing social fragmentation along cultural lines, should prevent states from supporting socially just institutions and policies?

THE GLOBALIZATION ARGUMENT treats individuals and firms as economic maximizers whose choices about where to work or invest depend entirely on the returns they can gain under different economic regimes. They are not treated as having allegiances to particular nation-states that might limit these choices. Notice, however, that the argument may hold provided that some, not necessarily all, economic actors think in this way. For a state to be threatened by a flight of capital or skilled labor as a result of its enacting certain policies in the name of social justice, it is only necessary that a sufficient proportion of actors display their willingness to exit from the economy to raise the cost of these policies beyond the realms of the possible: behavior at the margin may be enough to cause a stock-market collapse or an economic recession. Merely to observe that many people are loyal to their own nation, and would not leave it even if they could make more money working or investing somewhere else, does not rebut the argument. We need to show instead that social justice and economic efficiency do not clash in the way that the globalization argument assumes. We need, in other words, to show that even an economic maximizer might have good reason to work or invest in a state where socially just policies were being implemented (or at least to show that he would fare as well there as in a state that disregarded social justice). This is not to say that there can be a perfect marriage of social justice and economic efficiency. There will be points at which justice requires some people to sacrifice gains they might have made through the single-minded pursuit of economic advantage. When we reach those points, the question about what can bind people to one another in such a way that they will agree to cooperate within a just basic structure will re-emerge. But it is important to show that for part of the way along the road these two aims can walk together.

My case for social justice will in certain respects draw upon those critics of crude globalization theses who point out that states continue to play a crucial role in sustaining the conditions under which successful economic activity can take place.[6] Firms benefit from the stability that national systems of regulation provide, and communication and cooperation among employees are made easier when they share a distinct national culture; another body of evidence highlights the essential role of public education in creating a trained workforce that is then able to take advantage of international investment. Moreover, successful economic regimes are not all of a piece. There can be quite substantial variations both in the institutional structures of different market economies, and in more specific policies such as tax rates.[7] This evidence suggests that even stereotypical profit-maximizing entrepreneurs or multinational corporations would make their investment decisions not simply on the basis of a narrow tax-and-revenue calculation, but by considering more broadly the social environment in different possible locations; the same applies to a stereotypical highly paid professional deciding where in the world to offer her services.

To see the extent to which economic globalization might damage the prospects for social justice, I shall divide up the demands of justice in a slightly different way than hitherto, distinguishing equal citizenship, meritocratic justice, need-based justice, and material equality: as we shall see, the difficulties increase as we proceed down the list. Take equal citizenship first. Insofar as this refers to an equality of civil and political rights, there seems to be no conflict between justice and economic efficiency—no reason asset-holders should prefer to place their assets in regimes that do not grant the full set of civil and political rights to their members. The arguments of some East Asian leaders that economic progress is best promoted by a benign autocracy are widely recognized as self-serving. Indeed, the generally stable and pacific nature of liberal democracies suggests that they should be favored by investors and professional people. It might be argued (as it often was a century and a half ago) that democratic government means majority rule, and this in turn is likely to mean redistribution from the rich few to the poorer many. But this argument is not well-founded either in theory or in practice. Majorities can coalesce across different stretches of the scale of income and wealth, and the amount of redistribution they demand will depend partly on where the coalition forms and partly on the received economic wisdom of the moment (if people believe Hayek, then even a coalition of the poor will eschew government redistribution in favor of the trickle-down effect of the free market).

If equal citizenship includes social rights as well as civil and political rights, then the cost of protecting those rights might make the regime less attractive to the global economic maximizers whose behavior we are contemplating. On the other hand, social citizenship might be seen as a cost worth bearing for the sake of social stability. I shall return to this issue below when I discuss need-based justice.

Consider next meritocratic justice, by which I mean the idea that people should have equal opportunities to develop their skills and talents, and that jobs and other sought-after positions should be assigned on the basis of merit. There are good reasons to work and invest in a society that approximates to this ideal. Investors need to invest in something—a business, say—and workers need collaborators and partners to maximize their own returns. In a meritocratic society, there is the greatest chance that natural abilities will be converted into productive talents, and that organizations will be staffed by the best-qualified people. An investor wants the capital he supplies to be combined with the most productive labor, and he will therefore welcome measures such as antidiscrimination legislation that help to ensure that the business he invests in hires the best employees. A top opera singer wants to work with excellent musicians, stage directors, and so on; she will perform best in these circumstances, draw the biggest audiences, and cut the best records. This is most likely to happen where meritocratic principles prevail.

There are some limits to this argument. A mediocre opera singer might prefer to work in a society in which local talent had been stifled: she would at least find work, albeit in productions of relatively low quality. More seriously, asset-holders may consider not only the direct returns on their assets in different places, but the implications for their families. Consider a successful entrepreneur deciding whether to locate his business in country A, which is governed by meritocratic principles, or country B, where the rich send their children to well-funded private schools not accessible to the poor, the old-boy network plays a large part in job recruitment, and so on. Which should he choose? From a business point of view, he should choose A: he will have a larger pool of talent from which to recruit his workforce, the people chosen to work for him will tend to be the best qualified, and so on. From a personal point of view, however, he may favor B: he may not welcome the restrictions placed on his own behavior by meritocratic principles, and in particular he may want to secure a privileged position for his children through private education and other means. In other words, there is a gap between the proposition that businesses located in regimes of meritocratic justice will tend to do well in global competition and the proposition that the owners or managers of such businesses must favor meritocracy.

Meritocratic justice, therefore, must be based on something more than a simple calculation of economic rationality. This is still more true in the case of need-based justice, as defined at the beginning of the chapter. Up to a point, need-based justice can go hand in hand with economic efficiency, because in order for employees to function successfully they must have access to adequate housing, decent health care, child-care facilities, and the like. If these things are not provided by the state, then either productivity is going to suffer or business organizations will have to begin providing their own housing and health-care facilities, which may prove a relatively expensive option. But there are two obvious limits to this argument. The first is that it will not apply to that section of the population that remains unemployed or only marginally employed—for instance, unskilled casual labor that can be dispensed with if the worker falls ill. If such a social stratum exists (as it does in all liberal states), providing for its members' needs will be regarded as a net cost from the perspective of international investors. In reply it might be said that considerations of social harmony and social stability require that the needs even of economically marginal individuals be met by the state: nobody wants to live in a society in which there are beggars on the street, and investors will be disturbed by the prospect of a revolt of the underclass if such measures are not taken. This reply, however, relies too much on contingencies to be fully convincing. A robust defense of social justice must begin by asserting that the meeting of every citizen's needs is a principled requirement of justice quite apart from its economic consequences, and then suggest ways of minimizing the numbers who fall into the economically marginal group. Forms of education and training that increase workers' human capital may bring it about that meeting these workers' needs counts as a productive investment rather than a drag on the economy. So rather than pretending that efficiency and justice are one and the same, we look for ways of narrowing the gap between them.

There is also a second limit to the argument that seeks to reconcile need-based justice with economic efficiency. The need principle of social justice can be given a weaker or a stronger interpretation. The weaker interpretation holds that everyone's needs must be met up to a socially defined minimum; no one should be allowed to fall below a threshold level of nourishment, housing, health care, and so on. The stronger interpretation—the one I have been defending—holds that social resources that can be identified as need-meeting resources must be distributed according to need, in other words, that there should be no preventable inequalities in the extent to which different people's needs are met. These two interpretations come apart in a case such as the distribution of health care. The weaker interpretation will require that everyone be provided with a basic standard of health care, but leave open the possibility of some people's purchasing superior health care out of their own pockets. The stronger interpretation rules out this possibility, because it entails that some medical resources are being allocated on grounds other than need; their allocation will be partly a function of money. The argument that economic efficiency requires public provision for need in order to maintain workers' productivity will only take us as far as the weaker interpretation. Our hypothetical cosmopolitan investor or professional who is deciding where to employ her assets will want to locate herself in a society whose infrastructure provides for her employees' or colleagues' basic needs, but she won't want to be prevented from buying better health care or social services for herself and her family. Thus she may resist joining a society that implements the need principle in its stronger form.

In the case of both meritocratic and need-based justice, therefore, we find that socially just policies may also serve economic efficiency, but that individual agents may have reason to resist their full implementation. It is not, I think, fanciful to see the compromise that has emerged in existing liberal democracies—in which the state promotes meritocratic ideals in education and employment and provides for a range of needs from public funds, while leaving loopholes for the better-off through its toleration of private education and medicine—as a reflection of that balance of forces. But we have still found no reason to contemplate an outright confrontation between social justice and economic globalization. For something closer to that, we must turn to the fourth item on my list, the demand for greater material equality.

Where does this demand emerge within the theory of social justice? That depends a great deal on which theory we are considering. Several popular recent theories have included quite strong egalitarian demands. Dworkin's theory of equality of resources holds that people should enjoy an equal quantity of material resources unless they are personally responsible for having a less-than-equal share, for instance, by choosing to consume or give away their quotas.[8] Rawls' difference principle holds that material inequalities are just only when they serve to raise the position of the worst-off group in society.[9] Although neither theory requires flat equality, on any reasonable interpretation each demands a considerable reduction in the economic inequalities that currently exist in liberal societies.[10] I reject both theories, not for that reason, but for other reasons given here and elsewhere—neither theory accurately captures our firmly held beliefs about social justice.[11] Yet the theory I have been advancing also contains egalitarian components, as the discussion in the last chapter makes clear. Economic inequalities must first of all be deserved—they must correspond to real differences in social contribution—and second they must not undermine equal citizenship. (That at least is what social justice requires; as I argued in Chapter 11, we may also be committed to a kind of equality that goes beyond justice, and that gives us reason to want to narrow economic inequalities still further.) So although the theory proposed here may be less demanding in this respect than those of liberal egalitarians like Dworkin and Rawls, it still must face the charge that economic globalization blocks any move in the direction of greater equality. Resource distribution, it is claimed, is a function of global market forces that national governments are powerless to challenge; thus even modest moves toward equality are now off the political agenda.

A piece of evidence that seems to support this claim is the widely observed drift toward increased income inequality in most liberal democracies. Although the drift has been much more muted in the countries of Continental Europe than in countries where the labor market is less regulated (the United Kingdom is the outstanding example here, with income inequality rising rapidly over the late 1970s and 1980s), commentators often argue that these societies, too, will in time be forced to follow the Anglo-American example if they are to remain internationally competitive.[12] Yet the cause of the drift toward inequality remains controversial. Some attribute it fairly directly to globalization, arguing that capital mobility, together with the increasing volume of international trade, is causing the wages of unskilled labor in the developed world to be undercut by cheap labor in the developing world.[13] Others argue that changing technology is primarily responsible: in particular, that technical change has facilitated the emergence of "superstars" in many fields, not only sports and entertainment, whose incomes are many times higher than those of their professional colleagues whose actual performance is at most marginally inferior.[14] Yet neither of these explanations seems able to account for significant variations in material inequality between countries whose economic profiles are broadly similar. We must also look at changes in institutions, practices, and social norms within countries that have served, and may still serve, to contain inequality.[15] If Sweden is today a less equal society than it was a decade ago, this is not just because unskilled Swedish workers face tougher foreign competition, or because Swedish superstars, like superstars everywhere, find they can command extravagant incomes, but also because the economic bargain struck between the Swedish unions and employers to limit income inequality has largely collapsed, and (whether as cause or effect of this, or both) the Swedish public has become more ready to accept substantial income differences as legitimate.[16]

Yet even if economic globalization turns out not to be the main cause of increasing inequality in the developed world, it is difficult to argue that measures designed to limit inequality—either to ensure that low-earners take home a living wage, or to prevent members of the superstar club from capturing all the economic rent they can command—have a positive effect on efficiency. If we again look at the question from the perspective of our hypothetical capital investor or high-flying professional, such measures will be seen as deterrents to investing or working in the regime in question. Inequality-reducing policies require that people be willing to forgo some of the gains they might make simply by auctioning their assets in the global market, and this can happen only if those individuals are moved by a robust sense of social justice. We come back to the communitarian setting within which the idea of social justice initially took shape, and in particular to the nation-state as its main embodiment. If the nation-state is indeed crumbling, as some extreme exponents of the globalization thesis argue, then the prospects for all the elements of social justice—but above all the fourth element, greater material equality—look bleak.[17]

HERE WE MUST TURN TO MULTICULTURALISM, which, as explained earlier, has been credited both with weakening people's identification with national communities and with destabilizing their belief in social justice. I shall begin with the second of these claims, which asserts that cultural differences between groups inevitably translate into conflicting understandings of social justice, so that there is no real prospect of uncovering the "common moral consciousness" or "overlapping consensus" to which, as I argued in Chapter 1, all theories of social justice make open or tacit appeal. John Gray has put this argument forcefully, referring specifically to the principles of merit and need that have featured prominently in the account given here:

> Conceptions of merit are not shared as a common moral inheritance, neutrally available to the inner city Moslem population of Birmingham and the secularized professional classes of Hampstead, but instead reflect radically different cultural traditions and styles of life. It defies experience to suppose that any consensus on relative merits can be reached in a society so culturally diverse . . . as ours . . . The objectivity of basic needs is equally delusive. Needs can be given no plausible cross-cultural content, but instead are seen to vary across different moral traditions.[18]

Although Gray himself would probably now wish to qualify these statements, they encapsulate a widely held belief about how justice is understood in multicultural societies. Yet to my knowledge no one, including Gray himself, has produced any hard evidence for its validity. The claim that members of different ethnic or religious groups subscribe to different understandings of notions like merit and need is not backed up by any empirical evidence, but presented as though it were a self-evident truth. The assumption must be that the cultural differences that define the various groups in plural societies—differences in language, religion, cuisine, patterns of family life, and so on—inevitably translate into conflicting conceptions of social justice. But this assumption is a very dubious one.

Unfortunately, there is a dearth of hard evidence that could be brought forward to settle the issue. Sociologists and social psychologists, who, as we have seen, have studied popular conceptions of social justice in considerable detail, have not specifically explored the effects of cultural membership on the principles of justice people hold. We do know that there are some cross-national differences in beliefs about justice, particularly if comparisons are made between societies with radically different cultural backgrounds, for instance, the United States and India. This would lead us to expect some contrasts between, for instance, long-established ethnic groups in liberal democracies and groups of recent immigrants from third-world countries. In other words, national origins are likely to make a difference in how people think about justice, but why should this be true of ethnic or other such cultural differences themselves? The obvious parallel to draw here is with class and gender differences and their impact on conceptions of justice. As we saw in Chapter 4, these cleavages do not produce much disagreement about principles of justice in the abstract, but they do give rise to somewhat contrasting perceptions about the extent to which the principles are realized in practice. For instance, we find widespread agreement between rich and poor, men and women, on the principle that jobs and offices should be allocated on the basis of merit, but significant disagreement about the extent to which jobs and offices are actually allocated by meritocratic criteria— the worse-off groups being more likely to think that their society operates in unjust ways. We would expect the same pattern to appear in the case of cultural groups, depending on whether they are relatively advantaged or disadvantaged by existing social institutions. Disadvantaged groups—black Americans, for instance—will have more critical views about the existing opportunity structure or the welfare system than will other groups, but these views will be informed by the same underlying principles of social justice as are held by citizens generally.[19]

Such limited evidence as we have tends to confirm this picture: one American study explored the preferences of different ethnic groups— Europeans, Asians, Hispanics, and African Americans—for various norms of procedural justice, and found a very high degree of convergence.[20] According to the authors of this study, the main problem posed by multiculturalism for social justice is not that different groups will be drawn toward different principles, but that where group identities become very strong at the expense of inclusive national identities, it becomes harder to motivate people to extend the universe of distribution to include members of other groups. In other words, the scope of distributive justice tends to contract so that people become indifferent to the treatment given to those outside their group. It is also harder to win support for authoritative procedures that can be used to allocate resources across groups; the more fragmented identities become, the more people tend to look at how large a slice of the cake they are getting, rather than at whether a fair procedure has been used to divide the cake.[21]

The real challenge of multiculturalism, then, is not that it makes agreement about principles of social justice impossible to achieve, but that it makes it harder for people to see themselves as members of an inclusive community across which these principles are to be implemented. We do have evidence about the relationship between identification and justice: the more closely A identifies with B, the more willing A will be to practice justice toward B, in whatever form is appropriate to their relationship.[22] Wherever distinct cultural groups form within a political community, they tend to exaggerate both the degree of cultural homogeneity within the group and the degree of difference with nonmembers. This will lead to a contraction of the ethical universe within which conceptions of justice are applied unless it is counteracted by a strong overarching identity that pulls the various groups together. In practice, only common nationality can serve this purpose. What is required for the pursuit of social justice is not the elimination of cultural differences, but the opening up of national identities so that they become accessible to the members of many (ideally all) cultural groups within existing democratic states.

In other writings I have examined how this might be achieved, and also why integration on this model will very often be welcomed by members of the cultural groups in question.[23] A strong and inclusive form of citizenship, supported by a shared national identity, creates the conditions under which previously marginalized and disadvantaged groups have the greatest chance to have their just demands recognized and acted upon. So rather than taking it for granted that multiculturalism spells the end of the nation-state in its traditional form, we should look at how that institution can be rebuilt to accommodate a more culturally diverse array of citizens. At least we should do that if we are concerned about the prospects for social justice.

IN THE FIRST CHAPTER OF THIS BOOK, I explored the circumstances of social justice—the conditions under which the idea of social justice first entered the vocabulary of social ethics and political theory, and then became an operative ideal, shaping public policy and social practice. There were three main conditions: the idea assumes a bounded society with a determinate membership, an institutional structure whose impact on the life chances of each individual can be understood, and an agency capable of changing that structure in intended ways. The task of the present chapter has been to see whether current trends, specifically globalization and multiculturalism, are taking us beyond the circumstances of social justice. My verdict is that globalizers and multiculturalists are both wrong in one way but right in another. Globalizers are wrong to assume that the promotion of social justice is impossible in a globalized economy, because some elements of social justice have a positive (or at least a neutral) effect on economic efficiency; but they are right to point out that other elements, particularly the reduction-of-inequality element, become problematic to the extent that economic agents are able to escape the constraints imposed by nation-states. Multiculturalists are wrong to claim that cultural differences must inevitably translate into disagreement about the meaning of justice, but right to point out that we can no longer take for granted the culturally homogeneous nation as the primary universe of distribution.

In these circumstances, the pursuit of social justice requires a two-handed strategy. On the one hand, we have to look to new ways of promoting old principles, and in some cases we must look afresh at the principles themselves, to see whether they can realistically be followed in the contemporary world. Political instruments that have sometimes proved successful in the course of the last century—progressive taxation, for instance, or corporate bargaining as a means of compressing the primary distribution of income—may no longer be viable, in which case we must look for new mechanisms, such as measures to enhance the skills and talents that the less able bring with them to the labor market. Again, the old idea of the welfare state as an institution whose function was to provide uniform services to different sections of the community may have to be replaced by a more diverse set of institutions supplying different services to different groups, even if this means moving away from simple ideas of equal treatment.[24] On the other hand, recognizing that nation-states have so far been the main instruments of social justice, we must look for ways of reinforcing their authority and effectiveness in the face of the global economy. This may mean creating new political units that correspond better than existing ones to the identities that matter most to citizens, or it may mean more cross-national institutions that can cope better with the challenges posed by globalization and multiculturalism.

My conclusion is that the pursuit of social justice in the twenty-first century will be considerably tougher than it has been in the last half of the twentieth; that the principles we defend ought to be ones that do not fly directly in the face of the economic and social changes I have been considering; and that we will have to think much harder about questions of scope, about what the universe of social justice should be in a world in which economic, social, and political boundaries no longer neatly coincide.

Notes

Credits

Index

Notes

1. The Scope of Social Justice

1. See, for instance, J. Rawls, *A Theory of Justice* (Cambridge, Mass.: Harvard University Press, 1971), in which he talks indiscriminately about "justice," "distributive justice," and "social justice."
2. Aristotle first distinguished universal justice, which coincided with ethical virtue as a whole, from particular justice, which singled out one particular virtue among others. Within particular justice, the main division was between distributive justice, as explained in the text, and rectificatory justice, which concerns the putting right of injuries inflicted by one person on another (for instance, restitution in cases of theft). Aristotle then added a third category, commercial justice, requiring reciprocity when goods were exchanged in the market. In later writers Aristotle's second and third categories were often combined under the heading "commutative justice." See Aristotle, *Ethics,* trans. J. A. K. Thomson (Harmondsworth: Penguin, 1955), book 5, and the discussion in W. F. R. Hardie, *Aristotle's Ethical Theory,* 2nd ed. (Oxford: Clarendon Press, 1980), chap. 10, whose interpretation I follow here.
3. St. Thomas Aquinas, *Summa Theologica* (London: Burns, Oates and Washbourne, 1918), Qus 61 and 63 (vol. 10, pp. 157–167, 186–194). I discuss Aquinas' conception of distributive justice in greater detail in Chap. 6.
4. These continuities will be explored in the chapters that follow, especially Chap. 4.
5. See, for example, J. S. Mill, *Utilitarianism,* chap. 5 in J. S. Mill, *Utilitarianism; On Liberty; Representative Government,* ed. H. B. Acton (London: Dent, 1972); J. S. Mill, *Principles of Political Economy,* ed. J. Riley (Oxford: Oxford University Press, 1994), book 2; L. Stephen, "Social Equality," in *Social Rights and Duties,* vol. 1 (London: Swan Sonnenschein, 1896); H. Sidgwick, *The Methods of Ethics,* 7th ed. (London: Macmillan, 1963), book 3, chap. 5; H. Sidgwick, *Principles of Political Economy* (London: Macmillan, 1883), book 3, chaps. 6–7.

6. See J.-Y. Calvez and J. Perrin, *The Church and Social Justice* (London: Burns and Oates, 1961), chap. 6; L. W. Shields, *The History and Meaning of the Term Social Justice* (Ph.D. diss., University of Notre Dame, Indiana, 1941), chap. 3. Catholic social philosophers tended to equate social justice with legal justice, but following Aquinas they interpreted the latter in a broad, natural law sense. The idea was applied centrally to the division of property and other economic rights between different social classes.

7. Here I am oversimplifying greatly a complex issue. For proper discussion of Marx and Engels' views about justice, see, *inter alia,* A. Wood, *Karl Marx* (London: Routledge and Kegan Paul, 1981), chap. 9; A. Buchanan, *Marx and Justice* (London: Methuen, 1982); G. A. Cohen, review of A. Wood, *Karl Marx, Mind,* 92 (1983): 440–445; J. Elster, *Making Sense of Marx* (Cambridge, England: Cambridge University Press, 1985), chap. 4; S. Lukes, *Marxism and Morality* (Oxford: Clarendon Press, 1985), chap. 4. My point is that whatever Marx and Engels actually believed about justice, their pronouncements had the effect of deterring those socialists whom they influenced from appealing to ideas of distributive or social justice in their critiques of capitalist society.

8. W. W. Willoughby, *Social Justice* (New York: Macmillan, 1900). Other American texts from this period include T. N. Carver, *Essays in Social Justice* (Cambridge, Mass.: Harvard University Press, 1915); and J. A. Ryan, *Distributive Justice* (New York: Macmillan, 1916).

9. Willoughby, *Social Justice,* p. 7.

10. See also A. Menger, *The Right to the Whole Produce of Labour,* ed. H. S. Foxwell (London: Macmillan, 1899). Foxwell's Introduction underlines the need to respond to the challenge of socialism by scrutinizing the "notions of justice and fairness" on which it rests. According to Foxwell, the most stable society is one "in whose legal structure and economic relations the prevailing notions of equity or axioms of justice are most faithfully mirrored" (p. xiv). This seems to me to pinpoint the context in which early theories of social justice were elaborated. The passage from which these phrases are taken is quoted at length by Willoughby in his Introduction to *Social Justice,* "so brilliantly do they express the motives, which have led us to undertake the present work" (pp. 4–5).

11. L. T. Hobhouse, *The Elements of Social Justice* (London: Allen and Unwin, 1922).

12. For a Catholic example, consider the following from Pius XI's encyclical *Divini Redemptoris:* "Now it is of the very essence of social justice to demand from each individual all that is necessary for the common good. But just as in the living organism it is impossible to provide for the good of the whole unless each single part and each individual member is given

what it needs for the exercise of its proper functions, so it is impossible to care for the social organism and the good of society as a unit unless each single part and each individual member—that is to say, each individual man in the dignity of his human personality—is supplied with all that is necessary for the exercise of his social functions. If social justice be satisfied, the result will be an intense activity in economic life as a whole, pursued in tranquillity and order. This activity will be proof of the health of the social body" (cited in Shields, *History and Meaning*, pp. 49–50).

13. There is also sometimes an undercurrent of social Darwinism, the suggestion being that establishing just social institutions does not simply ensure fair treatment for individuals but also contributes to national survival and national prosperity. In Carver's work this becomes the dominant theme. According to Carver, "justice is that system of adjudicating conflicting interests which makes the group strong and progressive rather than weak and retrogressive whereas injustice is a system of adjusting conflicting interests which makes a nation weak and retrogressive rather than strong and progressive" (Carver, *Essays in Social Justice,* p. 30).

14. J. Rawls, *Political Liberalism* (New York: Columbia University Press, 1993), p. 68.

15. Rawls, *Theory of Justice,* p. 457. Rawls' failure to offer an explicit defense of this assumption is highlighted in M. Canovan, *Nationhood and Political Theory* (Cheltenham: Edward Elgar, 1996), chap. 4.

16. Rawls, *Theory of Justice,* p. 7.

17. This idea of a potential political consensus on social justice is very prominent in the later work of Rawls, but we can find a similar assumption being made by theorists through the concept's career. Early exponents like Mill and Sidgwick, for instance, took themselves to be systematizing the deliverances of the "common moral consciousness" on questions of justice and applying them to social institutions. The claim was not that people would spontaneously endorse the theory that was on offer, but that they could be rationally persuaded to accept it, because its basic components were already present in their everyday thinking about justice. This ruled out in particular the possibility that people might be deeply divided on questions of justice, say along class lines.

18. Compare here Brian Barry's defense of what he calls "resourcism": "[W]e do not look behind the division of the resource to ask what people will do with it or what they will get out of it. Once they have their 'fair share' they can do what they like with it. Each person has purposes of his or her own, and the fair way of dividing scarce resources is to give each person an equal chance to use those resources to fulfil his purposes, whatever they are. . . . This position is surely in line with commonsense thinking on

the subject" (B. Barry, *Theories of Justice* [Hemel Hempstead: Harvester-Wheatsheaf, 1989], p. 87.)

19. A good example of garbage collectors' taking pride in their work is presented in M. Walzer, *Spheres of Justice: A Defence of Pluralism and Equality* (Oxford: Martin Robertson, 1983), pp. 177–181. Walzer thinks that pride in work in cases like this is relevant to justice, partly because it stops the work from being experienced as degrading, and partly because it may help to lower the rate of accidents. But he would not, I am certain, want to suggest that it should be taken into account when assessing a fair wage for collecting garbage.

20. A major problem is the radical heterogeneity of public goods, even those that fall into the same broad category, for instance, environmental public goods. I have tried to tackle the issue of how such goods might be incorporated into a theory of social justice in "Social Justice and Environmental Goods," in A. Dobson, ed., *Fairness and Futurity: Essays on Environmental Sustainability and Social Justice* (Oxford: Oxford University Press, 1999). I argue there that three categories of goods must be distinguished: basic environmental goods (like clean air), access to which is required for the enjoyment of other primary goods such as liberty and property; goods for which an agreed social value might be established through public discussion; and goods whose value will vary radically according to individual preferences and conceptions of the good. Goods in these categories must enter the theory of justice in quite different places.

21. According to Rawls, primary goods are "things which it is supposed a rational man wants whatever else he wants." In general terms these are "rights and liberties, powers and opportunities, income and wealth" (Rawls, *Theory of Justice,* pp. 92, 62). This characterization of primary goods has drawn much criticism, and its shortcomings can be seen if we take as an example higher education, access to which is surely a concern of social justice, and yet it appears not to satisfy Rawls' criterion: there are many rational plans of life to which higher education is an irrelevance. On my view what brings a good within the scope of social justice is not that it is instrumentally valuable to all rational persons, but that it has a social value that can be recognized even by those who choose not to claim it.

22. Rawls' own answer to this question is not clear, as G. A. Cohen has shown in "Where the Action Is: On the Site of Distributive Justice," *Philosophy and Public Affairs,* 26 (1997): 3–30.

23. I include here the family, whose internal division of labor and distributive practices have very substantial effects on the respective life chances of

men and women, as Susan Okin has shown in *Justice, Gender, and the Family* (New York: Basic Books, 1989).

24. See, for example, R. Nozick, *Anarchy, State, and Utopia* (Oxford: Blackwell, 1974), chap. 7.

25. I have argued for this position in *Market, State, and Community: Theoretical Foundations of Market Socialism* (Oxford: Clarendon Press, 1989), chap. 1. For a full discussion of the responsibility view of freedom, see K. Kristjansson, *Social Freedom: The Responsibility View* (Cambridge, England: Cambridge University Press, 1996).

26. I. M. Young, *Justice and the Politics of Difference* (Princeton, N.J.: Princeton University Press, 1990), esp. chap. 1. See also the contrast that Nancy Fraser draws between claims for redistribution and claims for recognition in "From Redistribution to Recognition? Dilemmas of Justice in a 'Post-Socialist' Age," *New Left Review*, 212 (July/August 1995): 68–93.

27. See my discussion in *Market, State and Community*, chap. 6.

28. It might help here to think of a society whose members belonged to two distinct religious groups, each holding contrasting views about which forms of work were legitimate and which were taboo. We might think that the resulting segregation of labor was somewhat artificial and even absurd, but it would be hard to describe it as unjust. The real cases Young describes differ from this hypothetical one insofar as certain groups tend to end up holding menial jobs while others have good jobs, and it is this feature that makes us ask critical questions about how the division of labor has come about.

29. Young, *Justice and the Politics of Difference*, p. 20.

30. J. S. Mill, *On Liberty*, chap. 3 in Mill, *Utilitarianism; On Liberty; Representative Government*.

31. I have addressed the underlying issues more fully in *On Nationality* (Oxford: Clarendon Press, 1995), chaps. 3–4.

32. Part of the reason for this is cognitive—he probably won't know what workers doing comparable jobs in Germany or America are earning, or be able to assess the real purchasing power of these money wages—but this is not the whole reason. I am claiming that inequalities with comparable Spaniards are experienced as unfair in a way that inequalities with comparable Germans or Americans are not, primarily because of the common identity and sense of belonging to a group that (most) Spaniards share. (There are some obvious exceptions to this claim: a Spaniard working for a multinational corporation will expect to be paid the same wage as other nationals doing similar work for the corporation.)

33. See D. Miller, "Justice and Global Inequality," in A. Hurrell and N. Woods, eds., *Inequality in World Politics* (Oxford: Oxford University Press, 1999);

D. Miller, "The Limits of Cosmopolitan Justice," in D. R. Mapel and T. Nardin, eds., *International Society: Diverse Ethical Perspectives* (Princeton, N.J.: Princeton University Press, 1998).

2. A Sketch of a Theory of Justice

1. Empirical research shows that in any case Rawls' two principles of justice would be very unlikely to emerge from such an experiment. See N. Frohlich and J. Oppenheimer, *Choosing Justice: An Experimental Approach to Ethical Theory* (Berkeley and Los Angeles: University of California Press, 1992); and my own discussion of this research in Chap. 4.

2. "To invoke justice is the same thing as banging on the table: an emotional expression which turns one's demand into an absolute postulate. That is no proper way to mutual understanding. It is impossible to have a rational discussion with a man who mobilizes 'justice,' because he says nothing that can be argued for or against" (A. Ross, *On Law and Justice* [London: Stevens and Sons, 1958], p. 274). A similar position can be found in H. Kelsen, "What Is Justice?" in Kelsen, *What Is Justice?* (Berkeley and Los Angeles: University of California Press, 1957).

3. B. Pascal, *Pensées,* trans. A. J. Krailsheimer (Harmondsworth: Penguin, 1966), p. 239. More pithily still: "Justice is as much a matter of fashion as charm is" (p. 47).

4. F. Nietzsche, *The Birth of Tragedy and the Genealogy of Morals,* trans. F. Golffing (New York: Doubleday Anchor, 1956), p. 207.

5. There is controversy about this in the case of Marx. On some accounts, Marx's belief in a final, highest stage of society allowed him to present the ideal of justice appropriate to *that* society as the correct one. I cannot pursue this issue here, but see A. Wood, *Karl Marx* (London: Routledge and Kegan Paul, 1981), chap. 9; A. Buchanan, *Marx and Justice* (London: Methuen, 1982); G. A. Cohen, review of A. Wood, *Karl Marx, Mind,* 92 (1983): 440–445; J. Elster, *Making Sense of Marx* (Cambridge, England: Cambridge University Press, 1985), chap. 4; S. Lukes, *Marxism and Morality* (Oxford: Clarendon Press, 1985), chap. 4.

6. This is the portrait given by "postmodernists;" a good example can be found in J.-F. Lyotard and J.-L. Thebaud, *Just Gaming* (Manchester: Manchester University Press, 1985). While claiming that "there is first a multiplicity of justices, each one of them defined in relation to the rules specific to each game" (p. 100), Lyotard seeks to avoid complete skepticism by speaking also of "the justice of multiplicity." This requires us to respect the autonomy of the different language games and prohibits the regulation of one by another (Lyotard claims that such boundary crossing always involves the use of "terror"). As Stephen White has observed,

there is some convergence here with Michael Walzer's much less skeptical defense of a pluralist account of justice. See S. K. White, *Political Theory and Postmodernism* (Cambridge, England: Cambridge University Press, 1991), chap. 7.

7. S. Hampshire, *Innocence and Experience* (London: Allen Lane, 1989), p. 63.

8. See the fuller discussion of this question in Chap. 5.

9. Where political disputes have to be resolved by negotiation, this can take the form of disagreement over who should get a seat at the negotiating table, or indeed what shape the negotiating table should be.

10. See the evidence cited in Chap. 4.

11. M. Walzer, *Spheres of Justice: A Defence of Pluralism and Equality* (Oxford: Martin Robertson, 1983).

12. I have discussed Walzer's position at greater length in the Introduction to D. Miller and M. Walzer, eds., *Pluralism, Justice, and Equality* (Oxford: Oxford University Press, 1995).

13. These are modes of relationship that typically obtain between fellow members of a political society. I do not here address the question of what justice requires of us in the case of people outside our society; see my paper "Justice and Global Inequality," in A. Hurrell and N. Woods, eds., *Inequality in World Politics* (Oxford: Oxford University Press, 1999), in which I argue that its requirements are quite different from those of social justice.

14. This is not because the institutional claims have less force, but because their content is derivative. I return to this question in Chap. 5 when considering the relative importance of procedural and outcome justice.

15. I expand upon this claim in Chap. 10.

16. Walzer, *Spheres of Justice,* pp. 71–78.

17. This claim raises a number of difficult questions, some of which I address in Chap. 9. Note in particular that we cannot use marginal productivity *in a particular case* to measure desert, for this would have the absurd consequence that if employing an electrician is essential to making the product the team is producing, then the electrician's marginal contribution—the difference between her working and not working—will be the whole of the product's value. To get around this problem, we need to look at marginal contributions across the entire range of uses to which a particular set of skills may be put.

18. For more on the latter idea, see Chap. 8.

19. On these grounds I argue in Chap. 6 against Alasdair MacIntyre's claim that desert must be understood internally to "practices" such as sports, medicine, or science.

20. In Chap. 7 I argue that the attempt to factor out native talents from the

basis of desert ends by undermining the very idea of desert. Efforts and choices, too, are affected by circumstances over which the individual making them has no control. Thus if the contribution version of the desert principle is held to be undermined by the arbitrariness of the distribution of native talents, the corrosive effect will be carried across to all versions of that principle.

21. See also C. Taylor, "The Nature and Scope of Distributive Justice," in C. Taylor, *Philosophy and the Human Sciences: Philosophical Papers 2* (Cambridge, England: Cambridge University Press, 1985), esp. pp. 305–306.

22. Thus suppose that A and B are partners in some enterprise and that they work equally hard and conscientiously, but because of A's superior (innate) talents, she is able to produce $3x$ units of output whereas B can only produce $1x$. If we say that by the effort criterion they are equally deserving, and so should receive the equivalent of $2x$ each, this treats the $2x$ of output resulting from A's superior talents as a common asset to be shared equally between the partners.

23. Compare here Michael Sandel's claim that Rawls' difference principle, which relies in a similar way on a view of talents as a common asset, could only have a place in a community in the "strong, constitutive sense" (M. Sandel, *Liberalism and the Limits of Justice* [Cambridge, England: Cambridge University Press, 1982], pp. 147–152).

24. For a fuller discussion, see my paper "Citizenship and Pluralism," *Political Studies,* 43 (1995): 432–450.

25. T. H. Marshall, *Citizenship and Social Class,* ed. T. Bottomore (London: Pluto Press, 1992).

26. Walzer, *Spheres of Justice,* pp. 69–71.

27. As I argue in Chap. 10, determining the relative strength of different people's need-claims is not a simple matter; more than one factor has to be considered.

28. See D. Miller, "Democracy and Social Justice," *British Journal of Political Science,* 8 (1978): 1–19, reprinted in P. Birnbaum, J. Lively, and G. Parry, eds., *Democracy, Consensus and Social Contract* (London: Sage, 1978).

29. *The Institutes of Justinian,* trans J. B. Moyle (Oxford: Clarendon Press, 1937), p. 3. Similar definitions can be found in the writings of Cicero, Ulpian, Aquinas, and many other classical authors.

30. The most comprehensive study of this kind is J. Elster, *Local Justice: How Institutions Allocate Scarce Goods and Necessary Burdens* (Cambridge, England: Cambridge University Press, 1992).

31. See Chap. 4. In the social psychological literature, this is most frequently studied in terms of a contrast between equality and contribution rules of distribution. For a recent comprehensive review that also cites some ap-

parently disconfirming evidence, see K. Tornblom, "The Social Psychology of Distributive Justice," in K. Scherer, ed., *Justice: Interdisciplinary Perspectives* (Cambridge, England: Cambridge University Press, 1992).

32. I develop this point at greater length in the following chapter.

33. To repeat, I am not claiming that members of an instrumental association are *compelled* to use this criterion. They might choose simply to bargain with one another over the allocation of the association's resources. But if they want to base the allocation on a principle of distributive justice, then what fits the bill is a suitably tailored version of desert.

34. R. Jowell, L. Brook, G. Prior, and B. Taylor, eds., *British Social Attitudes: The 9th Report* (Aldershot: Dartmouth, 1992), pp. 137–138. One should not push the point too far. Lobbying on behalf of a relative is a less venal form of nepotism than actually awarding him the job yourself, and there is also evidence that this permissive attitude to nepotism rests on the assumption that the relative is competent to hold the job.

35. These are the simple cases, and it is easy to think of more complex arrangements falling somewhere between these poles. In the case of pensions, a compromise between the two principles is far more readily available than in the case of medical aid.

36. See Chap. 4.

37. Another factor may aid this misconception. Suppose I have to decide between offering a job to the best qualified applicant and my less qualified nephew. If I turn the nephew down, I harm him in a direct and obvious sense: he will have to settle for a less desirable job that matches his deserts. If I turn down the strongest candidate, however, I can comfort myself with the reflection that the next employer is bound to recognize his merits—hence no real harm (or injustice) is done to him. There is a fallacy of composition at work here. The injustice of nepotism emerges clearly only if we take it that everyone will follow the rule that I am now proposing to follow, but this again requires abstract thought.

38. See P. J. Conover, I. M. Crewe, and D. D. Searing, "The Nature of Citizenship in the United States and Great Britain: Empirical Comments on Theoretical Themes," *Journal of Politics,* 53 (1991): 800–832; and P. J. Conover, "Citizen Identities and Conceptions of the Self," *Journal of Political Philosophy,* 3 (1995): 133–165, for evidence that this is indeed the case.

39. It should not, however, address questions of social justice *exclusively* from this direction. Later in the book I suggest that liberal egalitarian political philosophers like Rawls and Dworkin may have fallen into error by developing theories of justice solely from the perspective of citizenship: see Chap. 11, n. 21.

3. Social Science and Political Philosophy

1. K. Törnblom, "The Social Psychology of Distributive Justice," in K. Scherer, ed., *Justice: Interdisciplinary Perspectives* (Cambridge, England: Cambridge University Press, 1992), p. 177.
2. Ibid., p. 191.
3. B. Barry, *Theories of Justice* (Hemel Hempstead: Harvester-Wheatsheaf, 1989).
4. See, for instance, G. Mikula, "On the Role of Justice in Allocation Decisions," in G. Mikula, ed., *Justice and Social Interaction* (Bern: Hans Huber, 1980).
5. J. Elster, *Local Justice: How Institutions Allocate Scarce Goods and Necessary Burdens* (Cambridge, England: Cambridge University Press, 1992).
6. Two points need to be made to back up this claim. First, once a line or a waiting list is in place as a means of determining access to a desired good, it is clearly unjust to attempt to break into the line or circumvent the waiting list; rules that are not themselves rules of justice can generate opportunities for just or unjust behavior when they are in operation. Second, it may in some circumstances be possible to argue that lining up, say, does represent a just procedure for allocating a resource. The length of time one has spent in a line may be seen as an indicator of one's level of desire or need for the resource in question (see Elster, *Local Justice*, p. 74, for this point; for the different argument that lines may be seen as fair because they act as randomizing devices, see A. Weale, *Political Theory and Social Policy* [London: Macmillan, 1983], pp. 145–147). But this cannot be generalized to all cases. The reason the first hundred people in the cinema line should get the hundred seats that the cinema has available is that no one has an intrinsically better claim to a cinema seat than anyone else, and lining up is a clear-cut, easily understood way of cutting the demand for cinema seats down to meet the supply. In itself, the procedure is neither just nor unjust. I discuss criteria of procedural justice in Chap. 5.
7. However, the fact that there are (fairly weak) class differences in the responses people give even to abstract questions about just social distribution shows that the effect of interests on beliefs about justice may be indirect as well as direct. I discuss the evidence on this question in the following chapter. For a useful summary see W. Arts and R. van der Veen, "Sociological Approaches to Distributive and Procedural Justice," in *Justice: Interdisciplinary Perspectives*, pp. 151–152.
8. See R. J. Harris and M. A. Joyce, "What's Fair? It Depends on How You Phrase the Question," *Journal of Personality and Social Psychology*, 38

(1980): 165–179. This reports experiments in which subjects had separately to allocate profits and expenses among the members of a five-person partnership. The data revealed that, for instance, many subjects advocated an equal sharing of expenses even in cases where this led to *unequal* outcomes overall for the partners. See also D. M. Messick and T. Schell, "Evidence for an Equality Heuristic in Social Decision Making," *Acta Psychologica,* 80 (1992): 311–323; and D. M. Messick, "Equality as a Decision Heuristic," in B. A. Mellers and J. Baron, eds., *Psychological Perspectives on Justice: Theory and Applications* (Cambridge, England: Cambridge University Press, 1993), for further investigation of this topic.

9. See S. T. Allison, L. R. McQueen, and L. M. Schaerfl, "Social Decision Making Processes and the Equal Partitionment of Shared Resources," *Journal of Experimental Social Psychology,* 28 (1992): 23–42.

10. I return to this question in Chap. 4.

11. See the evidence presented in the following chapter.

12. I borrow this from my paper "Complex Equality," in D. Miller and M. Walzer, eds., *Pluralism, Justice, and Equality* (Oxford: Oxford University Press, 1995), which presents the argument that justice and social equality are independent values. See further Chap. 11.

13. A. Swift, "Public Opinion and Political Philosophy: The Relation between Social Scientific and Philosophical Analyses of Distributive Justice" (unpublished paper), p. 11. Although Swift presents this as the final riposte of the social scientist, his account of the reasons social scientists should pay attention to philosophical discussion of justice has contributed greatly to the present chapter.

14. I. Kant, *The Metaphysical Elements of Justice,* trans J. Ladd (Indianapolis: Bobbs-Merrill, 1965), p. 102. Kant's position is particularly dramatic because he is applying it in a case of deserved *punishment;* if it holds in that case, then it must surely hold *a fortiori* in a case of deserved *reward.*

15. See, for instance, B. Moore, *Injustice: The Social Bases of Obedience and Revolt* (London: Macmillan, 1979). K. Soltan, in *The Causal Theory of Justice* (Berkeley: University of California Press, 1987), relies on the converse of this proposition when he suggests looking at *objections* as a way of building an empirical theory of justice: "Instead of studying what people believe is just, we ought to study the incidence of objections to different decisions that allocate harms and benefits and objections to rules governing those decisions" (p. 31).

16. This is a controversial view that I cannot defend here fully. In particular, it may be argued that to see justice in this way is to abandon its most basic critical function: our theory cannot judge an entire society, *including its beliefs,* to be radically unjust.

17. Bambrough expresses this contrast as follows: "Plato was influenced by the conviction of Socrates that the road to moral knowledge was narrow and steep; and he was led ultimately to an exaggerated form of the Socratic view that goodness is a special skill or branch of knowledge, accessible only to the gifted and highly trained philosopher. Aristotle held fast to the common-sense view that the good life is within the reach of ordinary men. At each stage of his enquiry, he appeals to common experience and common opinion, and he will abandon these *endoxa* for some philosopher's paradox only if the reasons are very strong indeed" (R. Bambrough, ed., *The Philosophy of Aristotle* [New York: Mentor, 1963], p. 281).

18. See Aristotle, *Ethics,* trans. J. A. K. Thomson, (Harmondsworth: Penguin, 1955), book 5. Note especially Aristotle's appeals to linguistic usage and popular opinion as a way of distinguishing justice from other virtues; e.g., "In the popular mind the description 'unjust' is held to apply both to the man who takes more than his due and to the man who breaks the law" (p. 140).

19. See Aristotle, *The Politics,* trans. and ed. E Barker, (London: Oxford University Press, 1978), pp. 117–118.

20. At the very least someone seeking to defend the Platonic view would have to develop an error theory to explain how people have come to misapply these shared criteria, to the extent that their conclusions are not even approximations to the truth. Adam Swift has suggested to me that political philosophers might want to give weight to popular opinion when it is expressed in conditions favorable to serious thought—for instance, during exercises in political deliberation of the kind that James Fishkin has been sponsoring—but not otherwise. This would yield an interesting third alternative to the positions identified in the text. For Fishkin's approach see *Democracy and Deliberation: New Directions for Democratic Reform* (New Haven: Yale University Press, 1991).

21. I shall not describe the content of Rawls' theory of justice, which I assume is familiar to most readers. The major statement is J. Rawls, *A Theory of Justice* (Cambridge, Mass.: Harvard University Press, 1971). My focus here is exclusively on Rawls' method of arguing for his two principles, and in particular the question what role, if any, empirical evidence about what people ordinarily regard as just should play in that argument.

22. J. Rawls, *Political Liberalism* (New York: Columbia University Press, 1993), p. 13.

23. Admittedly there is some ambiguity as to what Rawls means when he refers to "the public political culture." He could be referring to the political principles that people commonly subscribe to, or else to the institu-

tional embodiment of principles in a society's laws and constitution. The latter interpretation does not sit so easily with his idea of public justification.

24. One could of course argue that the contractarian device is itself at least partly justified by its congruence with popular beliefs. The argument would be that people see agreement behind a veil of ignorance as a way of capturing the quality of impartiality that a theory of justice should possess. Even if this is true—I think it is reading a good deal into the common person's sense of justice—it would still not follow that the output of the original position (supposing it does have a determinate output) corresponds to the substantive beliefs that people hold.

25. This procedure has been well described and clarified in N. Daniels, "Wide Reflective Equilibrium and Theory Acceptance in Ethics," *Journal of Philosophy,* 76 (1979): 256–282.

26. Rawls, *Theory of Justice,* p. 50.

27. Rawls, *Political Liberalism,* p. 28. In his unpublished manuscript "Justice as Fairness: A Restatement" (Cambridge, Mass.: Harvard University, 1990), Rawls introduces the idea that reflective equilibrium is *general* when the same conception of justice is affirmed in everyone's judgments (pp. 25–26). While clearly regarding this as a desirable goal, Rawls does not explain how we are supposed to move from individual reflective equilibrium to general reflective equilibrium.

28. Cf. J. Elster, "The Empirical Study of Justice," in D. Miller and M. Walzer, eds., *Pluralism, Justice, and Equality* (Oxford: Oxford University Press, 1995), pp. 93–94.

29. Contractarian theories of justice are examined most fully in Barry, *Theories of Justice.*

30. The most likely alternative is some form of utilitarianism, as argued for in J. Harsanyi, "Can the Maximin Principle Serve as a Basis for Morality? A Critique of John Rawls' Theory," *American Political Science Review,* 69 (1975): 594–606. (Rawls attempted to prevent his contractual theory from collapsing into utilitarianism by distinguishing choice under *uncertainty* from choice under *risk,* but few commentators have found this a convincing maneuver. Among the many critiques of Rawls' treatment of this issue, the most trenchant is probably still B. Barry, *The Liberal Theory of Justice* [Oxford: Clarendon Press, 1973], chap. 9.)

31. Rawls, *Political Liberalism,* p. 306.

32. An interpretation of this kind is proposed in T. M. Scanlon's paper "Contractualism and Utilitarianism," in A. Sen and B. Williams, eds., *Utilitarianism and Beyond* (Cambridge, England: Cambridge University Press, 1982), and more recently endorsed in Barry's *Justice as Impartiality* (Ox-

ford: Clarendon Press, 1995) as the best explication of the contractarian motif in Rawls. My view, in contrast, is that testing principles by applying a reasonable rejection test is not genuinely contractarian. There is an ambiguity in the test that obscures this. On the one hand, we could envisage people objecting to principles of justice according to how they personally would fare if the principles were implemented. Suppose that applying a particular principle of justice would leave a few people very badly off. If there are feasible alternative principles that do not have this consequence, it would be reasonable, on this first interpretation of the test, for the losers under the original principle to reject it. So it looks as though individuals are being given a veto on principles under which they would do very badly (relative to some alternative), and we appear to have an independent contractarian test of the validity of principles of justice that does not depend on our already embracing any substantive notions of justice.

On the other hand, consider someone whose well-being depends chiefly on carrying out activities that are damaging to others—a pedophile, for instance, or someone who takes great delight in destroying works of art. A rule prohibiting these activities lowers that person's welfare very considerably, perhaps leaves it very low in absolute terms. Can such a person reasonably reject the rule? To avoid answering this question in the affirmative, we need to switch to a different and moralized sense of "reasonableness" according to which rejection of the rule would not be reasonable no matter how bitterly the person in question might complain. But on this second version of the test independent moral criteria are being used to determine what counts as reasonable rejection and what does not. It may for certain purposes be illuminating to say that valid principles of justice are those that no one who was going to be subject to them could reasonably reject as a basis for cooperation, but because "reasonableness" here already embodies substantive moral criteria it is misleading to present this as a contractarian account of justice. I have discussed Barry's use (or misuse) of Scanlon at greater length in "The Limits of Cosmopolitan Justice," in D. Mapel and T. Nardin, eds., *The Constitution of International Society: Diverse Ethical Perspectives* (Princeton: Princeton University Press, 1998).

33. Cf. Barry: "[The original position] is merely a device for representing in a dramatic form the constraints that impartial appraisal imposes on anything that can count as a principle of justice" (*Theories of Justice,* p. 214).

34. Rawls, *Political Liberalism,* p. 26.

35. I am not alone in thinking this. For a discussion that focuses attention on the divergence between the priority assigned to basic liberties in Rawls'

principles of justice and what we know about the public culture of the society for which he is primarily writing, see G. Klosko, "Rawls' 'Political' Philosophy and American Democracy," *American Political Science Review,* 87 (1993): 348–359.

36. More precisely, this is what Walzer's approach requires of him, even though the account of justice that he actually gives is derived somewhat impressionistically from the shared meanings that he claims are embodied in different social goods.

37. See R. Nozick, *Anarchy, State and Utopia* (Oxford: Blackwell, 1974).

38. The research project that has come closest to meeting these desiderata is the International Social Justice Project, findings from which are presented in J. R. Kluegel, D. S. Mason, and B. Wegener, *Social Justice and Political Change: Public Opinion in Capitalist and Post-Communist States* (New York: Aldine de Gruyter, 1995). I discuss some of the evidence generated by this project in the following chapter.

39. I assume here that political philosophy has a practical aim: its purpose is not only to get at the truth, but to improve the thinking of those who are not professional philosophers.

40. I take this suggestion from Swift, "Public Opinion and Political Philosophy," pp. 4–6.

41. See C. Burgoyne, A. Swift, and G. Marshall, "Inconsistency in Beliefs about Distributive Justice: A Cautionary Note," *Journal for the Theory of Social Behaviour,* 23 (1993): 327–342.

4. Distributive Justice: What the People Think

1. See J. Elster, *The Cement of Society: A Study of Social Order* (Cambridge, England: Cambridge University Press, 1989), for an analysis of this kind.

2. More generally it has been suggested (see P. Brickman et al., "Microjustice and Macrojustice," in M. and S. Lerner, eds., *The Justice Motive in Social Behavior* [New York: Plenum Press, 1981]) that people may apply one criterion of justice when considering how resources are allocated individual by individual, and another criterion when looking at the overall distribution that results (for example, an allocation that gives each person what he or she deserves may be judged to be excessively inegalitarian overall). The macro-considerations at stake here may not necessarily be considerations of *justice,* however; they may, for instance, involve an ideal of social equality that is independent of justice, as I suggested in the last chapter.

3. See the general claim to this effect in M. Walzer, *Spheres of Justice: A Defence of Pluralism and Equality* (Oxford: Martin Robertson, 1983), and the copious evidence collected in J. Elster, *Local Justice: How Institutions*

Allocate Scarce Goods and Necessary Burdens (Cambridge, England: Cambridge University Press, 1992).

4. I examine the rationale for choosing an equal division of resources in circumstances of uncertainty more fully in Chap. 11.

5. Helpful reviews include G. Leventhal, "Fairness in Social Relationships," in J. Thibaut, J. Spence, and R. Carson, eds., *Contemporary Topics in Social Psychology* (Morristown, N.J.: General Learning Press, 1976); G. Mikula, "On the Role of Justice in Allocation Decisions," and T. Schwinger, "Just Allocations of Goods: Decisions among Three Principles," in G. Mikula, ed., *Justice and Social Interaction* (Bern: Hans Huber, 1980); K. Törnblom, "The Social Psychology of Distributive Justice," in K. Scherer, ed., *Justice: Interdisciplinary Perspectives* (Cambridge, England: Cambridge University Press, 1992).

6. See K. Törnblom and D. Jonsson, "Distribution versus Retribution: The Perceived Justice of the Contribution and Equality Principles for Cooperative and Competitive Relationships," *Acta Sociologica,* 30 (1987): 25–52. One should note, however, that switching to a team context may also imply that individual contributions are harder to disentangle, so that equality may be preferred not so much as an expression of group solidarity but by default (see above). In the Törnblom and Jonsson experiment, the contribution principle was operationalized in the proposal that bonuses should be allocated to goal-scorers, but people who know about soccer might reasonably think that winning depends on the whole team's performance, while who scores the goals is largely a matter of chance (and assigned position). There is less ambiguity in the work experiments referred to below.

7. See W. I. Griffith and J. Sell, "The Effects of Competition on Allocators' Preferences for Contributive and Retributive Justice Rules," *European Journal of Social Psychology,* 18 (1988): 443–455; M. Lerner, "The Justice Motive: 'Equity' and 'Parity' among Children," *Journal of Personality and Social Psychology,* 29 (1974): 539–550; Schwinger, "Just Allocations of Goods."

8. See M. Deutsch, *Distributive Justice* (New Haven: Yale University Press, 1985).

9. See Ibid., chap. 11; Mikula, "On the Role of Justice in Allocation Decisions," pp. 153–154.

10. See E. Kayser and H. Lamm, "Causal Explanation of Performance Differences and Allocations among Friends," *Journal of Social Psychology,* 115 (1981): 73–81.

11. See Mikula, "On the Role of Justice in Allocation Decisions"; E. G. Shapiro, "Effect of Expectations of Future Interaction on Reward Alloca-

tion in Dyads: Equity or Equality," *Journal of Personality and Social Psychology*, 31 (1975): 873–880.

12. See Deutsch, *Distributive Justice*, chap. 10.

13. See G. Leventhal, "The Distribution of Rewards and Resources in Groups and Organizations," in L. Berkowitz and E. Walster, eds., *Advances in Experimental Social Psychology*, vol. 9 (New York: Academic Press, 1976).

14. See G. Leventhal and J. Michaels, "Locus of Cause and Equity Motivation as Determinants of Reward Allocation," *Journal of Personality and Social Psychology*, 17 (1971): 229–235; S. Rest et al., "Further Evidence Concerning the Effects of Perceptions of Effort and Ability on Achievement Evaluation," *Journal of Personality and Social Psychology*, 28 (1973): 187–191; K. Y. Törnblom and D. R. Jonsson, "Subrules of the Equity and Contribution Principles: Their Perceived Fairness in Distribution and Retribution," *Social Psychology Quarterly*, 48 (1985): 249–261.

15. I say "presumably" because if achievements differ while effort is held constant, the only explanations available are that performers differ in ability or that external factors are affecting the outcome. Since I assume that no one would regard the latter as relevant to desert, it follows that ability is being allowed to count. The only other way of interpreting the results would be to argue that "achievement" is somehow picking up an additional aspect of "trying" besides that represented by "effort" (for example, that over and above physical effort achievement depends on something like concentration). I can see no reason for adopting such a forced reading of the data, however.

16. Leventhal and Michaels, "Locus of Cause and Equity Motivation."

17. Rest et al., "Further Evidence Concerning the Effects of Perceptions."

18. Presented with this choice, 78 percent of American subjects preferred income inequality and only 7 percent preferred equality. (See H. McClosky and J. Zaller, *The American Ethos: Public Attitudes toward Capitalism and Democracy* [Cambridge, Mass.: Harvard University Press, 1984], p. 84.) In contrast, 19 percent of Americans agreed strongly or somewhat with the first statement about equal shares. (See *International Social Justice Project: Documentation and Codebook* [Ann Arbor: University of Michigan Institute for Social Research, 1993], p. 171, which gives comparative figures for thirteen countries.) Notice that in addition to not being presented in the form of an either/or choice, this statement refers to the distribution of *wealth* and income, and one may speculate that people are more likely to believe that wealth (which suggests fixed holdings of capital assets) should be equally distributed than that income (which suggests a flow of money from work, primarily) should be.

19. A good sample of the reasons offered spontaneously by American work-

ing men for rejecting material equality can be found in R. Lane, *Political Ideology* (New York: Free Press, 1962), chap. 4.

20. A. Swift, G. Marshall, and C. Burgoyne, "Which Road to Social Justice?" *Sociology Review,* 2 (1992), p. 29.

21. T. W. Smith, "Social Inequality in Cross-National Perspective," in D. Alwin et. al., *Attitudes to Inequality and the Role of Government* (Rijswijk: Sociaal en Cultureel Planbureau, 1990), p. 25. The countries surveyed were the United States, Britain, Hungary, West Germany, Australia, Holland, and Italy. Of these only the Dutch stood out against inequality, with agreement rates averaging less than 50 percent.

22. S. Svallfors, "Dimensions of Inequality: A Comparison of Attitudes in Sweden and Britain," *European Sociological Review,* 9 (1993), p. 272.

23. McClosky and Zaller, *American Ethos,* p. 84.

24. J. Kluegel and E. Smith, *Beliefs about Inequality: Americans' Views of What Is and What Ought to Be* (New York: Aldine de Gruyter, 1986), p. 107. Note that the propositions here refer to *greater* equality; one may surmise that analogous propositions about *complete* equality would attract still higher degrees of support.

25. See G. Jasso and P. Rossi, "Distributive Justice and Earned Income," *American Sociological Review,* 42 (1977): 639–651; W. Alves and P. Rossi, "Who Should Get What? Fairness Judgments of the Distribution of Earnings," *American Journal of Sociology,* 84 (1978): 541–564; W. Alves, "Modeling Distributive Justice Judgments," in P. Rossi and S. Nock, eds., *Measuring Social Judgments* (Beverly Hills: Sage, 1982).

26. Alves, "Modeling Distributive Justice Judgments," pp. 216–217.

27. S. Verba and G. Orren, *Equality in America: The View from the Top* (Cambridge, Mass.: Harvard University Press, 1985), chap. 8.

28. In the Verba and Orren study, a fair income for an executive was judged to be $95,320, but for a doctor only $52,798. Removing executives from consideration almost halves the range of fair incomes.

29. The reason for thinking this is that respondents tended to be "tolerant" in the sense that they were biased toward judging the randomly assigned incomes fair rather than too high or low.

30. J. Hochschild, *What's Fair: American Beliefs about Distributive Justice* (Cambridge, Mass.: Harvard University Press, 1981).

31. Kluegel and Smith, *Beliefs about Inequality,* p. 113.

32. Hochschild, *What's Fair,* p. 112.

33. Ibid., p. 115.

34. Ibid., p. 118.

35. Kluegel and Smith, *Beliefs about Inequality,* p. 112.

36. McClosky and Zaller, *American Ethos,* p. 91. This proposition does not

refer specifically to equality of income, and so it may be picking up commitments to equality of opportunity, for example, alongside belief in the desirability of a narrower income range.

37. J. Mack and S. Lansley, *Poor Britain* (London: Allen and Unwin, 1985), p. 223. For figures for other countries, see T. Smith, "Inequality and Welfare," in R. Jowell, S. Witherspoon, and L. Brook, eds., *British Social Attitudes: Special International Report* (Gower: Aldershot, 1989).

38. As I will show later, there is a contrast here with ex-communist states.

39. Kluegel and Smith, *Beliefs about Inequality,* p. 120. Very similar opinions can be found in Verba and Orren's study of group leaders.

40. Kluegel and Smith, *Beliefs about Inequality,* p. 106. The majority was, however, a fairly slim one—55 percent in favor, 45 percent against.

41. McClosky and Zaller, *American Ethos,* p. 66.

42. In Verba and Orren's study, only business leaders were against raising the pay of the worst-paid occupation: see *Equality in America,* p. 160.

43. This conclusion is well represented in the interview material presented in L. Rainwater, *What Money Buys: Inequality and the Social Meanings of Income* (New York: Basic Books, 1974), esp. pp. 178–184.

44. The precise figures depend on how the question is put. There is somewhat greater support for the proposal that government should require firms to take on unemployed workers and then subsidize their wages than for the proposal that everyone who wants to work should be guaranteed a job, but both proposals get majority assent (see McClosky and Zaller, *American Ethos,* p. 276, and Kluegel and Smith, *Beliefs about Inequality,* p. 153). By contrast, the proposition that everyone who works should be guaranteed an income above the poverty line is considerably more popular than the proposition that everyone, regardless of employment status, should have a guaranteed minimum income, but neither attracts majority support (see Kluegel and Smith, *Beliefs about Inequality,* p. 153, and McClosky and Zaller, *American Ethos,* p. 275).

45. See especially Rainwater, *What Money Buys,* pp. 179–182.

46. See T. Schwinger, "The Need Principle of Distributive Justice," in H. W. Bierhoff, R. L. Cohen, and J. Greenberg, eds., *Justice in Social Relations* (New York: Plenum Press, 1986).

47. Deutsch, who was the first social psychologist to distinguish equity, equality, and need as principles of justice, proposed that equality would be favored in relationships in which "the fostering or maintenance of enjoyable social relations is the common goal," whereas need would be favored when "the fostering of personal development and personal welfare is the common goal." See M. Deutsch, "Equity, Equality and Need: What Determines Which Value Will Be Used as the Basis of Distributive

Justice?" *Journal of Social Issues,* 31 (1975), p. 143. It is difficult, however, to see how these alternatives could be distinguished experimentally.

48. G. Mikula and T. Schwinger, "Intermember Relations and Reward Allocation: Theoretical Considerations of Affects," in H. Brandstatter, J. Davis, and H. Schuler, eds., *Dynamics of Group Decisions* (Beverly Hills and London: Sage, 1978).

49. H. Lamm and T. Schwinger, "Norms Concerning Distributive Justice: Are Needs Taken into Consideration in Allocation Decisions?" *Social Psychology Quarterly,* 43 (1980): 425–429.

50. Some divided the surplus equally between the two students, others gave the whole of the surplus to the one who had not yet received any money. The latter option represents a kind of compromise between need and equality.

51. M. Yaari and M. Bar-Hillel, "On Dividing Justly," *Social Choice and Welfare,* 1 (1984): 1–24.

52. Yaari and Bar-Hillel refer to this as the "maximin solution," whereas I am taking it to represent the principle of distribution according to need. In a case such as the one described, where it is a question of dividing a fixed stock of goods between two individuals with the same basic needs, these two principles are bound to coincide. In defense of my interpretation, I would point out that if maximin were the fundamental principle at stake here, it would be difficult to explain why respondents shifted their ground so radically when needs were replaced by tastes. The rule "maximize the welfare of the worse-off individual" makes no distinction between differences in need and other kinds of utility difference.

53. Interestingly, however, there is a limit to this. In one variant, Smith was described as being very poor at converting fruit into vitamin, so that to achieve equal vitamin levels almost all the fruit had to be given to him, and of course the level of vitamin achieved by both parties was low. Although equality of need fulfillment remained the most popular option, there were many defections in favor of more efficient outcomes giving Jones a higher proportion of fruit. This is the equivalent of the battlefield policy of triage, whereby scarce medical resources are allocated to those they can help the most, at the expense of very seriously injured combatants who would require extensive treatment to have any chance of recovery. See further my discussion in Chap. 10.

54. See, for example, S. Schwartz, "The Justice of Need and the Activation of Humanitarian Norms," *Journal of Social Issues,* 31 (1975): 111–136.

55. H. Lamm and T. Schwinger, "Need Consideration in Allocation Decisions: Is it Just?" *Journal of Social Psychology,* 119 (1983): 205–209.

56. See, for instance, T. Campbell, "Humanity before Justice," *British Journal*

of Political Science, 4 (1974): 1–16. I criticize Campbell's argument in Chap. 10.

57. McClosky and Zaller, *American Ethos,* p. 272.

58. P. Taylor-Gooby, "Citizenship and Welfare," in R. Jowell, S. Witherspoon, and L. Brook, eds., *British Social Attitudes: The 1987 Report* (Gower: Aldershot, 1987).

59. P. Taylor-Gooby, *Public Opinion, Ideology and State Welfare* (London: Routledge and Kegan Paul, 1985), chap. 2.

60. See N. Jaffe, "Attitudes toward Public Welfare Programs and Recipients in the United States," appendix to L. M. Salamon, *Welfare: The Elusive Consensus* (New York: Praeger, 1978), and Kluegel and Smith, *Beliefs about Inequality,* pp. 152–158, for American evidence; Mack and Lansley, *Poor Britain,* pp. 209–221 for British evidence.

61. Mack and Lansley, *Poor Britain,* chap. 3.

62. The spectrum shifts with time, as certain items previously considered luxuries come to be counted as necessities. This process reveals itself, too, in changing perceptions of the minimum income needed to avoid poverty. See Rainwater, *What Money Buys,* chap. 3.

63. Mack and Lansley, *Poor Britain,* p. 258.

64. There are many examples of reasoning along these lines in Hochschild, *What's Fair,* esp. chaps. 6 and 8.

65. Few studies explicitly investigate the way people aggregate justice concerns of different kinds into an overall judgment, but for a micro-experiment see G. Elliot and B. Meeker, "Achieving Fairness in the Face of Competing Concerns," *Journal of Personality and Social Psychology,* 50 (1986): 754–760.

66. This is not the place to consider the various slightly different interpretations that can be given of the difference principle, since they do not bear on the main conclusion reported below.

67. See P. Brickman, "Preference for Inequality," *Sociometry,* 40 (1977): 303–310.

68. See N. Frohlich, J. Oppenheimer, and C. Eavey, "Choices of Principles of Distributive Justice in Experimental Groups," *American Journal of Political Science,* 31 (1987): 606–636; N. Frohlich, J. Oppenheimer, and C. Eavey, "Laboratory Results on Rawls's Distributive Justice," *British Journal of Political Science,* 17 (1987): 1–21; N. Frohlich and J. Oppenheimer, "Choosing Justice in Experimental Democracies with Production," *American Political Science Review,* 84 (1990): 461–477; N. Frohlich and J. Oppenheimer, *Choosing Justice: An Experimental Approach to Ethical Theory* (Berkeley: University of California Press, 1992).

69. This is true of all the original North American experiments. When the

project was replicated under slightly different conditions in Poland, one solitary group appears possibly to have opted for the difference principle, although other evidence suggests that this may have been a recording error. See Frohlich and Oppenheimer, *Choosing Justice,* pp. 58–59, 79.

70. Frohlich, Oppenheimer, and Eavey, "Choices of Principles of Distributive Justice in Experimental Groups," p. 630.

71. More radically still, it might be claimed that Rawls is specifying *what it would be rational to choose* under certain circumstances, and so his argument cannot be defeated by observations about what people do in fact choose in these circumstances. We may note, however, that Rawls wisely eschews any attempt to show that maximin is in general the rational strategy for choosing under uncertainty (J. Rawls, *A Theory of Justice* [Cambridge, Mass.: Harvard University Press, 1971], sect. 26). Instead, he appeals to certain empirical features of the original position as he has identified it that, he claims, make it reasonable to adopt such a conservative strategy. This seems to me to involve an empirical claim about how human beings will in general respond to uncertainties of the kind described, and so is open to empirical confirmation or falsification. (I am grateful to Andrew Williams for bringing this possibility to my attention, even though it is not one he would endorse himself.)

72. J. Rawls, *Political Liberalism* (New York: Columbia University Press, 1993), p. 282. Another change in Rawls' thinking concerns the status of the difference principle, which he no longer regards as a "constitutional essential" but as a principle whose validity is open to political discussion. Interestingly, the principle that there should be "a social minimum providing for the basic needs of all citizens" *is* taken to be a constitutional essential (see pp. 227–230). Whether this constitutes a weakening in Rawls' attachment to the difference principle is more moot. The case to the contrary is well put in D. Estlund, "The Survival of Egalitarian Justice in John Rawls's *Political Liberalism," Journal of Political Philosophy,* 4 (1996): 68–78.

73. Constraints of space mean that I have had to exclude another issue that merits investigation, namely, differences between men's and women's conceptions of justice. I discussed this briefly in the paper upon which this chapter is based, and concluded that men and women held broadly similar beliefs about distributive justice, though there were some significant differences in justice behavior. See D. Miller, "Distributive Justice: What the People Think," *Ethics,* 102 (1991–1992), pp. 581–582, and the references cited there.

74. See Elster, *The Cement of Society,* chap. 6.

75. See G. Høgsnes, "Wage Bargaining and Norms of Fairness: A Theoretical

Framework for Analysing the Norwegian Wage Formation," *Acta Sociologica*, 32 (1989): 339–357.

76. See R. Hyman and I. Brough, *Social Values and Industrial Relations* (Oxford: Blackwell, 1975).

77. See J. Kelley and M. D. R. Evans, "The Legitimation of Inequality: Occupational Earnings in Nine Nations, *American Journal of Sociology*, 99 (1993): 75–125.

78. Ibid., p. 116.

79. Ibid., p. 107. These figures are averages for nine countries covered by the International Social Survey Programme (ISSP) and equivalent surveys: Australia, Austria, Britain, Hungary, the Netherlands, Poland, Switzerland, the United States, and West Germany.

80. See the general discussion in M. Dornstein, *Conceptions of Fair Pay: Theoretical Perspectives and Empirical Research* (New York: Praeger, 1991), chaps. 6–7.

81. In the ISJP survey 68 percent of respondents thought that they were paid much or somewhat less than they deserved, as compared with 2 percent who thought they were paid more than they deserved. There was not much variation among countries in the latter figure. In relation to the former, people in the economically advantaged capitalist countries were more likely than those in ex-communist countries to say that they were paid about what they deserved. See *International Social Justice Project: Documentation and Codebook*, p. 139.

82. On comparable-worth policies, see S. M. Evans and B. J. Nelson, *Wage Justice: Comparable Worth and the Paradox of Technocratic Reform* (Chicago: University of Chicago Press, 1989); S. E. Rhoads, *Incomparable Worth: Pay Equity Meets the Market* (Cambridge, England: Cambridge University Press, 1993).

83. Hyman and Brough, *Social Values*, p. 37.

84. Rhoads, *Incomparable Worth*, pp. 83–84.

85. J. R. Kluegel and P. Matějů, "Egalitarian vs Inegalitarian Principles of Distributive Justice," in J. R. Kluegel, D. S. Mason, and B. Wegener, *Social Justice and Political Change: Public Opinion in Capitalist and Post-Communist States* (New York: Aldine de Gruyter, 1995).

86. McClosky and Zaller, *American Ethos*, pp. 154–156.

87. A. Swift, G. Marshall, C. Burgoyne, and D. Routh, "Distributive Justice: Does It Matter What the People Think?" in Kluegel et al., *Social Justice and Political Change*.

88. In McClosky and Zaller's survey only 9 percent of low-income Americans assented to this proposition. See McClosky and Zaller, *American Ethos*, p. 156.

89. See Smith, "Inequality and Welfare," pp. 72–74.

90. P. Whiteley, "Public Opinion and the Demand for Social Welfare in Britain," *Journal of Social Policy,* 10 (1981): 453–476.

91. P. Beedle and P. Taylor-Gooby, "Ambivalence and Altruism: Public Opinion about Taxation and Welfare," *Policy and Politics,* 11 (1983): 15–39.

92. Alves and Rossi, "Who Should Get What?" pp. 557–562. See also M. Dornstein, "Perceptions Regarding Standards for Evaluating Pay Equity and Their Determinants," *Journal of Occupational Psychology,* 58 (1985): 321–330, which reveals that blue-collar workers are far more likely than white-collar workers to mention "family need" when asked an open-ended question about fair pay.

93. See J. Rytina, W. Form, and J. Pease, "Income and Stratification Ideology: Beliefs about the American Opportunity Structure," *American Journal of Sociology,* 75 (1970): 703–716; Kluegel and Smith, *Beliefs about Inequality,* chaps. 3–4.

94. S. Verba, *Elites and the Idea of Equality: A Comparison of Japan, Sweden, and the United States* (Cambridge, Mass.: Harvard University Press, 1987), chap. 6.

95. I have looked at the evidence in greater detail, and provided some tables that summarize the responses in each country to a variety of justice-related questions, in "Popular Beliefs about Social Justice: A Comparative Approach," in S. Svallfors, ed., *In the Eye of the Beholder: Opinions on Welfare and Justice in Comparative Perspective* (Umea: Bank of Sweden, 1995).

96. Here the two halves of Germany diverged quite sharply: 60 percent of East Germans agreed with the proposition as compared with 32 percent of West Germans, despite high levels of agreement on general propositions about equality and desert.

97. For a fuller discussion, see D. S. Mason, "Justice, Socialism and Participation in the Post-Communist States," in Kluegel et al., *Social Justice and Political Change.*

98. On this issue East Germans already had "capitalist" attitudes, and indeed thought very much like West Germans.

99. See J. R. Kluegel et al., "Accounting for the Rich and Poor: Existential Justice in Comparative Perspective," in Kluegel et al., *Social Justice and Political Change.*

100. See also the general conclusions reached about conceptions of social justice in capitalist and ex-communist states in G. Marshall, A. Swift, and S. Roberts, *Against the Odds? Social Class and Social Justice in Industrial Societies* (Oxford: Clarendon Press, 1997), Appendix J.

101. For Hayek's argument, see *Law, Legislation and Liberty, vol. II: The Mirage*

of Social Justice (London: Routledge and Kegan Paul, 1976). Hayek did not attempt to deny that notions of social justice were widely shared; he tried to explain why this "mirage" seemed so plausible.

102. See Elster, *Local Justice,* passim.

103. Hochschild, *What's Fair,* chap. 6.

5. Procedures and Outcomes

1. This is the view of, for instance, Robert Nozick when he writes that "for an entitlement theorist any set of holdings that emerges from a legitimate process (specified by the principle of transfer) is just. . . . whatever comes out is to be accepted because of its pedigree, its history" (R. Nozick, *Anarchy, State and Utopia* [Oxford: Blackwell, 1974], p. 207). In the same camp stands F. A. Hayek's claim that justice is an attribute of human actions and the rules of behavior that human beings follow, so that outcomes can be called just or unjust only insofar as they are the intended results of such behavior. (See F. A. Hayek, *Law, Legislation and Liberty,* vol. II.: *The Mirage of Social Justice* [London: Routledge and Kegan Paul, 1976], chap. 8.) I shall return to the views of both thinkers later in the chapter.

2. There is a sustained argument to this effect in Hayek, *Law, Legislation and Liberty,* vol. II, chap. 9.

3. A variant on this occurs when the procedure uses a readily applicable criterion as a proxy for the less easily detectable quality that justice demands. In the example given, we might use objective testing that requires no judgment on the part of the marker, but whose results do not correlate perfectly with academic ability. For other examples of this phenomenon, see J. Elster, *Local Justice: How Institutions Allocate Scarce Goods and Necessary Burdens* (Cambridge, England: Cambridge University Press, 1992), p. 65.

4. That this example is more than hypothetical is shown by J. Le Grand, *The Strategy of Equality* (London: Allen and Unwin, 1982), chap. 3.

5. Several instances of this kind are collected in Elster, *Local Justice,* chap. 4.

6. J. Rawls, *A Theory of Justice* (Cambridge, Mass.: Harvard University Press, 1971), sect. 14. Later I shall examine an attempt to explain away pure procedural justice as simply a manifestation of the principle of free agreement.

7. I think, in fact, that we might be reluctant to describe the outcome as positively fair in cases such as this; the double negative "not unfair" better captures the sense that the outcome cannot be criticized on grounds of justice because of the nature of the procedure used to reach it, while on

the other hand it is intrinsically no more or less fair than any other outcome that might have been reached using the same procedure. Rawls also hedges on this point in *Theory of Justice,* p. 86.

8. For this argument see R. Dworkin, "Equality of Resources," *Philosophy and Public Affairs,* 10 (1980–1981): 283–345. I say "tends to produce" because the envy-free outcome will occur only if the auction is run repeatedly until everyone is satisfied with the outcome, in the sense that there is no better way in which he or she could have made his or her bids.

9. It might be objected here that even if the prison sentence imposed on the rapists was equivalent to that which would have been imposed for rape, the punishment as a whole is not equivalent because it does not carry the moral condemnation that goes along with a conviction for rape. The outcome, therefore, was not fully just and this is what grounds the victim's complaint. It is certainly true that the victim wanted the three men to be exposed as rapists. Nevertheless, she also has a separate ground for objecting to the procedure that was followed, namely, that a fair procedure in cases like this should respect the victim by giving her the opportunity to tell her side of the story, and in general to seek to establish the truth about what has occurred.

10. This example is inspired by John Broome's discussion in "Fairness," *Proceedings of the Aristotelian Society,* 91 (1990–1991): 87–102.

11. These are not, of course, the only possibilities. An intermediate procedure would be to conduct a *weighted* lottery in which each patient's chances of winning varied according to the likelihood of his or her being a successful recipient. Broome thinks weighted lotteries are appropriate where individuals have differentially strong claims on the good being allocated, although he is doubtful whether this would apply in the case we are considering.

12. At first glance it might seem that favoring the younger patients is justified simply on efficiency grounds—it is the policy that is likely to deliver the greatest benefit in aggregate. But one can also defend it on grounds of justice. People with defective kidneys are arbitrarily disadvantaged by comparison with the rest of the population. Each successful kidney transplant eliminates one case of arbitrary disadvantage. Thus the policy that maximizes transplant success is also the policy that creates the most outcome justice—that is, minimizes the number of people who are unfairly disadvantaged. See my fuller discussion in Chapter 10.

13. I am looking here at the immediate properties of procedures for assigning benefits, and not at institutional features that may help to guarantee those properties, such as the requirement that the person who administers a procedure should have no vested interest in a particular outcome, or that

potential beneficiaries should have a right of appeal if they believe that they have been unfairly treated. A complete account of procedural justice would need to incorporate these second-order features too.

14. For discussion see J. Lucas, *On Justice* (Oxford: Clarendon Press, 1980), pp. 84–94.

15. J. Elster, *Solomonic Judgements* (Cambridge, England: Cambridge University Press, 1989), chap. 3.

16. Let me stress, therefore, that accuracy in this context means "using procedures that elicit as much relevant personal information as possible," not "employing methods that in aggregate yield the greatest number of 'correct' outcomes."

17. In a helpful discussion, David Resnick marks this distinction by contrasting "unjust procedures" (those that are morally objectionable) with "unfair procedures" (those that violate procedural rules such as the impartiality of the judge who decides a case); see D. Resnick, "Due Process and Procedural Justice," in J. R. Pennock and J. W. Chapman, eds., *Nomos 18: Due Process* (New York: New York University Press, 1977). He thinks, however, that procedural unfairness can be accounted for in terms of its tendency to produce wrong or unjust outcomes, whereas my own account of procedural justice is intended to highlight those aspects of good procedure that cannot be explained by reference to outcomes. Moreover, although the dignity requirement differs from the other three aspects of procedural justice in the way indicated in the text, I shall shortly suggest that all four requirements can be justified morally in broadly the same terms.

18. I take this example from R. S. Summers, "Evaluating and Improving Legal Processes—A Plea for 'Process Values,'" *Cornell Law Review,* 60 (1974–1975): 1–52.

19. For a similar suggestion, see A. Weale, *Political Theory and Social Policy* (London: Macmillan, 1983), p. 142.

20. See E. A. Lind and T. R. Tyler, *The Social Psychology of Procedural Justice* (New York and London: Plenum Press, 1988), for a wealth of evidence on this subject.

21. C. Beitz, *Political Equality* (Princeton: Princeton University Press, 1989), chap. 5.

22. Nozick, *Anarchy, State, and Utopia,* chap. 7. I include the qualifier "largely" because although Nozick's central idea is that any outcome that arises from just procedures is *ipso facto* just, he includes among the conditions for the initial acquisition of resources a "Lockean proviso" which holds that an acquisition should not materially worsen the position of other persons who are thereby prevented from acquiring the resource in

question. This proviso may in certain circumstances allow us to deem unjust an outcome whose pedigree would otherwise be faultless—for instance, someone's having acquired by legitimate means a monopoly of a vital natural resource such as the only water hole in the desert, and then charging needy customers an exploitative price for the water.

23. I have explored this point in *Market, State, and Community: Theoretical Foundations of Market Socialism* (Oxford: Clarendon Press, 1989), chap. 7.

24. See A. M. MacLeod, "Distributive Justice, Contract and Equality," *Journal of Philosophy*, 81 (1984): 709–718.

25. W. N. Nelson, "The Very Idea of Pure Procedural Justice," *Ethics*, 90 (1979–1980): 502–511.

26. Responding to this point, Nelson suggests that wherever goods are indivisible, it may be thought that each person has an equal right to the good, and this requires that it be allocated by a random procedure. Each person has an equal right to the first serve at tennis, and so spinning an unweighted racket is the fair way to allocate this good. This seems to me a very implausible way out. Since I have no general right to goods that emerge only through the free agreement of the parties (like tennis matches), I cannot have an equal right with others antecedently to the agreement we reach. To invent rights in this way saves the entitlement explanation only by trivializing it.

27. If all transactions are voluntary, how can such unintended and undesired outcomes come about? No one, in making his or her own transactions, can grasp the overall results of many such transactions. To give a simple case, persons A–M may transfer to person N the entire supply of some particular resource, making N into a monopolist. No one, not even the last transactor, may know that this (unwanted) outcome will ensue. On this point see G. A. Cohen, *Self-Ownership, Freedom, and Equality* (Cambridge, England: Cambridge University Press, 1995), chap. 2.

28. If a decision has to be made between just two policies, then there is a strong, though not conclusive, case for regarding simple majority voting as the fairest decision procedure. With three or more policies to choose among, Arrow's Impossibility Theorem (which proves that no decision rule can simultaneously satisfy a small number of weak and apparently incontrovertible requirements) also implies that no rule can be singled out as uncontestably the fairest. For discussion of this point, see my paper "Deliberative Democracy and Social Choice," *Political Studies*, 40 (1992): 54–67.

29. Elster, *Solomonic Judgements*, p. 121. This is also the upshot of Brian Barry's discussion of procedural justice in *Political Argument*, 2nd ed. (He-

mel Hempstead: Harvester Wheatsheaf, 1990), chap. 6, sect. 2. Let me add that the argument for the priority of outcome justice does not apply in cases where a procedure is valued as an expression of social justice over and above its instrumental contribution to just outcomes. The example I gave earlier concerned equal voting rights: these not only help to ensure the fairness of political decisions, but represent a central application of the principle of equality that applies in the sphere of citizenship. If someone is deprived of voting rights without good cause, this not only makes the decision procedure less fair, but in itself constitutes an unjust outcome.

30. There is a helpful survey and analysis in Elster, *Solomonic Judgements,* chap. 2. Elster believes that people in modern societies tend to suffer from a form of hyper-rationalism, which leads them to reject random allocation even when there are good reasons to support it. For advocacy of increased use of lotteries (in conjunction with other mechanisms) in determining people's life chances, see B. Goodwin, *Justice by Lottery* (Hemel Hempstead: Harvester Wheatsheaf, 1992).

31. My position here coincides with that of John Rawls in "The Basic Structure as Subject," *Political Liberalism* (New York: Columbia University Press, 1993), pp. 281–285, who effectively exposes the defects of a purely procedural conception of justice.

32. Hayek, *Law, Legislation and Liberty,* vol. II, chaps. 9–10.

33. This has been argued in several places by Raymond Plant. See, for example, R. Plant, *Equality, Markets and the State,* Fabian Tract 494 (London: Fabian Society, 1984); R. Plant, *Modern Political Thought* (Oxford: Blackwell, 1991), pp. 80–97.

6. Virtues, Practices, and Justice

1. A. MacIntyre, *Whose Justice? Which Rationality?* (London: Duckworth, 1988), p. 39.

2. I have not considered MacIntyre's later book, *Three Rival Versions of Moral Enquiry* (London: Duckworth, 1990), which has much less to say on the topics that are my concern here.

3. See MacIntyre, *Whose Justice? Which Rationality?* Preface.

4. A. MacIntyre, *After Virtue* (London: Duckworth, 1981), p. 175.

5. See MacIntyre, *Whose Justice? Which Rationality?* esp. chaps. 3 and 7.

6. MacIntyre, *After Virtue,* pp. 170–173.

7. A. MacIntyre, *After Virtue,* 2nd ed. (London: Duckworth, 1984), p. 275.

8. So are the qualities needed to sustain family life such as to exclude success in games or exploration? MacIntyre plainly thinks not: he distin-

guishes "ruthlessness and relentlessness" (which for the reason given cannot count as virtues) from "the phronetic quality of knowing when to be ruthless or relentless." The latter quality is, presumably, sufficient to enable its possessor to succeed in practices such as those referred to above.

9. MacIntyre's discussion of this point is fairly cryptic (see *After Virtue,* p. 188), but presumably what he has in mind is that someone who entirely subordinates his pursuit of the goods internal to politics to his pursuit of the goods internal to sports, say, fails to manifest fully the virtue of justice; so equally does a society that esteems and rewards sportsmen more highly than politicians, even though within each category it treats individuals fairly.

10. MacIntyre, *After Virtue,* pp. 141–143.

11. Although *on the whole* the best player is the one who wins most often or who contributes most to his team's victory, this equation is not a precise one. Devotees will judge a player by his skill, his inventiveness, and so forth, as well as by his brute effectiveness.

12. This is confirmed in his response to my earlier critical appraisal ("Virtues and Practices," *Analyse und Kritik,* 6 [1984]: 49–60), where he is perfectly ready to describe as "self-contained" the practices that he relies upon to underpin his account of the virtues. See A. MacIntyre, "Rights, Practices and Marxism: Reply to Six Critics," *Analyse und Kritik,* 7 (1985): 234–248.

13. MacIntyre does not consider the problem posed by someone who simply refuses to recognize a putative internal good *as* a good—that is, as a valuable human end—and who therefore rejects any virtue that is uniquely connected with the practice in question. Apparently he presupposes that there is a (shifting) consensus about which practices are worth sustaining, so the only problem that may arise is how different practices are to be threaded together in the life of a particular person or of a community.

14. To avoid misunderstanding here, I should emphasize that my claim is a claim about the primary arenas in which virtues such as courage and justice are displayed. It is not a claim about what may motivate particular virtuous acts. A person may act courageously without looking beyond what his or her immediate circumstances seem to require, without considering the wider ends which acts of that kind serve to promote. When I dismiss "courage displayed merely for its own sake," I mean that someone who deliberately seeks out dangerous predicaments in order to show how plucky he is does not exhibit the moral quality of courage.

15. "Il faut noter que les jeux des enfants ne sont pas jeux, et les faut juger en

eux comme leurs plus sérieuses actions." Montaigne, *Essais,* ed. P. Villey (Paris: Presses Universitaires de France, 1965), p. 110.

16. At least initially. We have observed that a complete account of justice (according to MacIntyre) will also need to inquire into the ordering of practices within a person's life and within a community.

17. I am thinking, for instance, of a race official who tries to bring it about that the person who in his judgment is the fastest runner wins the race by advantaging her in some way.

18. MacIntyre, *After Virtue,* pp. 235–236.

19. Aristotle, *The Politics,* ed. E. Barker (Oxford: Oxford University Press, 1978), p. 118.

20. Ibid., p. 117.

21. For a view of Aristotle's *Politics* as an inevitably unsuccessful attempt to reconcile oligarchic and democratic principles, see J. Ober, *Mass and Elite in Democratic Athens* (Princeton: Princeton University Press, 1989), esp. pp. 293–295.

22. See A. W. H. Adkins, *Merit and Responsibility: A Study in Greek Values* (Oxford: Oxford University Press, 1960).

23. See Aristotle, *Ethics,* trans. J. A. K. Thomson (Harmondsworth: Penguin, 1955), book 5, chap. 3 (p. 146).

24. For evidence that this is indeed so, see Chap. 4.

25. MacIntyre, "Rights, Practices and Marxism," p. 245.

26. There are various possible reasons one might think it was indeed inconceivable, some of which are obliquely hinted at in the way that MacIntyre puts his case in the quotation above. These need to be brought out into the open and discussed. For a defense of the view that market allocations may in principle reward participants in proportion to their deserts, see my *Market, State and Community: Theoretical Foundations of Market Socialism* (Oxford: Clarendon Press, 1989), chap. 6, as well as Chap. 9 below.

27. Aquinas, *Summa Theologica* (London: Burns, Oates and Washbourne, 1918), II-II, Qu. 58 (vol. 10, p. 115).

28. Ibid., II-II, Qu. 58, art. 11, 66, art. 7 (vol. 10, pp. 133, 232–233).

29. Ibid., II-II, Qu. 63, art. 1 (vol. 10, p. 187).

30. Ibid., II-II, Qu. 63, art. 4 (vol. 10, p. 193).

31. Ibid., II-II, Qu. 61, art. 2 (vol. 10, p. 160).

32. Ibid., II-II, Qu. 61, art. 2 (vol. 10, p. 162).

33. MacIntyre, *Whose Justice? Which Rationality?* p. 200. Although I agree with the general claim, the particular argument he offers in support appears to be based on a misreading of Aquinas. MacIntyre (ibid.) asserts that Aquinas would have counted as usury the profits one might receive from investing in a partnership. But in Qu. 78, art. 2, reply to obj. 5,

Aquinas distinguishes receiving interest on a simple loan from entrusting money to a merchant or craftsman "so as to form a kind of society" in which, because one does not transfer ownership of the capital, one is entitled to receive a share of the profits. (For a general discussion of Aquinas' attitude toward profit-making, which confirms this point, see J. Coleman, "Property and Poverty," in J. H. Burns, ed., *The Cambridge History of Medieval Political Thought, c. 350c.–1450* [Cambridge, England: Cambridge University Press, 1988], pp. 621–625.)

34. It would be possible to modify this conclusion somewhat by playing down Aquinas' account of distributive justice and placing the emphasis instead on his general conception of justice as legality, which as we have seen belongs firmly within the tradition of natural law. This would bring him closer to early liberal thinkers such as Locke. I do not think MacIntyre would be at all sympathetic to such a reading.

7. The Concept of Desert

1. Besides A. MacIntyre, *After Virtue* (London: Duckworth, 1981), chap. 17, see, for instance, W. A. Galston, *Liberal Purposes: Goods, Virtues, and Diversity in the Liberal State* (Cambridge, England: Cambridge University Press, 1991), chaps. 8–9, and S. Scheffler, "Responsibility, Reactive Attitudes, and Liberalism in Philosophy and Politics," *Philosophy and Public Affairs,* 21 (1992): 299–323.
2. See, for instance, J. Baker, *Arguing for Equality* (London: Verso, 1987), chap. 6; T. Honderich, *Conservatism* (Harmondsworth: Penguin, 1991), chap. 8.
3. Scheffler, "Responsibility, Reactive Attitudes, and Liberalism."
4. H. Sidgwick, *The Methods of Ethics,* 7th ed. (London: Macmillan, 1963), p. 284.
5. The best recent expression of the pluralist view can be found in G. Sher, *Desert* (Princeton: Princeton University Press, 1987).
6. For this view see J. Griffin, *Well-Being: Its Meaning, Measurement and Moral Importance* (Oxford: Clarendon Press, 1986), chap. 12.
7. Although not explicitly stated, this view seems to be implicit in R. Nozick, *Anarchy, State and Utopia* (Oxford: Blackwell, 1974), chap. 7. Nozick would, I think, concede that where benefits have to be assigned, it is often morally desirable to do so in accordance with desert. But he would deny that the recipients have a *right* to this kind of distribution, and since justice is defined in terms of rights, the assignor commits no injustice if he allocates the benefits in some other way.
8. Since my underlying interest is in distributive justice as opposed to the

justice of punishment, I shall examine what it means to deserve benefits without asking how far the analysis can be extended to desert of harms. My method is to attempt to identify the core idea that lies behind everyday judgments of desert, and then to see if this idea can survive the various critical attacks that philosophers have launched against it. At the same time I appeal to these judgments in order to set aside various restrictive or revisionary accounts of desert found in the philosophical literature.

9. In cases of coercion some desert may persist, since the coerced agent may, for instance, still have choices to make, albeit from a restricted range of options, or may be able to display a greater or lesser degree of skill in carrying out the task she is coerced into performing. It remains true that if one is coerced into doing X one's deserts are typically less extensive than if one does X freely.

10. Although under the rules of the competition I am obviously entitled to receive it. The relationship between desert and entitlement will also be explored more fully later on.

11. Among these is Rawls, who formulates the desert principle as "Justice is happiness according to virtue" (*A Theory of Justice* [Cambridge, Mass.: Harvard University Press, 1971], p. 310) and then proceeds to criticize it on this interpretation. I have discussed Rawls' critique of desert briefly in *Market, State, and Community: Theoretical Foundations of Market Socialism* (Oxford: Clarendon Press, 1989), pp. 158–159, and will return to it below. Hayek is another who assumes that desert must be moral desert; I discuss his views in Chap. 9.

12. This argument is well made in J. Lamont, "The Concept of Desert in Distributive Justice," *Philosophical Quarterly,* 44 (1994): 45–64.

13. P. Strawson, "Freedom and Resentment," in G. Watson, ed., *Free Will* (Oxford: Oxford University Press, 1982). The connection between desert and a view of human beings as free agents is also stressed in J. Lucas, *On Justice* (Oxford: Clarendon Press, 1980), chap. 11: "If we deny people their deserts, we are not really treating them as persons because we are taking them for granted. They are not in our eyes autonomous agents who had it in their power to act or not to act, but merely natural phenomena which we have been manipulating at our will" (p. 202).

14. Lucas, *On Justice,* p. 166. See also J. Lucas, *Responsibility* (Oxford: Clarendon Press, 1993), pp. 124–126.

15. Notice, however, that statements such as "A deserves to win the 1500 meters" may have different meanings and invoke different desert-bases in different contexts. The desert at issue can be based on past performance: "Jones has trained far harder than the other competitors; though he's not

likely to, he really deserves to win this race." It can be based on present performance viewed retrospectively: "Smith deserved to win; it wasn't his fault that he got badly boxed in on the last turn." Finally, as indicated in the text, it can be based on anticipated future performance: "Brown is the outstanding athlete in the field; he really deserves to win."

16. J. Feinberg, "Justice and Personal Desert," in *Doing and Deserving: Essays in the Theory of Responsibility* (Princeton, N.J.: Princeton University Press, 1970).

17. Thus for present purposes I do not distinguish, as Alasdair MacIntyre does, between "practices" and "institutions": see *After Virtue,* pp. 175–183, and my discussion of MacIntyre's notion of a practice in the previous chapter.

18. Rawls, *Theory of Justice,* sect. 48. As Rawls puts it, "when just economic arrangements exist, the claims of individuals are properly settled by reference to the rules and precepts (with their respective weights) which these practices take as relevant. . . . it is incorrect to say that just distributive shares reward individuals according to their moral worth. But what we can say is that, in the traditional phrase, a just scheme gives each person his due: that is, it allots to each what he is entitled to as defined by the scheme itself" (p. 313).

19. For a more extended analysis along these lines, see R. Goodin, "Negating Positive Desert Claims," *Political Theory,* 13 (1985): 575–598 (revised version in R. Goodin, *Reasons for Welfare: The Political Theory of the Welfare State* [Princeton: Princeton University Press, 1988], chap. 10).

20. See, for example, Feinberg, "Justice and Personal Desert"; J. Kleinig, "The Concept of Desert," *American Philosophical Quarterly,* 8 (1971): 71–78; and my own earlier discussion, drawing upon these, in *Social Justice* (Oxford: Clarendon Press, 1976), chap. 3.

21. As he later sums up the position, "desert is understood as entitlement acquired under fair conditions" (J. Rawls, *Justice as Fairness: A Restatement* [Cambridge, Mass.: Harvard University, 1990], p. 64).

22. It might be thought that this was ruled out in Rawls' case by another principle, that of fair equality of opportunity. But the latter holds simply that unequal rewards should be "attached to offices and positions open to all under conditions of fair equality of opportunity" (*Theory of Justice,* p. 302). This requires that men and women have an equal opportunity to compete for jobs, but it does not rule out adjusting the wages and salaries attached to those jobs to take account of the differential willingness of men and women to take them—in the case described, paying male incumbents more than female incumbents. There is in any case a problem in showing why, within the Rawlsian framework, the principle of fair

equality of opportunity should be treated as a principle of justice rather than as a principle of efficiency. What makes it *unfair* (as opposed to merely inefficient) if some people have greater opportunities to compete for jobs and offices than others, once we have given up the idea that people *deserve* (in a pre-institutional sense) an equal chance to compete for such positions?

23. The literature on kibbutzim reveals the tension between their official egalitarianism and the *de facto* emergence of inequalities of influence and prestige, which, however, are rarely sufficient to satisfy those holding managerial and other positions of authority—partly, I suspect, because they are not sanctioned by public opinion within the kibbutzim. See, for example, E. Yuchtman, "Reward Distribution and Work-Role Attractiveness in the Kibbutz—Reflections on Equity Theory," *American Sociological Review,* 37 (1972): 581–595; Y. Talmon, *Family and Community in the Kibbutz* (Cambridge, Mass.: Harvard University Press, 1972); E. Ben-Rafael, *Status, Power and Conflict in the Kibbutz* (Aldershot: Avebury, 1988).

24. See my discussion in Chap. 4.

25. It is not clear to me whether the factoring out goes all the way, or whether a residue is left in the sense that the actual performance still counts for something despite its elements of contingency. In the case in which someone does something harmful, it seems that there is a residue. To use an example of Nagel's, we think that a negligent truck driver who kills a child deserves more blame and punishment than an equally negligent driver who is lucky enough not to have a child cross his path (T. Nagel, "Moral Luck," in *Mortal Questions* [Cambridge, England: Cambridge University Press, 1991]). This can be explained partly on epistemic grounds: we know that the first driver was acting dangerously, whereas we can't be certain in the second case that some countervailing factor might not have eliminated the negligence (for example, that a driver who drove too fast by normal standards didn't have exceptionally good reflexes). (See N. Richards, "Luck and Desert," *Mind,* 95 [1986]: 198–209, for an explanation along these lines.) My view, however, is that the epistemic explanation doesn't account for everything, and that desert in such cases irreducibly depends, in part, on the actual nature or consequences of the actor's performance; I am less sure, though, whether this is also true when we are considering desert of prizes and other advantages.

26. As Nagel puts it, "we judge people for what they actually do or fail to do, not just for what they would have done if circumstances had been different" ("Moral Luck," p. 34).

27. These include Rawls, *Theory of Justice,* sects. 17 and 48; J. Rachels, "What People Deserve," in J. Arthur and W. H. Shaw, eds., *Justice and Economic*

Distribution (Englewood Cliffs, N.J.: Prentice-Hall, 1978); W. Sadurski, *Giving Desert Its Due: Social Justice and Legal Theory* (Dordrecht: D. Reidel, 1985), chap. 5; T. Campbell, *Justice* (London: Macmillan, 1988), esp chap. 6.

28. In an interesting discussion of the causes of social inequality, Nagel gives reasons that inequalities deriving from differences in talent are commonly regarded as less unjust than inequalities arising from discrimination or from inherited class differences. See T. Nagel, *Equality and Partiality* (New York: Oxford University Press, 1991), chap. 10.

29. On this point see A. T. Kronman, "Talent Pooling," in J. R. Pennock and J. W. Chapman, eds., *Nomos 23: Human Rights* (New York: New York University Press, 1981).

30. See the discussion of Kant in Nagel, "Moral Luck." The original source is I. Kant, *Foundations of the Metaphysics of Morals* (Indianapolis: Bobbs-Merrill, 1959), first section.

31. Wrong about the nature of morality. But one might also ask, more specifically, whether he is correct in supposing that a person's capacity to will rightly is unaffected by contingent facts about him such as his preferences and capacities.

32. I present this as a stark choice, though there may be intermediate possibilities: for instance, it is sometimes argued that because of worries about desert we should not allow people's incomes to depend on differences in their economic performance, though we might permit such differences to be recognized in other ways—by tokens of esteem, for instance. (See, for example, G. Marshall, A. Swift, and S. Roberts, *Against the Odds? Social Class and Social Justice in Industrial Societies* [Oxford: Clarendon Press, 1997], p. 166.) I am not, however, convinced that this is a cogent proposal. Although there may be other grounds for preferring tokens to cash as a way of recognizing desert (considerations of need, for instance), if it is wrong in principle to reward people for their talent-dependent performances, then *any* form of reward, material or immaterial, is wrong. Conversely, if people do deserve differently on this basis, I cannot see what argument would rule out financial rewards as an appropriate form of requital.

33. As noted earlier, both Rawls and Sidgwick are happy to continue using the *words* "desert" and "deserves" so long as their meaning is transformed as each of them proposes.

34. As Sher puts this point, we need the idea of a self with its constitutive preferences and abilities: "No being that did not stand in some suitably intimate relation to its preferences, values, skills, talents and abilities could choose and act in the full sense" (*Desert,* p. 159).

35. Sidgwick, *Methods of Ethics,* p. 349.

36. By "elicited" here I mean *"appropriately* elicited." The bare fact that A admires B's performance is not enough to make B deserving. A's admiration is expressed in a judgment ("That was a terrific performance of the Emperor concerto"), and that judgment can be validated or invalidated by interpersonal criteria.

37. The very ingenious attempt by George Sher in *Desert* to find such deeper values has two unwelcome consequences. First, the values promoted by the requital of different kinds of desert turn out to be radically heterogeneous, leaving the concept in an alarmingly fragmented state. Second, Sher is obliged by his program to abandon as lacking in normative force desert claims that one might well regard as fairly central uses of the concept. These include such claims as "that superior political candidates deserve to be elected, that authors of outstanding books deserve recognition, and that scientists who discover vaccines or generals who lead victorious armies deserve honors and awards" (p. 129). Sher's project is better seen, I think, as an attempt to find reasons that people who are skeptical about the moral force of desert itself might nevertheless come to acquiesce in many of the desert claims that we normally make. For some more specific problems with Sher's analysis see my paper "Recent Theories of Social Justice," *British Journal of Political Science,* 21 (1991): 371–391.

38. This is legislation aimed primarily at eliminating the gap between men's and women's levels of pay by applying the principle of equal pay for work of equal value, regardless of whether the work is traditionally done by men or by women.

39. For a careful elaboration of the distinction between comparative and noncomparative judgments of justice, see J. Feinberg, "Noncomparative Justice," *Philosophical Review,* 83 (1974): 297–338.

40. In Chap. 9 I return to the question whether the contributions made by people in different jobs can be objectively compared.

41. Compare here the empirical findings on people's beliefs about deserved inequalities reported in Chap. 4. I concluded there that these beliefs are not determinate enough for us to do more than establish top and bottom limits to the range of income differences that people would regard as socially just.

42. Can we imagine a society in which manual labor is genuinely valued more highly than medical practice? Hypothetically we can, but it is interesting to find that in the Soviet Union, which in its heyday went to great lengths to glorify manual labor, the occupation of doctor was still ranked considerably above that of manual worker. See A. Inkeles, *The Soviet Citizen: Daily Life in a Totalitarian Society* (Cambridge, Mass.: Harvard University Press, 1959), pp. 76–80, for evidence to this effect.

43. See Feinberg, "Noncomparative Justice."

44. In this respect there is a clear contrast with cases of deserved punishment, where there is normally no parallel problem of scarcity.
45. Feinberg, "Noncomparative Justice."
46. I discuss briefly how desert and social equality may be reconciled in Chap. 9. For a fuller discussion see my papers "Complex Equality," in D. Miller and M. Walzer, eds., *Pluralism, Justice and Equality* (Oxford: Oxford University Press, 1995), and "Equality and Market Socialism," in P. Bardhan and J. Roemer, eds., *Market Socialism: The Current Debate* (New York: Oxford University Press, 1993).

8. Deserving Jobs

1. G. Eliot, *Middlemarch* (Oxford: Oxford University Press, 1988), p. 417.
2. Political philosophers often reject the claim that the best-qualified candidate *deserves* the job in any proper sense of desert. For a recent example, see A. Gutmann and D. Thompson, *Democracy and Disagreement* (Cambridge, Mass.: Harvard University Press, 1996), p. 313.
3. H. Sidgwick, *The Methods of Ethics* (London: Macmillan, 1907), chap. 5. For a more recent exposition see N. Daniels, "Meritocracy," in J. Arthur and W. Shaw, eds., *Justice and Economic Distribution* (Englewood Cliffs, N.J.: Prentice-Hall, 1978). Daniels brings out clearly how the fitness principle (which he terms the "Productivity Principle") differs from the principle of desert.
4. The injustice of the outcome and the unfair treatment of the candidate are separate issues from a moral point of view, even though they are often concurrent in practice. If, for instance, the committee conscientiously tried to hire the best candidate but (say, because of incomplete information) made the wrong decision, the outcome would be unjust, but it would be inappropriate for the thwarted candidate to complain of unfair treatment. In other cases the onus will lie on the unfair treatment (see note 16).
5. Cf. G. Sher, *Desert* (Princeton: Princeton University Press, 1987), p. 121.
6. For this argument, see R. Goodin, "Negating Positive Desert Claims," *Political Theory,* 13 (1985): 575–598 (a revised version appears as R. Goodin, *Reasons for Welfare: The Political Theory of the Welfare State* [Princeton: Princeton University Press, 1988], chap. 10).
7. As I argued in the previous chapter, this should not, properly speaking, be counted as a claim of desert at all; rather, it should be seen as a claim of entitlement (see also J. Kleinig, "The Concept of Desert," *American Philosophical Quarterly,* 8 [1971]: 71–78 on this point). As noted, however, the loose use of "deserves" in ordinary speech tends to blur this important

conceptual distinction in a way that is helpful to the position I am criticizing.

8. For this interpretation of the desert principle, see J. Rachels, "What People Deserve," in Arthur and Shaw, *Justice and Economic Distribution*.

9. Unless the future performance gave us reason to think that we had wrongly characterized the original one—that the author's successful books had been ghost-written, or that the winning athletic performance was some sort of fluke, for instance.

10. I shall shortly consider reasons other things may not be equal, that is, various factors that qualify predictable performance as the appropriate basis of desert.

11. I return to this question in the following chapter, where I try to rebut some of the criticisms that have been leveled against the use of market prices in estimating people's relative economic deserts. I also address the difficulty posed by jobs that are not market based.

12. This is obviously very crude, but a more plausible measure, giving greater weight to the injustice suffered by those who are relatively worse off, would simply strengthen the example as it is presented.

13. To the extent that individual incomes can be adjusted after the event to reflect performance, hiring by merit becomes less important as a principle of justice. Thus if I am hiring people to pick grapes in my vineyard, and I pay each of them according to the weight he or she picks individually, my hiring practice need only comply with criteria of procedural fairness (for instance, I could choose the pickers by lot). But more commonly a jobholder's contribution depends on the way his job fits in with the rest of the organization to which he belongs, and here it makes sense to identify the relevant competence (and set the appropriate salary) first, and then to hire the person who best meets the requirements of the job so defined.

14. What if the same institution or committee is making a series of appointments and is fairly confident that the best-qualified candidate for job X will subsequently also be best qualified for job Y, which is better paid? The right policy here is surely to bring the facts to the candidate's attention and allow her to withdraw from the competition for X if she wishes, rather than to try to engineer overall justice directly. After all, she may prefer job X to job Y for some reason other than pay. This brings out the point that the principle of occupational choice trumps the principle that rewards should be proportional to contributions in cases of conflict.

15. Can such a consequentialist justification of the hiring-by-merit rule be squared with the overall aim of my argument, which is to explain and justify a certain principle of desert? Yes, because the consequence that is sought is a state of affairs in which economic rewards are adjusted as

accurately as possible to deserts. For the reasons given, this consequentialist argument will normally converge with the nonconsequentialist injunction to do the just thing regardless of what we expect others to do. In special circumstances, however, there might be a divergence—say, if we know that the second-placed candidate for a job has been blacklisted by other employers so that this represents his only chance of getting a decent job. Here a consequentialist might employ the person, whereas a Kantian would not. I do not take sides on this issue (I am grateful to Philip Pettit for drawing it to my attention. His own defense of the consequentialist position can be found in J. Braithwaite and P. Pettit, *Not Just Deserts: A Republican Theory of Criminal Justice* [Oxford: Clarendon Press, 1990], chap. 3).

16. Note that the questions "How much injustice has the appointing committee brought about?" and "How much injustice has been done to the best-qualified candidate?" are different. If the committee appoints someone who is only marginally less qualified than the best candidate, the amount of injustice created, as measured by the discrepancy between future contributions and rewards, may be quite small. Nevertheless, the decision may represent a serious injustice to the best-qualified candidate, for instance, in a case where the committee allows racial or sexual prejudice to influence the outcome.

17. Cf. Sher, *Desert*, p. 59.

18. I ignore here other respects in which a job may constitute a benefit, for instance, the opportunity it may give for personal self-realization. For reasons given in Chap. 1, it is contestable whether a theory of social justice should try to take such benefits into account.

19. As we shall see, this criterion has to be qualified to take into account influences on future performance that are *not* relevant to desert.

20. One way to see this is to vary the causal story that links the individual in question to the future performance. Suppose that there is a chemical treatment that can turn average runners into champion athletes, but this treatment works only with those of a certain rare blood type. To say "Because I have blood type X I deserve to become a champion sprinter" would make no sense, even if the prediction on which it was based was well-founded. The reason is that the connection between my present feature and the future performance is purely one of physical causation in this case, whereas in the case of deserving a job, the valuable quality I now possess (managerial skill, for instance) is precisely the one that I will deploy if given the job.

21. It follows, of course, that if we are deeply skeptical about the extent to which the economic system does indeed reward people according to their contributions, then we will give little weight to the claim that the best-

qualified applicants deserve the jobs being offered. Alternatively, if we understand desert in such a way that it is poorly measured by economic contribution, the same conclusion will follow. This second line of argument is pursued in T. Nagel, "Equal Treatment and Compensatory Discrimination," *Philosophy and Public Affairs,* 2 (1972–1973): 348–363 (reprinted as chap. 7 of his *Mortal Questions* [Cambridge, England: Cambridge University Press, 1979]). I return to this question in the following chapter.

22. By this I mean that the desert claim of the future job-holder to the rewards of the job is a necessary precondition for the desert claim of the best-qualified candidate. As observed above (note 16), the force of the latter claim cannot be reduced to the size of the desert-reward mismatch that will ensue if someone else is given the job.

23. For a more thorough discussion of the use of statistical information for predictive purposes when hiring decisions are made, see G. Sher, "Predicting Performance," *Social Philosophy and Policy,* 5 (1987–1988): 188–203.

24. What, however, if we ask her the question and she tells us, yes, she is quite likely to want to take a career break in a few years' time? We do then have information specific to the person, and on the view I am defending, which links present desert to future performance, she is less deserving than an otherwise equally qualified candidate who does not plan to take a break. There are two ways of avoiding the unpalatable policy implications of this concession. One is to say that in such cases employers ought to be flexible and be prepared to pay people what they are worth at any particular moment, and so the woman should be hired on full pay and then offered a fair proportion of that over the period of reduced performance. The other is to say that employers should bear some of the costs of raising children by supporting women (especially) over the period when their careers are interrupted. In the case we are considering the woman would, strictly speaking, be less deserving, but other considerations of social justice, especially equality of opportunity, would tell us to ignore that fact. Perhaps this is the reason that in countries such as the United States employers are prohibited from asking women about their child-bearing and child-rearing intentions. They are required to assess relative deserts with that piece of information blocked out.

25. For this distinction see A. Wertheimer, "Jobs, Qualifications and Preferences," *Ethics,* 94 (1983–1984): 99–112.

26. Wertheimer's careful discussion suggests that there is no one criterion but rather a range of factors that together determine what we allow to count as reaction qualifications for jobs.

27. M. Walzer, *Spheres of Justice: A Defence of Pluralism and Equality* (Oxford.

Martin Robertson, 1983), p. 136. The limits Walzer later specifies take the form of qualities that must be considered irrelevant to the selection committee's decision: "abilities that won't be used on the job, personal characteristics that won't affect performance, and political affiliations and group identifications beyond citizenship itself" (pp. 145–146).

28. Walzer might of course be *recommending* that application committees engage in forward-looking, not backward-looking, reasoning, or in other words should apply something like Sidgwick's principle of fitness rather than desert. My point about this is (a) that there is nothing in the nature of the task they have to accomplish to compel them to do so; and (b) that this is not how most people would regard the hiring decision: they would regard it as unfair if candidates were assessed on consequentialist grounds alone. Given his general stance, this last consideration should weigh with Walzer.

29. I shall not consider all the policies that fall into the category of "affirmative action" except to say that many of these policies are consistent with, and indeed may be required by, the principle of giving jobs to those who most deserve them. For instance, requiring employers to search actively for applicants from different social groups when drawing up their lists of job candidates is a way of ensuring that no deserving candidates are being overlooked merely because they were not informed about the existence of the job or felt that they would automatically be rejected.

30. The idea of a role model may mean different things in different contexts, as Anita Allen shows in A. L. Allen, "The Role Model Argument and Faculty Diversity," in S. M. Cahn, ed., *The Affirmative Action Debate* (London: Routledge, 1995). Here I am considering a role model to be a person who inspires others to follow her educational or career choices.

31. There are circumstances in which it could be argued that groups have suffered an injustice if their members have been discouraged from applying for particular occupations—say, if women have it drummed into them at home and at school that no woman will ever have a successful career in science. It does not follow, however, that positive discrimination policies aimed at counteracting this indoctrination treat their gainers and losers justly, even if the consequences are broadly favorable to social justice.

32. A critic might argue that I am relying here on a narrow notion of desert, and that on a broader interpretation desert should attach to socially valuable attributes and performances even if these are not connected to the job. For a view of this kind, contrasting narrower and wider notions of merit, see R. H. Fallon, "To Each According to His Ability, from None According to His Race: The Concept of Merit in the Law of Antidiscrimination," *Boston University Law Review*, 60 (1980): 817–877. In reply I

should say that if employers try to reward desert in this broader sense, rather than specific, job-related desert, then (a) the form of the reward (income, job-satisfaction, and so on) will very often be an incongruous response to the desert in question; and (b) in the absence of common standards of reward, there will be arbitrary inequalities in the way different people are treated by their employing institutions. What, and how much, does someone deserve for acting as a role model?

33. R. Dworkin, "Bakke's Case: Are Quotas Unfair?" in R. Dworkin, *A Matter of Principle* (Oxford: Clarendon Press, 1986), p. 299.

34. For discussion of this point, see Gutmann and Thompson, *Democracy and Disagreement,* pp. 324–327.

35. This assumes that the effect of the unfavorable treatment is to reduce examination grades but not permanently to lower either ability or motivation. Or, to put the point the other way around, the assumption is that, given a job, members of these groups would reveal their hitherto submerged potentialities. This is an empirical matter, but I am less skeptical than Alan Goldman about the chances of such an assumption's holding true. See A. Goldman, *Justice and Reverse Discrimination* (Princeton: Princeton University Press, 1979), pp. 58–59 for the counterargument.

36. It may be argued that rather than applying a corrective weighting to every candidate's examination grades or other performance indicators, we should assess in each individual case the extent to which past performance under-represents present potential (for instance, we should not discriminate in favor of black candidates who have attended expensive private schools). But since this information is likely to be very hard to obtain, using a standardized weighting may be the fairest policy, even though it overcorrects some candidates' performances and undercorrects others. The issue here—what counts as fair treatment of members of different groups in circumstances where the best available indicators correlate only imperfectly with actual performance—is a complex one, and I do not have the space to deal with it properly. For two illuminating discussions, see M. Kelman, "Concepts of Discrimination in 'General Ability' Job Testing," *Harvard Law Review,* 104 (1991): 1158–1247, and M. Selmi, "Testing for Equality: Merit, Efficiency and the Affirmative Action Debate," *University of California Los Angeles Law Review,* 42 (1995): 1251–1314.

37. It may be the case, of course, that past injustice is the direct or indirect cause of the underperformance for which we are attempting to correct. But the distinction between rectifying past injustice and doing justice in the present remains crucial. For a similar distinction, and some pertinent remarks on the difficulties of the compensatory argument, see G. Sher,

"Justifying Reverse Discrimination in Employment," in Cahn, *The Affirmative Action Debate.*

38. In using this example, I assume there is a relevant similarity between deserving a job and deserving a place at a university or college, though I should immediately concede that there are also important points of difference. It might be argued that the relevant consideration in assigning university places should not be the opportunity to acquire grades but the opportunity to develop talents and acquire skills. (Jobs, too, could be looked at in this way—not as opportunities to earn income, but as vehicles for self-realization—and this would radically alter our approach to the question of who deserved them. But such a shift in perspective would be less plausible here.) So although I believe that the argument of this chapter can throw useful light on the question of college admissions, I don't want to say that it entirely settles that question.

9. Two Cheers for Meritocracy

1. C. A. R. Crosland, *The Future of Socialism* (London: Cape, 1956).
2. See the evidence presented in Chap. 4.
3. For a very lucid treatment of the issues here, see G. Marshall, A. Swift, and S. Roberts, *Against the Odds? Social Class and Social Justice in Industrial Societies* (Oxford: Clarendon Press, 1997).
4. As far as Britain is concerned, Marshall and Swift appear to have much the better of Saunders in their recent exchange. See P. Saunders, "Might Britain Be a Meritocracy?" *Sociology,* 29 (1995): 23–41, and G. Marshall and A. Swift, "Merit and Mobility: A Reply to Peter Saunders," *Sociology,* 30 (1996): 375–386.
5. F. A. Hayek, *Law, Legislation and Liberty,* vol. II: *The Mirage of Social Justice* (London: Routledge and Kegan Paul, 1976), chap. 9; F. A. Hayek, *The Constitution of Liberty* (London: Routledge and Kegan Paul, 1960), chap. 6.
6. J. Rawls, *A Theory of Justice* (Cambridge, Mass.: Harvard University Press, 1971), p. 104.
7. Jencks, for instance, estimated that family background accounted for nearly half of people's advantage in occupational status and between 15 and 35 percent of their earnings advantage (in 1970s America). See C. Jencks, *Who Gets Ahead? The Determinants of Economic Success in America* (New York: Basic Books, 1979), chap. 3.
8. Fishkin has given a robust expression of this argument in the form of a "trilemma": it is impossible simultaneously to satisfy the following three principles: (a) the Principle of Merit (positions should be allocated on the

basis of job-related criteria); (b) Equality of Life Chances (children's prospects of achieving positions should not depend on arbitrary native characteristics such as race or family background); and (c) the Autonomy of the Family (the development of children within the family should not be interfered with coercively). See J. Fishkin, *Justice, Equal Opportunity, and the Family* (New Haven: Yale University Press, 1983).

9. C. Offe, *Industry and Inequality: The Achievement Principle in Work and Social Status* (London: Edward Arnold, 1976), pp. 41–42.

10. I do not intend this as a decisive rebuttal of either critique, because it could be said in reply that Hayek's picture applies to some segments of the economy and Offe's picture to other segments. At this point I simply want to highlight the way in which attacks on the merit principle rest on possibly controversial assumptions about how market economies distribute resources to individuals.

11. Hayek, *Constitution*, pp. 94–95.

12. See also my discussion in *Market, State and Community: Theoretical Foundations of Market Socialism* (Oxford: Clarendon Press, 1989), chap. 6.

13. Hayek, *Law, Legislation and Liberty II*, p. 76.

14. This is clearly not the case for goods or services whose creation depends upon combining the unique skills of two or more individuals. If a composer and a librettist join forces to write an opera, that particular opera could not have been created if either had withdrawn from the cooperation, and so each can apparently claim the whole value of the opera as his or her marginal product. In these circumstances it is clearly inappropriate to try to use marginal product as a measure of contribution, and indeed it may be impossible to separate the value of the two contributions. In contrast, wherever the skills required to produce a good or service are possessed by many, then normal market forces will tend to ensure that the price someone can command for joining a production team measures that person's contribution to the team's product.

15. But, it might be said, if we take the bakers collectively, they have provided the consumers of bread with more value than is reflected in its market price; given this, doesn't each baker deserve his or her proportional share of that enhanced value? The answer is that, if we measure desert by productive achievement, this does not extend to the unintended collective consequences of action. Compare the following case. A beggar sits on the street and a number of people throw coins into his tin. Unbeknownst to these donors, he has made a bet with a rich friend that if he can raise $100 in this way the friend will double his takings. He succeeds in doing so. But if we wanted to record each donor's credit in the book of charitable giving, we should surely write in the amount that each actually gave, not

the doubled amount that he or she helped the beggar to realize. Jones intended to confer $1 of benefit on the beggar, even though in the event his action produced one-hundredth part of $200. This example shows that value can be created without anyone's deserving anything as a result.

16. I am not competent to set out the conditions under which this will hold, but economists will be.

17. Note that this argument doesn't depend on invoking qualitative judgments of value of the kind that I ruled out earlier, nor does it depend on the value that *particular* individuals may derive from a good or service, which is not relevant to its suppliers' deserts.

18. Note that the ideal of meritocracy itself says nothing directly about the scale of social inequalities that may justifiably obtain. It is therefore quite consistent to defend meritocracy while simultaneously arguing that the size of income and other inequalities should be reduced; and indeed, as the point under discussion shows, meritocratic ideals may give us indirect reasons for wanting this. I return to the relationship between meritocracy and inequality at the end of the chapter.

19. C. Jencks, *Inequality: A Reassessment of the Effect of Family and Schooling in America* (Harmondsworth: Penguin, 1975); Jencks acknowledged the error himself in *Who Gets Ahead?*

20. Offe, *Industry and Inequality,* chap. 4.

21. See, for instance, M. J. Piore and C. F. Sabel, *The Second Industrial Divide: Possibilities for Prosperity* (New York: Basic Books, 1984); J. Mathews, *Tools of Change: New Technology and the Democratization of Work* (Sydney: Pluto Press, 1989).

22. It might be argued that on a strict reading the merit principle doesn't exclude even discriminatory criteria of selection in such cases; it is simply silent when judgments of relative merit cannot be made. In my understanding (which I think is the common one), however, it works in tandem with the principle of equality of opportunity, which would be violated if the methods of selection referred to in the text were used.

23. I. M. Young, *Justice and the Politics of Difference* (Princeton: Princeton University Press, 1990), p. 204.

24. See my discussion in the previous chapter.

25. Since I have been arguing that the value of people's services should be measured by the extent to which they satisfy other people's preferences, why ignore preferences such as those described? These are not, however, mere preferences; they are preferences informed by theories or beliefs that directly contravene the principle of merit—for instance, the belief that there is a whole category of persons who are unfit to take on work of a

certain kind. It is surely not paradoxical to exclude such preferences when the principle is applied.

26. See, for instance, T. Sowell, *Markets and Minorities* (Oxford: Blackwell, 1981).

27. The main alternative solutions are discussed in R. A. Musgrave's classic textbook *The Theory of Public Finance* (New York: McGraw-Hill, 1959).

28. Thus I leave aside here theoretical solutions that depend on taxing each consumer according to the benefit he or she receives from a particular good. It is of course possible in some cases to convert public goods into goods for which identifiable users can be charged, as when tolls are imposed on roads. In such cases the problem we are addressing disappears, since market mechanisms can then be used to determine the optimal supply.

29. This solution was endorsed by A. C. Pigou—"expenditure should be pushed in all directions up to the point at which the satisfaction obtained from the last shilling expended is equal to the satisfaction lost in respect of the last shilling called up on government service" (*A Study in Public Finance*, 3rd ed. [London: Macmillan, 1947], p. 31)—though he went on to qualify it on practical grounds.

30. Or as an economist would say, we need to specify a social welfare function. See P. Samuelson, "The Pure Theory of Public Expenditures," *Review of Economics and Statistics*, 36 (1954): 387–389.

31. See Musgrave, *Theory of Public Finance*, chap. 1.

32. I have looked at this question in somewhat greater depth in "Social Justice and Environmental Goods," in A. Dobson, ed., *Fairness and Futurity: Essays on Environmental Sustainability and Social Justice* (Oxford: Oxford University Press, 1999).

33. M. Young, *The Rise of the Meritocracy* (London: Thames and Hudson, 1958).

34. See M. Walzer, *Spheres of Justice: A Defence of Pluralism and Equality* (Oxford: Martin Robertson, 1983), and my own discussion of Walzerian equality in "Complex Equality," in D. Miller and M. Walzer, eds., *Pluralism, Justice and Equality* (Oxford: Oxford University Press, 1995).

35. For an argument that the merit principle points toward market socialism, see *Market, State and Community*, chap. 6.

36. A similar point can be made about cumulation across generations. Both egalitarians and meritocrats will want to see inherited wealth taxed as heavily as possible to prevent favored members of the next generation from starting life in a position of inequality or undeserved advantage.

10. "To Each According to His Needs"

1. For a sustained polemic to this effect, see A. Flew, *The Politics of Procrustes: Contradictions of Enforced Equality* (London: Temple Smith, 1981).

2. J. Gray, "Classical Liberalism, Positional Goods, and the Politicization of Poverty," in A. Ellis and K. Kumar, eds., *Dilemmas of Liberal Democracies: Studies in Fred Hirsch's "Social Limits to Growth"* (London: Tavistock, 1983), p. 182.

3. This criticism is pressed in C. Fried, *Right and Wrong* (Cambridge, Mass.: Harvard University Press, 1978), chap. 5.

4. See K. Marx, *Critique of the Gotha Programme,* in D. McLellan, ed., *Karl Marx: Selected Writings* (Oxford: Oxford University Press, 1977), p. 569.

5. D. Hume, "An Enquiry Concerning the Principles of Morals," in *Enquiries Concerning the Human Understanding and Concerning the Principles of Morals,* ed. L. A. Selby-Bigge (Oxford: Clarendon Press, 1975), p. 184. For discussion of whether Marx agreed with Hume about the circumstances of justice, see A. Buchanan, *Marx and Justice* (London: Methuen, 1982), chap. 4; S. Lukes, *Marxism and Morality* (Oxford: Clarendon Press, 1985), chap. 2; and G. A. Cohen, *Self-Ownership, Freedom and Equality* (Cambridge, England: Cambridge University Press, 1995), chap. 5, sect. 10.

6. I do not mean to suggest that the principle is only ever applied in circumstances of scarcity and competing demands on resources. In a small, close-knit community such as a kibbutz, there may be sufficient consensus about what should count as needs, and people may be sufficiently responsible in advancing their claims, that all requests for additional resources can be met out of the kibbutz's budget (or the kibbutz may expand its output to meet them). Here I think we have a case in which the need principle still operates in the background as a principle of distributive justice—it regulates the demands that members put forward—but it is not explicitly invoked to resolve conflicts. This is a happy state of affairs, but it does require a very high degree of mutual trust and solidarity. In any case, my concern in this chapter is with the use of the principle as a principle of social justice in circumstances where conflicting demands on resources (for example, medical aid) cannot be reconciled so harmoniously.

7. D. Miller, *Social Justice* (Oxford: Clarendon Press, 1976), chap. 4; D. Wiggins, "Claims of Need," in *Needs, Values, Truth: Essays in the Philosophy of Value* (Oxford: Blackwell, 1987); G. Thomson, *Needs* (London: Routledge and Kegan Paul, 1987).

8. Here I follow Wiggins, "Claims of Need," sects. 5–6. There has been some debate about whether the grammar of need statements always takes the form "A needs X in order to Y" (see, for instance, B. Barry, *Political Argument* [London: Routledge and Kegan Paul, 1965], chap. 3, sect. 5a, and my critique of this view in *Social Justice,* chap. 4, sect. 2). The point to make here is that whereas with instrumental needs expansion from "A needs X" to "A needs X in order to Y" explains the need for X and gives it moral force, in the case of intrinsic needs such expansion at most helps to reveal the precise character of the need in question. Thus if I say, "Jones urgently needs medical attention," it would be somewhat obtuse to ask, "What does he need it for?" Possible replies to this question—"To stay alive," "To get back to a healthy condition," "To avoid crippling pain"— would have no purpose other than to indicate more exactly the *kind* of medical need Jones has. In the end the strictly grammatical question matters less than the question whether the formula "A needs X in order to Y" prompts us to think of all need claims, instrumental and intrinsic, as having the same moral standing. My view is that it does. For the contrary view see J. Griffin, *Well-Being: Its Meaning, Measurement and Moral Importance* (Oxford: Clarendon Press, 1986), p. 327.

9. Thomson, *Needs,* pp. 21–22.

10. I do not say that these are the only possible ways to understand "need." An alternative approach that has proved popular in recent political philosophy is to try to understand (basic) needs by reference to the generic conditions of moral agency (for this approach, see especially A. Gewirth, *Human Rights: Essays on Justification and Applications* [Chicago: University of Chicago Press, 1982], chap. 1; and R. Plant, *Modern Political Thought* [Oxford: Blackwell, 1991], chaps. 5 and 7). The idea is that there are certain preconditions that must be satisfied for anyone to function as an autonomous moral agent, regardless of his particular purposes. It is unclear to me, however, that any determinate list of needs can be derived in this way. On the one hand one could point out that autonomous agency is possible whenever someone is conscious and has some choices to make, even if in other respects that person is physically tightly constrained or deprived of resources. On the other hand if the conditions of agency are expanded to include everything that an agent needs (instrumentally) to achieve his purposes, then we have an inflated view of needs that corresponds to the second position described in the text. Any intermediate point between these extremes must be regarded as arbitrarily chosen so long as we stick to the agency approach.

11. For a defense of the biological model, see N. Daniels, *Just Health Care* (Cambridge, England: Cambridge University Press, 1985), chap. 2.

12. See A. Maslow, *Toward a Psychology of Being*, 2nd ed. (New York: Van Nostrand Reinhold, 1968).

13. As I did myself in *Social Justice*, chap. 4.

14. This is common ground between the political philosophies of Rawls and Dworkin, for instance.

15. As a test case, consider the following example, suggested to me by Andrew Williams. Suppose we have two candidates for a hip replacement whose medical condition in identical, but whereas one has throughout his life been an enthusiastic hill walker, the other is a couch potato. Should we say that the former has a stronger need for the operation than the latter? In my view their chosen lifestyles do not affect their needs, and if we did give priority to the first man our decision would be based on welfarist grounds rather than on grounds of need and justice.

16. In his very carefully argued analysis, Thomson defines needs in terms of individuals' inescapable basic interests (where "interests" are seen as the motivations that underlie specific desires). This has the virtue of preserving the objectivity of need while still allowing that, because of variation in basic interests, individuals have different basic needs. The price, however, is if we take seriously the idea that the interests that ground needs are inescapable (meaning not merely "unchosen" but "unalterable"), we will end up with a narrow set of needs—perhaps not much more than the biological core referred to above. See Thomson, *Needs*, passim.

17. See A. Sen, *Inequality Reexamined* (Oxford: Clarendon Press, 1992), chap. 3. Sen wants to use a functionings-capability metric to measure individual well-being, whereas I believe it is better suited to defining needs and related notions such as poverty.

18. As Cohen has pointed out, "functioning" has to be interpreted in a wide sense to do the job for which it is required here: it must cover not only activities but also conditions such as not being afflicted with disease or chronic pain. See G. A. Cohen, "Equality of What? On Welfare, Goods, and Capabilities," in M. C. Nussbaum and A. Sen, eds., *The Quality of Life* (Oxford: Clarendon Press, 1993).

19. A. Smith, *The Wealth of Nations*, ed. R. H. Campbell and A. S. Skinner (Oxford: Clarendon Press, 1976), vol. II, pp. 869–870.

20. This third claim holds only within certain limits. It is worth recalling here that the full statement of the principle of need originally read, "From each according to his ability, to each according to his needs." This implies that people who ask as a matter of justice for resources to satisfy their needs should acknowledge a reciprocal obligation to use their capacities to create those resources. This implies in turn that people do have an obligation to meet their needs when failure to do so prevents them from contributing to social welfare—where undernourishment means that they are unfit for

work, for instance. At what level this obligation should be pitched, and how far its performance should be enforced, are difficult questions that are outside the scope of the present discussion.

21. As Griffin points out, when we act in an individual capacity it may sometimes be right to satisfy preferences instead of needs: "If the cripple is my son, and he says that he would much prefer an education in philosophy to lifts and wheelchairs, and I am satisfied that he knows what is involved, I should use my resources as he wants" (*Well-Being*, p. 46). But he concedes that the social obligation in cases like this may nonetheless be to fulfill needs.

22. See M. Walzer, *Spheres of Justice: A Defence of Pluralism and Equality* (Oxford: Martin Robertson, 1983), chap. 3.

23. For the claim that needs must be understood in terms of the current standard of living in the relevant community, see S. I. Benn and R. S. Peters, *Social Principles and the Democratic State* (London: Allen and Unwin, 1959). This claim has been criticized by several authors: see Thomson, *Needs*, p. 95; and Miller, *Social Justice*, p. 138. Benn and Peters' error lies not in recognizing that needs depend on social norms, but in supposing that the relevant norm is the living standard that most people in a particular society actually enjoy, rather than the set of functionings that is recognized to be minimally adequate. Thus on Benn and Peters' view, in a society in which a disease like bilharzia is endemic, we could not speak of a need for treatment, because suffering from bilharzia will be the norm, whereas on my view there is such a need wherever bilharzia impairs bodily functionings (of the lungs and liver, for instance) that are recognized in that society as part of the basic set.

24. See L. Doyal and I. Gough, *A Theory of Human Need* (Basingstoke: Macmillan, 1991), chaps. 2–3, for this charge.

25. The issues here are quite complex, and I have tried to address them in D. Miller, "Justice and Global Inequality," in A. Hurrell and N. Woods, eds., *Inequality in World Politics* (Oxford: Oxford University Press, 1999). I argue there that the relevant international obligations should be defined in terms of *basic rights*, where these in turn are understood as the conditions that are universally necessary to allow men and women to lead minimally adequate lives. In the terms of the present discussion, this means that basic rights correspond to biological or quasi-biological needs, along with those socially defined needs that are replicated across human societies—needs for certain personal freedoms, for instance. Needs that are specific to particular societies, by contrast, give rise to obligations of justice only against fellow members, not against the world at large.

26. Sen, *Inequality Reexamined*, chap. 3.

27. I use negative numbers to underline the fact that we are talking about degrees of deficiency: A falls short of full functioning (for example, physical health) by 50 degrees, and so forth.

28. For discussion, see G. Winslow, *Triage and Justice* (Berkeley: University of California Press, 1982).

29. For instance, the San Francisco Office of Emergency Services has a triage plan to be used in the event of a major earthquake. See Winslow, *Triage and Justice,* chap. 2.

30. The ambiguity may be deliberate because from the point of view of those who actually have to decide whom to treat and whom not to treat, it is obviously of some comfort to believe that those who are placed in category 1 will die no matter what is done for them.

31. The severely wounded may have a claim to morphine, for example, to ease their pain. The point is that they cannot demand surgical treatment if there is no hope that the surgery will be effective.

32. For full discussion of this issue, see A. Sen, *On Economic Inequality* (Oxford: Clarendon Press, 1973), chap. 2; L. Temkin, *Inequality* (New York: Oxford University Press, 1993), esp. chap. 5.

33. This is equivalent to the Gini coefficient of inequality frequently employed by economists.

34. See Temkin, *Inequality,* for a persuasive argument that our concern for equality may be multifaceted, so that no single measure can capture it accurately.

35. Elizabeth Anscombe once argued, in effect, that there could not be injustice of this second kind. Discussing the case of a drug that is used to save the life of one person when it might have been used to save five, she claims that none of the five has been wronged: "Why, just because he was one of five who could have been saved, is he wronged in not being saved, if someone is supplied with it who needed it? What is *his* claim, except the claim that what was needed go to him rather than be wasted? But it was not wasted. So he was not wronged" (G. E. M. Anscombe, "Who is Wronged?" *Oxford Review,* 5 [1967]: pp. 16–17). If this were the end of the matter, "to each according to his needs" would mean only "use your resources to meet needs rather than waste them on something else." But it cannot be the end of the matter. What would Anscombe say about a case in which a resource is used to meet A's less urgent need instead of B's more urgent need? Would this be wasting the resource? If so, why not in the original case, too? (On this question see also B. Barry, "And Who Is My Neighbour?" *Liberty and Justice* [Oxford: Clarendon Press, 1991], sect. 1).

36. See my discussion in Chap. 5 of the way in which just procedures show equal respect toward those to whom they are applied.

37. Good examples are J. R. Lucas, "Justice," *Philosophy,* 47 (1972): 229–248; and T. D. Campbell, "Humanity before Justice," *British Journal of Political Science,* 4 (1974): 401–416. Campbell also maintains this position in *Justice* (Basingstoke: Macmillan, 1988), but Lucas retreats somewhat in *On Justice* (Oxford: Clarendon Press, 1980), allowing there that need is "a logically proper basis of apportionment," but arguing that it should not be seen as "the only, or the prime, one" as far as justice is concerned (p. 183).

38. One might fail to see this by thinking about a limited range of cases, for instance, people starving in a famine, where degree of need and degree of suffering will largely coincide. But consider needs of other kinds, such as needs for education. Here there is no simple correlation between being needy and suffering.

39. Campbell, "Humanity before Justice," p. 15.

40. In an illuminating discussion of such a principle, Parfit calls it simply the Priority View. See D. Parfit, "Equality or Priority?" (Lindley Lecture, University of Kansas, 1991). I prefer the term "weighted priority principle" to emphasize that it requires us not to give *strict* priority to the worst-off or neediest, but to let improvements in people's position count for more or less depending on how badly off they were before the intervention.

41. T. Nagel, *Equality and Partiality* (New York: Oxford University Press, 1991), esp. chap. 7.

42. The contrast between priority principles and egalitarian principles proper is well brought out in Parfit, "Equality or Priority?" sects. 9–11. Parfit thinks that many self-proclaimed egalitarians in fact hold a version of the Priority View, but he concedes that there is a comprehensible form of egalitarianism that cannot be reduced in this way.

43. Lucas, "Justice," p. 237.

44. Ibid., p. 242.

45. A more sophisticated appeal to rational self-interest might attempt to explain why most people would prefer an inclusive needs-based public health service—for instance, one might argue that prospective parents cannot predict the health needs of their children, or that people know themselves to be bad choosers and therefore want to avoid being exposed to a market in health insurance. It would take me too far afield to address these arguments here, so let me simply say that they strike me as unnecessarily ingenious in the face of the simpler explanation that people just think it's fair for health care to be allocated on the basis of need rather than ability to pay.

46. See my discussion in Chap. 4 of the more secure position of desert criteria and the less secure position of need criteria in popular thinking about justice in contemporary liberal societies.

47. I mean here no question that might give rise to claims of *desert*. In a wider sense of "opportunity," the opportunities available to the elderly do of course matter: hip replacements are justified, among other things, by the fact that they restore opportunities for mobility. These are what I have described above as "functionings."

48. There have been cases in which desert criteria have been included among those used to select patients for scarce medical operations such as kidney transplants or dialysis. A frequently cited example is the Seattle committee that in the early 1960s used criteria such as past and expected future contribution to society to select patients for dialysis. This was widely condemned at the time: for discussion see Winslow, *Triage and Justice,* chap. 1, and J. Elster, *Local Justice: How Institutions Allocate Scarce Goods and Necessary Burdens* (Cambridge, England: Cambridge University Press, 1992), pp. 156–157.

49. For evidence that members of the public do discriminate between those who are personally responsible for their condition of need and those who are not, and give priority to the latter, especially when resources are scarce, see L. J. Skitka and P. E. Tetlock, "Of Ants and Grasshoppers: The Political Psychology of Allocating Public Assistance," in B. A. Mellers and J. Baron, eds., *Psychological Perspectives on Justice: Theory and Applications* (Cambridge, England: Cambridge University Press, 1993).

50. To avoid confusion here, let me say that the first farmer may have a claim of desert as well as a claim of need. We may believe that a hard-working farmer hit by drought deserves to enjoy the fruits that his labor would have produced had it not been for this unforeseeable piece of bad luck. His claim of need, by contrast, extends only to the point of restoring him to normal functioning, and its condition is merely that he should not have behaved irresponsibly and thereby brought his needs upon himself.

51. See, for instance, A. Gutmann, "Justice Across the Spheres," in D. Miller and M. Walzer, eds., *Pluralism, Justice and Equality* (Oxford: Oxford University Press, 1995).

52. It counts in favor of this second approach that, in the cases referred to, people are not wholly responsible for the needs that they incur, because it is unpredictable who in particular will contract heart disease as a result of smoking, or who will injure themselves parachuting. This suggests that it would be wrong to acknowledge only a humanitarian obligation, and not an obligation of justice, in the case of those who turned out to be unlucky.

53. The range of possibilities here is illuminatingly discussed in B. Barry, "Chance, Choice, and Justice," *Liberty and Justice* (Oxford: Clarendon Press, 1991).

11. Equality and Justice

1. See, for instance, J. Lucas, *On Justice* (Oxford: Clarendon Press, 1980), chap. 9; A. ·Flew, *The Politics of Procrustes: Contradictions of Enforced Equality* (London: Temple Smith, 1981), chap. 3.

2. See, *inter alia,* R. Dworkin, "Equality of Welfare," *Philosophy and Public Affairs,* 10 (1981): 185–246; R. Dworkin, "Equality of Resources," *Philosophy and Public Affairs,* 10 (1981): 283–345; A. Sen, "Equality of What?" in *Choice, Welfare and Measurement* (Oxford: Blackwell, 1982); G. A. Cohen, "On the Currency of Egalitarian Justice," *Ethics,* 99 (1988–9): 906–944; G. A. Cohen, "Equality of What? On Welfare, Goods and Capabilities," in M. Nussbaum and A. Sen, eds., *The Quality of Life* (Oxford: Clarendon Press, 1992); R. Arneson, "Equality and Equal Opportunity for Welfare," *Philosophical Studies,* 54 (1988): 79–95.

3. R. Dworkin, "What Is Equality? Part 3: The Place of Liberty," *Iowa Law Review,* 73 (1987–1988), p. 6 (my italics).

4. The epithet is borrowed from C. Taylor, "The Politics of Recognition," *Philosophical Arguments* (Cambridge, Mass.: Harvard University Press, 1995), p. 254.

5. I mean that only people in these two categories think that all our concerns about distributive justice can be captured by a suitably formulated principle of equality. Those outside (the vast majority) are likely to value certain specific types of equality—for instance, equality of opportunity, or political equality—without making equality the core principle of their political morality.

6. Others who have drawn distinctions among kinds of equality that run parallel to this include T. Nagel, "Equality," in *Mortal Questions* (Cambridge, England: Cambridge University Press, 1991), and T. M. Scanlon, "The Diversity of Objections to Inequality" (Lindley Lecture, University of Kansas, 1996).

7. For this contrast see L. Temkin, *Inequality* (New York: Oxford University Press, 1993), esp. chaps. 9–10; for a similar contrast between individualistic and communal egalitarianism, see J. Broome, *Weighing Goods: Equality, Uncertainty and Time* (Oxford: Blackwell, 1991), chap. 9.

8. Sometimes (though not always) showing that A has a just claim to more resources will involve comparing her position with that of B, C, D, and so on, but the contrast still remains between arguments for greater equality that rest on the (comparative or noncomparative) claims of individuals, and arguments that focus on the overall character of the society in question.

9. For a more extended argument to this effect, see J. Kane, "Justice, Impartiality and Equality: Why the Concept of Justice Does Not Presume Equality," *Political Theory,* 24 (1996): 373–393.

10. For views of this kind, see C. Ake, "Justice as Equality," *Philosophy and Public Affairs,* 5 (1975): 69–89, and W. Sadurski, *Giving Desert Its Due: Social Justice and Legal Theory* (Dordrecht: D. Reidel, 1985), chaps. 4–5. The most elaborate attempt to analyze deserved income as a form of compensation is J. Lamont, "Incentive Income, Deserved Income and Economic Rents," *Journal of Political Philosophy,* 5 (1997): 26–46.

11. Might it be argued here that showing equal respect requires only a procedural form of equality, and that this would be satisfied so long as the manna were distributed by lottery or some other arbitrary device even without mutual consent? This argument would of course narrow still further the claim that justice entails equality as a default. I do not find it fully convincing, however. My intuition is that in cases where some generally valuable resource becomes available to a group in such a way that no member has any better claim to it than any other, each member has a concrete claim to an equal share, not merely a claim to equal treatment. Thus if one person is able to control the distribution of the good and imposes a (fair) lottery without consent, he inflicts a mild form of injustice by overriding that claim. But I find it difficult to separate this intuition from the different consideration that the lottery is a poor allocative mechanism because giving all the manna to the lucky winner is likely to generate less welfare than would an equal distribution.

12. Parfit says in a similar vein that in such cases "equality is the default: what we should aim for when we cannot justify distributing unequally." D. Parfit, "Equality or Priority?" (Lindley Lecture, University of Kansas, 1991), p. 15.

13. *Exodus,* chap. 16, v. 18.

14. In saying this I am not denying that each person has a basic right to resources that are adequate for subsistence. This, however, does not involve a demand for equality. I have developed this distinction, and the case against global egalitarianism, more fully in D. Miller, "Justice and Global Inequality," in A. Hurrell and N. Woods, eds., *Inequality in World Politics* (Oxford: Oxford University Press, 1999).

15. This is not the only way in which the injustice of a distribution could be measured, but I believe that my argument will apply to all plausible measures—for instance, those that count in surpluses as well as shortfalls, or those that weight bigger shortfalls more heavily than smaller ones.

16. I hope in another paper to give a formal proof of this result, but its

intuitive plausibility can be seen as follows. Suppose we start with an equal distribution of the product, so that Λ, B, C, D, and E get 5 units each. Now break the equality by moving A to $5 + X$ and B to $5 - X$. Will expected injustice increase or decrease? For some pairs of contributions the effect of the change will be to decrease injustice, for others it will increase injustice, and for yet others the effect will be neutral. It turns out, however, that every case in which injustice is decreased can be mirrored by a case in which injustice is increased, simply by reversing the contributions of A and B—and *ex hypothesi* for any array of contributions that includes A9, B6, say, there is an equally likely array that includes A6, B9. Meanwhile, if A and B have both made contributions that fall within the range $5 - X$ to $5 + X$, the effect of the move away from equality is to produce a preponderance of cases in which injustice is increased: within this range worsening cases are rarely matched by improving cases. Thus overall the result of departing from equality must be to increase expected injustice. The next step is to generalize this result to cover more complex moves away from equal distribution.

17. I have pointed to the evidence on this issue in Chap. 3.

18. I don't mean that states must necessarily be the direct suppliers of these goods, but they must assume responsibility at least in the sense of setting the terms and conditions under which private suppliers can operate.

19. Mill set out his scheme most elaborately in "Thoughts on Parliamentary Reform," in G. Himmelfarb, ed., *Essays on Politics and Culture by John Stuart Mill* (New York: Doubleday Anchor, 1963). A simpler version is given in J. S. Mill, "Considerations on Representative Government," in *Utilitarianism: On Liberty; Representative Government,* ed. H. B. Acton (London: Dent, 1972), chap. 8.

20. This idea has been explored in greater depth by Taylor in "The Politics of Recognition."

21. It may perhaps be illuminating to see recent liberal egalitarian theories of justice—for instance, the theories of Rawls and Dworkin—as specifying what justice requires from the perspective of citizenship. This would help to explain Rawls' view that justice fundamentally requires an equal distribution of social goods (with the rider, of course, that for some goods inequalities are permissible if they work to everyone's advantage), and Dworkin's claim that "equal concern and respect" underlie more specific criteria of distributive justice (such as equality of resources); see, for instance, J. Rawls, *A Theory of Justice* (Cambridge, Mass.: Harvard University Press, 1971), p. 62, and R. Dworkin, "Liberalism," in *A Matter of Principle* (Oxford: Clarendon Press, 1986). As general claims about jus

tice, and indeed about social justice, these views seem to me mistaken. But taken more narrowly, as attempts to capture the core meaning of equal citizenship, they are more defensible. It may be significant here that in his more recent work, Rawls always prefers to use the language of citizenship to expound his theory: whereas in *A Theory of Justice* the subjects of his theory are variously described as "persons," "men," or "parties," they are now consistently referred to as "citizens" (see *Political Liberalism* [New York: Columbia University Press, 1993], passim). Along with this has gone a shift toward seeing the principles of justice as laying down the "constitutional essentials" of a just society, rather that as principles that should regulate social institutions in a wider sense (see *Political Liberalism,* Lecture 6, sect. 5).

22. M. Walzer, *Spheres of Justice: A Defence of Pluralism and Equality* (Oxford: Martin Robertson, 1983), chap. 11.

23. *Oxford English Dictionary,* 2nd ed. (Oxford: Clarendon Press, 1989) vol. III, p. 681.

24. See my discussion of desert judgments in Chap. 7.

25. As I have pointed out elsewhere, the causal link between inequalities in material distribution and social inequality is not simple: it is mediated by cultural factors that vary from one society to the next. See D. Miller, "Arguments for Equality," in P. A. French, T. E. Uehling, and H. K. Wettstein, eds., *Midwest Studies in Philosophy, VII: Social and Political Philosophy* (Minneapolis: University of Minnesota Press, 1982), pp. 84–85.

26. D. Miller, "Complex Equality," in D. Miller and M. Walzer, eds., *Pluralism, Justice and Equality* (Oxford: Oxford University Press, 1995).

27. See the evidence cited in Chap. 4.

28. Walzer, *Spheres of Justice,* chap. 1.

29. The first practice is empirically more liable to degenerate into injustice—if the donations are used to buy special favors from the party in power—but we can imagine a case in which all we have is honors being used as a cheap and effective way of securing funding for political parties. Here the chief objection is that those who already score highly on the dimension of money are being permitted to translate that into a high score on the dimension of recognition, and that objection appeals to an ideal of social equality.

30. I have explored the way in which writers in the social-democratic tradition such as Richard Tawney and Anthony Crosland understood equality in "Equality and Market Socialism," in P. K. Bardhan and J. Roemer, eds., *Market Socialism: The Current Debate* (New York: Oxford University Press, 1993).

12. Prospects for Social Justice

1. Some have argued, more ambitiously, that social justice actually requires a market economy: see, for instance, R. Dworkin, "Liberalism," in *A Matter of Principle* (Oxford: Clarendon Press, 1986). I do not wish to enter that debate here. For the purposes of this chapter, which concerns prospects for social justice in liberal democracies at the end of the twentieth century, we need only say that there is no feasible alternative to the market economy on the horizon. Our question must be: given such an economy, what can be done to bring its procedures and outcomes closer to social justice? (For a contrary view—one that maintains that we must continue to look for a form of justice beyond the market—see G. A. Cohen, "The Future of a Disillusion," in *Self-Ownership, Freedom, and Equality* [Cambridge, England: Cambridge University Press, 1995].)

2. There is an excellent discussion of this issue in Cécile Fabre's forthcoming book *Social Rights under the Constitution: Government and the Decent Life* (Oxford University Press).

3. For this version see J. D. Davidson and W. Rees-Mogg, *The Sovereign Individual: The Coming Economic Revolution: How to Survive and Prosper In It* (Basingstoke: Macmillan, 1997).

4. "Multiculturalism" can be used descriptively, to refer to the social and political processes referred to in the text, or it can be used normatively, to identify a certain favored political response to these processes. I have criticized multiculturalism in its normative sense in *On Nationality* (Oxford: Clarendon Press, 1995), chap. 5, sects. 3–5. Here I am chiefly concerned with the implications of multiculturalism in its descriptive sense for social justice.

5. I. M. Young, *Justice and the Politics of Difference* (Princeton: N.J.: Princeton University Press, 1990), esp. chap. 1; N. Fraser, "From Redistribution to Recognition? Dilemmas of Justice in a 'Post-Socialist' Age," *New Left Review*, 212 (July/August 1995): 68–93.

6. The best general study in this vein is P. Hirst and G. Thompson, *Globalization in Question: The International Economy and the Possibilities of Governance* (Cambridge, England: Polity Press, 1996).

7. A common theme in recent writing in this area has been the contrast among Anglo-American, Continental European, and East Asian models of capitalism; for an accessible presentation, see W. Hutton, *The State We're In* (London: Jonathan Cape, 1995), chap. 10. For evidence of significant variation in tax regimes, see S. Steinmo, *Taxation and Democracy: Swedish, British and American Approaches to Financing the Modern State* (New Haven and London: Yale University Press, 1993).

8. See R. Dworkin, "Equality of Resources," *Philosophy and Public Affairs,* 10 (1981): 283–345.

9. J. Rawls, *A Theory of Justice* (Cambridge, Mass.: Harvard University Press, 1971), sect. 13.

10. This is perhaps clearer in the case of Dworkin's theory than in the case of Rawls'. It would be very implausible to argue that the inequalities we see around us are the effect simply of personal choice and responsibility in the use of resources that were initially equal. In Rawls' theory everything depends on how one fills out empirically the principle that economic inequalities are just only when they serve to raise the position of the worst-off. If one thought that the long-term material position of the worst-off group is best promoted by allowing free rein to the market, then the principle would cease to demand egalitarian redistribution. But Rawls himself, and most of his followers, have assumed otherwise. Indeed, some have claimed that the principle properly understood allows only compensatory material inequalities. (For the latter interpretation, see G. A. Cohen, "Incentives, Inequality, and Community," in G. B. Peterson, ed., *The Tanner Lectures on Human Values,* vol. 13 [Salt Lake City: University of Utah Press, 1992]: 263–329.)

11. My reasons for rejecting the Rawlsian difference principle have been given in earlier chapters of the book. For my disagreements with Dworkin, see D. Miller, "Equality," in G. M. K. Hunt, ed., *Philosophy and Politics* (Cambridge, England: Cambridge University Press, 1990).

12. See A. B. Atkinson, *Incomes and the Welfare State: Essays on Britain and Europe* (Cambridge, England: Cambridge University Press, 1995), chaps. 1–2, for evidence on this.

13. See A. Wood, *North-South Trade, Employment and Inequality* (Oxford: Clarendon Press, 1994).

14. See R. H. Frank and P. J. Cook, *The Winner-Take-All Society* (New York, The Free Press, 1995).

15. Here I follow A. B. Atkinson, "Bringing Income Distribution in from the Cold," *Economic Journal,* 107 (1997): 297–321.

16. See the evidence presented in S. Svallfors, "Dimensions of Inequality: A Comparison of Attitudes in Sweden and Britain," *European Sociological Review,* 9 (1993): 267–287. It should be said that Swedish opinions about the absolute size of fair income differences remain comparatively egalitarian by international standards.

17. See, for instance, K. Ohmae, *The End of the Nation State: The Rise of Regional Economies* (London: Harper Collins, 1995).

18. J. Gray, "Classical Liberalism, Positional Goods, and the Politicization of Poverty," in A. Ellis and K. Kumar, eds., *Dilemmas of Liberal Democracies:*

Studies in Fred Hirsch's "Social Limits to Growth" (London: Tavistock, 1983), pp. 181–182.

19. When asked to choose between "preferential treatment" and "ability" as grounds for getting jobs, black Americans by a large majority endorse "ability," showing their commitment to meritocratic principles of social justice. At the same time they are more likely than whites to believe that blacks need special help from the government to overcome the economic barriers they face. See S. M. Lipset, "Equal Chances versus Equal Results," *Annals of the American Academy of Political and Social Science,* 523 (September 1992): 63–74.

20. T. R. Tyler, R. J. Boeckmann, H. J. Smith, and Y. J. Huo, *Social Justice in a Diverse Society* (Boulder, Co.: Westview Press, 1997), chap. 10.

21. Ibid.

22. I have learned here from Yuen Huo's unpublished paper "Justice and Exclusion: Exploring the Boundaries of Our Moral Community."

23. See D. Miller, *On Nationality,* chap. 5; D. Miller, "Group Identities, National Identities and Democratic Politics," in J. Horton and S. Mendus, eds., *Toleration, Identity and Difference* (London: Macmillan, 1999).

24. See B. Rothstein, *Just Institutions Matter: The Moral and Political Logic of the Universal Welfare State* (Cambridge, England: Cambridge University Press, 1998), chap. 8, for further thoughts along these lines.

Credits

Some of the chapters presented here appeared in an earlier form elsewhere. I would like to thank the publishers of the following essays for permission to include and adapt material from them in the present book:

"Distributive Justice: What the People Think," *Ethics,* 102 (1991–1992), 555–593. Copyright © 1992 by the University of Chicago. All rights reserved.

"Deserving Jobs," *Philosophical Quarterly,* 42 (1992), 161–181. Copyright © *The Philosophical Quarterly,* 1992.

"Virtues, Practices and Justice," in J. Horton and S. Mendus, eds., *After MacIntyre* (Cambridge, England: Polity Press, 1994).

Review of K. R. Scherer, *Justice: Interdisciplinary Perspectives,* in *Social Justice Research,* 7 (1994), 167–188.

"Popular Conceptions of Social Justice: A Comparative Approach," in S. Svallfors, ed., *In the Eye of the Beholder* (Umea: Bank of Sweden, 1995).

"Two Cheers for Meritocracy," *Journal of Political Philosophy,* 4 (1996), 277–301.

"Equality and Justice," *Ratio,* 10 (1997), 222–237.

Index

Harvard University Press is a member of Green Press Initiative
(greenpressinitiative.org), a nonprofit organization working to
help publishers and printers increase their use of recycled paper
and decrease their use of fiber derived from endangered forests.
This book was printed on 100% recycled paper containing
50% post-consumer waste and processed chlorine free.